D1520326

Louis Bouyer

TRANSLATED BY PIERRE DE FONTNOUVELLE

C O S

The World and

M O S

the Glory of God

ST. BEDE'S PUBLICATIONS
Petersham, Massachusetts

Originally published in France under the title *Cosmos, Le Monde et La Gloire de Dieu* © 1982 by Les Editions du Cerf. All questions concerning the rights of translation, reproduction, adaptation, in any language or in any manner other than what appears in this volume, must be addressed to the editor of the original French edition. This translation was approved by the author.

B Q T
6 0 3
. B 72 /
/ 9 8 8
Cop. 2

Nihil Obstat: Lawrence A. Deery
                  Vicar for Canonical Affairs
Imprimatur: +Timothy J. Harrington
                  Bishop of Worcester
Worcester, Massachusetts
August 12, 1988

The *Nihil obstat* and *Imprimatur* are official declarations that a book or pamphlet is free of doctrinal and moral error. No implication is contained therein that those granting the *Nihil obstat* and *Imprimatur* agree with the content, opinions or statements expressed.

Scripture quotations contained herein are from the Revised Standard Version Bible, Catholic Edition, copyright © 1965 and 1966 by the Division of Christian Education of the National Council of the Churches of Christ in the USA, and are used by permission.

Cover design by Basil Atwell, OSB
        monk of Assumption Abbey, Richardton, ND

LIBRARY OF CONGRESS CATALOGING IN PUBLICATION DATA

Bouyer, Louis, 1913-
   [Cosmos. English]
   Cosmos : the world and the glory of God / Louis Bouyer :
translated by Pierre de Fontnouvelle.
      p.   cm.
   Translation of: Cosmos.
   Includes index.
   ISBN 0-932506-66-6
   1. Creation.   2. Cosmology.   3. Cosmology, Biblical.   4. Fall of man.
5. Glory of God.   6. Religion and science—1946-   I. Title.
BT695.B6413   1988
231.7—dc19   88-18592
CIP

Published by St. Bede's Publications
        P. O. Box 545
        Petersham, Massachusetts 01366-0545

Contents

Introduction

This is the final volume in my attempt to interpret what the Fathers of the Church called the economy of salvation, studied in conjunction with theology in its original sense as the doctrine of God. The title *Cosmos* designates first of all the systematic whole which we experience as the universe. According to St. Thomas, and in this he agrees with Aristotle, everything in our intelligence comes to it through the senses, a postulate which is in complete harmony with the biblical view of man. Conversely, the cosmos is the essentially integrated whole, the infinitely complex system which we are aware of through the perception of our senses as interpreted by the intellect. God himself can be known to us only in or through our indivisible experience of the world and of ourselves as being in the world. For God is knowable to his creatures, and particularly to man, only in and through his creation.

On the other hand, what the Bible calls the glory of God is but the divine radiance of the cosmos when we contemplate it in its infinite vastness and depth, a radiance emanating from all existence, from the entire cosmic being. And this is precisely why the created world can be called "cosmos," meaning order and beauty.

For those with a knowledge of the modern history of science, it may seem naive or pretentious to have selected this title, since it is the same one Alexander von Humboldt gave to the first scientific attempt to describe the world as such. But as his own brother Wilhelm pointed out, although the scientist presented his major work as a general survey of everything brought into existence by the Creator, there is no further mention of God in the entire book. It has therefore been my purpose to show that there is another side to the picture. As Father Jaki has recently emphasized in his Gifford Lectures, if at first sight the vision of the world provided by modern science seems to leave no place for God, his angels, or our souls—for anything spiritual or hypercosmic—this vision and science itself can be understood only if we remember that science necessarily assumes something beyond or outside its reach. This transcendent element supports the coherence of the entire scientific undertaking, which would falter and dissolve irreparably if it were to persist in ignoring this silent but radiant presence behind everything scrutinized by science. It is a presence that also underlies, even more directly, the scientist's own capacity for fruitful endeavor. One may suspect that the repeatedly alleged "death of God" portends the imminent death of countless men undermined in their humanity by their excessive and exclusive self-confidence.

Finally, even if our minds were to succeed—like the Platonists, or like Augustine and Monica in the famous vision of Ostia—in reaching through the cosmos to the One who lies beyond it, Wordsworth's comment would still hold true: "The world is too much with us..." In spite of what we may think or imagine, we remain inseparable from the world, to which we belong through everything we are, even in our most sublime mystical ecstasies and our loftiest metaphysical speculations. This being, who may be capable of reaching the most perfect vision of the Being of beings, must nevertheless remain in and of the world. Knowledge of any kind is accessible to us only if we ourselves, through our spirit, are grafted onto cosmic materiality; or, more accurately, since we are as it were "breathed" into this cosmic reality, if we are able mysteriously to identify with it, just as the creative Spirit saturates it with his active presence. Even in the most dematerializing Christian conceptions, such as that of Origen—according to which God, in the fullness of time, will draw to himself out of the present world the vast throng of those who have experienced salvation—this multitude would remain essentially cosmic in the sense indicated above, emerging from the world we know as a butterfly from its cocoon.

The last word in connection with these considerations is that the glory of God, the light he shines upon all things, and without which we cannot sense, reflect upon, and finally see his own light face to face, is in fact this very light itself: *in lumine tuo videbimus lumen.*

COSMOS

Chapter I: The World as Question

The World and Man

What is the place occupied by the world in a Christian view of life? In a well-known formulation, Newman stressed the crucial and indeed unique importance of "the thought of two and only two beings, absolute and luminously evident in themselves: myself and my creator,"[1] and one may well wonder whether this insight implies that for a Christian the world is irrelevant. To maintain that such is the case would, however, betray a deep misunderstanding of Newman's works.

Is this to say that the world does have a role in our concerns, but only as the setting in which the drama of human existence is played out, a drama about each of us and God? Or, since the world, i.e., the physical universe, is obviously linked in its own evolution to the emergence of man, is it also linked to his ultimate destiny? In other words, might the development of man's relationship with God be simply a part, albeit the main one, of the world's history?

Does history, then, have a field extending from man to the entire universe (human nature being considered as specifically historical, i.e., as finding its fulfillment only in and through history, whose unfolding is actually before all else our own)? This question leads to another, which is obviously fundamental: what precisely is meant by "the world," in the context of Christian faith and, even more significantly, how does this meaning evolve when a deeper expression of that faith is sought?

The very question is enough to bring out a dual meaning of the term, one which is already found in the New Testament. On occasion it seems that "the world" denotes the universe which surrounds and contains man, while remaining alien or even hostile. This is clearly the sense applicable in the First Epistle of St. John: "Do not love the world or the things in the world. . . [for] the whole world is in the power of the evil one."[2] Elsewhere, on the contrary, the world appears so closely linked to us as to be practically synonymous with mankind: "For God so loved the world that he gave his only Son, that whoever believes in him should not perish but have eternal life,"[3] (again according to St. John, but this time in the Gospel). Here we become aware of a second duality underlying the world: from one viewpoint, which emphasizes the definite structure and order implied by the Greek word *cosmos*, the world is intrinsically evil and appears condemned beyond any possibility of remission. From another viewpoint, however, the world as created by God appears saveable, though perverted, and is seen as good, indeed fundamentally good.

The World and God

This raises another major question, also of prime importance, concerning the world: what, precisely, is its relationship to God? This question, once voiced, breaks down into a series of other ones. First, is the world a reality distinct from God? In other words, is the world—that unified whole we experience—the supreme reality, or is it only its harbinger or faint image? As soon as one replies that the world is not God, a new constellation of questions arises. To start with, is the world independent of God, does it have a distinct or even separate existence, is it completely apart? If this is not the case, if the world, while essentially distinct, is still dependent on God, is this dependence total or merely partial? This question can be split again into two very different parts. Is the world's course inevitably predetermined by God? Or is it, though dependent on God, endowed with some degree of real freedom? Regarding its origin, and not only its evolution or history, is the world totally dependent on God, in the specific sense of having received its entire existence from him, or is this only partly so? According to Greek cosmogonal theories, the matter (whatever meaning one gives the term) of the universe is not only eternal, just as God himself is, but also completely separate from him.

If one does not espouse these theories, but on the contrary believes that the world is entirely dependent on God in its genesis, even though it may be endowed with a certain freedom in relation to him, how should this original dependence be viewed? Is the world God's creation, owing its distinct existence to him? And if so, was it created *ex nihilo*, in the sense that nothing, not even God, can be considered the principle of its existence? This gives rise to two further questions. On God's part, was this creation a free or a necessary act? In other words, could God have refrained from creating the world? And, assuming he was free to create it or not, could he, after deciding to do so, have made it quite different from what it actually is?

Still another question obtrudes: regardless of whether the act of creation was free or necessary, has the world always existed, just as God has, or did it begin at some point in time? Which brings up a symmetrical question: will this world have an end and, if so, will it be followed by one or more other worlds? If so, will these other worlds be entirely different, or will they in some unknowable way proceed from the world we know? Finally, will these future worlds continue forever, or is all creation destined to be reabsorbed, either into nothingness, or into God himself?

If one were to leave aside this entire speculation regarding creation, what other possible relationships between the world and God can we contemplate? Might the world be simply an emanation of God or a projection, so to speak, of something within the godhead? Rather than a divine emanation, should the world not be viewed as a mere phase in the immanent development of the divine being? When asked about the existence of God, Renan answered: "He may not exist yet, but never fear, he will one day!" In Hegel's philosophy, God, or rather the Absolute, is at the root of all things. In a deeper sense, however, he can be considered as the goal toward which all existence tends. In S. Alexander's philosophy,[4] perhaps the strangest in this respect, God does not now exist, nor has he ever existed in the past, but, in this philosophy also, he will be the end, the ultimate target and destination of all things, although it seems less than certain that this end will ever be attained.

The World and Our Knowledge of God

Following upon this first group of connected questions, all bearing on the relation between the existence, the very being of the world and that of God, we come to a second family of questions, dealing with the world and our knowledge of God.

Is it really through our knowledge of the world, one may ask, that we attain the knowledge of God? Or might it not be, on the contrary, by withdrawing as much as possible from the world into the deepest core of our inner selves, or even beyond, that we will find God? The God whom St. Augustine described as *intimior intimo meo*,[5] and whom Evagrius Ponticus saw in the same light, may well be identical to the deepest point of the soul,[6] the *Grund* dear to German mystics,[7] and even dearer to their not always entirely faithful disciples, the nineteenth-century idealists,[8] or rather to an *Urgrund* which would turn out to be, as Jakob Boehme called it, an *Ungrund*:[9] literally a bottomless abyss.

There are, of course, intermediate attitudes. These recognize that knowledge of God can arise partly from our experience of the world, but partly also from abilities which are apparently ours alone and which allow us to discover God within ourselves.[10] Others, however, deny that any knowledge of God can arise either from the world, from ourselves, or from a combination of both, and see it exclusively as the result of revelation, totally and radically transcending both the world and the self.[11] Yet, granting the validity of this approach, one would have to wonder whether the alleged revelation really falls to earth, coming into man's ken, quite like a meteorite. It seems that this is how Moslems view the Koran, and Fundamentalist Christians adopt very similar positions regarding the Bible.[12] Nevertheless, the problem of our knowledge of the world and of God cannot fail to arise again, at least where the manner of revelation is concerned. For even if the Koran and the Bible are deemed wholly divine, they use everyday words, and it does seem that divine revelation, as reflected in these books thought to have come from heaven, borrows a great deal from earthly visions.

Man in the World

Once more, a new cluster of questions comes to the fore. After considering the relationship between God and the world, then our knowledge of God and of the world, we may well wonder about the nature and the manner of our relationship to the world, and first about that relationship as it stood originally.

Are we a product of the world, the result or a result of its immanent evolution?[13] Or have we been thrust into the world, fallen from elsewhere? If so, should we consider our bodies as simply alien, or actually hostile, to that transcendental element, our soul?[14] Or, rather, is there an affinity, or even a mutual complementarity between the two?[15] In the latter case, what is the degree of their association, of their compenetration or symbiosis? Even if the body is not a tomb for the soul, as it is described in a Greek play on words, probably Pythagorean in inspiration (*sēma* = tomb and *sōma* = body), is it but the soul's temporary envelope, or is it essential for man to be a soul in a body? Is the soul made for the body as the body is made for the soul? And even if it were so, is the soul's participation in the world through the body so close, so intimate, that the soul can live and know only in and through the body? Does the soul possess a degree of real autonomy from the body, and if so, how much?[16]

The Problem of Evil

This brings up once again the question, is the existence of the world in itself fundamentally good? Or does the world contain some elements that are good and others that are not? Or is it we who have introduced all evil into the world? Is evil present quite independently of us? Finally, is the origin of evil inextricably mixed? Does evil exist in the world partly without our having any hand in the matter, and partly because of us? And assuming we opt for this view, is there a link between the evil which is in us and arises from us and the evil which is in the world and comes from the world? If there is such a link what is its nature?[17]

This brings back, under another aspect, the question of the historicity of the world. To put the matter differently, has the world always been in the same apparently unsatisfactory relationship to God as now, or did this relationship arise at some point, as it were, accidentally? If so, is it possible to make good the fault (seen as not inherent in existence), to overcome the fall (seen as distinct from creation)? And now we find the ultimate question: once man has made his appearance in the world, even if his entire being is but a product of the world, does he have the power to alter it?[18]

Underlying all these questions are others, more disturbing still. We have already wondered whether this world is the only one ever to have existed, assuming there was a time before its inception. But is it the only one to exist here and now? And if there are other worlds, have they or can they have any connection with ours, and if there is such a connection, what is its nature?[19] Conversely, is the world of our daily existence really endowed with unity, consistency, and coherence? How are we to interpret the frequently alleged antinomies between matter and spirit, the real and the ideal, the physical realm and the moral, etc.?[20]

From that level of reflection, we reach (or return to) more complex and deeper questions, although they are but subtler forms of earlier ones: in speaking of the world, do we have in mind an object facing us, so to speak, or a reality which includes us? In other words, can we count on the common presupposition of nineteenth-century German idealist philosophers, that there is a basic opposition between Nature and Spirit, with man seen as the emergence of the Spirit (*Geist*) into the world of Nature, while still in unavoidable tension with the world?[21]

Rational Reflection and Revelation

To be sure, this does not exhaust the questions raised by the world. But we have at least identified the main ones. And even at this early stage in our endeavor, it may already be noted that Christianity, or more generally the whole of biblical revelation, before suggesting an answer to any of these questions, first unexpectedly modifies them. Although the most traditional Christian philosophers generally agree in accepting as rationally demonstrable the proposition that the world in its entirety was created by God, who saw it as good both as a whole and in all its parts, this revelation actually brushes aside all the questions which man had previously raised about the original relationship between the world and God. Instead it proposes, in creation *ex nihilo*, a free creation that exhibits freedom both in itself and in its Maker, an insight no one had ever considered, either to affirm its validity or to deny it![22]

This leads us to consider, without further ado, the complexity—in certain respects a paradoxical one—displayed by the relationship between the knowledge of the world arising directly from the actual experience of man as he is living in the concrete world, and the revised and completed knowledge given by the Word of God, the revelation received from Israel and continued, we believe, to its fulfillment in the Christian Church. The two levels of knowledge are both continuous and discontinuous. By entering into the experience of man naturally present in the world, biblical and evangelical revelation becomes accessible to man. And this is readily understandable when we realize that a basic point of this revelation is that God is the creator of the entire world, including the whole of man. It follows that the world and man are both fundamentally good in their very nature, i.e., inasmuch as they proceed from God the Creator, and could not continue to exist unless this link with God (whatever may have subsequently occurred) remained at the root of their enduring existence and their permanent essence.[23]

Here, however, lies the paradox of revelation: precisely because it shows God as creator, revelation is obviously, from the outset, an essentially redeeming process. It does not simply reestablish an authentic view of the original, permanent relationship between man and the world on the one hand, and their Creator on the other: by the very fact that this restoration of truth compels recognition, it shines forth as an intervention of the Creator in the history of his creation, which has in effect become the history of creation's estrangement or alienation from the One from whom it continues to draw its very being. Through this intervention, God seeks to reinstate the relationship he willed in creating the world and man, but from which creation has deviated. This is what gives revelation—although it is fundamentally a restoration or renewal of the primitive truth expressed by creation itself, i.e., the original revelation of God precisely as creator—its healing, indeed redeeming, quality. It bears witness, by virtue of its relative novelty, that a catastrophe took place in creation, which once again alienated it from its Maker. And revelation specifically identifies the nature of this calamity: the God-made creature turned to false gods, away from the true God on whom it was, and always remains, dependent, even in the act of rebellion. This is why revelation heals and redeems: it leads to deliverance from bondage, then to restoration of man's vocation, which is to adhere freely to God, discovering its filial character as the goal of evangelic revelation.[24]

Knowledge and Tradition

The preceding comments are of particular significance as partly capturing the traditional nature of our knowledge of the world. At a later stage, these remarks will also be of interest in respect to the historical development of this "primitive" knowledge: namely, when we consider the development of what may be called our revealed knowledge. For the latter will be closely linked to the growth of historical knowledge emerging, so to speak, from the very historicity of our fundamental knowledge of the world.

We must first elucidate the historical authenticity of our knowledge of the world, whose traditional nature is accounted for by this historicity. At first sight, there is nothing more personal, indeed more individual, than our elementary knowledge of the world and its maturation into a more thoughtful form of knowledge. This happens as a result of the progressive emergence of the multitude of questions we have identified, through which our basic experience of the world challenges our intelligence. Nevertheless, however valid and primary this aspect may be, we should not overlook its complement, the collective or, more specifically, social aspect. Indeed, for each of us, the discovery of the world—a quest by which the world becomes a kind of language, allowing the full reality to impinge on our intelligence and incite it to grapple with a host of relevant issues—is in fact inseparable from the discovery of human language, and so from the intercommunication of minds. This discovery is a necessary concomitant of our awakening to thought and life, so that it proves actually impossible to separate our most personal experience of the world from our experience of personal life. This arises and develops only within the fundamental relationship between self and humankind, as initially represented by parents and close relatives.[25]

Once we become aware of this fact, which is basic to our entire experience of the world, it becomes clear that the development of our knowledge of the world, however personal it may be fundamentally, is nevertheless traditional to an equally essential degree. Moreover, this leads us immediately to note what precisely tradition is *per se*[26] and what it is not. This, despite preconceptions so widespread as to seem invincible; indeed, for our contemporaries, whether or not they consider themselves traditionalists, the general tendency is to assume an opposition between accepting traditional ideas and acquiring, through individual experience alone, ideas viewed as personal. In actual fact, this opposition does not prevail; the only valid contrast is between complementary aspects of one and the same reality. This is not a case of distinct and intrinsically antagonistic realities.

Tradition is viewed by both traditionalists and their opponents as somewhat like a coin passed on from hand to hand, which one hesitates to handle more than necessary for fear of blurring its design. The comparison, however, is highly inappropriate, since tradition cannot be separated from a true knowledge of the world. For the transmission of such a knowledge, and of any accretions that become grafted onto it, can take place only through a process which is not mechanical, but organic, and even spiritual, insofar as it seems that individuals as conscious beings can exist only in a constant reciprocity of relations, as the question of tradition illustrates perfectly. All the questions we have raised, which the world actually puts to us, accumulate in the course of human history, and reappear over and over again in the personal history of each individual consciousness. This occurs only through an indivisible process, a shared openness of every mind. Each of us awakens to the knowledge both of the world and of our fellowmen, and moreover becomes aware of what all men, in their individual consciousness, acting and interacting, can feel and think of this world.[27]

The paradox inherent in this discovery is most striking when we move from an elementary consciousness of the world in its initial confusion to a higher, scientific, essentially rational knowledge. For although all reasoning arises from an individual consciousness operating freely on its own, it is nevertheless obvious that all science is ultimately the result of a constant collaboration between the most diverse minds. Science progresses through a gradual sifting, carried out thanks to intercommunication, of the most personal intuitions granted to the creative geniuses of every age. And these intuitions stir up, so to speak, the basic assumptions produced by the cooperative pursuit of experiences, even the most personal, of all mankind evolving in unison.

Scientific, Mythic, and Revealed Knowledge

So-called scientific knowledge, as we shall subsequently note, always arises in the wake of a widely received and generally accepted cognition, which we may call the initial knowledge of cosmic reality. This primary stage is that of mythic knowledge, whose processes and development we intend to examine comprehensively in a subsequent chapter. It is a development that grows from the deep roots of individual and collective experience of the world (or, more accurately, of individual experience within the human community). After the way is opened by this mythic knowledge, which thus remains fundamental in every respect, revealed knowledge, biblical and evangelical, will develop. And, as we shall see, though both revealed and scientific knowledge of the world develop to some extent independently from mythic knowledge—even finding fault with it or opposing it altogether—this is not the end of the matter. Even when there seems to be outright opposition, they never cease to adhere to it. It is on a mythic base that both scientific and revealed knowledge unfold, the former through the exercise of critical reason and the latter by virtue of a mysterious inspiration. They transform our consciousness of the world, and what might be called our consciousness as beings in the world. Nevertheless, neither can totally disregard mythic consciousness nor, without risking disintegration, break away from a fundamental link to that mode of consciousness which is refined and corrected by science or totally transfigured through revelation.[28]

As to the interrelationship between the consciousness and tradition of science on the one hand, and of revelation as vouchsafed to Israel and the Church on the other, these two forms of man's cosmic consciousness are of necessity linked in their origin and in their development, despite certain appearances as deceptive and misleading as those invoked to establish the total independence of science and revelation from myth. This is evident first of all from the history of the wisdom of antiquity, taken up, along with mythic knowledge, by revelation, which assumed and transcended them both. Conversely, the same close link is brought to light by the history of science, whose general outline Whitehead was one of the first to perceive in modern times,[29] and whose details have been masterfully sketched just recently by Stanley Jaki. It is clear that modern science of the cosmos was able to take shape and progress only after medieval scholasticism had succeeded in giving scientific form—i.e., a form as fully reasoned as possible at the time—to our knowledge of Jewish and Christian revelation.[30]

We shall now attempt to advance step-by-step in the study of these complex processes, striving never to lose sight either of their intricacy or of their fundamental unity.

Chapter II: The World as Object of Human Experience

The World and Individual Experience

From the foregoing, it follows that any knowledge we may attain of the world necessarily arises from our personal experience and, moreover, can be nothing more than and nothing else but an elaboration of that experience. It is because there are human beings, or rather human minds with individual experience of cosmic reality, who have pondered their own experience while enriching it with the shared experience and thinking of others, that *mythos*—organically linked knowledge in its primary stage—and *logos*—the same knowledge sifted by discursive reasoning—eventually develop. And it is through a mysterious transmutation involving first *mythos* and then *logos* that revealed knowledge (as we eventually called it) emerged in the fullness of time. And, as we shall see, revealed knowledge itself will evolve in theology into a scientific and rational form of knowledge (though never completely) which will paradoxically give rise to the only truly mature developments in the science of the cosmos.[1]

All this does not mean that in our knowledge of the world there will never be, or can never be, anything more than what arises from immediate experience of the world. It does mean, however, that nothing can be real to us except insofar as it is linked to that experience and appears as its extension, either in myth or in the logos of science or in the word of revelation.

Knowledge, the Senses, and the Mind

A second and equally important point is that this primitive and elementary experience, which remains the necessary basis for any real development of our knowledge of the world, is by no means what is commonly known as a pure sense experience. One cannot even claim that primitive experience starts out by being purely sensory. For the "pure facts" or "raw facts" which were the alleged foundation of positivist science, and on which it was assumed that scientific reasoning could subsequently operate in an appropriate manner, do not and cannot exist.

Indeed, what is referred to as sense experience in its pure state, far from being a given, an elementary datum of consciousness, is but a by-product of thought focusing on our actual experience, which is always, from the very first, not a joint experience of the senses and the intellect, but an organic and single reality which reflective intelligence subsequently and somewhat artificially breaks down into a sensible component and an intelligible component. Both are in fact initially received by us *per modum unius*: in the pristine perception of the world, the mind and the senses act together, both unable to distinguish at first what comes from the senses and what from the intellect intervening after the event to focus on a datum assumed to be perceivable only by the senses.

On the other hand, any perception of reality available to us initially forms a unified whole, or rather a unit. Reflection will allow us first to distinguish in the abstract, then to attempt to separate concretely (though it is doubtful that we will ever fully succeed in this endeavor) the components of this initial perception. The contemporary experimental school of psychology has emphasized a basic truth that each of us could quite easily have reached, if we were more aware of the spontaneous manner in which we experience reality through our responses. We encounter nothing in our actual experience of the world which first occurs as a mere perception of the senses, and then draws a response from our intellect. On the contrary, everything we perceive is grasped as a single and total act of our consciousness, so that what we think of as a strictly intellectual activity is already present with and in the perception of the senses. William James has shown the presence of mental perceptions underlying, so to speak, any perception of the senses,[2] but it seems necessary to go further and to assert that, from the most elementary awakening of human consciousness, every perception is leavened with intellectual activity.

So-called sensible illusions are a consequence of this primary connection between the senses and the mind. We do not view a stick partly immersed in water by means of an accurate perception from which we then conclude that the stick is bent, improperly applying a certain line of reasoning to unusually complex sensory data; we immediately see the stick as bent. For we see everything through an activity of the mind which at once distinguishes groupings of color spots within the overall perception. But how is this achieved?

From Mere Unity to Unity Through Multiplicity

Since our awareness of the world is shaped by the flow of time, the all-encompassing whole we perceive in both its unity and its diversity is also seen by us as ever-changing. And this appears to be what leads us from an indiscriminate perception of unknown chaos to a consciousness of distinct objects and beings, and indeed of the world as such. At each moment, our perception of reality is integrated. But this unified vision shatters when we compare, by means of memory, two different stages of reality's constant mutation, both of which become successively the focus of our reflective attention, and are in a sense immobilized or frozen in the process, at a second level of consciousness. At a third stage, we are able to reconstruct the world by synthesis into a unity of the parts which had been previously recognized as distinct.[3]

After the changing but cohesive image of our primary perception is repeatedly severed by successive flashes of double perception—hence a fragmentation into successive views resembling many different landscapes —we reach a clear consciousness of the world as a unit, and recognize the permanence and consistency underlying its many different faces. In other words, we now recapture on a conscious level what had earlier been a semi-conscious view of reality.

When we reach this third stage, where consciousness oscillates or pulsates steadily between complexity and unity, reflective cognition, which perceives distinctions as a way to reestablish unity, comes fully into its own. At this highest stage, the world reveals itself as essentially one, though complex, and indeed monistic in its very complexity.

The Birth of Myth

This synthetic view of reality, whose inner and native unity reemerges in the explicit discovery of its multiplicity, is first expressed in mythic form. More precisely, as soon as this spontaneous synthetic reconstruction of reality by the human mind—as yet unaware of itself, but becoming conscious of its own activity—rediscovers the primary oneness of experience, a unity perceptible indissolubly to both our senses and our minds, the stage is set for the appearance of myth as a first manifestation of our explicit consciousness of the world.

Myth is a synthetic elaboration of our experience of the world, reestablished in unity through the integration of successive and discrete views of reality into one intuitive and all-inclusive vision, so that the world may then be formally acknowledged in its primordial unity, rather than being just mysteriously sensed.[4]

Our fundamental experience is therefore essentially temporal, as well as successive, which does not mean that it is "simply" sensory, for it is the experience of a continual flux of total, though still only half-conscious, perception. Our experience tends toward full consciousness, and prepares for it through sudden and deliberate interruptions of this flux when reflective attention comes into play. But it reaches an awareness of the world as such only at a higher or deeper level of consciousness, i.e., when we succeed by a supreme intuition in recovering the still indistinct unity which underpinned and encompassed each one of those transitory views, as well as the flow of our habitual semi-consciousness, and beyond the latter, or perhaps this side of it, a boundless and undefinable unconscious. This unconscious is the backdrop and foundation of our usual semi-conscious existence, punctuated by successive flashes of normal consciousness, and exceptionally with "third-stage" supra-conscious intuitions through which we recapture and appropriate the primal unity of the ineffable perception that allows our intelligence to attain reality directly though still obscurely.

Solidarity of Individual Consciousnesses

The foregoing is only a part, a thread, though perhaps the central one, in our experience. For we may well wonder whether, at any of these levels or phases of development, our experience is separate or separable from the influence exercised by the individual consciousness of other human beings. A child's first impressions are both superficially stamped and deeply colored in their substance by its mother's consciousness; these initial impressions will focus on the same objects which had previously drawn the mother's attention.

The major problem is to ascertain whether it is through the same process—whereby intelligibility is drawn out of the sensory data which it permeated—that we attain an elementary awareness of the individual consciousness of other human beings, i.e., through the mechanism, or one resembling it, used in verbal communication. Or is this awareness gained through a process of direct intuition which lies at the root of language itself and indeed makes language possible? It should be noted, however, that this intuition would fall within the scope of parapsychology rather than within what may be considered the normal, or at least usual, realm of our psychology. According to the Jungian school, it takes children a certain amount of time to acquire an awareness which is completely distinct and autonomous in relation to that of their parents.[5] Similarly, there is ample evidence that psychoanalysts experience, between themselves and their patients, communications which do not appear to rely on the usual channels of an external sense perception even permeated with intelligence.[6]

One may wonder whether the acquisition of language and of everything related to language does not assume or imply this original integration of individual consciousnesses, and of the contents of each individual consciousness, as a basis for our intuitive perception of multiplicity and unity, or rather of multiplicity as a sign of reality's living unity. By the same token, this would emphasize that, in the final analysis, any knowledge of the world which we appropriate is only linguistic in nature,[7] from which it would follow that of itself the world is, as it were, but a language shared by the minds immersed in it. But how could this be so unless the world is first and foremost the expression or manifestation of a Spirit whence all others proceed and in whom they are joined together through their fully developed knowledge, just as they were originally pre-united in the first awakening of their consciousness?

Importance and Knowledge

None of this, however, deals directly with the dynamic process which leads the spirit to a full intuition of the world as such. In order to reach the heart of the matter, we must turn to one of the most penetrating insights reached by Whitehead, in the first few pages of his highly significant *Modes of Thought*.[8] He suggests that this reconstruction, by the fully conscious mind, of reality's underlying unity, first glimpsed in the as yet confused primal perception of it, always develops from a detail endowed with special importance by that mind, and selected for that very reason among countless others. This detail is made the focus of a complex reality; all other details are then seen only in relation to the privileged and chosen one, and in the process consciousness recovers the unity of the whole. The importance ascribed to the chosen detail is not determined merely by the intellect, however. It is the result of a free choice by the spirit, and depends on the angle or viewpoint from which the spirit decides to consider the universe. According to the choices made, different schemes will emerge, and at first sight they will appear incompatible. But it would be an error to conclude that they are subjective. Indeed, they relate to various aspects of reality and various approaches to it. Far from simply revealing different minds or diverse states of mind, these schemes do picture reality. Wittgenstein likened them to heterogeneous linguistic games, all legitimate, and each with what may be called its objective truth, as long as one remains absolutely faithful to the logic of the unifying principle adopted in each case.[9]

Symbol and Knowledge

It is therefore clear that the process will yield endlessly diversified views of reality. In *Symbolism*, another of his works, Whitehead points out that these various views will all have a common characteristic: the knowledge they provide is symbolic. None of them will fully coincide with the whole of reality.[10] This does not in any way mean that the views are inadequate or that they are the stuff of dreams or figments of the imagination; instead, they are suggested by the data which they seek to capture. But they bring into play different kinds of symbolism, each one being appropriate to the actual aspect of reality which has held our attention, rather than relating to a mere projection of our imagination. For example, the technologically-oriented symbols used as the tools of contemporary science conform to the various ways in which we approach the world in order to harness nature for the benefit of our utilitarian endeavors. Religious symbols are also selected, as are all other imaginable symbols, according to the use we intend to make of the world. This is to say that they conform to the so-called ritual intelligence, which by definition is not narrowly utilitarian.[11] For rites, in this context, are an activity of man in the world, through which he attunes his being and his life to the main coordinates of cosmic life and being. In ritual observance, human activity therefore tends to follow divine activity, through which reality is formed.[12] It follows that man's entire life and his very being find in rites—and recognize in the myth which expresses the inner content of rites—their foundation in the world. Man then feels in complete harmony with his own principle and that of the world.[13]

Hence the unique value attaching to the mythic expression of cosmic reality. And hence also the explanation of the fact that man finds his place in the universe and feels at home there only by virtue of mythic representation. The latter is essential to man, so that his various activities may tend toward a common goal, may be mutually compatible, and may be in harmony with the cosmos, which is the ultimate frame of reference of these activities. These in turn must accord, if they are to prove truly significant, with the laws governing the development of the cosmos.

It may be said that myths, whose nature is essentially religious, are the fulfillment and consolidation of a vision of the universe which recognizes in them something like a common and universal language shared by all men. For myths allow us to recapture in that language the beginning and the end of all things, the alpha and the omega; they provide an initial and permanent communication between the absolute Spirit and the divided, changeable, and inconstant spirits that we are.

Knowledge and Will

Enough has been said for us to realize that the activity of the human intellect, aiming at cognition or recognition of the world, is inseparable from the activity of our senses, which allows us to cleave to cosmic reality through the very reality of our physical being, and is equally inseparable from the activity of our will. One must not hesitate to say it: our knowledge of the world is determined by what we want to achieve in respect to the world.[14] Which is why that type of knowledge, which will furnish a foundation for all others, will be mythic knowledge, a thoroughly religious one in the most literal sense, since it is bound up with an effort of the will to connect with the activity that upholds and leads the world, thus endowing the world with structural and final unity.

Myth and Rites

The human activity which coincides with divine activity is ritual activity. For the latter is by no means artificial, an activity outside everyday life, as assumed by some of our contemporaries who have lost contact with reality. For them religious matters, which relate to the divine dimension, the truest dimension of all, have lost all meaning. On the contrary, ritual activity is one in which man feels, knows, and wills himself to be "acted upon" by the same activity which makes him a being in the world, by bringing the world into being. Finding himself not only immersed in total reality, but also in tune with it, man sees himself as capable of gaining the widest and deepest vision of this reality, insofar as it emanates from the super-reality which is God.[15]

The myth giving form to this vision is therefore the framework in which human life, the world whence it issues and where it unfolds, and the eternal and transcendent source which animates and joins them together, each for the other, are put in orderly and systematic arrangement, a perspective which is not only the truest, but also the only one which applies to the first and supreme truth.

Reason and Language

This prompts us to take a further step and to recognize that there is a close connection between language and reason, i.e., the intellectual activity in closest harmony with the main thrust of reality. This assertion is verified by a study of the rare cases of those abandoned children who are reared without any human contact.[16] Since they were taught no human language during the formative stage of their intelligence, their mind is forever impaired and permanently incapable of acquiring any knowledge on a human level. It is therefore hardly surprising that the Greek word *logos* means both reason and articulated speech.

Language is a system of communication between individuals as conscious beings, a system reflecting the dual fact that they recognize one another as such and can share the contents of their thoughts and wills. This is indeed why mythic knowledge is fundamental to all other systems of knowledge of the world, each focusing on one of its multiple facets, which our own multiform activity can adapt to, since it recognizes the activity which underpins the world and, within the world, our own life, as a personal activity.

It should be noted that at this point we touch upon a relationship which will become increasingly clear in the course of our study and which Maurice Nédoncelle has described as the essential reciprocity between conscious beings.[17]

Magic, Myth, and Idol

By the same token, we become aware at once of both the strength and the weakness of mythic knowledge. It obviously takes shape when man recognizes himself as a consciousness endowed with free will and capable of thought, in other words as a personal being. He will then inevitably be tempted to want to become, or to already think that he is, the only person that counts, and therefore to draw to himself everything in the world, including the mysterious power he senses in ritual activity, a power beyond compare. This is the temptation of magic, which affects all cultures in the process of becoming a civilization, i.e., an organization of the world in terms of an individual and collective human life centered on itself.[18]

Myth, which proclaims on the contrary that ritual, even when practiced by man, remains a fundamentally and properly divine activity, contradicts and counters this magical tendency. Obviously, however, myth can achieve this only by representing divine activity and divine personality according to the image man has formed of himself. This entails a downgrading of God in myth, although the latter reaffirms the divinity as against the growing "imperialism" of human consciousness, an evolution which leads to polytheism and idolatry, i.e., a process of reducing the one and transcendent God to what is multiple and partial.[19]

Myth and the Fall

It may therefore be asserted that mythic consciousness is innately troubled by what can be referred to as the Fall: the involution of man, whereby he retires within his own being, which prevents effective and authentic communication between God and himself, and leaves him defenseless against cosmic "powers," whose willfulness led to their own downfall. The emancipation from the All-powerful which they urge on man would make man a slave to their tyranny.[20]

Mythos and Logos

The dim perception of the inner contradiction involved in the very development of myth leads the *logos*, or discursive reasoning, to seek to unravel it. Is this to say that *mythos* and *logos* are alien to each other? If they really were, they would not exhibit such a striking congruity, even in their opposition. We are inevitably dependent, Ortega y Gasset claimed, on that which we oppose, and his insight is certainly pertinent at this point.[21] Indeed, myth, or more precisely the mythopoetic function of the mind producing it, presupposes the existence of the *logos*. But at this primary and fundamental stage of the process, it is through a participatory logic—rather

than an analytic and dialectic separation—that the *logos* not only distinguishes before reuniting, but also establishes further distinctions only in
order to bring together more effectively.[22]

This will remain characteristic of poetry, even after it breaks away from
mythogenesis: the re-creating imagination which is the soul of poetry will
always involve a recovery of the living and indeed spiritual unity underlying matter, something entirely different from the dead unity of a world
atomized and mechanized by dialectics, even when the latter tries to
achieve a synthesis through a succession of separate analyses.

Here, on the contrary, the unity of reality is rediscovered in its very
principle, as an inexhaustible creation of harmonies, which do not develop
through a disintegration of the primal living unity, but through a multiplication of that unity within itself.

All the same, we must take care not to believe that the only possible
development of the human mind gradually forming a concept of the universe is the one so remarkably exemplified by Greek thinkers, an evolution
in which a dialectic logos emerged from myth, then turned against it, and
finally took its place. Let us not forget that for Plato himself, the logos was
to emerge from myth only to return to it subsequently and prepare the
transposition and transfiguration of myth on a higher plane.[23] In fact, the
failure of this program in the later evolution or involution of the Academy
itself, which was to lead to the total skepticism of Carneades, may well have
been due only to the inner impoverishment already suffered in ancient
Greece by the myths inherited from the Indo-European tradition.

In India itself, the relationship between logos and mythos has been quite
different. The analytic and dialectic logos developed not outside and against
myth, but within it. In the dizzying metaphysics of Hinduism, the result
was to be a peculiar pseudo-morphosis, so that intellectuality was never
divided in India as it was in Greece. This result was even more disconcerting, however, since it altered from within myth's very substance: eventually myth became a mere poetic gloss, and a beguiling but superficial unity
covered a schizoid acceptance of the most bewildering constellation of
contradictions in terms.[24]

Developments were again different in Egypt. The emergence of the
dialectic logos, in typically Egyptian wisdom, not only also took place from
within, and not outside myth and in reaction to it, but always followed the
mythic impulse, even though by degrees the logos boldly corrected the
direction of that impulse.[25]

In China, the scholarly Taoism of the Tao-te-Ching was assimilated with
popular Taoism, rather than emerging from it, and we no longer see a
correction of the mythos by the logos, but instead a purification or decanta-
tion, a process whose material counterpart or projection is found in the

operations of alchemy. It is true that in Confucianism with its complete humanism, a feature which takes the place held by pancosmism in the Tao, an unmistakable tension appears between logos and mythos.[26] In a manner most characteristic of China, however, the humanization of the cosmos, carried to the highest degree, finds a deep echo in the widening of humanity to cosmic or even hypercosmic dimensions and fullness. This is the tendency to endow the human emperor with the attributes of the absolute in a celestial identification with the ideal emperor: the elevation of the entire human reign into a true celestial kingdom.[27]

With the advent of neo-Confucianism, which involves an invasion of Chinese thinking by India's intemperate rationalization, harmony is not destroyed, but becomes frozen into a kind of sublimation difficult to distinguish from pure and simple inflexibility.[28]

On the other hand, due to the Chinese soul's humanism, and even more its innate realism, in China, more durably and better still than in India itself, the Buddhist criticism of all myths and rituals was to lead, in Amidism, to a seeming denial of all human and cosmic reality, but only by visibly pointing the way to the hyper-cosmic superhumanity of a mysterious and wholly divine compassion.[29]

Turning back to Greece, and particularly to its rationalizing humanism, which Western civilization was to carry further from the Renaissance onward, it is there and nowhere else that the development of our knowledge of the world was to go through the three phases recognized and described by Auguste Comte: the theological, metaphysical, and positivist stages. However, because myth from the start was to weaken into mythology (a reduction of the divine to wholly human images), rational criticism—before which myth was forced to give ground by its own decadence—was to purge myths only by exhausting or diluting them in a fog of abstractions. Inevitably, after mankind succeeded only too well in asserting its humanity by demythicizing the cosmos, this fog would in turn dissipate and leave behind the residuum of a fully materialized world, where man can but proclaim the death of God, just before realizing that he is in fact announcing his own demise.

Myth and Divine Word

In the interval between the first retreat of Greek humanism, so typical of the Hellenistic age, and its contemporary revival, fore-doomed after a late flowering in the Renaissance and its aftermath, an utterly different development has occurred, one that remains supremely vital, although apparently ignored in our post-Christian civilization. And we may confidently believe it will subsist till the end of time, as the ultimate sign of the rediscovery of the divine, or rather of the true God discovered at last through the darkened transparence of a fallen universe, one to which he has returned under a progressively translucent veil. We obviously refer to the revealed knowledge of the universe, which stands against the defeat of both "logical" and "mythic" knowledge, though following the channels which they had both prepared.

Chapter III: From Myths to the Word: From Deified Kings to God the King

We have already emphasized the need—if we are not to doom every effort of the human mind to understand the cosmos—to recognize in myths much more than a mere preamble to the development of rational thinking or of biblical revelation. Even though, in their concrete and historical manifestations, myths must be criticized by the former and transfigured by the latter, it is on the basis of the mythopoetic process, an absolutely fundamental form of thought, and on no other basis, that rational thinking and revelation must stand. This is so true that if one were to insist on the existence of an irreducible opposition, in order to build an entirely rational science or to receive a revelation assumed to be totally demythologized, the science would collapse and the revelation would evaporate.

Permanent Value of Myth

Mythopoetic thinking approaches cosmic reality first through a sure instinct that there exists a spontaneous harmony between our spirit and that reality, then through the very quality which allows our spirit to grasp reality, not only from one specific and superficial viewpoint, but by means of a deep sympathy with its inner structure and its fundamental evolution.[1] This is indeed why the purging of mythopoetic thinking from human consciousness can only be apparent. Once he has turned to rationalism, man may think he has cast out of his intelligence the patterns of mythic thought. His dreams show this to be an illusion: mythic constructs remain at the root of human consciousness, even if they are repressed into the subconscious—to reemerge whenever there is a relaxation of the conscious mind—or into the unconscious, from which they arise again only when the reflective and deliberate consciousness is totally inoperative.[2]

Even in the waking state, a resurgent mythopoetic consciousness bursts forth in the daydreams of poetry, the only form of consciousness through which we continue to hold onto the deepest realities, although in a semi-darkness which protects them from an over-rational awareness. These concern our innermost being, the most secret but most authentic reality of this world, and we are perhaps fully ourselves only when we rediscover this reality in its proper dimension. This is what Jung tried to describe in his stimulating but not wholly satisfactory study of what he called the archetypes of the unconscious.

Archetypes and Hierophanies

The description and enumeration attempted by Carl Jung himself, and especially by his disciples, are at the same time somewhat simplistic and excessively detailed.[3] This is not to say that the object of their endeavor was imaginary, though their forays into the unknown frequently yielded nothing more than a semblance of what they sought, a rough and at times whimsical facsimile. It is unquestionable, however, that through a process of trial and error the Jungian searchers often came very close to the hierophanies described, in the most trustworthy histories of comparative religion, as the basis for a wide variety of myths.[4]

Concentrating on the major hierophanies, it is certain that the importance (in Whitehead's sense) ascribed to one or the other of them at various stages in the development of religious awareness is related to the successive and corresponding stages reached by human cultures. This is according to the most reliable findings of Father Schmidt's research which posited, however, the highly questionable existence of an initial monotheism.[5]

Since the latter stages may be defined in terms of humanity's means of subsistence, the sky—all-encompassing in its transcendent unity—became the symbol of the divine when man still had to rely on the picking and gathering of food, and therefore felt wholly dependent for his livelihood on that mysterious unity underlying and ruling the universe.

In his first attempt to domesticate nature, man reached the hunting and fishing stage. Though still dependent, in this new endeavor, on the cosmic powers, he started to "immanentize" and thereby divide them. Without ever completely forgetting the presence and sovereign power of the celestial god, he turned for success in his activities to a moon and water goddess of the night and of springs—whom he saw as the mother of the living, permanently free from every marriage, and therefore permanently independent.

Although pastoral nomadism no doubt represents a further step to control nature for man's own ends, it may be assumed that sun worship, linked to the renewal of vegetation sought by the periodically moving nomads, marks a return, along a different path, to a more thoughtful sense of divine transcendence and unity. Pettazoni is therefore not entirely wrong when he sees in the first explicit forms of monotheism the results of this mutation.[6] It may be noted, however, that a belief in the gods of wind and rain (and of a single one combining their attributes, i.e., the god of storms)—which first appeared elsewhere during this period—could also have led to the same stage.[7]

On the other hand, the next hierophany—which relates to the shift to a sedentary life, with the soil being systematically cultivated for the first time—engulfed the divine in the chthonian powers (both terrestrial and subterranean) of vegetation: these are mother images again, but of death as much as of life, or of a life arising only from or for death.[8]

A kind of summation of this entire past takes place with the transition from cultivation to civilization proper, i.e., to the establishment of a small city, in which a coordinated hierarchy of specialized functions emerges. Paradoxically, it is at this point that the tendency to polytheism becomes fully explicit, while magic seems about to absorb religion completely. Through incipient industry, *homo faber*, the blacksmith becomes the key to all other activities: construction of a dwelling (finally mastered to meet the growing needs of man), agriculture, fishing and hunting, and of course war.[9] But it is also at this stage that the king makes his appearance, succeeding the primitive shaman, who inspired the most ancient forms of worship in the first human communities.[10] The king was to be the cornerstone of the city, as the blacksmith was its foundation. The stellar hierophanies then became dominant, though associated with lodes of metallic ore in the earth through a system of astrological correspondence.

The Royal Myth

The shaman was an inspired being who maintained and ceaselessly renewed the contact—easily lost by other men—with the cosmic and hypercosmic powers. In contradistinction, at the dawn of the first civilizations the king became the permanent link, the living nexus between, on the one hand, the cosmos and whatever transcends it and, on the other hand, the small world man fashions for himself, in the city, within and at the heart of the macrocosm.[11]

It is noteworthy that in countries with an even climate, such as Egypt, the identification of the city with the cosmos appears so perfect that the king becomes the epiphany of the supreme god.[12] In other areas, where there is less security and the weather is more variable, the king never reaches such high status. But he remains, nevertheless, the chosen instrument of the deity, the usual channel for divine intervention, which he can therefore count upon.[13]

At this stage, myths reach what may be called their classical form, for the king provides a dominant hierophany which defines the relationship in human ritual, from the viewpoint of both the organized community and the individual, with the various cosmic hierophanies, whose successive emergence and hierarchy we have already referred to. Indeed, before being the leader in wartime and the organizer of the city during peace, the king is always the institutor of rites, and particularly of the fundamental one: the ritual of sacrifice, around which all the others gravitate.[14] For a long time, the king remained both the agent of sacrifice, like Saul,[15] and its lyrically inspired commentator, like David,[16] before delegating specialized priests, at least for daily celebrations, and professional prophets to interpret these.

Nature and Meaning of Sacrifice

At this point, it is essential to indicate the primitive meaning or meanings of sacrifice,[17] for it contains implicitly all the themes that fully-developed myths will orchestrate around the heroic deeds supposedly performed by the king, along with the gods he represents or embodies, as well as the adversaries he meets in combat and the goddesses he marries.

It can never be overemphasized that the inspirational fruitfulness of the ritual experience, and particularly of the sacrificial experience, illustrates the total inanity of the contemporary theological quarrel between proponents of the Eucharist as sacrifice and those of the Eucharist as banquet.[18] For a phenomenological study of primitive sacrifice and of its implications precludes any opposition between the two concepts; indeed, a sacrifice is a ritual banquet, that is to say, not an artificial festivity, but a celebration recognized as the quintessential feast in which men meet the gods to enter into a profound vital association with them. Such a view is obviously fully consonant with the close link between each hierophany and man's various means of existence in the cosmos.[19]

This deep significance of sacrifice is fully supported, as far as Israel is concerned, by the whole of Leviticus, which has been called, on the literal level, a handbook for the perfect butcher, one that describes the various ways of preparing a repast with which God is associated. Either it is entirely dedicated to him (as in the case of the holocaust), or the priest alone shares it with him (penitential sacrifices), or else those who make the offering also participate (sacrifices of communion or of thanksgiving).[20] Basic to this ritual diversity is the Paschal sacrifice, indistinguishable from the family meal taken at the springtime renewal of vegetation, but a rite which was to become, for the entire people, the founding sacrifice, offered for the establishment and renewal of the Covenant, through which Israel may be said to have received its collective identity and was consecrated to its God.[21]

In their material aspect, however, the sacrifices of the Hebrews were a continuation of the sacrificial system prevalent in Canaan, or indeed in the entire Near East. The most diverse *thusiai* of the Greeks and the *sacrificia* of the Romans are obviously related to that system.[22] Earlier, the same pattern is found all over the ancient Orient. The Vedas of aryanized India are but an elaborate sacrificial theology, which introduces all human, cosmic, and even supra-cosmic reality into the pre-eminent sacrifice of the *soma-haoma*.[23]

For those we call primitive peoples, whose entire consciousness is filled with the most fundamental experiences of life in the world, an awareness subsequently repressed into the unconscious, it can be said that the deeply sacral experience of the ritual meal is pregnant with everything the most sophisticated religious developments would ever express.

The meal, that central activity through which the human family constantly replenishes and recenters itself in the cosmos, shows first that the cosmos, in its deepest nature, is a community of apparently inexhaustible life. This life, which suffuses the world to reach its highest development in man, is revealed through the meal as something inherently of this world, yet necessarily originating outside and above it. Conversely, it may be sensed through the significance of the meal that divine life, the very life of the gods, of God, is entirely directed toward communication and the giving of that which is most precious, i.e., of oneself.

In receiving together the same gift, men reach their fullest dimension and become aware of their unity as human beings and of their oneness with cosmic reality. They themselves become regenerated and may even bring about a regeneration of cosmic reality, in that total community, communion in and with transcendence. They are thus caught up in the same process of communication and exchange, which becomes manifest to them as the connection between man and the world and between the cosmos and the divine. Renewing their life as they do, living in this fashion, how could men not feel that they themselves are called to a divine life?

Eros and Thanatos

In this context, and on the basis we have just described, the king, originator of the sacrifices, and therefore representative of the divine among humans, will be described by myths as renewing and embodying the divine combat through which life perpetually triumphs over death, or, more fundamentally still, an inexpressible divine marriage which regenerates at its maternal source the gift of life.

We unquestionably find here, in all fully-evolved religions, a confirmation of the validity of Freud's last intuition, reached after his discovery of the crucial nature of sexuality as the mystery of life, both human and cosmic, to the effect that this mystery may simply be, in the last analysis, the intrusion, underlying both the cosmos and human existence, of a death instinct into the quintessential vital instinct.[24]

The Myths of the Near East and the Bible

We are now in a position to examine, among the many forms of the universal myth that are characteristic of the Near East, those in contrast to which divine revelation (as we consider it) was to stand. An unexpected fertilization was thus to take place, whose fruit is in the biblical Word, and particularly the account of creation. In the first few pages of the Bible, the Word proclaims that it created everything that exists.

We can outline the royal myths of the Near East, and indicate the main thrust of what was to be the primordial message of the Bible: that the God revealed to Israel is in fact the only true king. But first we need to describe in some detail the various populations which successively settled in the area and established a series of civilizations that intensely interacted until the emergence of biblical revelation.

Pre-Biblical Cultures

The birth of the Egyptian civilization and monarchy go back to approximately 4000 B.C., although it is not possible to trace the course of their history until about 2500 B.C. In Mesopotamia also, the start of the fourth millennium B.C. witnessed the beginning of the establishment and growth of Sumer, which handed down to its successors, thanks to cuneiform writing, epics that were to enjoy the most extraordinary success.

Somewhat later, a first wave of Semitic peoples, the Akkadians, reach Ur in Chaldea. They settled there, adopting the writing and culture of Sumer, but not its language. Toward 2200 B.C., a second wave occurred, that of the Amorites, who settled in Babylon, and whose greatest king and lawmaker was to be Hammurabi. Their ascendency was a short one, however, and around 2000 B.C. they were replaced by the Assyrians, a third wave of invaders, who conquered Babylon. Meanwhile, Canaan had undergone parallel invasions. The last of these, around 1400 B.C., was to be that of the Ugarites, who settled in northern Syria. Earlier, however, between 3000 and 1225 B.C., the non-Semitic Hittites had infiltrated Asia Minor and settled in Hattusa.[25]

The Egyptian King: God Made Manifest

In Egypt, probably due to the particularly effective regularity—made possible by the periodic floods of the Nile—in irrigation and agriculture, both completely controlled by the king, he was himself divine and identified with the most powerful gods. For this reason, he first embodied Horus, son of Osiris, the god of vegetation. But he was also the manifestation of Ra, the sun god, and the epiphany of the fecundating Nile. Through his identification with these gods, the entire life of the Pharaoh was a ritual, seen as maintaining the life of the Egyptian land, wrested from the deadly desert. Upon his death, however, the Pharaoh would become Osiris himself, the god put to death but brought back to life through the magic of his sister and consort Isis, who then conceived Horus by him. The new king, the successor of the Pharaoh, was then identified with Horus.

So it was that the king, with his inherited knowledge of *Maat*, the cosmic order established in the world by these gods, imparted it to the Egyptian microcosm, whose harmonious life he ensured, in spite of the powers of death inhabiting the deserts of sand which surrounded the fertile land on every side. Egypt was therefore the only successful world, just as Egyptians were the only ones to deserve the name of men (the same word was used to designate "a man" and "an Egyptian").

From this viewpoint there was, strictly speaking, no history, since the kings embodied, successively and interminably, the same divine powers. This continuity was duly emphasized in the chronicles which record the accomplishments,[26] and occasionally the failures, of later pharaohs, and which systematically make use of the formal language initially introduced to glorify the heroic or ordinary deeds of the earliest kings.

The Babylonian or Canaanite King: Servant and Son of God

The rulers of Babylon and Canaan were seen in a substantially different light. The climate being unpredictable and characterized by violent storms and devastating droughts, the kings were considered less as heirs to an ancient royal line (which was the case in Egypt) than as self-made men, so to speak, and their gods resembled them in this respect. This shift in image or perception is already clear with the first of the area's monarchs to emerge as a truly outstanding historical figure, the cunning and pious Sumerian Gudea. These kings were in effect tribal chieftains whose leadership had been brought out by a major crisis, either a sudden invasion which was successfully repulsed, or a natural disaster. They are therefore not gods incarnate, but at best were adopted by the gods, whom they represented as eminent servants; were called sons through ritual courtesy, but with a filiation as uncertain as their tenure.

It is here that history takes its start. The history of these kings and of their subjects remained eventful and uneven; it could never have been reconciled with undisturbed cycles similar to those of Egyptian liturgy. Although attempts were made by these peoples to maintain such a link, it is characteristic of these other civilizations that attention was not focused on the daily ritual of the awakening, the ceremonial rising, and the various stately events of the royal day, serenely unfolding through set stages, but rather on a single exceptional celebration, that of the new year. By virtue of his personal power and as champion of the local god, the king was seen to reestablish the balance of a kingdom in continual need of being brought back to the purity and vigor of its origins.

Particularly in Babylon, the king, like Marduk the tutelary deity, was required to struggle against the powers of death represented by Tiamat, the goddess of Chaos. Marduk first undergoes a mysterious humiliation, is stripped of his royal insignia, and confesses his fault and that of his people; in a dramatic reversal of fortune, he emerges victorious from the conflict, he recovers everything wrested from him, and his regenerating power asserts itself in a hierogamy, through which he evokes from Tiamat, as goddess of the primordial waters, a renewed vitality for his land and his entire empire.[27]

This is evidently the origin (or perhaps one of the earliest reoccurrences) of the theme of the barren Earth and the languishing King, whose personal wound makes his entire kingdom sterile, including the soil; it is a figure that recurs in the medieval legend of the Grail. In *The Golden Bough*, Sir James Frazer attempted to trace through various civilizations this universal theme of the king who suffers with his people, and with the whole cosmos, and whose personal victory saves all things and all men.[28]

The Feast of the New Year and the Divine Kingship

The great Norwegian exegete Sigmund Mowinckel believed that the Babylonian and Canaanitic feast of the New Year was introduced into Israel much earlier than the Bible suggests, but that its liturgical application, not to a human king but to the invisible king symbolized by the Ark of the Covenant, was the origin of the specifically Hebrew concept of God's reign superseding and abolishing all other reigns. God, who revealed himself to Abraham and his sons through his Word, is therefore the only true King.[29]

That the New Year celebration was indeed of major importance in Israel from the earliest times is a subject discussed at length by exegetes, but has not won the status of a majority opinion.[30] On the other hand, the kingship of the Lord of the Jews—the God who showed himself to their fathers, delivered them from Egypt, settled them in Canaan, and was finally enthroned in Zion under the symbolism of the Ark of the Covenant—was a central theme whose primordial importance is certainly attested by the entire book of Psalms, as studied by Gunkel, then by Mowinckel. More specifically, God's eschatological enthronement at the completion of history, foreshadowed and even initiated in the Yahwist cult, is the essential theme of the psalms which start with *Cantate Domino* or *Dominus regnavit*, and which are at the very heart of the psalter.[31]

God, Israel's Only King

Israel is closely related to the surrounding peoples, in their sacral and definitely regal civilizations, by the central nature of the king's role in the cult and by the entire religious literature. But it also stands sharply apart since, for Israel, no human king can be God. On the contrary, the God who revealed himself to Abraham precisely by forcing him to distance himself from the developing cities of the Fertile Crescent, by drawing him and his sons into a long period of wandering in search of an unworldly kingdom, this mysterious and omnipotent God, the only wise one, is alone king.

Moreover, it must be recognized from the start, and with increasing clarity as the prophetic Word unfolds, that not only will Israel itself never have any other king, but also that the one who revealed himself to Israel is in fact also the king of all peoples, whether they realize it or not, and therefore the master of the entire human history. Nor is this all: it must be emphasized, and this is the key concept, that God is supremely the King of the cosmic powers themselves, i.e., of those whom the other peoples of the world consider as their gods, but who in reality are but the servants of the only true God. Willingly or not, in the fullness of time, they will have to fall into line with his laws.[32]

In these assertions, we have the entire revelation already latent in the first manifestations of the biblical Word. And by the same token a totally renewed cosmology will replace that of the myths, while yet taking up again all their images and symbols.

The Living God

In order fully to understand the foregoing, one must bear prominently in mind that, in contrast to the gods of Canaan and Babylon and Egypt, the God of Israel appears as the living and life-giving God.[33]

The Canaanitic and Babylonian deities, and particularly their mother-goddesses, were above all else fertility gods. They embodied the life of the world—plant life, born of the soil—but in its relation to animal life, as it is transmitted to man himself and finds in sexuality its most striking expression for the semi-primitive peoples. This was reflected at the lowest level in the sacred prostitution of the hierodules—priests and priestesses dedicated to the worship of the goddess known as Astarte in the Bible.

The view of life as a divine manifestation was no less important in Israel. Its obvious reaction against orgiastic cults never led to any form of puritanism. Those who later attempted to find in this reaction a justification for collective repression were totally mistaken, for there is in the Bible no trace of contempt for the body. Human life is the life of the body, to such an extent that the idea of a soul distinct from the body—even though it may be neither as recent in the Bible as the exegetes of the early twentieth century were inclined to believe, nor a concept introduced from Iran or Greece—

became explicit only at a fairly late stage, without the soul and the body ever being considered as alien, let alone antagonistic, to each other.

Nor can one detect in Israel any aversion to sexuality. There has been a long-standing misconception in this regard concerning the purification procedures required by Leviticus in connection with sexual activity, in particular for women following childbirth. However, it is not because the Bible saw sexuality and procreation as in any way impure *per se* that these procedures were required. Quite the opposite, in fact. Since everything related to life is sacred and belongs to God, sinful man is under suspicion of unworthiness, having ventured with his usual presumption into an area in which he is even less his own master than elsewhere. The purification required of him parallels the one priests must undergo, for the same reason, after carrying out their sacred duties. In order to distinguish a holy book from one not inspired, the Jews would say that the former soiled one's hands. In precisely the same sense, the rubrics of Catholic liturgy speak of "purifying" the sacred vessels, when the actual purpose is to remove all remaining traces of the Blessed Sacrament they had held.[34]

The point is that the God recognized by Israel is not simply living, as we are, albeit superabundantly. He is not a mere receptacle and transmitter of cosmic life. He is the master of life, because he is its source, a transcendent source in whom life infinitely surpasses the characteristics and limitations of life as it is ordinarily received and imparted. Which is why Leviticus prohibits the drinking of blood, which is life itself, and life, even in us, belongs only to God.[35] Henceforth, our adoration will no longer be exclusively directed toward cosmic life; created life, seen as radically surpassing us, gains a totally unprecedented dignity.

Highly significant in this regard is the special abhorrence inspired in Israel by the divinities and cults of Egypt, and by Osiris in particular.[36] To be sure, Osiris is a god of life, and especially of plant life renewed in the spring. But the myth of Osiris' sister-spouse Isis seeking and gathering the fragments of his body that were scattered by Seth, his brother and enemy, then magically bringing them back to life so as to allow the infant Horus to be conceived in her by the revived Osiris, presents a picture totally alien to the sovereign, intangible and invulnerable life which the Angel of God was to reveal in the burning bush.[37] In sharp contrast to Egypt, funeral home of gods, men, and animals, all equally mummified, the promised land beyond the desert will appear as the land of life, a life flowing inexhaustibly from its source. The God who will inhabit that land with his people will be, according to the prophets Isaiah and Jeremiah, the source of these living waters, a source having absolutely nothing in common with the broken cisterns built by man, unable to hold even stagnant water.[38] God therefore appears as completely transcending all our forms of life and all forms of cosmic life.

There is no feminine deity, no sexuality in God, but a virginal Paternity requiring no other divine partner.

Sexual imagery, and more precisely the relationship between husband and wife, will indeed play a role in biblical tradition, and will display a hitherto unknown breadth and purity. But this imagery will make its appearance at a second stage of revelation, not to illustrate divine life in itself, nor the original relation between the creator and his creation, but only to exemplify the wholly eschatological relationship, arising through the grace of God, which will freely unite creation to its creator at the end of time.[39]

From these various considerations it follows that divine life will appear in the Word heard by Israel as totally incommensurable with our life and that of the entire universe, to such an extent that, for ourselves and for the universe, divine life will be as overwhelming as a thunderbolt. It is a common theme in the earliest narratives of the Pentateuch, and even more in the book of Judges, which is markedly primitive in its mode of expression, that no mortal may see God without dying—because of the infinite power of the divine life when it meets directly our own merely relative and wholly dependent life.[40] And yet, once again, the supreme revelation toward which the entire Old Testament points with increasing emphasis is the Living One who imparts life to created man in order to adopt him, not simply in a purely formal and ultimately fictitious way but, quite mysteriously, in the truest and most literal sense of the word. This revelation is already apparent in Exodus 24:10, where the ancients of Israel are allowed to see the place where God stands. It will be superabundantly clear in the promises of resurrection and of new and immortal life with God expressed in the apocalypse of Isaiah. These promises become fully explicit in Ezechiel's visions: first of Jerusalem rebuilt, when a flow of life-giving waters issuing from the Temple shall heal the symbolic waters of the Dead Sea, then, and even more importantly, of the dead arising and being clothed again with flesh at the command of the Word and finally receiving the Spirit, the very breath of the life of God.[41]

The Glory of God

This leads us to the other major biblical theme, that of God's glory. It is a theme linked to the previous one, for glory, a characteristically royal trait, is but the manifestation in the king of an extraordinary vitality. In this sense Semitic kings, at the stage when the first civilizations were taking shape, were clearly the successors and heirs of the primitive shamans. These were the inspired men who seem to have initiated the earliest cultures by displaying a form of life superior to that of ordinary men, one recognizable as the life of the spirits, or of the Spirit.

Etymologically, the Hebrew word *kābôd*, which we translate as *glory*, means "weight." It opposes the divine reality of the true God to the triviality and changeability of the false gods, the idols. God is "full," he is plenitude itself, whereas they are emptiness.[42]

Quite early, however, this figure was supplemented with the image of an effulgent supernatural light emerging spontaneously from God's infinite vitality. Psalm 104, which closely imitates (so it seems) a hymn by Ikhnaton (the Pharaoh who attempted to introduce a first solar monotheism), shows God in his course, giving light with life, in the manner of the sun. The earliest origins of this theme, later taken up by Israel, are found in the celebration of the sun's radiance (in the traditional Egyptian cult), and perhaps even more directly in the faint and mysterious light visible in the heart of darkness and prevailing over night itself: in the light of the stars, and particularly of Venus, the evening star, which the Sumerians identified with their mother-goddess Inanna, and which the Babylonians later saw as Ishtar (the Astaroth or Astarte of the Bible).

It has been quite properly noted by S. Hooke that the divine glory, as understood by Israel, was to find adequate representation only in an imagery fully appropriate to some of the most ancient biblical accounts, which are ascribed both to the so-called Elohist and to the earliest sacerdotal tradition. This is the imagery of the pillar of cloud by day and the pillar of fire by night, guiding and protecting Israel in the desert. This pillar is obviously related to the manifestation of the Lord in the supernatural storm which surrounded his descent on Sinai, and to the luminous cloud which covered first the tabernacle set up by Moses, then the most holy place of the Solomonic Temple. After Moses himself was summoned to meet face-to-face the God who spoke to Israel from within the darkness, it was within that cloud that both Isaiah and Ezechiel, in their visions of the Temple, believed they saw, in Ezechiel's words, "a likeness as it were of a human form."[43]

The Transfiguration of the Cosmos

This admittance to the luminous cloud, this paradoxical vision of the otherwise inaccessible light it reveals to the elect, has as its counterpart the theme of glorification, the supernatural resplendence of those to whom this direct meeting has been vouchsafed. Glorification is reflected in the blinding radiance of Moses' countenance after he has spent forty days on the mountain, "talking with God."[44] The same theme reemerges explicitly in the New Testament, when St. Paul asserts that we are called to behold, under the features of the risen Christ, the very glory of the divine face, so as to be ourselves transfigured "from one degree of glory to another; for this comes from the Lord who is the Spirit." The Apostle emphasized the very different mode of the Old Testment by pointing out that the Hebrews were not even permitted to look upon the reflection of God's countenance in the face of Moses, which was covered with a veil. This fundamental shift in the New Testament is illustrated in the account of the Transfiguration of Jesus on the mount, in the presence of his chosen disciples, on the eve of the Passion.[45]

As for St. John, he writes in his First Epistle that the Christians' certainty of becoming similar to God in the risen Christ, which is also their goal, is because they shall see God as he is.[46] In this respect, it should be stressed that many exegetes were mistaken in believing that a Hellenistic, more precisely a Platonic, influence could be detected in this theme. Although both Plato and the Bible, and particularly the Gospel, show a close link between contemplating God and resembling him, the relation between the two terms is diametrically opposed in their viewpoints. For Plato and his successors, down to Plotinus, man finally succeeds in knowing God, and therefore resembling him, through a long ascetic endeavor initiated and controlled by man himself.[47] In the Bible, on the contrary, God's spontaneous and free revelation to man, in spite of the latter's unworthiness, leads man to resemblance of God, who illuminates his creature to the point of conferring divine likeness upon him and making man his true son. In the words of Psalm 36 (35), "For with thee is the fountain of life; in thy light do we see light."[48]

First in the apocalyptic texts, then in the New Testament, we shall later examine the subsequent development of these two closely associated themes: the light of glory and the divine life.

Cosmic Law and Moral Law

It remains for us to bring out a third feature of the divine kingship according to the Bible, which is found in the law arising therefrom and which rules both the hearts of the faithful and the conduct of the entire universe. As we have said, it was already a basic theme in Egyptian religion that the king reigned by virtue of his innate knowledge (since he was divine) of *Maat*, the divine law ruling the universe. Similarly Marduk, the Babylonian god who turned the kings he adopted into his servants, received from Ishtar the tablets of destiny, the *Me*, which allowed him to rule the city effectively. This myth was later popularized in Babylonian astrology, which claimed to read in the stars the laws governing earthly events.

This same viewpoint is expressed, with the utmost clarity, in Psalm 19 (18), which too many modern exegetes, their vision clouded by Western rationalism, have seen as including two unrelated psalms, whereas it simply voices, with typically biblical precision, the early Semites' indistinct perception that the purpose of religion is essentially to foster in human hearts the freely-accepted reign of the same divine law which endows the physical universe with coherence and harmony.[49]

The Divine Word

The ultimate significance of biblical revelation, however, is to recognize in God's Word heard by Israel the one and only source of both the law which holds sway in all things and the law which rules the lives of those men to whom God has made himself known. Hence the truth, adumbrated earlier but made fully explicit and literally fundamental in the Bible, that nothing exists except by the sovereign will of God and as an expression of that will. He has but to speak for all things and beings to come into existence. Conversely, everything which exists is but a concrete realization of the Word through which God expresses his plan. As one of the psalms puts it:

> [The Lord] sends forth his command to the earth;
>   his word runs swiftly.
> He gives snow like wool;
>   he scatters hoarfrost like ashes.
> He casts forth his ice like morsels;
>   who can stand before his cold?
> He sends forth his word, and melts them;
>   he makes his wind blow, and the waters flow.[50]

And Psalm 19 (18) says:

> The heavens are telling the glory of God...
> Day to day pours forth speech...
> There is no speech, nor are there words;
>   their voice is not heard;
> yet their voice goes out through all the earth,
>   and their words to the end of the world.[51]

This is where we see biblical revelation, as revelation of the divine kingship, in its exclusive splendor, lead to the biblical doctrine of creation.

Chapter IV: From Cosmogonic Myth to Creative Word

Myth and Biblical Word

It is still a temptation for historians of comparative religion to find diverse influences everywhere, on the basis of occasionally striking analogies. Some monuments of pre-Columbian America show the likeness of a man and a woman standing on either side of a tree laden with fruit which they seem to covet, and reportedly also of a woman conversing with a snake.[1] Does this indicate the likelihood of an uninterrupted primitive tradition, shared by all peoples, which might be at the root of the accounts in Genesis?[2]

In fact, things are more complex. Jungian psychologists, in spite of their over-simplifications and undue generalizations, are quite right to note the universal presence of certain symbolic representations, which are astonishingly constant through time and space.[3] These phenomena may not exactly attest to the existence of the archetypes Jung claimed to identify in what he called the collective unconscious, but they do point to a structure of the human soul which produces similar images, everywhere and independently, in response to the same universe. As Georges Dumézil[4] has emphasized, however, in order to speak of an influence or a continuous tradition, it is not enough to find the same symbolism in various parts of the world. The same groups of symbols must also be similarly arranged. As a matter of fact, we can be certain of not being misled by false analogies—unwittingly projected by us onto the documents being analyzed—only if a lexicological analysis verifies the historical connections suggested by analysis of the symbols themselves. Otherwise, the derivation of myths or of any other representation can never be considered as fully established.[5]

In this respect, Dumézil has thrown into particularly sharp relief—against the background of the spread and diversification of the Indo-European languages—a mythic heritage whose substance remains unchanged from the earliest civilizations of India to the Greeks and Romans.[6] This holds true even though the substance is colored differently at each stage, and even when it seems debilitated by an endless repetition of formulas whose original meaning has become unclear even to those who persist in using them.

The same comment applies to those myths that have become typically Semitic, although they seem to have been borrowed from Sumer, a different racial group; the Semites adopted Sumer's overall culture, even its writing, but not its language.[7] These myths therefore show a connection with Indo-European myths, though differing from them in adaptations not peculiarly Semitic, having been foreshadowed in Sumer. Still, they reflect conditions of life specific to the Fertile Crescent, and especially to Mesopotamia. A highly developed sense of drama and heroic character shows that what we call history probably originated in these cultures.[8]

In each area, shared myths were altered, and these alterations reveal the specific experiences and responses of each population.[9] These variations are in a sense preparations for the last and most important mutation of all, the shift from myths proper to what Israel considers the Word of God. One comment should immediately be added, however: this latest development implies such a radical transformation of fundamental views on cosmic and human reality that, even allowing a most remarkable and elaborate gestation, it is clear we are dealing with something absolutely new.

The Cosmogonic Myth in Sumer

In Sumer, as in most early cultures, the basic conviction was that everything comes from the sea, whose waters were seen as the source of all beings; the goddess Nammu appeared as the universal mother.[10] Peculiar to the Sumerians was the importance they ascribed to certain prescribed limits, whose various combinations brought into being everything that exists. The sea itself is bounded by the celestial horizon and the terrestrial shore; both were personified and sexed, and became An, the god of heaven, and Ki, the goddess of earth. Their union produced Enlil, the god of the air that separates them. Enlil carries off another goddess, Ninhil, who seems to represent the sky. She is cast down with Enlil into the depths of the underground world, where she gives birth to Nanna, also known as Sin, the moon goddess. In turn Nanna begets Utu, the sun god, from her union with Ningal, another divinity.

At this point, a new deity makes its appearance: the god of wisdom, Enki. He is very different from the other members of the Sumerian pantheon, who merely personify powers of nature. Enki suggests that Enlil produce a god and a goddess, both benevolent, in apparent atonement for his folly, which had led him to send forth a multiplicity of gods from heaven to the earth. The two beneficent deities are Lahar, the god of cattle, and Ashnan, the goddess of grain. Finally Enlil produces man, fashioned of clay by Nammu, the goddess of primeval waters, and by Ninmah, who tends to births. Man will offer sacrifices to all the gods.

Meanwhile, Enki continues his beneficial activity. He launches civilization by suggesting that Enlil make the first tool, a pickax. Inanna, daughter of Enki, plies her father with wine and takes from him the tablets of destiny, *Me*, which she gives to man...

The Babylonian Cosmogonic Myth

Sumer's rudimentary cosmogony, which is also (as with all myths) a theogony, is known to us only in fragments, and may raise more questions than it answers. But it is obviously the origin of the much more sophisticated version that was to emerge in Babylon[11] and may be considered as a close antecedent of the first biblical account of creation. It has reached us in the form of an Akkadian epic, *Enuma Elish*, that describes a celebration of the new year in which Marduk had become the central and probably the most powerful divinity. This major poem was found on seven tablets discovered in Nineveh by George Smith in 1876.[12]

This literary monument brings out, better than any Sumerian prototypes, the dualistic nature of the myth. Initially Apu was the god of rivers and Tiamat the goddess of the sea who gave birth to the demon Kingu, the dark power of the depths. However, Apu and Tiamat had first begotten Lahmu and Lahamu, who dwelt on either side of the line separating the sea and the rivers; then Anshar and Kishar, abiding above and below the horizon; and finally Aun, representing the sky, and Nadimmud-Ea, representing both the earth and wisdom, to whom Marduk was born.

As related on the second tablet, this initial phase led to a conflict between the first-born of the gods and the next in line, who ordered Marduk to lead the battle. The third tablet describes his investiture, which closely follows the royal liturgy of the coronation and enthronement. The fourth pictures Marduk cleaving Tiamat in two, thus separating the waters of the sky from those of the earth. In the fifth tablet, Marduk establishes the calendar, on which the entire ritual is based. In the sixth, to ensure that the ritual will be faithfully carried out, he produces man, fashioned of clay and the blood of Kingu, who was slain in combat with his mother.

It will be noted that the Babylonian version of the Sumerian myth emphasizes the revolt of the later gods against the primordial ones. The latter appear decidedly ambiguous: they are the first source of life, yet that life develops only through conflict with a principle of death which springs from the same origin.

The Celebration of the New Year

The outgoing year establishes the apparent victory of death, deeply rooted in cosmic existence. After a ritual battle, the new year renews faltering life, but each time must repeat its victory over death, which derives, together with life itself, from the source of all things. As we have already indicated, Mowinckel assumes that, Israel having taken up the celebration of the new year, biblical inspiration refashioned this myth into the first account of creation in the initial chapter of Genesis. The celebration then became, according to him, the feast of the enthronement, not of an earthly king, servant and vicar of Marduk, but of God himself, the hidden God whose special presence with Israel was reflected in the choice of Zion as the repository of the Ark of the Covenant.[13]

From Myths to the Biblical Cosmogony

Mowinckel's position has been vigorously disputed by other exegetes.[14] They point out that the new year celebration appears to have been adopted belatedly by the Israelites, who never seem to have given it the fundamental importance it presumably had in Babylon. Instead, as early as the exodus from Egypt and the arrival in Canaan, the Passover was seen by Moses and the prophets as a sort of founders' day celebration. And the so-called sacerdotal account of creation[15] highlights every week, not just the first week of the year. This is an equally novel viewpoint: everything is directed toward the Sabbath, i.e., toward the affirmation that God does not have to consolidate or renew ceaselessly a creation fundamentally divided against itself, as in the Babylonian myth, but has established the universe out of his omnipotence, with no possible opposition. What he has wrought therefore remains stable and permanent, so that God is now resting endlessly from his work.

Man was not born to maintain the life of secondary, dependent gods through the preparation and offering of sacrifices. Having been called by the one and all-powerful God to participate in the achievement, or rather the fruitful perfecting of divine creation, man is not required to sustain a divine life which has no need of his assistance. On the contrary, man's worship will be to partake in the divine repose; God's Sabbath is extended to include man, and becomes the day of worship. Once this general frame of reference is clarified and set straight, all the rest will follow.

Like its forerunners, the Bible devotes considerable attention to *tôledôth*, genealogies. These no longer concern gods, however, but creatures, and the lineage leads to man, whose service to God already appears, not as a slavery which the deity needs in order to survive, but as a friendship, a reciprocity of pure thanksgiving toward pure benevolence. For this is the most salient point in the entire biblical account: the world does not proceed from a primal divinity, i.e., a single deity, but one indistinguishable from the disorder of still-unformed matter. It does not reach concrete existence only through a dialectic process of precarious separations and combinations, even less from a conflict between secondary and primordial divinities. The concept of discord in the pantheon presumably resulted from the fusion of two successive stages in the myth's development that increasingly emphasized the fundamental dualism. In Genesis, on the contrary, even though the abyss of undifferentiated waters, the primeval chaos (*tehôm*), remains the first creature, or the first phase of creation,[16] this chaos, far from being the primal deity, is but the initial product of the divinity, which shows itself from the start as completely transcending the entire cosmic existence. The latter proceeds from this transcendent God, not through some necessity, and even less through a kind of degradation of the divine being itself, but as a result of God's generosity. The first product of creation, though initially formless, will therefore unquestionably be seen as fundamentally good.[17] And this goodness, essential to the creature as it is to the creator, becomes more and more pronounced, going from amorphous matter to man created in God's own image and called upon to imitate him in his bountiful action.[18]

In this context, cosmic existence does not arise from a division within the mother principle of all things, nor does it diversify through an alternation of sexual fertilizations and conflicts, so overlapped that they seem to be two faces of a single reality, in which death and life not only interchange endlessly, but indeed represent two poles of a single reality. On the contrary, a distinction freely effected by the transcendent God within a created but still indefinite being—always progressing in the same direction, as through an incubation of his Spirit,[19] his own life-breath—will bring forth beings increasingly capable of spiritualizing this *materia prima*, i.e., the abyss or the primal chaos. Instead of a merciless struggle, we see the gradual development of an ascending ladder of life. At the top stands the one who carries God's image in himself; being able to understand the divine task and to perceive its benevolent purpose, he will assist in the completion of the undertaking, thereby perfecting himself through a cooperation which leads to friendship with the Lord.[20]

It seems to be at this point that sexuality is transfigured into a reciprocal friendship;[21] sexuality had appeared at the start of creation, was typical of it, as opposed to the creator, and developed with the beings which originated through sexual generation. Through the later prophets[22] it was revealed that this relationship immanent to humanity, and thereby elevated and refined, was to become the image of the relationship intended by God between himself and mankind. By the end of the first chapter of Genesis, it may be said that this narrative of creation has laid the groundwork for this final revelation. Man's participation in the divine Sabbath, upon the completion of creation, leads us toward the ultimate revelation, by expressing both man's innate likeness to his creator and the reciprocal assimilation which God is proposing to man.

It is clear that we have moved from a world view in which the development of the material universe is but a fragmenting or scattering of a divine reality to the concept of a single transcendent God who produced all things through a gradual communication of his benevolence. Instead of sharpening the confrontational aspect, i.e., the conflict inherent in the very development of life, the high point of creation is in man created in God's image and destined, in God's beneficence, actually to resemble God. Man's destiny is therefore anything but that of a slave serving a fundamentally needy divinity. On the contrary, man is intended to be the friend of God, associated with him in both his blissful repose and his wholly generous activity. Sexuality no longer appears, in the divinity itself, as part of a dichotomy that produces life only to abandon it to death. It is distinctive of the creature, and evolves to become the image of the ultimate relationship which this creation is destined to enter into with the God who made it.

The Creative Word

The most original feature in the text of Genesis, however, is clearly the idea that God creates all beings by his Word alone.[23] First, here is the most solemn affirmation that the divine Word, the source of Israel's entire history, including its existence as God's people, is the origin of all existence. Conversely, every created being is but the expression and materialization of the omnipotent benevolence of the God who showed himself to Abraham and his children.[24] This being so, the whole world exists and has a definite identity, at least in its principle, only because God thinks and wants it. This world is the expression of the conjoined thought and will of the Most High, the Only One.

We have here the most fully developed and explicit statement, in respect to the world as divine creation, of this fundamental truth about the Word received in faith by Israel. God is the king, the only true king, and his kingdom, that of his sovereign will, includes not only Israel but all men, even those who know him not. It includes everything that exists, beginning with those cosmic powers that are simply among God's earliest servants, although treated as gods by other peoples.

The Second Biblical Account: Anthropogenesis

The Bible adds to this account of creation an appendix, a very different version.[25] It was included by the so-called sacerdotal redactors of the first account, even though it came from another source, probably from what modern critics refer to as the Yahwist document.[26] The most striking feature of this second account is that it does not merely culminate in the creation of man but is almost entirely absorbed by that crowning episode of the creative process. This may well be because the second account is given not mainly for its own sake, but as a necessary introduction to the story of the Fall, which shows how the world, created wholly good by God, was corrupted and fell prey to evil.[27]

Further, the new text's recasting of the myth, although as marked in content as the first account, is less extensively so as to its form. Images deliberately excised by the sacerdotal writer, because they seemed to detract from God's transcendence, have been preserved (as is done in a few other parts of the Bible, and particularly in the Psalms). The second account, for instance, shows God, as the myth does, forming man out of the slime of the earth. But a twofold correction is immediately apparent. It is not by fashioning him with supposedly divine blood that God gives man life (as with Kingu), but by breathing into him the breath of life. Moreover, and this is also highly significant, the biblical writer avoids using the same term to designate God's breath (rûah) and the created soul (nephesh) which the Spirit will call forth in man as an echo of the Maker's own life. In a very real sense, this is the counterpart of the idea, found in the first account, that man was created in God's image and likeness.

It should be further noted that the immediate parallel to the second account is no longer the Babylonian myth, but that of Canaan. Life does not come from the waters of the sea (Tiamat or Tehôm), but sprouts in the desert from life-giving rain. And the description of the place where man first appears goes back to the Sumerian epic of Emmerkar. There the god Enki eats of the fruit of eight plants created by the mother goddess Ninhursag, who curses and slays him. Repenting of her deed, she revives him by producing eight divinities to cure Enki's eight injured organs. Ninti, the name of one of these divinities, means both rib and life. This is obviously the derivation of the biblical Eve, whose name means life, and who is pictured as being fashioned from a rib taken from man.

The theme of man warned not to pluck the fruit of divine knowledge and to keep away from the tree of life—i.e., prevented from seeking immortality through magic—suggests the plants eaten by Enki as well as the Akkadian and Babylonian theme of man seeking divine immortality (a theme which inspires the entire epic of Gilgamesh). It is also related to the theme, already mentioned as Sumerian in origin, of the tablets of destiny stolen from the gods and given to men by a goddess who betrays her trust. Finally, the name of the garden where God placed newly-created man, Eden, is derived from the Akkadian Eddin, which designates a plain or steppe.[28]

This multiplicity of borrowed themes, used with relatively minor adaptations, emphasizes that the account in Genesis 2 is no less original than the one in the previous chapter. Here again we have a genealogy of man rather than of the gods. But man's kinship with God is brought out more clearly than in any of the mythic accounts. Although blood remains for the Hebrews the specific sign of divine vitality in both the human and non-human world, it is not blood that man receives from God. Rather, life in man is the breath initiated by the very breath of God.[29] It is thus quite natural that man and woman—whose oneness is so strongly emphasized even in the difference between them—are set apart from other living creatures and called upon to rule over them. Adam gives them their names, which is to say that he knows them somehow as God knows them, and he is called upon to keep and perfect creation through his work.[30] But mankind must resist the temptation to gain knowledge fully similar to God's. Any such effort to become God's equal, far from bringing man immortality (as in the myth), would cause him to lose all hope of acquiring it. This obviously assumes that the true God is willing to give man this immortality, this life that is with himself and like his own, provided that man remains obedient to his commands.

The last characteristic of the biblical revelation in Genesis is therefore that creation has of itself nothing in common with any kind of Fall. But the biblical account hints at the manner in which, through pride and greed, the Fall could take place in a world created essentially good, and how the Fall could be brought about by the one who is creation's highest achievement, man himself.

Chapter V: The Fall in Myths and According to the Biblical Word

Just as mythic cosmogony is also, and even principally, a theogony, the genealogy of the gods, so the description of Fall is merged with that of creation. In fact, mythic accounts see in creation a Fall of the divinity.

Sumerian and Babylonian Views of the Fall

We have already seen how, in Sumerian mythology, Ninhil (the goddess who appears to represent the sky) is carried off by Enlil, the god of air, and is then cast into the depths of the earth with him. She gives birth first to the moon goddess, who in turn begets the sun god, from whom will proceed all the inferior divinities, and finally man, who is called upon to serve them.[1] Also, the goddess and queen of the heavens, Inanna, identified with the morning star, sinks into the subterranean world, where she is stripped of her jewels and royal vestments and put to death. After she has been absent from the heavens for three days, her vizier Ninshubur prevails on Enki, the god of wisdom—an eminently magical wisdom—to bring her back to life by giving her miraculous revivifying food and drink. She re-ascends to heaven, and must therefore send her consort Dumuzi, god of vegetation, to her place underground.[2]

The Babylonians carried out a striking shift in this myth. It is in order to save her brother and husband Tammuz from a similar fate that Ishtar gave herself up to the infernal powers, but managed to defeat them in the end.[3] Another theme, that of the flood, already plays a major role in both Sumerian and Babylonian myths. In Sumer, Enlil, the god of air, angry at mankind's noisy turbulence which disturbs the gods' repose, decides to destroy men by torrential rains. Enki, god of wisdom, wishes to save the pious Ziusudra, who on his advice builds a huge ship and thus survives a seven-day flood. Ziusudra then offers to make sacrifice on his ship to the sun god, who bestows immortality on him.[4]

The Babylonian gods make the same decision for a similar reason. The hero whose life is saved is Utnapishtim, and Ea (the counterpart of Enki) teaches him to build an enormous structure in which he gathers all kinds of animals. After the flood has lasted six days, the building runs aground on the top of mount Nizir. Utnapishtim sends forth in turn a dove, a swallow, and a raven to reconnoiter. He then offers a sacrifice on the mountain, where the gods gather like flies, we are told. Immortality is conferred on him and his wife, to whom Ishtar gives her necklace of lapis lazuli (the rainbow) as a token of that promise.[5]

In all these early accounts, one finds the snake, as god of the underground world and of sexuality, and the tree, symbol of ascent toward heaven, of magical knowledge, of life-defying death.[6] When the Semites adopt the theme of paradise, the latter becomes the abode of the immortals, to which Utnapishtim is admitted after the flood.[7]

Once again, and perhaps more than ever, the similarities with the biblical account stand out, but the differences are even more striking. A point should be emphasized that is too often overlooked. In the Bible, creation and the Fall are absolutely separate; moreover three different Falls, distinct though related, may be identified. There is the Fall of the first man and woman, in Genesis 3; the Fall of the celestial powers, in Genesis 6; and, finally, the Fall of human society, and more specifically of civilized society, in Genesis 11.

The Fall of the First Man and Woman

It is obvious that the Fall of man, or rather of the human couple, in Genesis 3, was precipitated by the suggestion of the serpent. He was therefore previously perverted, which is underscored in the Hebrew text by the contrast between the serpent's provocative nudity, equivalent to vicious guile, and the initially innocent nakedness of man and woman.[8] Contrary to mythic accounts, moreoever, they are placed in paradise from the start, by God himself, which is to say that they are, if not already immortal, at least intended for immortality.

It is clear that man and woman could not achieve eternal life by satisfying their desire for a magical knowledge which would make them the equals of the divinity. Quite the opposite: it is precisely that desire, encouraged by the serpent, which made them lose their immortality. It therefore seems that their union, occurring as the conclusion of their sharing of the forbidden fruit, far from completing God's work by cooperating with his plan, will express a wish to dominate the world in his place. The result will be that they themselves will be ruled by a wholly animal desire; their initial dominion over vegetative life is destroyed and they are cast out of paradise into an arid land.[9]

Consequences of the Initial Fall

Generally considered to be Yahwist in origin, the account of the first murder follows upon the rivalry between Abel and Cain, the original couple's first two sons. It illustrates the fact that mankind, starting out under such auspices, was doomed to internal strife. But this story has a threefold mythic background, and a close study of the elements emphasizes and sharpens its meaning immeasurably.[10]

The occupations of the two brothers—Abel raised cattle and Cain tilled the soil—provide a reflection of the ritual murders through which the first farmers sought to refertilize the land impoverished by the grazing of the nomadic herdsmen's livestock. More specifically, the account calls to mind the rivalry apparent in Sumerian mythology between Enkadi, god of farmers, and Dumuzi, god of shepherds, who both courted Inanna, goddess of the sky. Finally, Cain's flight after the murder parallels the ritual flight of the Babylonian priest, following the purification of the sanctuary, smeared with the blood of a lamb. He is protected by a special mark, which originally distinguished ritual murderers from common murderers.

Besides recognizing in Abel's murder by Cain the consequence of their parents' transgression, the Yahwist writer clearly has in mind the prophets' opposition to the adoption by Israel of primitive forms of agriculture, linked to worship of the natural powers, instead of the creator, with the additional abomination of ritual murders.[11]

Fall of the Powers

The second account of the Fall, or rather of a Fall, this time involving the cosmic powers (Gn. 6:1-4), should also be read in the light of Canaanitic nature cults. Of the entire Bible, this is certainly the part which has most blatantly kept the coloring of Babylonian and Canaanitic myths. It describes the "sons of God," embodying superhuman powers, drawn to the earth by the desire to take to themselves the "daughters of men," whose beauty had fascinated them. These unions brought forth prodigious beings, the giants or "mighty men of old," renowned for their feats of valor and their longevity. But their power is clearly evil, just as their origin is unnatural.

Although the downfall of Inanna and Ishtar may have inspired this account, in the biblical version the fallen powers are masculine, while femininity resides in the daughters of men, who have been seductive before being seduced. The story brings out a constant biblical theme: the opposition and connection between the masculine and feminine is always seen as a contrast between, on the one hand, the element representing the divinity in human and material creation and, on the other hand, creation itself.[12] In his transcendence, God is above this distinction, but in his relationship with creatures, he cannot be feminine, any more than his creatures can appear masculine. The same holds true for the beings who should be his representatives to human beings, but who turn the latter away from the Only One worthy of being worshipped, and seek to arrogate this worship to themselves while flattering them by the promise of an alliance which meets their own desires.

The biblical interpretation of this episode assumes that the prophets identify idolatry (worship of the created powers seeking to take the place which belongs only to the Uncreated One) with adultery, and even prostitution.[13] For the hierodules of many Babylonian or Canaanitic sanctuaries were in effect nothing but prostitutes. And Hosea, Jeremiah, and Ezechiel stress that Israel, the faithful people, must accept betrothal only to God, for the eternal nuptials which will ensure—in the total and confident surrender of the creature to God—mankind's only possible accession to immortality.[14]

Thus pride, the wish to usurp God's place and so dominate the world possessively, first corrupted the highest creatures, meant to protect and lead toward the creator the more humble beings that we are. Conversely, a selfish and egotistical wish for immediate gratification led us into slavery, instead of gaining for us the illusive freedom we sought far from God. Mankind then multiplied, but it was a multiplication in sin. And men drew upon themselves the punishment of the flood. It was a punishment, however, that held out a first hope of salvation.

The Flood in Myths and in the Bible

Today, the biblical account of the flood is generally explained by the insertion into a priestly narrative of a Yahwist narrative, whose details are not always compatible.[15] The two narratives agree in presenting the cataclysm as a judgment of God intended to condemn a long series of transgressions. Noah found grace before the Lord, since he was the only "just" man, the only one faithful to the true God.[16] According to the priestly writer, Noah was forewarned of the flood and received from on high a detailed description of the ark of salvation, which he built in accordance with the divine instructions.[17]

In the Yahwist portion of the text, "of all clean animals" Noah was to take into the ark "seven pairs...the male and his mate," but he was directed to bring in only two of "the animals that are unclean." The priestly writer, however, reported that two pairs of all animals, without distinction, were to be saved.[18] For the Yahwist, the flood was the result of a torrential rain.[19] The priestly writer indicates that "the windows of heavens were opened," and that the primal abyss (the tehôm) reappeared:[20] "the fountains of the great deep burst forth." For the Yahwist, the flood lasted forty days, and the waters ebbed for seven days,[21] whereas the priestly writer speaks of a hundred and fifty days in each case. Only he specifies that the ark landed on

Mount Ararat.[22] On the other hand, the Yahwist relates that a dove was released after the raven, mentions the sacrifice offered up by Noah, and adds that God "smelled [the] pleasing odor" of the holocaust and promised not to repeat such a curse.[23] The priestly writer, however, concludes with the establishment of the first covenant, to be attested for all time by the rainbow.[24]

Once again, it should be noted how the sacerdotal writer seeks to tone down or to eliminate altogether the mythic imagery applied to divine action, while the earlier Yahwist writer is markedly less concerned in this regard. However, when the priestly redactor finds an image which might suit his purpose, e.g., the rainbow as sign of the covenant, he keeps it. They are both in agreement in transposing the significance of the events they relate: God saves an innocent remnant from the punishment brought on by the "wickedness of men." The priestly narrative goes one step further and sees in this episode an occasion for the first covenant, the foundation of all those that were to follow.

The Tower of Babel: The Fall of the Human City

The subsequent story of the tower of Babel, where the two strands of Hebraic tradition appear so closely interwoven that it is difficult to tell them apart (chapter 11), shows that the city built by the descendants of Noah, the just, repeated the fault of mankind's sinful ancestors who lived before the flood.[25] Men established an earthly city to assert their mastery here below, thus seeking to usurp God's dominion over all things. But mankind is once again punished, this time through dissension and the confusion of tongues, the inevitable result of the common rebellion.

Clearly the Bible had in mind Babylon, with its ziggurats, its colossal towers topped by platforms for the celebration of a magical cult that sought to rob the gods of their power and utilize it for the selfish benefit of themselves. The play on words is eloquent in this respect: the Hebrew noun *Bābel*, which means "confusion," replaces the Babylonian term *Babili*, or "door to God."

This whole set of biblical accounts of the Fall thus stresses once again revelation's most constant and distinctive theme: the Fall of the cosmos was not caused by some kind of divine degradation; instead, the downfall of the more powerful creatures led to that of the weaker ones. Conversely, neither the world's multiplicity nor its materiality are the essence or the source of evil, which resides in the arrogance and selfish greed of the created spirits. Their sins are all the more serious, since these spirits are more spiritual and closer to the divinity.

Mythic and Biblical Cosmogony

We are now in a position to draw an illuminating parallel between the separate concepts of the world which emerge from myths and from the biblical Word.

Myths fundamentally confuse the divinity, or the many gods, with the realities of nature. The divine Word springs entirely from the initial assertion that there is but one God and that he transcends all natural reality.

According to myths, there is no distinction between the creation of the world and its fall, since the world comes into existence through the fall of the gods, who either divide and degenerate, or enter into conflict with each other. According to the Word, creation is, on the contrary, a free act of God; since it proceeds from his pure benevolence, creation is entirely good in itself, though in a limited and dependent way.

For myths, evil is inherent in the existence of gods and men. For the Word, there is no evil in God, and there was initially none in the creature he fashioned.

Myths imply that multiplicity, and perhaps also materiality or materialization, are the source of evil.[26] The Word asserts that the most spiritual part of creation, and the very quality which draws it close to God's unity and oneness, are at the root of evil, through the initial temptation of pride, followed by selfish cupidity.

In myths, man is but the last step in the degradation of the divine. The Word affirms that man is but a creature, but one made in the image of God.

Myths hold that the divine spreads and diversifies itself through many downward gradations. The Word proclaims that the divine is entirely in the One, and that other spirits, high though they may be, remain his creatures and his servants, whether faithful or not.

Finally, myths describe creation, and the gods also, as essentially a mixture of good and evil. But the God who speaks to man is himself the Good, and what he has wrought is good in itself, since it comes from him; it becomes evil only by accident, because of the pride of the rebellious powers.

Chapter VI: From Wisdom to Apocalypse

Wisdom and Kingship

The Egyptian kings were assumed to lead their kingdom in the same way the divinity ruled the world, since the Pharaoh partook in the *Maat*, the divine order immanent in all things. Similarly, the kings of Mesopotamia were supposedly able to carry out their duties as servants or adoptees of a tutelary god only because a divine accomplice had given them the *Me*, or tablets of destiny.[1] These two related terms are best translated as "wisdom." It is therefore clear that wisdom is supernatural in origin, not to say divine. However, the establishment of the various kingdoms meant that wisdom was increasingly humanized, and eventually became identical with the practical experience of life in the world, progressively filtered and sifted by rational meditation.[2] For kings cannot exercise their kingship without the establishment around them of a whole caste of officials, responsible for interpreting and applying in practice the sovereign's supposedly-inspired instructions. As it comes up against the realities and limitations of daily life, wisdom acquires a wealth of practical experience; in order for this to be passed on (and indeed, in the very process of being communicated), it is organized and interpreted through a constant rumination that involves critical reasoning. Wisdom thus evolves into a tradition of government and administration that is fed by an accumulation of experience and is itself assimilated through an ever-alert rational intelligence. This tradition nevertheless continues to proceed from the mythic data on which the monarchy is based.

Wisdom and Myth

In some civilizations, wisdom ultimately freed itself to a substantial degree from its roots. There were even cases where wisdom sought to discredit myths and to displace them; yet wisdom undeniably originated in myths, and its origin shows clearly even in the process of attempted rejection. For the very foundation of wisdom remains that the universe in which we live makes sense. Myths express that meaning, and they alone seem to have the power to make it explicit.

One should therefore not accept too readily the idea that the rationalizing *logos* of wisdom inevitably enters into conflict with the *mythos*. This does not seem to have occurred in Egypt[3] or Mesopotamia. In fact, just as contemporary anthropology has determined that the primitive mind is by no means pre-logical, but rather metalogical—i.e., that the emergence of mythic vision occurred at about the same time as the earliest instances of a rational ciriticism of experience—wisdom in those two countries, and particularly in Egypt, appears to have developed along with mythic knowledge. And if wisdom has on occasion, in Egypt or Mesopotamia, criticized myths, it was not to eliminate them and take their place, but simply to explain their meaning, even if this required a correction.

The significance of this continuity of the *Maat*, from its inspired introduction into the mind of the Pharaoh to its detailed formulation, after it was strengthened by experience and purified by reasoned criticism, is brought out by the fact that the earliest known compilation of Egyptian wisdom is ascribed to Ptahhotep, vizier to king Izezi of the fifth dynasty, who lived around 2500 B.C., in the form of a prophecy given by the Pharaoh to his minister.[4] Somewhat similar is the Assyrian wisdom of Ahikar, who is believed to have been in the service of Sennacherib (704-681) and his successor Esarhaddon (680-669).[5]

Nevertheless, from these archaic writings to the latest Egyptian wisdom of Amenemope, later than the tenth century and perhaps even than the seventh, and strikingly similar to the biblical book of Proverbs (particularly 22:17—24:22), wisdom was a realistic knowledge, based on a duly pondered experience of the world, passed on from father to son, or by the older officials to their younger colleagues just admitted to join them.

At that stage, wisdom may be described as a technique for the organization of human life in the world, and more specifically in the new cities, which constituted a world in the process of humanization. Being the work of a caste whose survival it defended, this wisdom was very soon in danger of deteriorating into a set of skills necessary for personal success, or even a handbook of social etiquette. Even so, it remained fundamentally religious in its essence, though including various specialized techniques concerning first and foremost ritual procedures, but also war and agriculture (a basic requirement for urban living), as well as architecture and trade, both linked to the development of the cities. In connection with its agricultural interest, wisdom was to evolve (and to include for some time) meteorology and astronomy, and even geometry, derived by the Egyptians from the methods for agrarian mensuration. Wisdom was to culminate in the art of government, and particularly of dispensing justice, thus achieving a synthesis of wisdom's many ramifications.[6]

Wisdom Comes to Israel

Wisdom was to reach Israel as a natural concomitant of monarchy and of the king's retinue. This is why initially it was looked on by the prophets with as much suspicion as monarchy itself. To Samuel, the Israelites' wish to follow the example of other nations and be ruled by a king first seemed tantamount to a denial of the God who had spoken to their fathers.[7] Similarly, the quest for wisdom was considered as one more instance of a refusal to heed his word.[8]

The Word itself finally accepted the concept of monarchy, though modifying it thoroughly: the Israelite king became one of God's servants (rather than *the* servant), and therefore also the people's representative before God (rather than the converse), on the basis of faith in his Word.[9] In the same way, the Word accepted wisdom, but changing it and identifying it progressively with itself.

The earliest Hebrew proverbs, when they are read after the prophets, seem rather worldly, if not materialistic. To be sure, Egyptian wisdom, which inspired the proverbs, was religious in its own way. But Egyptian religion was precisely of the kind against which the religion of the Word took a firm stand.

Yet even Egyptian wisdom, from Ptahhotep to Amenemope, had evolved considerably: from a formula for earthly success, it had become a school of detachment. In Israel, the "fear of the Lord" remained the foundation of wisdom, but this fear became identified with the "knowledge of the Lord," which derives exclusively from his Word,[10] so that the transformation of wisdom went much deeper. It has been quite correctly noted that in Israel the wise men tended to meet with the deuteronomists, whose ambition it was to order the entire life of the people exclusively in terms of obedience to the prophetic Word.[11] The two schools of thought soon merged. For both, divine holiness became identified with justice, and *hesed*, loving piety toward God and compassionate pity for men, surpassed sacrifices and gave them their full meaning.

The feasibility of this merger was due to the fact that neither wisdom nor prophecy aimed at a purely objective knowledge; they both sought to learn enough of ultimate reality to model human life according to the laws governing the cosmic order, recognized as divine in its principle. In Egypt, in particular, wisdom was shaped by the vision of an order primitively imposed on chaos by the gods, an order which had to be maintained against all the forces of disintegration.[12] A connection with the cosmic order was ensured through tradition, for which the kings and their uninterrupted line of succession were the channel. This tradition made it possible to establish a distinction between what was both primitive and permanent, on the one hand, and what was merely accidental and contingent on the other. The wholly predictable floods of the Nile seem to have at least promoted this view. As a consequence, the essential virtues of a wise man, in Egyptian eyes, were attentive silence and patience.

Due probably to the irregularity of the seasons, wisdom took a more dramatic turn in Mesopotamia. Hence the vision of an imperfect world order needing to be constantly corrected, and the importance of loyal obedience to the hero capable of overcoming adversity.[13] In Israel, since wisdom was entirely dependent on the divine Word, it was based on humble prayer and a piety having contrition as a leading feature. In contrast to Saul, David, though certainly not free of sin, was a king after God's heart, because he recognized his transgression before the divine judgment and humbled himself.[14] At the beginning of his reign, Solomon was a model king in the Davidic sense, for in prayer he asked for the wisdom which is received from God, rather than for any other gift.[15] Conversely, at the height of his glory he was condemned for yielding to pride and covetousness, instead of remaining, as at first, totally dependent on God.

Wisdom and the Problem of Evil

It should be noted at this point that first in Egypt, then even more so in Mesopotamia, wisdom veered increasingly toward pessimism and seemed more and more preoccupied with the problem of evil, which was seen by Egyptians as a progressive and irresistible decadence. The desecration of the tombs of the great ancestors was the most dismaying sign of this evil.[16] In contrast, the pessimism typical of Israelite wisdom, as expressed in Ecclesiastes, stressed the permanence of an evil order, in spite of the temporary and superficial changes which the best human wisdom could bring to bear on this order.[17] Whatever ephemeral comfort one might take from the basic righteousness remaining in God's creatures, the only real hope was in the divine Word and the only wisdom to conduct one's life in accordance with the Word.[18]

Egyptian wisdom was far from ignoring the problem of innocent suffering,[19] particularly distressing to pious men, but it was in Mesopotamian wisdom that the enigma was approached with the most boldness. The Akkadian *Ludlul bel nemeqi* (I will praise the Lord of wisdom) hesitates between two possible conclusions.[20] Either the gods judge according to different standards than our own, or else one must hope against hope that evil will not endure, that the good shall prevail in the end.

Wisdom and Mystery

In its final development, Israel's wisdom was much more daring: it acknowledged this existential mystery, yet proclaimed an indomitable hope, one based entirely on faith. For the cosmic view so distinctive of the biblical religion—every creature is fundamentally good in its principle, for all existence is totally and exclusively dependent on the will of a God who is Goodness itself—far from solving the mystery of evil, and particularly of innocent suffering, made it even more agonizing. Hence the lesson of Job.[21]

The main thrust of this lesson is that no human wisdom—even if it is firmly established on assertions of the Word, but then developed according to purely human reasoning—can lead anywhere but to a dead end. This is clear in the case of Job's friends: God himself mocks their arguments.[22] To be sure, as they emphasize, all the evil in the world is rooted in sin committed by creatures. But it does not follow that those who suffer most are the greatest sinners.

Yet one may not conclude that God himself does not judge according to the principles he revealed to us. The truth of the matter is that knowledge belongs to him alone, because he alone holds the final keys to human destiny, or rather to the history of which we are all a part.

As a matter of fact, the solution to the problem, as suggested by the book of Job, cannot be a speculative one. As far as we are concerned, it is a question of accepting with unshakable faith, hard as that may be, the suffering we can neither master nor understand, without ceasing to place all our trust in God. He alone, in his own time and by means he alone knows, since he alone has mastery over them, will then restore justice.

We have already referred to the progressive merger which took place in Israel between wisdom (in the process of being deepened and widened) and prophetic revelation, itself being enriched through a constant pondering of the Word of God in the light of the actual experience of life. It may be said in this regard that the teachings of Second Isaiah on the salvific efficacy of the innocent suffering of the faithful and humiliated Servant provide an answer to Job's suppliant and trusting prayer.[23]

From Wisdom to Apocalypse

More generally, the development of Israelite wisdom into a new type of prophecy—viz., the apocalypse, the revelation of the end of history (or what we call eschatology), rather than its beginning—answers the problem raised by Ecclesiastes about the decidedly unsatisfactory and unacceptable world order we live in. It belongs to God alone to modify it, when and as he chooses. The shift from wisdom to apocalypse had been prepared, in the same way as Israel's entire maturation, by the ordeal of the exile in Babylon. But the change took place only when it became clear that any hope of a restoration of the earthly kingdom of Judah and Israel had to be abandoned. At that time, the expectation of a catastrophic end to history replaced the anticipation of the coming of God's reign in history. Thus would come about the judgment, the ultimate defeat of the powers of evil, and so the establishment of the divine kingdom.[24]

Instead of simply hoping for the appearance of a son of David, a Davidic king after God's heart, Israel therefore decisively raised its sights, so to speak, to a supernatural Messiah, a king anointed with the very power of God.[25] This figure emerges in the last prophetic texts, and again in the apocalyptic writings themselves. In the latter, however, the vision is even more sublime, and we learn in chapter 7 of the book of Daniel that only from a "son of man," one coming with the clouds of heaven, can the advent of the kingdom be expected.[26]

At about the same time, Israel drew from its experience of the purifying trial required as preparation for this coming the mysterious image of a Servant of the Lord who, through his innocent sufferings, would atone not only for the sins of Israel, but for those of the entire world.[27] At that stage, when all the wise men's calculations seemed to be disproved, wisdom, along with the abolished earthly kingship, was as though elevated to heaven. In other words, God appeared as the only wise one and the only king: the only one to know the ultimate secret of human and cosmic history, since he is the only one able to unravel its web.

Henceforth, it was clearly no longer sufficient to pray for God's gift of wisdom, as Solomon had done. For true wisdom far exceeds any experience, any exercise of reason, even if illuminated by the divine Word. It may be imparted only through a new and supreme revelation, *the* revelation above all others, since it relates to the ultimate mystery, that of the only possible reversal of the human and cosmic Fall. Hence the designation of apocalypse, derived from the Greek word for revelation.

The transition from wisdom to the apocalypse can be seen in chapter 2 of the book of Daniel.[28] The Babylonian king had a premonitory dream which none of his diviners, magicians, or wise men could explain. They told him that only a god could decipher the enigma. But the Jewish captive Daniel, who was a wise man, appeared before the king and stated that neither the wisdom of the Jews nor any other wisdom could determine the meaning of the dream, but, he added, "there is a God in heaven who reveals mysteries." In a preparatory prayer, Daniel had already given the reason for this divine knowledge: God alone establishes the *kairoi*, i.e., he determines when and how decisive events are to take place.[29] The king's dream related to the ultimate events in history (*ta eschata*), and Daniel had been sent to him by God to shed light on the premonition through an apocalypse,[30] the revelation not just of any divine mystery, but of the ultimate mystery: how after the various human kingdoms have destroyed each other, the only definitive Reign, the Reign of God, would abolish and replace them forever.[31]

It is most remarkable that chapters 1 and 2 of I Corinthians, where St. Paul defines the Christian mystery as the last word of the Scriptures, the unexpected conclusion of the history of Israel, and the solution to the enigma of human and cosmic history in Christ and his cross, reintroduces all the themes of chapter 2 of the book of Daniel. And it maintains precisely the same connections between them: the wholly supernatural wisdom belonging only to God, the ultimate mystery to which wisdom leads and in which it is condensed, the decisive *kairos* through which the *eschaton* (the end of all things) comes about, the event whose final revelation will coincide with the definitive establishment of the divine kingdom.[32]

The apocalyptic literature, which in a sense filled the interval between the Old and the New Testaments, made more explicit the eschatological cast of Israel's supreme hope and turned it into a dominant element of all religious thought and experience.[33] Once again, this literature carried to its highest point the progressive supernaturalization started by the last prophets, and especially Third Isaiah, by transforming the idealized figure of the Davidic king into that of a king whose reign is literally that of God himself: the Messiah. But this was not enough for the apocalyptic authors. As an introduction to the eschatological reign, they therefore replaced this Messiah, anointed from on high but still of this world, with the image of the Son of man, who makes his first biblical appearance in chapter 7 of Daniel, the same book in which we were able to observe the transition from wisdom to apocalypse. The image is still that of a man, but a new and celestial one, coming from God.[34]

The Son of Man and the Saints of the Most High

The same chapter 7 of the book of Daniel also suggests the mysterious identification of this Son of man with "the saints of the Most High," a term which designates God's eschatological people.[35] And the various apocalypses will have in common an insistence on the dreadful trials these saints will have to go through before the coming of the Kingdom. This shows how much they owe, not only to the messianism of the last great prophets, but also to the highly enigmatic Deutero-Isaiah vision of the suffering and humiliated Servant of God. It can thus be said that the figure of the celestial Son of man and that of the humiliated Servant tend to converge throughout apocalyptic literature and throughout Israel's piety at its best, in the period immediately preceding the birth of Christ. Clearly, the main cause of this evolution was the persecution carried out by Antiochus Epiphanes and the ensuing martyrdom of the Jews who refused to abandon their faith.[36]

It is only in the Christian apocalypse, however, that the two figures actually merged, and were absorbed and superseded, together with the figure of the Messiah, in the person and destiny of Jesus of Nazareth.[37]

Victory over the Forces of Evil

Around these central figures, the eschatological theme of the reign of

God, replacing and abolishing all other kingdoms, was the theme in which apocalyptic literature caused the entire revelation of the Old Testament to focus and to prepare for an even more exalted revelation.[38] It should be noted that this theme is but the ultimate elaboration of the first and fundamental one set forth by the entire biblical Word: that of the exclusive and universal kingship of the God who spoke to Abraham, to Moses, and to the prophets.[39] But it was the last Jewish apocalypses, such as the *Testament of Levi*,[40] which stated explicitly that the present era (*aiōn houtos*, Greek translation of the Hebrew *'ōlām hazzeh*) is not ruled by God, but by his enemy Belial, the fallen prince of this world. In the coming era (*aiōn mellōn*, for *'ōlām habbā'*), God's reign will begin, on earth as in heaven, in accordance with the traditional vision of the psalms of the enthronement.

It needs emphasizing that we have here the exact framework of the first sermon given by Jesus, with the interpretation he suggested of his own role, that of the stronger man who comes to oust "a strong man" who "guards his own palace" in this world and "takes away his armor and... divides his spoil."[41]

This amounts to saying that the apocalypses, without reverting to the metaphysical dualism pervading the ancient myths, carried to its highest point and to its ultimate consequences the ethical and historical dualism with which the biblical accounts of the creation and the Fall had replaced the former dualism.[42] From this eschatological viewpoint, the apocalypses thus reactivated all the images of strife and victorious conflict which the biblical tradition had systematically purged from the description of the origins of man and the world. And it adapted these images to the eschatological conflict and its final solution of the problem of evil.[43]

So it was that the Leviathan had already appeared in the early apocalypse inserted into Isaiah 26, as also the "beast" of the abyss in Daniel 7. In general, the apocalypses appropriated all the dualistic images of the cosmogonic myths in order to apply them to the final conflict of judgment day; that is, to the hoped-for victory over the fallen cosmic powers, which will again be brought under the authority of the one God, king of the universe and of all ages.[44]

At the same time, the apocalypses ascribe to the mysterious divine messenger himself, who was to be the supernatural instrument of the heavenly kingdom's victory over all other kingdoms, all that the myths had said of the first man, likened to the king of paradise,[45] or of primordial Man, anticipating within himself all of cosmic reality, but in a state of unblemished innocence and divine glory.[46] Conversely, the apocalypses describe the final state of the world redeemed, transfigured by the purging of evil, as a world reminiscent of the garden of the gods described in Sumerian and Babylonian myths, to which their various human heroes—Ziusudra,

Utnapishtim, or Gilgamesh—had all sought to gain admittance in order to partake of divine immortality. But in Jewish apocalyptic thinking, this prospect does not appear as a reminder of a fabulous and vanished past, but as the revelation of God's supreme grace, present in the supreme victory of divine love and fidelity over the powers of depredation and unfaithfulness.[47]

Death and Transfiguration

At the same time as they all develop these themes of the messianic reign, and particularly of the celestial Man—which were already introduced into the Hebrew Bible by the last prophets or the last sapiential book of Daniel— the apocalyptic writings, and especially II Enoch and IV Esdras (so astonishingly close to the sermons of Jesus, whose introduction they might well be), become absorbed in a joint vision of the sufferings of the just (necessary to the birth of a regenerated world) and of the incorruptibility and glory issuing directly from a manifest divine presence characteristic of the renewed world.[48] One may say that death and transfiguration are the two inseparable faces of the apocalyptic view of cosmic and human destiny.

In the apocalyptic imagery, three relatively new traits distinguish these books from early biblical writings. The first is the explicit affirmation concerning the promise of eternal life for the just, in God's presence, and in the resurrection and transfiguration of all things which are distinctive of the eschatological viewpoint in the apocalypses.[49] The earliest expression of this assertion is probably the one found in the short apocalypse inserted in Isaiah 26.

> Thy dead shall live, their bodies shall rise.
> O dwellers in the dust, awake and sing for joy!
> For thy dew is a dew of light,
> and on the land of the shades thou wilt let it fall.[50]

Light and Darkness: Angels and Demons

The second trait is that the moral and historical dualism which sets apart the present time from the time to come is consistently described as a conflict between light and darkness.[51] The third, closely bound up with the previous one, is the progressive development, in place of the early mythological cosmologies, of an increasingly detailed angelology, in which may be noted a sharper and sharper division between the faithful angels, heavenly servants of God who assist the earthly elect, and the fallen angels, demons who tempt and accuse men, especially the faithful, and who are their bitter enemies.[52]

Some have seen in these three distinctive traits of the apocalypses the mark of an Iranian influence, following upon the victory won over Babylon by Cyrus, in 529 B.C., an event which had made possible Israel's liberation and return from exile. It is undeniable that, just as the Hebrew Scriptures used images and themes borrowed from the mythology and wisdom of Babylon or Sumer, as well as Egypt, so it also unhesitatingly appropriated material from Iranian religious thinking and, subsequently, as we shall see, from Greek thinkers.[53]

At this point, however, an elementary distinction must be drawn between the teachings of Zoroaster and the syncretistic Mazdaism which was to follow.[54] Above all, one must distinguish between the variety of expressions borrowed by the divine Word from diverse civilizations, and the Word's fidelity to itself, reflected again and again in the way it adapted and modified all the borrowed elements. On the first point, it now seems certain that in Iran, Zoroaster, who appears to have been a contemporary of the great prophets of Israel, preached a doctrine similar to theirs. Rejecting any metaphysical dualism, he taught the oneness of a God of light, creator of all things, and maintained that the evil in the powers of darkness was due to their fall, brought about by disobedience. This insubordination is subject to the final judgment, which those who are faithful to the only true God must prepare for by placing themselves at his service without reservation.

Zoroaster's successors distorted his religious legacy, reinstated the former mythic categories, and introduced a hierarchy of the powers of darkness, led by Ahriman, the spirit of evil, in perpetual conflict with the powers of light, which issued from Ormuzd, a wholly spiritual god embodying the principle of good.[55] Though the apocalyptic authors adopted Iranian images, they modified them so as to restore Zoroaster's doctrine and also to express the soul of the teachings of Israel's last and greatest prophets, who found in Zoroaster an exceptionally faithful echo.

Pursuing and correcting Iranian angelology and eschatology, these prophets elucidated the traditional expectation of the kingdom of God, inherent in Abraham's vocation and in the first teachings of the Word. They also developed, in accordance with a cosmology wholly imbued with this expectation, some of the earliest tenets in the doctrine revealed by the Word. For Judaic angelology is but an extension of Israel's primary assertion that the cosmic powers worshipped by their neighbors are at the root of the manifestations of sacrality and divine glory in the cosmos, far exceeding anything man can find on his own level, although these powers are no more divine than himself. To treat them as divine would therefore be to share in their downfall, brought on by their own pride and lust for domination.

Hence this ancient sense, so basic in Israel's mentality, of the evil spirit and the good spirit struggling against each other in every man, as in Saul.[56]

But Israel rejected any metaphysical dualism other than that of an absolutely good creator and a creature fundamentally good as long as it remains in its original state of dependence. Its earliest tradition held that the evil spirit itself comes from God,[57] which meant that it had been created by God and could continue its action in this world only with the tolerance of God, who would turn even the evil designs of the fallen spirit to his own ultimately good ends. In Persian times, the fully developed eschatology of Judaism, along with its angelology, made this explicit and carried it to its ultimate consequences. In the testing of the just, such as Job or the Servant in Isaiah 53, Judaic eschatology perceived the providential preparation of a final and total victory, not only of some or all spirits faithful to God over some or all evil spirits, but of the holy Spirit, the Spirit of God, over every perverted spirit. This struggle and victory is to be the prelude to the entrance of the saints themselves, glorified by the testing of their faithfulness, into the eschatological kingdom of holiness and immortality.[58]

Thus interpreted, the image of the conflict between light and darkness may indeed have been, if not exactly taken over from Iran, at least given its prominence in the apocalyptic vision by Israel's contact with the new Mazdean myths. It nevertheless remains true that this image was in harmony with the vision of divine glory, as a luminous and blazing radiance, and of the life of the God transcending all simply cosmic life, a vision that goes back to the earliest origins of Yahwist piety.[59]

All these developments in apocalyptic eschatology, by means of angelology, are continuously linked with the first biblical intimations of the fundamental revelation of God's exclusive kingship; moreover, they lead us to the threshold of the Gospel. In the process, as we have already noted, the apocalyptic writings—emerging as a new biblical revelation on the end of time and of cosmic history, and so preparing the solution of the mystery implied in the initial revelation of creation and Fall—have not hesitated to use even the most archaic images of a cosmic conflict and of the exaltation of man to a divine plane of existence, images which the initial revelation had simply brushed aside. The use of these ancient images is nowhere more striking (nor more thorough in the metamorphosis of the borrowed material) than in the depiction of the celestial Jerusalem, the city of God to which the elect gain entry, which is the concluding vision of the apocalypses.[60]

Chapter VII: The Heavenly City and Wisdom Personified

The Heavenly City

The Word of God and the history of salvation into which it had led Israel, following Abraham's vocation, had started with an initial break brought on by the construction of the first human cities. Babili, the divine door through which men hoped to reach immortality, was reduced in the Bible to Babel; the confusion of their languages (i.e., their thoughts) with their joint labors turned into fratricidal conflict.[1] Conversely, the pinnacle of God's Word in the Old Testament, and in the New Testament as well, was to be the vision of a celestial city whose only architect would be God in his wisdom. It would be a city descending to earth from God—rather than an earthly city aspiring to pierce the vault of heaven in some Promethean elevation. In that celestial city, the Word is to bring together, with each other and with the Most High, the host of his saints. These are the elect purified through the eschatological trial and identified with the truly divine life of that new and celestial Man who will also be, according to St. Paul, the new Adam, the ultimate and definitive Man. Thus, by the grace of the Creator who has made all things out of his infinite benevolence, the saints will finally find their home in the heavenly and divine city. They had left the earthly city to wander like perpetual nomads through the entire history of salvation, and arrived at the overwhelming realization of what seemed to be the wildest dreams of a fallen mankind and a fallen world.[2]

Asceticism and Eschatology

This evolution of apocalyptic thinking was to complete a paradoxical development in Israel's religiousness, but one in strict conformity with the teachings of the greatest prophets. It may be described as the transition from a fundamentally eudaemonistic concept of existence to an increasingly ascetic one.[3] Throughout the transition, however, the resolutely optimistic assertions in the Genesis account of creation remained unshaken. Consequently, biblical asceticism, even in its most extreme New Testament form, will never be centered on a condemnation or rejection of the world. It is rather a preference,[4] arising not from the idea that the world is evil, even in part, but from a conviction that God is preferable to all his gifts, even the most precious.

In the most archaic portions of Genesis, e.g., Jacob's blessings of his sons before his death,[5] the logical consequence of the assertion that all things were created good by God, and that man was placed in the world to make it bear fruit and to draw reward for his cooperation with the divine work, was reflected in the promise of ample worldly goods, large progeny, and a long and happy life. Much later, as may be seen in the Gradual Psalms, identical blessings are expressed: numerous children around the table of the just, like so many arrows in his quiver, a fruitful wife, like a vine on the sides of his house, are added to the blessings on the land and the flocks.[6] And in the last developments of Israel's piety, Jesus will maintain the *berakah*, the typical benediction, in full and turn it into the Christian Eucharist, invoking divine favor first upon the Word, which is light and life, then upon food and the land: the promised land, which is to renew for the faithful people the bounty of paradise and make it everlasting.[7]

Without in any way disputing this optimistic outlook or detracting from it, a complementary and contrasting view appeared as early as the arrival in Palestine. The prophets were quick to take note of it and to draw the inescapable conclusion, first for themselves, then for the entire people, or at least for the faithful remnant: though all the good things of the earth are indeed desirable, because they are gifts from God, they change into snares for sinful, selfish, and arrogant men who prefer unlimited enjoyment of these gifts to faithful obedience to their donor. Through them, God's enemy, the supreme prevaricator, easily deceives and enslaves us.

This is what Hosea expressed with consummate clearness and simplicity:

[Israel] did not know
    that it was I who gave her
    the grain, the wine, and the oil,
and who lavished upon her silver
    and gold which they used for Ba'al.
Therefore I will take back
    my grain in its time,
    and my wine in its season;
and I will take away my wool and my flax,
    which were to cover her nakedness.
Now I will uncover her lewdness
    in the sight of her lovers,
    and no one shall rescue her out of my hand.[8]

The people worshipped the powers of nature instead of their creator. They thought only of unrestrained gratification, thereby changing into a curse what should have been a boon. In order to draw the unfaithful back to the Bridegroom, who should have received the unlimited love only he deserved, the gifts which had been bestowed will have to be withdrawn, so that the unfaithful may learn to expect them only from God:

Therefore, behold, I will allure her,
    and bring her back into the wilderness,
    and speak tenderly to her.
And there I will give her her vineyards,
    and make the Valley of Achor a door of hope.
And there she shall answer as in the days of her youth,
    as at the time when she came out of the land of Egypt.[9]

More clearly still, Isaiah showed that injustice and unfaithfulness go together when man yields to selfish cupidity, or seeks to break away from the true God to worship divinities that are only the immediate sources of our interests and pleasures:

Their land is filled with silver and gold,
    and there is no end to their treasures;...
Their land is filled with idols;
    they bow down to the work of their hands,
    to what their own fingers have made....
And the haughtiness of man shall be humbled,
    and the pride of men shall be brought low;
    and the LORD alone will be exalted in that day.
And the idols shall utterly pass away.[10]

Moreover, Isaiah was the first to say that wealth and prosperity are not necessarily a sign of benediction but, on the contrary, that the rich man who becomes a slave to his wealth and worships only whatever he thinks can increase it, is accursed among all men:

Woe to those who join house to house,
    who add field to field,
until there is no more room,
    and you are made to dwell alone
    in the midst of the land....
Woe to those who draw iniquity with cords of falsehood,...
Woe to those who call evil good
    and good evil,
who put darkness for light
    and light for darkness,...[11]

By his example, when he was stripped of everything because of his faithfulness to the only true God, even more than by his explicit teaching, Jeremiah showed Israel that rich, egotistical and idolatrous men are cursed rather than blessed by God, while it is the one who carries faithfulness to God to the point of supreme deprivation who is blessed.

Contrary to what was still considered the only normal condition in life for an Israelite, Jeremiah was called to celibacy by God:

You shall not take a wife, nor shall you have sons or daughters in this place.[12]

He is instructed to announce the imminent punishment, and to prepare the people for massacres, captivity, and exile. And, by expressing in heart-rending terms the agonizing trial required by his own vocation, he empha-sizes that there can be no hesitation when the divine word is heard:

> O LORD, thou hast deceived me,
>   and I was deceived;
> thou art stronger than I,
>   and thou hast prevailed.
> I have become a laughingstock all the day;
>   every one mocks me.
> For whenever I speak, I cry out,
>   I shout, "Violence and destruction!"
> For the word of the LORD has become for me
>   a reproach and derision all day long.
> If I say, "I will not mention him,
>   or speak any more in his name,"
> there is in my heart as it were a burning fire
>   shut up in my bones,
> and I am weary with holding it in,
>   and I cannot.[13]

Such writings obviously laid the groundwork for the great vision of the Second Isaiah: the song of the supreme Servant of God, who appears broken, humiliated, rejected by both God and men, but whose innocent suffering will spell salvation, not only for the Jews, but for all peoples.[14]

Until the time of the Gospel, it seems that the Jews were so perturbed by this proposition that they did not know what to make of it. However, as Joachim Jeremias has emphasized, the idea nevertheless slowly made its way, inspiring in the apocalyptic authors a conviction that one can prepare for the coming times only by breaking deliberately with the present time.[15] What is more, those Jews who, in the words of St. Luke, awaited the consolation of Israel,[16] though they did not previously dare to apply directly to the Messiah or to the heavenly Son of man the mysterious image of the Servant suffering to redeem the sins of the people and of all mankind, would be fully convinced at the coming of Jesus that the sufferings of the just are necessary to hasten the consummation of all things in the eschato-logical salvation they expected.[17]

The Beatitude of the Poor

So it is that the last psalms focus on the poor man, who seems altogether defeated by life and who lacks everything, but whose inability to rely on anything but pure and invincible faith makes him the perfect prayerful petitioner:

> Incline thy ear, O LORD, and answer me,
>   for I am poor and needy. Preserve my life, for I am godly;
>   save thy servant who trusts in thee.
> Thou art my God; be gracious to me, O Lord,
>   for to thee do I cry all the day.
> Gladden the soul of thy servant,
>   for to thee, O Lord, do I lift up my soul.[18]

The evangelic beatitudes only make clearer the complete reversal which has taken place: whereas "blessed are the rich" seemed the logical consequence of the fundamental goodness of creation, there had been a shift to "blessed are the poor," especially the poor by choice, since it is only by freeing oneself beforehand from the world as it is that one may prepare to greet the renewed world of the kingdom of God. Further, the trusting acceptance of this extreme poverty enables us to prepare the coming of the divine kingdom better than anything else we can do.[19]

The novelty of the approach is not however as complete as it might seem. As Hosea implied, the principle of separation or liberation was already expressed in the exodus, through the fact that the original liberation, when God had shown himself as the Savior of his own, had led to the desert, which had to be crossed before the promised land could be reached.[20] And we have already noted how Abraham, the father of the people, in order to be faithful to the Word, and even to hear the Word, had to break with human society, which had settled into an organized and stable possession of earthly goods.[21]

The first Christian monks, such as St. Gregory of Nazianzus in his great theological and spiritual poem on *Aretē* (Virtue as the highest form of human life), saw this clearly.[22] In the exodus of Abraham, then in that of the entire people out of Egypt, and finally in the test of exile and adversity, all necessary to the separation of the faithful few from the mass of the unfaithful, they recognized the principle of monastic calling as it was understood by Christians of the Constantine era. Indeed, in early monasticism, voluntary poverty was considered the principle of all asceticism, a radical means of detachment from this world and of progression toward the world to come.[23] Therefore, only *xeniteia* (peregrination), the recognized and freely accepted status of a foreigner or traveler, defines monastic life, which is in effect a pilgrimage from the fallen city of Babel to the celestial city, the heavenly Jerusalem, whose architect and king is God.[24]

Just before the advent of Christ, his forerunner John, the last and greatest of the prophets, was also the definitive ascetic model for the kingdom.[25]

The fact that prophecy and asceticism go hand in hand had already been understood by the pre-Messianic communities, such as those of Qumran or of the Essenes. Also bearing witness to this link would be the first chapters of Luke, speaking revealingly of all those who awaited the consolation of Israel.[26]

This ascesis, however, like all unperverted forms of asceticism, has as counterpart a certain mystique. It signifies the pre-perception in faith of the ultimate mystery: that of the awaited kingdom, which will overcome the demonic reign when the *aiōn mellōn* replaces the *aiōn houtos*. The purpose of ascesis is to free us from the latter, so that we may go forward to the divine kingdom, by which this world will be destroyed.

In the symbolic description of the ultimate future, foreseen through the faith of the apocalyptic authors—more daringly than ever, though still in the mainstream of the greatest prophets, such as Hosea, Third Isaiah, and Ezechiel—we see revived and applied to eschatology still another mythic image, one that the revelation of creation had most strictly banned. It is the feminine figure of a beloved Bride of the Most High, an image which the sapiential books apply to wisdom itself, and which the apocalypses will subsequently connect with the heavenly Jerusalem, a city which will descend to earth when God's kingdom comes, in order to receive and gather all the elect.[27]

The Eschatological Nuptials

If there is a concept which the first stage of biblical revelation had made every effort to cast out, it was certainly the idea that the true God might have had a divine partner, a feminine one, and more generally that the created forms of vitality, such as the division of the sexes, might be ascribed to God's eternal and transcendent life. Yet, even the most adamant prophets in this regard, notably Hosea, in likening Israel's endemic idolatry to adultery and prostitution, conjured up a contrasting vision of a chosen nation, to be finally separated from the unfaithful and fallen nation; and they did not hesitate to present this nation—the immaculate virgin drawn by divine omnipotence on the last day from fallen creation—as intended for divine nuptials: the Chosen one, the Betrothed of the Lord himself. This Chosen one shall no longer call him "my Lord," but instead "my Husband."[28] Ezechiel stresses even more strongly the unworthiness of Israel, which he paints not only as unfaithful to its first love, but also as misbegotten and undeserving from birth of any compassion.[29] Yet Israel was adopted and reared by God, and continued to receive his untiring love, in spite of the original perversion of all its instincts. Ezechiel also shows that Israel is intended for purification, for regeneration by the all-powerful divine love, so that it finally becomes worthy of being the Bride of the Lord.[30]

The City as Bride

Chapter 54 of the book of Isaiah applies these nuptial images for the first time not just to the "spiritual" Israel of the eschatological times, but more precisely to the city built by God himself to gather therein all the elect, after the stage of the purifying trial. It is also the first to apply to the City as Bride the same paradisal images of a heavenly city applied by myths to the enticing abode of the gods:

O afflicted one, storm-tossed, and not comforted,
  behold, I will set your stones in antimony,
  and lay your foundations with sapphires.
I will make your pinnacles of agate,
  your gates of carbuncles,
  and all your wall of precious stones.[31]

A subsequent chapter continues in the same vein:

Arise, shine; for your light has come,
  and the glory of the LORD has risen upon you.
For behold, darkness shall cover the earth,
  and thick darkness the peoples;
but the LORD will arise upon you,
  and his glory will be seen upon you....
Your gates shall be open continually;
  day and night they shall not be shut;
that men may bring to you the wealth of the nations,
  with their kings led in procession. ...
they shall call you the City of the LORD,
  the Zion of the Holy One of Israel....
The sun shall be no more
  your light by day,
nor for brightness shall the moon
  give light to you by night;
but the LORD will be your everlasting light,
  and your God will be your glory.[32]

And the same series of prophecies repeats almost exactly Hosea's opening words:

You shall be a crown of beauty in the hand of the LORD,
  and a royal diadem in the hand of your God.
You shall no more be termed Forsaken,
  and your land shall no more be termed Desolate;

but you shall be called My delight is in her,
and your land Married;
for the LORD delights in you,
and your land shall be married.[33]

All these images reappear in the apocalypse of the New Testament, but it receives from the inter-Testamentary apocalypses, and particularly *Baruch's Syriac Apocalypse*, a further idea. It is that the eschatological city, where the faithful, redeemed by the Lord, will be gathered with him forever in a transfigured world, has remained hidden in him from time immemorial, as the ultimate preserve of his creative plan, the mystery of his wisdom.[34]

Wisdom as Bride

Since it was from the paradoxical evolution of wisdom in Israel that the apocalyptic writings were to derive, we may now grasp how this personification of the eschatological city is closely linked with that of wisdom itself.

Chapter 8 of the book of Proverbs already showed this Wisdom—the plan God conceived from time immemorial for his creative work—as his alter ego that has always been with him: his eternal thought concerning his work, the ideal he tends toward achieving in it:

The LORD created me at the beginning of his work,
the first of his acts of old.
Ages ago I was set up,
at the first, before the beginning of the earth.
When there were no depths I was brought forth,
when there were no springs abounding with water.
Before the mountains had been shaped,
before the hills, I was brought forth;
before he had made the earth with its fields,
or the first of the dust of the world.
When he established the heavens, I was there,
when he drew a circle on the face of the deep,
when he made firm the skies above,
when he established the fountains of the deep,
when he assigned to the sea its limit,
so that the waters might not transgress his command,
when he marked out the foundations of the earth,
then I was beside him, like a master workman;
and I was daily his delight,
rejoicing before him always,
rejoicing in his inhabited world,
and delighting in the sons of men.[35]

The comment is often made by modern exegetes that this personification of Wisdom in the book of Proverbs should not be taken too seriously since it has its counterpart in the personification of folly.[36] But this is not a valid objection, for this parallel obviously stems from one so archaic in Israel that there is reason to assume it goes back to the earliest times—namely, the parallel between the good and evil spirits; and the personification of each is obviously much more than metaphorical.[37]

As for Wisdom, the subsequent book of Ecclesiasticus, or Wisdom of Jesus ben Sirach, is not content to review and underscore its personal features. It clearly brought together Wisdom and both the divine Word and the specific divine Presence in Israel (and even more specially in the Jerusalem sanctuary), a Presence always linked with the biblical Word:

> I came forth from the mouth of the Most High,
>   and covered the earth like a mist.
> I dwelt in high places,
>   and my throne was in a pillar of cloud. . . .
> Then the Creator of all things gave me a commandment,
>   and the one who created me assigned a place for my tent.
> And he said, 'Make your dwelling in Jacob,
>   and in Israel receive your inheritance.'
> From eternity, in the beginning, he created me,
>   and for eternity I shall not cease to exist.
> In the holy tabernacle I ministered before him,
>   and so I was established in Zion.[38]

In other words, Wisdom is personified inasmuch as it is the total content of God's Word. God brings his works to perfection in his Word by making himself present in it and marking it, as it were, with a living reflection of his own countenance. Wisdom is therefore inseparable from the perfect Israel, from the cosmic city where God turns the life of the elect, assembled in unanimous praise, into one single voice with his own.

Thus, if Wisdom appears as the Daughter of God and the Bride of the perfect man, the man adopted by God, so the City which God planned to establish in his Wisdom to be the pinnacle of his works, the kingdom of the saints of the Most High,[39] appears as his own chosen Bride, beloved from time immemorial. This is how one may best understand the verse of Isaiah 62 which concludes the previous quotation:

> For as a young man marries a virgin,
>   so shall your sons marry you,
> and as the bridegroom rejoices over the bride,
>   so shall your God rejoice over you.[40]

It is certainly in this sense that Israel was to interpret King Solomon's impassioned search for Wisdom, as described in the book of Wisdom, which was therefore attributed to him. Solomon's search was to be viewed as a reflection of God's own eternal quest for his eschatological Bride, throughout the history of creation and salvation:

> I loved her and sought her from my youth,
> and I desired to take her for my bride,
> and I became enamoured of her beauty.
> She glorifies her noble birth by living with God,
> and the Lord of all loves her.
> For she is an initiate in the knowledge of God,
> and an associate in his works.[41]

In the same sense, the Song of Solomon, the nuptial poem of the exemplary king and his bride chosen among all women, was to become for Israel the Song of Songs, included in the Bible as the nuptial poem of the Creator and his redeemed creature, the heavenly City that includes all the elect in a cosmos, henceforth reconciled and integrated within itself, in a definitive union with the one God.[42]

Development of the Berakah

The *berakah*, that typically Jewish prayer in which the Christian *eucharistia* originated,[43] reflected these various developments. A response of faith to the Word, it encompassed from the beginning (as early as the return from exile, as shown by the prayer of Ezra in Nehemiah 10) the overall vision of the plan of divine Wisdom, including in a single design creation and redemption from the Fall. The synagogal prayers that follow this model, written either to follow the reading of the Torah and the prophets or to conclude the community meal, end with the vision of Jerusalem rebuilt, where all those who had been dispersed would be brought together forever, praising the only God in his eternal Kingdom.

Chapter VIII: Development of Greek Cosmologies from the Ionians to Plato

At the same time as Israel was translating wisdom into apocalypse, Greece was taking it in an entirely different direction. It was an interpretation that would exert influence on the last unfolding of the biblical Word, and eventually on the growth of Christian theology.

In Greece, attempts at rational criticism of experience, not content to supplement myth or even to correct and interpret it, took a stand against it and tried to displace it. But before reaching that point, Greek wisdom attempted to make myth more logical and, in fact, it never actually replaced myth, but simply incorporated it under another form.

The First Ionians

It is undeniable that the initiators of Greek thinking, the Ionians, no matter how varied the systems they presented, always used mythic data as a basis. Further, through the many developments of their views, they consistently projected onto reality a model that was both vitalistic and personalistic, the most fundamental characteristic of the mythic mentality.[1]

The first effort was that of Thales of Miletus,[2] according to whom the sky (*ouranos*), i.e., all-encompassing reality, is *empsychos*, a living reality, an animated organism, a *zōon*. As in the earliest Mesopotamian cosmogonies, starting with the Sumerian and including the works of Hesiod and Homer (who both believed that all gods, as well as all men, proceed from *Okeanos*), Thales held that water is the source of all life and all being. Collingwood explains this system as the divinity calling forth all beings from water, much as a magician would.[3] Indeed, Thales provides the first philosophical use of the word *physis*, or nature, and for him the term unquestionably designates the mysterious process through which everything derives from the divine power infused into the basic substance.

A little later, Anaximander, finding a contradiction in the view that one of the elements composing the physical universe could be the source of cosmic evolution, contended that the origin of everything was the infinite (the *apeiron*, i.e., that which is undefinable and has no ascribable limits), and he identified it with the divinity. Specific beings were seen by him as the result of local eddies, variously concentrating the infinite's primitively amorphous state.

Anaximenes objected that the supposed condensation of the infinite was an absurdity, and reverted to the concept that the principle of all things was in one of the actual elements: according to him, it was air which brought forth all things, through its various degrees of condensation or rarefaction.[4]

Pythagoras

In Collingwood's opinion, these various speculations on relative condensation seem to have led to the decisive shift Pythagoras was to introduce into Ionian cosmogony.[5] He held that the cosmological problem did not reside in identifying some supposedly primitive substance; instead, *physis* involved geometric and mathematical forms imposed on essentially amorphous matter. More precisely, in the Pythagorean school, numbers were the key to the differentiated yet unified structure of the universe. Further, numbers were linked to the arrangement and interrelation of figures in space. For two points determine a line, three a surface, and four a volume. In the final analysis, the *tetraktys* is therefore the source of all concrete forms of reality and the manifestation of the divine, conceived of as a mathematical intelligence.

This is one of the two sources of Plato's theory of Ideas, as Forms of things and beings. The other source was to be provided by the Socratic quest for the true Good, as the ideal toward which the harmony of Forms is oriented.

Heraclitus and Parmenides

Before moving on from Pythagoras to Socrates and Plato, we must consider the conflict between the diametrically opposed views of Heraclitus and Parmenides. The former was an Ephesian who lived at the turn of the sixth century B.C.; he was therefore an Ionian.[6] He may, in fact, be considered the last proponent of true Ionian philosophy, since he held that the entire diversified cosmos stemmed from a single element. For Heraclitus, this element was neither water (singled out by Thales), nor some *apeiron* (as in Anaximander's view), nor air (Anaximenes' basic substance), but fire. The heart of his system, however, lay in his conviction that perpetual change is essential to the life of the universe. Hence, the well-known formulation: "All flows, all passes away, nothing remains."[7] Or again: "One cannot bathe twice in the same river." Hence also the description of the universe as a huge battlefield,[8] and Heraclitus' choice of fire as fundamental element. And this perpetual mutation of everything that exists is governed by its own immanent law: a cosmic *logos* which provides all things with meaning and expresses the divine mind, unchanging behind the universal flux.

Totally opposite, at least to the first part of the Heraclitic doctrine, is the teaching of Parmenides.[9] For him change is only apparent, an illusion of our senses, needing to be corrected by the intellect. For "being" cannot derive from any form of "becoming," since nothing can become unless it pre-exists. Nor can being arise from non-being, since that would be absolutely meaningless. In Parmenides' view, the immutable being is spherical rather than infinite. This means, on the one hand, that the indefinite cannot exist and, on the other, that a distinction between material and spiritual being remains unknown.

In the subsequent period, Melissos of Samos[10] maintained (though he had few supporters on this point) that Parmenides' "being" can be only infinite. The other great member of the Eleatic school, Zeno, developed his celebrated paradoxes against the Pythagorean idea of an infinitely divisible space. If this concept held true, Achilles could never overtake the turtle, nor could an arrow reach its target, since they would both need infinite time to pass through the infinite number of intermediate points, whatever the speed at which they might both travel.[11]

Empedocles, Leucippus, and Anaxagoras

Meanwhile, two different attempts were made to reconcile the Heraclitean and Parmenidean visions of the world. According to Empedocles of Agrigentum,[12] the four elements (water, air, fire, and earth) are eternal, and everything results from their various combinations and separations, which are due to love (eros) or strife (palē).

Leucippus of Miletus introduced the concept of atoms, i.e., indivisible elementary particles, having different shapes and sizes. Their various combinations produce everything, including the four basic elements. Unlike his later disciples such as Democritus and Epicurus, he did not consider these permutations to be the result of pure chance, but to come from logos te kai anankē, reason and necessity.[13] But it is not clear what he meant by this.

Finally, Anaxagoras[14] maintained the Pythagorean concept of infinitely divisible particles, and asserted that they always belong to one or another of the four elements. These ubiquitous elements are present in variable and changing proportions, which explains the variability and mutability of the universe. The divine intelligence, the nous, is the only ultimate cause of these movements, with the variations they bring about.

The Sophists

The rapid succession of these conflicting hypothetical schemes, coinciding with a period of great political upheavals which produced moral laxity and religious skepticism, led to an inevitable reaction. The so-called

Sophists were both the initiators and the result of this backlash. But the merciless criticism Socrates was to level at their doctrines was simply an attempt to reduce their principles or tendencies *ad absurdum*, i.e., to ultimate conclusions which few Sophists, if any, would have found acceptable.[15] It is revealing that for his contemporaries, including Aristophanes, men neither malicious nor unintelligent, Socrates remained a Sophist, and perhaps the most dangerous of all, owing to his inexorable logic.[16]

It is clear that Sophists, at least initially, sought, as Socrates did, to return to the sources and purpose of primitive wisdom, leaving excessive rationalism for experience, and a detached consideration of the universe for concern about form in human life. Since they lived at a time when democratic government was being established, they gradually concentrated on the art of effective citizenship in the new city states. Hence Sophist emphasis on rhetoric, the art of persuasion. But this emphasis did not necessarily imply unscrupulous ambition. Indeed, Sophists were the first to take a stand against the diversity of local laws and to seek a "natural" law that would be in harmony with *physis*, the order of things, in general, and especially with human nature. According to Plato's dialogues, it seems that two Sophists in particular sharpened the critical focus of Socrates. They may therefore be considered as specially representative of the entire movement.

Protagoras and Gorgias

The major saying ascribed to Protagoras[17] in *Theaetetus* is that "man himself is the measure of all things." The proof he gives shows exactly what he means by this maxim: the same wind will seem cold to one man and warm to another. It appears, however, that in his view this extreme individualism and subjectivism applies only to the perceptions of the senses. For the *Protagoras* describes him as convinced that there can be no ethic unless it is socially oriented. Yet again, according to the *Theaetetus*, the only possible basis for this system of morals is "the surest," which seems to be simply what is most expedient in the specific circumstances. Given this tendency, the discussion in the *Protagoras* leads him to support local custom, while denying that it has any absolute value.

Gorgias,[18] his contemporary, became a total skeptic in respect to all realities external to ourselves. Nothing exists, he said, since nothing can come into being unless it has pre-existed, as Parmenides pointed out. The proof put forward by Melissos is no less cogent: permanent and eternal being should be infinite, but an existing infinite is a contradictory concept. This being so, what more could wisdom aim at than to persuade others of what we consider desirable? Wisdom then becomes a mere *psychagogia*, the art of influencing other minds. When sophistry reached that point, the Socratic protest arose.

Socrates

In discussing Socrates, we must first admit to being somewhat daunted by the multiplicity of divergent witnesses and of inconsistent evidence.[19] The figure of Socrates emerging even from the first few of Plato's dialogues is decidedly that of a metaphysician who takes ethical problems as a starting point. This trait becomes increasingly pronounced in the later dialogues. Xenophon, on the other hand, saw Socrates exclusively as a moralist, whose only interest was to produce or maintain a sound and harmonious society. To Aristophanes, he was merely another Sophist, but a particularly subtle one, deeply involved in physics.

Aristotle's scant testimony, found in his critique of Plato, puts us on the right track.[20] According to this evidence, Plato should receive exclusive credit for the theory of Ideas, with Socrates being above all a demanding moralist, intent on developing accurate definitions through a rigorous critical process; that is, he began by defining the good and proceeded inductively from the particular to the general. This is the right line of interpretation, but it should be pursued further. It is noteworthy that Socrates did not claim (any more than the biblical Daniel) to possess wisdom, but only to be wisdom's friend, or *philosophos*. Moreover, his cryptic utterances on the *daimōn* guiding and inspiring him, a being commanding absolute obedience, did not show that he was irreligious as has been charged. On the contrary, they were symptomatic of a vague but stubborn conviction that, in the quest for wisdom, it is not enough to avoid abstract rationality and reestablish contact with the reality of life. Neither is it a matter of turning back to myths with a sharpened sense of their permanent significance as the Pythagoreans had sought to do. Rather, it requires going beyond myths, so to speak, but still in the direction indicated by them. This is why we may assert that there is in Socrates a religious element that relates him to the prophets. This element is the overpowering attraction of a never-satisfied demand for purity and authenticity, which impels him to pursue a still unknown good, but one sufficiently foreshadowed so that any inferior substitute or caricature would be unhesitatingly rejected by critical reasoning. This twofold impulse, involving a return to myths and an effort to reach beyond them in a spirit of faithfulness to the essence of the mythic instinct, is characteristic of the entire period, but reaches its purest expression in the doctrine of Socrates.

Plato

More than anyone else, Plato drew inspiration from this impulse, but it may be doubted whether, in his thinking, the same purity and refusal to compromise were fully maintained.[21] The Pythagoreans had passed on to him the Orphic myth, which they had been the first to allegorize: in a jealous rage, the Titans, sons of the earth, killed and devoured Dionysus, son of Zeus, who then struck them down by lightning; the human race was subsequently born from their ashes. The Pythagoreans therefore asserted that we are a divine spark encased in an earthen shell. This is the principle of the entire Platonic anthropology.[22]

Yet another Ionian, Xenophanes of Colophon,[23] had been the first to criticize the figure of the mythic gods, claiming they were a mere projection of man, with all his shortcomings and virtues magnified. In fact, Heraclitus had already cast doubt on the virtually automatic salvation expected from the "mysteries" and their initiations, and questioned the concept of divinity implied by this salvation.[24] Plato would attempt a synthesis of these various elements: the initial efforts of Greek thinking, filtered by the realistic criticism of the Sophists, which in Socratic teaching seemed to lead to a humanism beyond the merely human.[25]

Born to an aristocratic family in Athens, or possibly Aegina, in 428 or 427, Plato was nevertheless educated according to the democratic traditions of Pericles, who had died a year earlier. Plato seems to have intended at first to become an artist, but he became associated with Cratylus, who carried to its ultimate consequences the Heraclitean philosophy of universal change. A friend and disciple of Socrates, Plato retired to Megara, living near the mathematician Euclid, after Socrates' trial and conviction. He may also have traveled to Egypt. In any case, he later visited Italy and Sicily, remained there for some time at the court of Dionysius of Syracuse, and became a friend of the latter's brother-in-law Dion. Back in Athens, Plato organized the meetings in the Academos gardens, where—according to Aristotle—he devoted himself increasingly to pure speculation. He returned to Syracuse to visit Dion and instruct Dionysius II. A third stay appears to have convinced him that it is impossible to effect, through enlightened despotism, a philosophical ideal of society or human existence. He died in 348 or 347.

Lutoslawski seems to have definitely established that Plato's philosophy underwent four successive stages of development.[26] The first remained Socratic, and is typified by the *Apology of Socrates, Protagoras,* and *Gorgias,* the initial dialogues. In these writings, Forms are immanent in our thinking, as they probably always were for Socrates, even though he may never have used the term himself. These Forms are produced by the *logos,* i.e., by the dialectics or critical dialogue. In the second phase, that of *Cratylus,* the *Symposium,* the *Phaedo,* and the first book of the *Republic,* we see Forms becoming Ideas which transcend experience and thought itself. The third phase, with books II to X of the *Republic,* the *Phaedrus, Theaetetus,* and *Parmenides,* is marked by the assumption (in the discussion with Parmenides) that

Forms must be in some way both immanent and transcendent: they are present in our thinking, and even in physical reality, yet remain above and beyond both.

In the fourth phase, the figure of Socrates (whose name had become an alias for Plato himself in his most distinctive thinking) disappears altogether. The *Sophist*, the *Statesman*, the *Timaeus*, and the *Laws* finally saw true reality only in a noetic world (where Forms have their proper place), of which this world can be, at best, a feeble and imperfect copy. The *Timaeus*, the only one of Plato's works to be known at firsthand in the Latin Middle Ages, where it had an enormous influence, sets forth a fundamentally Pythagorean cosmology. Within this fully developed theory of Forms, it took over many features from Ionian physics, and attempted to integrate Heraclitus and Parmenides.[27] The physical world of constant change and materiality lends itself only to perception through the senses, which can do no more than provide an inaccurate opinion of reality (*doxa* = appearance). It nevertheless tends to imitate (*mimēsis*) the transcendent Forms, and to this extent the physical world is said to participate or share (*metexis*) in them. The demiurge (*dēmiourgos*), more artist than creator, contemplates the Forms and models, according to them, a receptacle which *per se* is nothing but empty space; but he infuses into it a soul (*psychē*), both in this world and in the beyond, and thus provides the link between the noetic and physical worlds. And so we have time, defined as a changeable image of unchanging eternity, according to which Forms are totally but successively copied.

The Platonic demiurge is therefore clearly not responsible for the existence of Ideas or of what we call matter. One may, however, wonder about the precise relationship between the Good, the Ideas, and the demiurge[28]— especially since Plato explicitly asserts that the Good is the source of everything that exists, since the nature of the Good is to communicate itself. This has remained the major enigma of Plato's effort at integration or synthesis. His disciples tried ceaselessly to resolve the point, but it seems probable that Plato himself never developed a clear answer in this respect, just as we are left without an answer after studying the entire body of his teachings.

Chapter IX: From the Cosmos of Aristotle to that of Philo Judaeus

Aristotle expressed a second reaction of Greek thinking, a move toward realism following the excess of Platonic speculation.

Aristotle

It must be admitted that ascertaining Aristotle's final position may be even more difficult than determining the main and definitive thrust of Plato's teachings.[1]

Born in 384 or 383 in the Thracian city of Stagira, Aristotle was the son of Nichomachus, physician to the Macedonian King Amyntas II. From 368/367 to 348/347 he studied under Plato at the Academy of Athens. He subsequently stayed in Assos (Troad), then Mytilene, on the island of Lesbos. In 343/342 he was invited to Pella by King Philip of Macedonia to take charge of the education of Alexander, his son and future successor. In 336/335, after Alexander had become king, Aristotle returned to Stagira, then to Athens, where the following year he founded his own school of philosophy, the Lyceum. When Alexander died in 323/322, the philosopher retired to Euboea in Chalcis, where he died in 322/321.

The difficulty we find in interpreting his doctrine is due to the fact that only fragments remain of his *exoterikoi logoi*, the dialogues intended for the general public, whereas we know but indirectly, through his disciple Andronicos of Rhodes (middle of the first century B.C.), Aristotle's *akroamatikoi*, his teachings at the Lyceum. It nevertheless seems that his thinking went through three successive phases. In the first, he remained a disciple of Plato. In the second, he criticized the development of the Platonic doctrine of Ideas or Forms. In the third, beginning in the year 335, he seems to have concentrated on scientific studies of "physics" in the wider sense, i.e., the study of nature, and especially of living beings.

According to Werner Jaeger, Aristotle's major metaphysical essay on cosmology, the *Lambda Metaphysics*, was completely abandoned toward the end of his life, when he confined himself increasingly to strictly positive studies.[2] Yet Guthrie[3] seems to have demonstrated that the essay was a late contribution and that it therefore reflects Aristotle's final views on the universe. No consensus has developed on how to interpret his conceptualism, as opposed to what might be called Plato's realistic idealism. William Ross seems inclined to see in it a pure form of nominalism.[4] More generally, since the Renaissance, many commentators have favored a materialistic interpretation of Aristotle, one that precludes the notion both of a God existing independently of the physical universe and of an immortal human soul. On these points, however, the most recent research (such as that by Chroust[5]) indicates a return to an interpretation proposed by Thomas Aquinas, who saw in Aristotle a sincerely and deeply religious thinker and who recognized that his conceptualism amounted to a moderate realism. Be that as it may, five distinct points strike us as noteworthy, when viewing Aristotelian cosmology.

1. The first is the meaning Aristotle ascribes to *physis* (nature) in *Lambda Metaphysics*. He contrasts it with *techne* (the art of a craftsman or artist fashioning an object from the outside) and *bia* (violence, also acting from outside and forcing an object to behave in a way alien to it). Nature, as he means it, is therefore a principle of activity immanent to things themselves.

2. In Aristotle's view, as in that of the Ionians, the whole of nature is a living entity, and carries within itself the principle which actuates it. Nature successively takes on various forms, but each one *in posse* lies hidden in the previous one. In contradistinction to contemporary thinking on evolution, Aristotle considered that the structure and changes observed in nature are eternal. Any movement therefore tends toward the one he deemed perfect: circular movement.

At this stage, a first explicit objection to Plato's teaching emerges: in order to obtain the incessant process characteristic of nature, there is no need to postulate anything external to it. Such an outside influence would be needed only if the universe had not always existed (which Plato's *Timaeus* itself rules out, since it holds that there can never have been a time when there was no world). It follows that there can be no other efficient cause than *physis* itself, a process which is its own cause. It seems difficult not to deduce materialism and atheism from this view. *Lambda Metaphysics* nevertheless introduces God into the picture, but in an unexpected manner.

3. It is the very intelligibility of change, so characteristic of nature, which postulates God—or, at least, a certain kind of God. Indeed, according to Aristotle, becoming—i.e., the constant movement from potentiality to actuality—assumes the presence in matter of its future form. However, he added, form cannot already have been in matter itself; otherwise there would be no "becoming," or else the process of change would have reached its end even before occurring, which is obviously contradictory. But it is equally impossible for forms to exist independently. They must therefore be present in a cosmic intelligence, visualized as "thinking thought" (*noēsis noēseōs*), which Aristotle considers the prime mover (itself motionless) of the universe.

To comprehend this reversal, one must attempt to grasp how Aristotle, in criticizing Plato, came to a certain understanding of knowledge. As he saw it, there are two possibilities. The first involves the knowledge of something material, e.g., the sound of a bell. In such an instance, knowledge never bears on matter as such, but concerns only the form (*logos*) assumed by matter; in the example chosen, it concerns specifically the rhythm of matter's vibrations, to the extent that this rhythm is perceived by one's own body. In the case of anything immaterial, such as the good, knowledge is simply a complete correspondence or congruity between the known and the one who knows. Forms will therefore be found in divine thought.

How then does *physis* receive the forms? Aristotle answers that it does so through an *eros*, a love which is essentially desire and impels the *physis* spontaneously toward God, but leaves the divinity totally unmoved. Nature develops because it is moved toward God by its love for him. But since God lacks or needs nothing, he cannot love. He does not even know the world as such, i.e., as perpetual change. He knows only his own thoughts, which the world tends to imitate: God "moves all things, inasmuch as he is loved by them."[6]

4. The *nous*, the divine intelligence, does not exercise this attraction on our universe in a direct manner. The attraction is actually felt only by an intelligence lower than God's, i.e., by the soul of the upper heaven. The animate heaven is thus the first entity in motion, the only one to feel the direct influence of the unmoved and utterly unaware-of-it prime mover. In turn, the souls relating to various bodies (and first of all the planets) move in accordance with the desire impelling them toward a higher entity in motion, which similarly is unaware of them. The process produces an entire noetic cosmos, underlying the universe we see and touch but seeming to reach beyond it in the pure *noēsis noeseōs*.[7]

5. The apparent result, as Collingwood noted, is that nothing can be known of matter considered separately from the *logos* (i.e., from its various forms), except that it is only a limit: the term means simply that non-actual potentialities are unfulfilled. This being so, as Collingwood quite rightly emphasizes, everything we call matter—atoms, molecules, electrons, vibrations—is in fact immaterial, in Aristotle's view. Matter is replaced by forms.[8]

Democritus and Epicurus

After Aristotle, the atomic theory initiated by Leucippus was to be modified several times. Democritus of Abdera, a contemporary of Socrates, had already re-interpreted it, apparently by giving a dominant role to *blind necessity*.[9] Some time after Aristotle, Epicurus reworked the theory, introducing the idea that atoms converging toward the center of the earth may deviate slightly from a predetermined path, admitting some randomness and freedom. This cosmology does not deny the existence of the gods but gives them no role in the life of the cosmos. Aside from that, it is noteworthy that though Epicurean ethics stressed the cultivation of pleasure, Epicurus himself seems to have been a chronic invalid for whom pleasure was but an unstable balance between various painful passions and could be maintained only through the constant practice of austere discipline.[10]

Far more than these developments, and perhaps more markedly even than Plato and Aristotle, it was the thinking of the first Stoics that influenced the last stages of the wisdom of the Old Testament. This was particularly so in the sapiential books, soon translated into Greek (for instance, the book of Jesus ben Sirach), or even written directly in that language (e.g., the so-called Wisdom of Solomon).[11]

Stoicism

The three masters of the first period of Stoicism,[12] the only period to concern us here, focused directly on cosmology, while maintaining a deep interest in anthropology. The speculation engaged in by Zeno of Citium,[13] Cleanthes of Assos,[14] and Chrysippus of Soli[15] drew its main inspiration from Sicilian medical circles and their physiology. According to this school of thought, the vital principle is a kind of subtle fire which is a natural attribute of the body, and not (as Hippocrates believed) one borrowed from the surrounding universe through breathing. The Stoics held, however, that everything in the universe is endowed with a life that has much in common. In ourselves and in everything else, this life derives from the condensation of a sort of fiery air, the *pneuma*, which is at the same time *logos*: reason immanent in all things, the divine reason. This *pneuma*, this "spirit" (seen, however, as wholly material) unfailingly animates all things, by virtue of a supremely good necessity. Through the spirit in us, which makes us reasonable human beings, we must recognize this necessity and accept it. Our individual life will then be happy and successful. But we cannot avoid the necessity in question. To quote a formulation which became a Latin proverb in later Stoicism: *volentem fata ducunt, nolentem trahunt* (fate leads the willing, drags the unwilling).

The individual structure and vitality of the various parts of the universe are due to *logoi spermatikoi*, seminal reasons in which the universal *logos* is multiplied, without dividing *stricto sensu*. Our soul is thus but a fragment of the divinity. This kind of materialistic but dynamic pantheism would later be capable—as may be seen in the hymn to Zeus by Cleanthes—of paradoxically sustaining, if not inspiring, a profoundly religious sense of life and of the world.

One particular point which Stoicism was to develop would acquire considerable importance in the later development of Jewish and Christian ethics and asceticism. It was the distinction between two constantly opposed aspects or tendencies of human and cosmic life: the *poioun*, or positive activity working to fulfill the *logos*, i.e., the divine reason immanent in all things; and the *paschon*, a mere passivity tending to reabsorb all things into a diffuse and tensionless materiality and leading to absolute nothingness, nonexistence, or unconsciousness.[16] The entire universe thus periodically falls into an *ekpyrōsis*, a total dissolution, but one preparatory to a rebirth which reinitiates the same cycle.

Finally, even if it is the same *pneuma* which produces everything that exists, its various degrees of condensation nevertheless account for an ascending series of realizations. According to Chrysippus, these are a mere *hexis* (a coming into being in the inorganic world), a *physis* (a capacity for development in plants), a *psychē* (the instinctive soul of animals), and a *hegemonikon* (a capability of freedom and autonomy in man).[17]

Biblical Wisdom and Stoic Wisdom

The sapiential texts of the Stoics, as well as the speculations of Jewish religious thinkers who witnessed the beginning of Christianity, particularly those produced during and after the Diaspora, written in Greek and under the influence of Hellenistic culture, and even works of Palestinian Judaism—all these showed somehow the same willingness to use Hellenistic wisdom that earlier stages of revelation had exhibited toward ancient myths and archaic wisdom. It is remarkable that the same capacity for critical revision and creative reinterpretation is evident not only in the writings incorporated into the Bible, but also in the whole of this most Hellenized of Jewish thinking. It even seems increasingly certain that the last Hellenistic philosophy, neo-Platonism—which some have maintained could equally well have been called neo-Stoicism, and in which Aristotelian influence is hardly less important—would never have developed as it did, especially in the synthesis carried out by Plotinus, unless it had been exposed to a Jewish and Christian influence.

The Platonic theory of Ideas, the Aristotelian concept of thinking thought, and perhaps even more the *Logos-Pneuma* System of the Stoics, were all utilized by the Jews to define the characteristics of divine wisdom. They considered it as the ultimate and total object of God's thought on creation and the history of salvation, but without ever immersing God into the world or divinizing the world. Similarly, the dynamic character of the cosmos and of salvation history, as well as their final unity, were to be perceived in a way that owed much to the Aristotelian and Stoic notions of *physis*. But the vision of an eternal cyclical cosmos was to be replaced by the concept of a universe finite in both time and space, fulfilling definitively through the freedoms divinely created and sustained, the immutable plan of a wholly benevolent Wisdom. Finally, the eternal destiny of each human individual—within the framework of the master design of love and grace which gives direction to all things—was to be illuminated by the concept of a human soul specially related to divine spirituality, even though never identified with the divinity nor seen as separable in destiny or history from the body, intended for resurrection, nor from the entire universe, awaiting its own redemption and transfiguration.

Philo

Philo Judaeus (Philo of Alexandria) seems to represent an extreme case of the assimilation of Hellenism by a believing and practicing Jew. The studies devoted to him at the beginning of this century generally saw him as just another eclectic Hellenistic philosopher between Platonism and Stoicism, who prepared the ground for the subsequent synthesis of neo-Platonism.[18] This is largely true of his *Logos*, which combines the immanence of the Stoic *Pneuma-Logos* with the ideality, if not the strict transcendence, of Platonic Ideas. This also applies to his "powers," particularly the creative and the royal power, the latter governing whatever the former produces. It is as difficult to say to what extent these powers are distinct from the *Logos* as to ascertain the latter's relationship to God, whose main intermediary with the created world it seems to be.

More recent studies, such as those by Wolfson, Goodenough, and Jean Laporte,[19] have increasingly brought out another side to Philo's teaching. It is one that has been long neglected but which Philo himself considered basic to his entire doctrine. His mind was deeply permeated not only with the Bible, which he never ceased reading and commenting on, but also with the Judaism of his time, even that of the Pharisees, who concentrated increasingly on the Torah as Law. As Goodenough among others has shown, Philo was motivated above all by the justification of Judaism—in the eyes of the most religious and thoughtful pagans—as a form of life: the *hodos basilikē*, or royal road leading to the actual reign of God over all human existence, to match his reign over the cosmos. When due attention is paid to this aspect, which was certainly the most important to Philo, everything in his works takes on a different complexion. It becomes clear that his "powers" are but a Hellenized presentation of the angels of Judaism. His Logos, before being the intelligible world of the Platonists or the Pneuma-Logos of the Stoics, is unquestionably the creative Word of Genesis which illuminated patriarchs and prophets. He stated explicitly that it is also the Angel of the Lord, an immanent manifestation of the transcendent God according to the highest biblical tradition.

An element that seems totally absent from Philo's thinking is eschatolog-ical tension, the sense of conflict and of God's final judgment so dominant in apocalyptic literature. He may seem to carry to an extreme the tendency evident in the last sapiential books of the Greek Bible—and particularly in the Wisdom of Solomon—to reduce biblical history to a collection of indi-vidual destinies, typically faithful to the revealing and provident Logos. It should be said that, at the very least, he shows the tendency, found in the last prophets and indeed progressively in the whole Bible, of interiorizing and therefore individualizing the divine plan. Philo focuses strongly on the identification, by the believer turned philosopher, of the entire biblical history with the history of his own meeting with God and the perfecting of his resemblance to the Most High.

It nevertheless remains true that Philo's entire doctrine is wedded to the Bible. It has been claimed that the use of allegorical exegesis allowed him to introduce into the reading of the sacred text all the Greek ideas that were dear to him. This may on occasion be true. But it should not be forgotten that he interpreted the Bible from a predominantly Jewish viewpoint. These colored the borrowed philosophical elements much more than the Greek concepts distorted his Jewish thinking. As Laporte has noted, Philo's entire religious philosophy leads, in the same way as intertestamentary literature of Palestinian Judaism, to the *eucharistia*. This is God's blessing bestowed on everything he has made, in the creation of man and the world, entirely promoting the illumination of man—shaped according to God's plan for him—by the divine Logos, which takes possession of man's entire being to the extent that the Logos is revealed to man.[20]

Chapter X: The Evangelical Vision of the Cosmos

Modern criticism has made us acutely aware of the difficulty in determining precisely what Jesus himself taught and what is interpretation of his teaching. It is a difficulty linked to the problem of assessing his life and person as presented somewhat differently by various evangelists.[1] Concerning the world, however, we can be sure that Jesus' thinking has come down to us practically as it was expressed to his disciples. For it is remarkable that the four Gospel writers, despite their particular viewpoints and interests, are in perfect agreement on this. They all make clear that Jesus adopted the vision of the created universe that emerges from the intertestamentary apocalypses. This vision assumes the initial revelation on the creation and Fall as prelude and premise to the later eschatological view. But Jesus transfigured these elements in his assertion of the divine fatherhood, which would extend to all men.[2]

The Divine Fatherhood

This fatherhood itself demands both an absolute detachment from everything other than God and his love and an exultant recognition that God's love gives ultimate meaning to all things. Hence the paradoxical beatitude of the poor; for them everything acquires a transparency to the divine presence.[3] This Jewish piety, which saw in all things and in everything that happens to us the signs of God's benevolence, became in Jesus a filial reverence that recognized in all things God speaking to us, the Father addressing his children. Jesus' attitude became as it were the last word of this address, a perfect reflection of the Father's *agape*, the creative, saving and paternal love in which the Lord's justice and mercy join and are absorbed into a hitherto unimaginable and inconceivable generosity.

"Consider the lilies, how they grow; they neither toil nor spin; yet I tell you, even Solomon in all his glory was not arrayed like one of these."[4] One saying such as this is enough to express the essence of the teaching of Jesus in this regard. The parables in their diversity are the result of this approach; they require us to look at everything here below in the light that the world is a manifestation of its maker's inexhaustible liberality and generosity. Thus to enter into a personal relationship with God can be suggested only by the idea of fatherhood carried to a supreme degree of communication and communion.[5] This explains why the parables of the Kingdom, identifying it with the reign of this fatherly love, find something like an echo in the summary of the law, which calls upon us to respond to God's pure gift of love with a love of total surrender, and urges us to love everything he loves.

The fourth Gospel makes fully explicit this teaching of the Synoptics when it quotes a saying of Jesus in which the entire evangelical message opens up to us at once and in its deepest implications: "For God so loved the world that he gave his only Son, that whoever believes in him should not perish but have eternal life." And its counterpart: "And this is eternal life, that they know thee the only true God, and Jesus Christ, whom thou hast sent."[6]

The entire Gospel would be completely misrepresented and distorted if one were to equate God with the world or reduce him to our fellow-creature or neighbor. On the contrary, everything in the world must be seen only as a gift, having meaning for us only because it signifies the presence of the God of love. Our fellowman must be looked upon as someone God wants to turn into his own child, just as he does ourselves. This is why we must start by taking or regaining a child's view of things, which is possible only if Christ's essentially filial experience is shared by us. But this renewal of our vision, enlisting our entire being, has as its corollary the detachment of the poor, who know that they can gain what St. Paul calls "the glorious liberty of the children of God" only by breaking free from any selfish and vain-glorious attachments.[7] This is the inspiration for the four beatitudes of St. Luke and the eight of St. Matthew, which assume that poverty should extend to everything other than God himself, and further-more that poverty is all the more "in truth" as it must be "in Spirit." This indigence finds its counterpart—as the Cistercian Isaac of Stella has expressed it so eloquently in what is probably the most moving commen-tary on these texts—in a renewed possession of the entire universe. As St. Paul has also said: "all are yours; and you are Christ's; and Christ is God's."[8] In this sense and even now, for the New Testament faith, the world is capable of becoming for us, once again, the Kingdom of God. This will happen to the extent that its deep nature is again revealed to those who, while in the world, are restored through voluntary poverty to the spirit of childhood, which only the Son can bring us.[9]

Knowledge and Eucharist

Such is the knowledge imparted to us by the Son: he allows us to recognize God as Father, and all things as the result and token of the Father's love, that love that is the Son's alone and can be known only through a filial experience of love. This is the ultimate significance of the eucharist—the ultimate end of the entire teaching of the Word in the Old Testament—when it flowered into the filial thanksgiving that is the culmination of the message of the Synoptics, as well as being the heart of the fourth Gospel.

It is pertinent to quote the formula given by St. Luke,[10] based on the same key terms, and structured in the same way as in the Gospel according to St. Matthew:[11]

> I thank thee, Father, Lord of heaven and earth, that thou has hidden these things from the wise and understanding and revealed them to babes; yea, Father, for such was thy gracious will [*eudokia*]. All things have been delivered to me by my Father; and no one knows the Son except the Father, and no one knows the Father except the Son and any one to whom the Son chooses to reveal him.

God as Father is blessed for the revelation of his plan in all things, which is precisely that of the paternal *agape*: the unlimited communication of everything he is through everything he has, through his Son, in whom he is known with a knowledge that is an obedience of conformity, based on the closest union, or rather communion. We become his children in the Son, by knowing him as the Son himself is known to him, with a knowledge of love through which we receive everything in his person.

The Conflict with the Devil

But the Gospel of Jesus is no less clear about the fact that this restitution of the authentic knowledge of God in all things, in the knowledge of his love, through association with the Son and his perfect filiation, has as necessary counterpart a mortal struggle with the hostile power that has entered the world to oppose and set the world against all this. The Son came into the world, was given to us, and was delivered to this evil power, precisely to take up this struggle.

In this context the account given in the Synoptics of the temptation of Jesus acquires its full meaning.[12] As Riesenfeld has established, we must see in this temptation *the* crucial experience for Jesus, who in describing the episode disclosed to his disciples the full significance of his mission in 'the world. St. Mark stressed that it was the Spirit of God in Jesus which literally "drove him out into the desert" to undergo the ordeal.[13] There is an obvious correlation between this temptation and the original fall of man, as described in Genesis. This time, however, man emerges victorious. The hymn in Philippians 2 acclaims in Jesus the new Adam, the eschatological Son of man foreseen in the apocalypses, the *Gibbor* of Qumran's Midrashic literature;[14] for he chose (in contrast to the first man) faithfulness to the fatherly Word rather than surrender to the blandishments of the tempter, and in so doing exposed Satan's snares for all time.

Closely linked to this account of Jesus triumphant over the temptation which had caused Adam's downfall was the explanation—doubtless also going back to Jesus himself—that his ministry in this world was above all an exorcism: the casting out of the evil spirit by the Spirit of God. This is why the work of the apostles in announcing the good word is seen, in the same Gospel according to St. Mark, as involving inseparably preaching and the casting out of devils.[15]

Deeply significant is the answer given by Jesus to those who accused him of casting out Beelzebub only through the prince of the demons himself. In fact, this exorcism can be accomplished only by the divine Spirit. Jesus thus appears as the stronger one who, entering "into the house of a strong man"[16] (the devil in this world), expels him and turns his own weapons against him. Ths only unpardonable sin is thus a failure to acknowledge this action of the Spirit through Jesus, which is the world's only hope of salvation.

Pauline Cosmology

This creative reinterpretation carried out by Jesus, a task inseparable from what he is (the Son) and from his mission in the world (to bring us back to the plan of adoption by God, which is the true meaning of creation) is obviously the source of the Christian cosmologies already in the process of systematization and set forth in turn by St. Paul and St. John.

André Feuillet in particular has shown the influence exercised on St. Paul by the sapiential literature.[17] The apostle clearly adopted the view of creation and of its history contained in the books of wisdom. As D. Deden and Dom Jacques Dupont had already established, however, apocalyptic literature contributed no less to his vision of the world.[18] At this point, one may stress the close connection already noted between chapters 1 and 2 of the First Epistle to the Corinthians on the mystery of Christ where the last word of God's wisdom is revealed to us as the key that will turn the history of sin into that of salvation, and chapter 2 of the book of Daniel, where we see the shift from wisdom to apocalypse.

In a deeper sense, St. Paul preserved as the basis for his whole conception of the world the views of creation and the Fall which are so fundamental to the entire Old Testament. As the last books of wisdom had done, he introduced into these views some elements of Stoic thinking, e.g., the consonant notions of creation as *cosmos* and of man as *sōma*.[19] He was particularly conscious of the organic nature of the entire creation and of human life inserted into creation, so that only human life can express the ultimate meaning of the created world in its entirety and its unity. Hence his optimistic view of creation as a whole, and of the body of humanity. Not only did he see them both as good in themselves, inasmuch as they both issued from the hands of God, who created everything "in the Son," but he saw them as intended together for the glory of resurrection, and spreading, through the divine Spirit and from Christ the Son of God, to the far ends of the universe.[20]

According to St. Paul, this explains how we are spontaneously in tune, as is the whole of creation, with the aspirations of the Spirit of God in us and in the universe.[21] For example, the "unspeakable groanings" of the Spirit accompany an agony of all creation that can be compared only to the travail of childbirth. For in its present condition, creation is in a state of servitude from which it must be delivered, and this requires the deliverance of mankind itself.[22] We therefore find in St. Paul, along with the apocalyptic opposition between the present time and the age to come, a description of the former as a period of slavery and enmity and an identification of the latter with liberation, redemption, and glory, so that the current state of the world is one of impatient expectation (*apokaradokia*).[23]

The Enemies of God

Characteristic of St. Paul is the list he gives of the enemies of man that must be defeated so that the whole of creation may be free of them, enemies only Christ can bring down.[24] First come sin and death, the latter having been visited upon the world by the former.[25] At the root of both, however, is the flesh: our entire being as it collapses into its basest part, if not quickened by the divine Spirit; and the world: the whole of creation which has closed itself, around us and in us, to the presence of the Spirit.[26]

St. Paul saw the cause of this degradation—which includes our own downfall, though obviously preceding and exceeding it—in what he calls (in Galatians and Colossians) "the elements of this world."[27] They are identical with "the princes of this world"[28] of I Corinthians, as well as with "the spirits of wickedness" and "the rulers of the world of this darkness"[29] referred to in Ephesians. But their power merges into the domination exercised by the one whom St. Paul calls "the god of this world" in II Corinthians,[30] who is obviously the serpent of Genesis, Satan, Job's accuser and tempter, the apocalyptic Belial (or Beliar).

As Aulen notes in his *Christus Victor*,[31] however, it is clear that this enmity we suffer from is due to our own sinfulness and is in the final analysis a manifestation of God's anger,[32] indeed of his law.[33] This emphasizes that for St. Paul, faithful to the certainties rooted in Israel's consciousness by the divine Word, the evil spirit who presently dominates the world and man could not do so unless he were also a spirit proceeding from God, always remaining, whatever he may do and in spite of himself, in God's service. Conversely, St. Paul also asserts that God's anger, and even his law, were overcome by Christ on the cross,[34] along with "the principalities and powers" of this world.[35]

Two Contrasting Dispensations

A major question inevitably arises: why are we, and the universe with us, under the sway of the powers of evil, and subject therefore to God's anger, closely connected with what appears to be his law? This is what St. Paul calls "the mystery of iniquity."[36] It is also quite simply the most mysterious aspect of the Pauline view of the world in general and of its present state, a view which follows from the revelation of the Old Testament, but which makes that revelation more explicit than ever before.

One must first consider the idea, borrowed from Judaism by the Epistle to the Galatians,[37] that we received the law through the ministry of angels. The same idea is also found in the Acts of the Apostles[38]—specifically in Stephen's speech—and in Hebrews.[39] In Colossians,[40] and more explicitly in Galatians,[41] it is clear that St. Paul relates the observance of this law (which was largely a matter of observing times and involved weeks, months, and days) to the worship of astral powers. The key to the enigma is provided by a comment found in Hebrews: "For it was not to angels that God subjected the world to come...."[42] This implies that this world, the physical world to which we belong through our body, was "subjected" from its inception to the spiritual world of angels. The fall of a large number of angels made them the first evildoers. Man, by following their suggestion, was included in their degradation, along with the earth from which man had been drawn and which had been entrusted to him. He became the slave of the fallen angels, instead of being God's willing servant, recipient of a filial inheritance. This is man's deserved punishment, one that the rebellious angels must administer, in spite of their own rebellion. Their enmity toward us is therefore identified with God's just anger. Concurrently, however, the faithful angels remain witnesses (through communication of the divine law) to the continuing and true significance of the created world and to the kind of life we should lead in it. But in our state of servitude, this law and the knowledge of it, although countering the homage given to the satanic powers by our sinfulness, only confirm our condemnation with theirs. This explains the enmity ascribed to the law itself.

Christ appeared as the Second, or rather the Last Adam,[43] the eschatological Man, the celestial Man—as Daniel's Son of man who comes with the clouds of heaven. Henceforth, dominion over the universe no longer belongs to the angels, either faithful or fallen; through the victory of the cross and resurrection, this authority has passed into the hands of the new man and the renewed mankind which derives from him. The unfaithful

angels, intending his destruction,[44] thereby unconsciously divested themselves of their corrupt power. This is the main theme of the Epistle to the
Colossians.[45] Under these conditions, the faithful angels themselves
became merely the servants of the new dispensation, of the one who
established it, and of those who form one body with him, i.e., redeemed
men. So it shall be till the end of history, when Christ shall deliver up the
kingdom to his Father, so that forever "God may be all in all."[46]

The entire Gospel, seen from the typically Pauline viewpoint of the two
Adams and the two mankinds deriving therefrom, appears as the announcement of victory over sin,[47] leading to victory over death.[48] The Christological hymn in Philippians[49] urges us to recognize the victory of the divine
agape over the greed of sinful man, of the Son's humility over demonic pride,
of filial obedience over the rebelliousness which made us lose, like the
angels themselves, any right to immortality in the glory of the Father.

This explains the transition from a first preparatory dispensation, involving creation and the Fall, to the definitive divine economy, established by
the incarnation and the cross. It is a decisive shift from an order based on
the law and merit to the order of grace, a new dispensation in which mercy
and compassion fulfill and exceed justice.

The Pauline Eucharist

These various interrelated considerations were the source of the Pauline
"eucharist." It is the theme of all his letters, the very heart of his entire
doctrine, and in Ephesians we see it as literally all-pervasive.[50] The Pauline
eucharist glorifies the victory, in the world and through the cross of Christ,
of the Father's loving plan, which as it were bursts asunder the closed
universe of the fallen powers. It is therefore fully permeated and animated
by the Christological vision of the cosmos presented in the Epistles written
during St. Paul's captivity. It is a vision in which everything is subordinated
to the dynamic process which leads from creation in the Son, through the
Fall, to redemption by the Son, and to the freedom and glory of the children
of God. In this view, one sees the world more clearly than ever as the
creation of a supremely wise, good, and powerful God. It is the radiance of
the divine Wisdom, a radiance eternally expressed by the Son, an effulgence
whose temporal result is the world. This world is therefore fundamentally
spiritual; the angelic world appears as though clothed in the physical world,
which is thus the reflection of a reflection.

The pride of the celestial powers has distorted the meaning of the universe. When man subsequently appeared as the first resurgence of freedom, he yielded to their urging that he turn to idolatry and away from

worship of the Father. He thereby became the prey of death, instead of gaining the expected satisfaction of his immoderate greed. In accordance with the eternal plan of divine Wisdom, however, not only man and his world, but also the universe of higher powers, had been created for "the kingdom of the Son of his love."[51] Eventually, at the highest point in the history of the sinfulness of powers and men, when the cross was inflicted on the Son who became man in order to save the whole world, the ultimate revelation of the firstborn of all creation[52] who was made into "the last Adam,"[53] there is the supreme revelation of God's love. It is the voluntary humiliation, the *kenōsis* of the Son's obedience unto death, even to the death of the cross.[54] The universal reconciliation is thus accomplished in the crucified body of Christ: of men with each other and with the still faithful powers, and of the whole world with God. All things are recapitulated in their principle; the firstborn of every creature, who thus becomes the firstborn from the dead,[55] is revealed as the firstborn of countless brothers.

The Johannine Dualism: Light and Darkness

A differently constructed scheme, though one in harmony with the Pauline, is basic to St. John's writings. We shall dwell only on its two most distinctive features. The first is that the entire history of the world is revealed in the history of Christ as a conflict between light and darkness. This is what the book of Revelation shows us in the history of the Church, which appears as the completion and conclusion of cosmic history. The cross leads to glory those who follow the Lamb wherever he goes,[56] i.e., the faithful disciples. Their suffering allows them to triumph and to reach heaven, in the very presence of God. Until the last day, they are under the altar[57] where the Lamb sacrificed since the creation of the world[58] rests in the glory of the fulfilled immolation. For the other face of this immolation is the Lamb's victory, and that of all those who follow him, over death and the ancient serpent.[59] After that the celestial Jerusalem, the Bride of the Lamb, will come down out of heaven, prepared as a Bride adorned for her Husband.[60]

In the Gospel according to St. John, the conflict between light and darkness, announced even in the prologue,[61] breaks out as early as the preliminaries to the passion. The inevitability of the conflict became obvious with the symbolic healing of the man born blind.[62] This life, which is in God and is imparted by his Word, is the light of men—the light having shone in the darkness, which could not overcome it. And so it actually becomes, for mankind and the whole world, the light of life. This is why St. John's first Epistle proclaims: "God is light and in him is no darkness."[63]

Ambiguity of the World in John

This leads us directly to the second characteristic feature of the Johannine vision. It is the ambiguity of the biblical notion of the world carried to the highest point in these writings, but also finally resolved. In his first Epistle, St. John says, "Do not love the world or the things in the world. . . . [for] the whole world is in the power of the evil one."[64] Yet he asserted in the Gospel: "For God so loved the world that he gave his only Son, that whoever believes in him should not perish but have eternal life."[65] How is it possible to reconcile two such contradictory statements?

The Gospel's prologue, which obviously makes reference to Genesis, but from a higher viewpoint, assures us that all of creation was made by the divine Word, who is light and life, for he is the very Son of the Father, his only begotten Son, full of grace and truth.[66] According to St. John, however, the prince of the world[67] has become the father of lies.[68] He stood not in the truth,[69] apparently because he laid claim to the glory which belongs only to God, a glory which only the Son can give to those who acknowledge him.[70] The prince of the world has therefore corrupted created life at its source, by changing his own light into darkness. This is precisely why the Word of light and life became flesh of our flesh, so that the entire world might once again know (literally "see") God in him, and thus be saved and returned to life.[71]

The world sees God by contemplating in a spirit of faith the cross of Christ, which is the manifestation and triumph of divine love. It is the love eternally bestowed on the Son, which had created man originally and which at the end of history will make us all children of God in the only begotten Son.[72] The history of the world thus ends in the exaltation of the Son of man. On the cross he draws us all to him, raising us with him to meet the Father[73] and enter into the Son's own glory. This is the glory which was his before the beginning of the world, the glory of the only Son with his Father.[74] One may therefore conclude, with St. John as with St. Paul, that the world, in its principle, is but a reflection of the glory of God, and ultimately, in the redemption by Christ, the world will be entirely absorbed into God's glory.

The Expectation of Redemption

The question of when and how this will come about inevitably arises. St. John holds, as does St. Paul, that the fulfillment of our expectation will occur when Christ appears in his glory, at the Parousia or second coming. St. Paul does not elaborate on his statement.[75] As we have already mentioned, however, St. John adds: " . . . it does not yet appear what we shall be, but we know that when he appears we shall be like him, for we shall see him as he is."[76] This seems fully consistent with what II Corinthians has to say about the Christian's present life: "And we all, with unveiled face, beholding the glory of the Lord, are being changed into his likeness from one degree of glory to another; for this comes from the Lord who is the Spirit."[77]

In other words, the transfiguration will be an accomplished fact for us only on the last day, but it is being prepared for even now, to the extent that faith takes hold of us and causes us somehow to anticipate the vision itself. In St. Paul's writings, this seems to be in line with the description of the gift of the Spirit by the glorified Christ as both a pledge (*arrabōn*), and a first fruit (*aparchē*) of eternal life.[78] In St. John the transition seems even smoother: faith appears simply as a link between the physical vision of the Word made flesh and an anticipated vision of his divine reality, and thereby of the Father himself. Significant in this respect are the words spoken to Philip in the meeting after the Last Supper.[79]

Realized or Anticipated Eschatology?

These various comments should be sufficient to disprove a concept generally accepted by exegetes at the beginning of this century, in reaction against the minimizing interpretations of liberal Protestantism, namely that the entire expectation of the first Christians, and of the Jewish apocalyptic writers before them, was directed toward a catastrophic future, considered to be imminent. Contemporary exegesis, on the contrary, is increasingly aware that this viewpoint is one-sided and overly literal. In actual fact, although after a time the Jews placed all their hopes in a divine intervention which seemed about to take place, this attitude did not emerge in Christ's lifetime, nor even to any marked degree before the first siege of Jerusalem by the Romans in 70 A.D., but only around the time of the rebellion led by Bar Cocheba nearly fifty years later.[80]

One should, however, avoid a contrary reaction which would deny this eschatological expectation—so essential to the New Testament and to the purest intertestamentary Judaism—and replace it with the idea of an eschatology fulfilled in the death and resurrection of Jesus, as C. H. Dodd has expressed it.[81] It would be far more correct to note, as Cullmann did, that the whole Church had the feeling of being henceforth in a paradoxical position, in which the predicament facing all Christians parallels the situation of Christ during his earthly life.[82] From the moment that the Spirit of Christ descended on those who believe in him, the time to come and the present time have been, as it were, brought together for them—as it had been for him. The kingdom of God is already here, in us through the Spirit and in him before his Passion and glorification. But it "suffereth violence,"[83] i.e., it is hidden by the still persisting externals of Belial's reign.

Just as death was swallowed up by the resurrection after the Passion of Jesus, so that henceforth everything is absorbed into the kingdom, so will it be for us when Christ appears. We will pass through the fire of judgment, so that naught will remain in us except the new man, who is Christ in us, "the hope of glory."[84] For the time being we remain in our "inner nature," hidden from view by the declining "outer nature."[85]

In the fullness of time, when all things are done, the whole universe will be transfigured, with our own bodies of flesh, but already the miracles of the saints bear witness to an anticipation of this glorification, wherever the energies of the kingdom are released to the highest degree. In this situation, as the Gospel makes clear, we must be ready at any moment for the end, and even ardently hope for it. "But of that day or that hour no one knows, not even the angels in heaven, nor the Son, but only the Father,"[86] in the words of St. Mark.

This seems to be the last word of what may be said—on the basis of the New Testament—concerning the future of the cosmos, a future of which Christians have a kind of foreknowledge or even a preperception, to the extent that they are truly followers of Christ.

Chapter XI: The Struggle Against Gnosticism and Arianism: From St. Irenaeus to St. Athanasius and St. Augustine

From the first centuries when Christianity started spreading, what may be called evangelic cosmology was to encounter two heresies: Gnosticism and Arianism. The major accomplishment of the Fathers of the period—St. Irenaeus before the Nicene Council, and immediately after it a series of Doctors of the Church, from St. Athanasius to St. Augustine—was to defeat both doctrines. It may be said that these two errors stem from two opposite tendencies of the human mind, both equally deep-rooted; they therefore reflect two temptations chronically facing Christian cosmology, each being a kind of mirror-image of the other.

Gnosticism finds it impossible to concede that God the savior and God the creator are one and the same. Arianism refuses to acknowledge the transcendence of the God who not only appeared to us, but also gave himself up for us and to us in Jesus Christ. Gnostic salvation is therefore only a counter-creation, a decreation. And Arian salvation cannot really bestow on us anything exceeding even slightly the created world. The Gnostic savior cannot become involved with anything created; his incarnation must be either an illusion or a sham. As for the Arian savior, when all is said and done, he is simply the first among creatures.

Gnosticism: God Alien to the World

In discussing gnosis and Gnosticism, one should always bear in mind a highly pertinent comment by R. P. Casey,[1] to the effect that those we are now accustomed to call Gnostics actually have no right to this designation, in the view of the Fathers opposing them. Their gnosis was an unfounded claim, these Fathers emphasized, since gnosis, far from being something heretical, can be found only in the true Church.

Going back at least to St. Paul, authentic gnosis is the heritage and the Christian development of the knowledge of God typical of the last great prophets. As St. Paul explained, this deeper knowledge implies, on the basis of a life entirely suffused by faith, the availability of an experience anticipating eternal life and affording a glimpse of what God is in himself and wants to be for us. This is the experience of *agape*, the love that gives of itself without reservation.[2] In contradistinction, the pseudo-gnosis of the first- and second-century heretics claimed to be an esoteric knowledge, passed down through occult tradition, with the purpose of supplementing and correcting the substance of the Christian faith openly preached to all by the apostles and their successors.

Since the end of the last century, four main explanations of the origin and nature of the heretical gnosis have been put forward one after the other. Eugène de Faye, the first to have studied Gnostic texts comprehensively, sought to bring out in them the hasty and inconsiderate Hellenization of Christianity which had already been denounced by Adolf von Harnack as the initial reaction of Hellenism to evangelization.[3] Without abandoning this version, but shifting the focus of research from the traditional philosophical area to the syncretistic religious context of the Hellenistic period, Wilhelm Bousset and Reichardt Reitzenstein[4] tried to update this first hypothesis. Toward the end of his life, Reitzenstein changed his own way of thinking, however, and inclined to the belief that Gnosticism had an Iranian origin and derived from an advanced form of Mazdaism.[5]

Nowadays, the most highly regarded specialists in this field, such as Quispel[6] in the Netherlands and R. M. Grant[7] in the United States, have come around to recognizing the soundness of the opinions developed at the beginning of this century by Friedländer,[8] whose ideas found little following at first, but were revived and pursued before World War II by O. Cullmann.[9] Friedländer held that the heretical Gnosticism we are discussing was the result of a breakdown of Judaism shortly after the start of Christianity, and more specifically of apocalyptic Judaism.

Grant went to great pains to establish that these Gnostic concepts are a recasting of the essentially historical and ethical dualism of the apocalypses, reduced to an even more extreme and explicit version of the metaphysical dualism which (as we have seen) was a major feature of all ancient myths. More precisely, Grant felt that this recasting was triggered by the loss of all hope—after the defeat of Bar Cocheba's rebellion and of the intemperate messianic expectations which had led to it—that God would ever intervene in this world to save the elect here below. The idea of a historical and eschatological salvation was then replaced by the non-temporal hope of a return from a fallen level of existence to the pure and original divine existence.

A feature of the Gnostic systems is that they are largely shaped by the same failure we have already noted in all ancient myths to make and maintain essential distinctions in three fundamental areas. These systems confuse cosmogony with theogony, and therefore creation with the Fall, and conversely any possible salvation with a decreation pure and simple. But the apocalyptic texts, like the earliest prophetic writings, borrowed mythic images and reinterpreted them to express the completely different biblical viewpoint on creation, the Fall, and now salvation. The Gnostics on the contrary make use of typically biblical expressions to cover a reaffirma-tion and a hardening of the mythic elements that biblical revelation had undertaken to correct.

This process, first applied to Jewish apocalyptic utterances, soon spread to the Gospel of Christ, himself disguised as a Gnostic savior. Retaining a certain amount of this biblical and evangelic substance, Gnosticism in the third stage of its development reverted to the old paganism, but in the syncretistic form typical of the period. A major example is the gnosis of pseudo-Hermetic writings such as the *Poimandres* and the *Asclepius*.[10]

As Carsten Colpe[11] recently noted, this underscores the monumental error of Bultmann and his successors, when they claimed to see in the figure of the Gnostic savior the origin of what they present as the mythic expression of Christianity in the writings of the New Testament. In actual fact, the most reliable chronology of the pertinent texts confirms irrefuta-bly that the Gnostic savior, who does not make his appearance until late in the second century, is but a distorted copy of Jesus obviously plagiarized from our Gospels, and cannot possibly have been a source of the Gospel Christology (or worse, the only source of the entire Gospel, as the most extreme mythologists of the last century such as Van den Berg, van Eysinga, and their few followers claimed).

Gnostic Salvation and Savior

In these so-called Gnostic texts, extremely varied in form but unchang-ing in substance, we see the end result of the tendency—explicit in the Orphic myth—to explain the spiritual part of man by a divinity not only completely transcendent but absolutely alien and hostile to the world of bodies, a divinity which has nevertheless somehow fallen into the material world. In fact, according to all these Gnostic writings, the only savable persons are those who have a kind of spark of a divine *pneuma*. At present this divine spark is separated from its pleroma, its transcendent plenitude, and held in the dark prison of a material world, which is itself condemned by its materiality without any possibility of remission. In order to save that spark, it is enough to restore to it its knowledge (or gnosis) of its origin and true nature. Consequently, the divine spark will have no other aim but to break free from the body, from the entire world of bodies, so as to be reabsorbed into the pleroma from which it should never have separated. Its knowledge or consciousness of itself, thus revived, is the only possible principle of this salvation.

In later Gnostic systems—such as those of Basilides, Valentinus, or Carpocrates[12]—which feature a savior, he deliberately descends from the pleroma to the world of bodies where those like him are held. He can save them by recalling them to what they have actually never ceased to be, but only if he takes on no more than a mere appearance of corporeity. He cannot obscure the light of his own being and of those in whom it has been progressively darkened by an unnatural misalliance between body and soul, since he seeks to revive that light through his teaching.

The word aeon (from the Greek *aiōn*)[13] is characteristic of the Jewish or Christian pseudomorphosis assumed in Gnosticism by this revival of the earliest myths. In the most sophisticated Gnostic systems, the term designates the increasingly adulterated emanations from the pleroma through which it is linked to our material world. These nontemporal stratifications of a divine being who has fallen into an essentially anti-divine matter, without ceasing to be fundamentally itself, are therefore now given a name which, in the Greek translations of the apocalypses, designated just the opposite of this metaphysical dualism, viz., a mere historical and moral dualism of free beings rebelling against their creator, then brought back to him through his incarnation into the very matter they are made of.

With Marcion, heretical Gnosticism tried to escape from this obviously mythological framework, revealing in the works of Valentinus and his followers the entirely borrowed nature of their biblical concepts and images. In so doing, however, Gnosticism merely betrayed its fundamentally anti-biblical inspiration; it drew a sharp opposition between the Old Testament's God, creator of the universe, whose spiteful justice, though not evil, dooms us to live with evil, and the New Testament's God the Savior, whose love alone can deliver us, a love assumed to be totally uncontaminated by the other Old Testament God.

St. Irenaeus and His Recapitulation

In his *Adversus Haereses*,[14] St. Irenaeus was the champion of Christian orthodoxy against what he thought was a pseudo-gnosis. He opposed to it the idea, borrowed from the Epistle to the Ephesians,[15] of a recapitulation (*anakephalaiōsis*); this seems to denote both a re-establishment from its principle of the divine work, thwarted by the Fall, and a summation of that work in the adoption—meant literally, and not merely in a legalistic sense—of the human creature in the Son of God made man,[16] "to make the children of men into children of God."[17] In contrast to static Gnosticism, Irenaeus presents Christianity as a progressive history, specifically as an education of man by his creator, a process which will lead man, in spite of his initial fall (and any subsequent falls), to the shared sonship conferred by the incarnate Son of God.

St. Irenaeus thus held that there exists a flawless continuity in the creator's plan. It leads through redemption, and in spite of the first defection, to what the creator had in mind from the beginning. There is on the contrary an absolute discontinuity, Irenaeus maintained, between God's eternal life (extended in the Son and the Spirit, both "begotten" by him) and the life of the cosmos ("produced" by him through an entirely gratuitous creation). This production reaches its highest point in man made in God's image and brings about, in accordance with the biblical vision and in response to the creator's invitation, a living resemblance, making mankind the body of the Son and the temple of the Spirit.[18] This outcome is prepared for by the fact that man is drawn from cosmic matter through the joint action of the Son and the Spirit, working together like the two hands of the invisible Father. The Son comes to meet us in history, as it were, to shape us from without, and the Spirit emerges from the deepest part of our being to elicit from our freedom a joyous consent to this formation, which is, in the final analysis, a conformation.[19]

Man fell by yielding to the arrogant prompting of the cosmic powers to seek only the sensual gratification they offer; this cut him off for a time from God's intended adoption and removed him from the active presence of the divine hands. Since that fall, however, the Son has descended to us, in the Word which appears through the entire Old Testament, and has thus become accustomed to living with the children of men[20] in their self-inflicted exile. The Virgin, by her *Fiat*, joyfully accepted the angel's announcement of the incarnation. She was a new Eve whose faith made possible the Son's coming in the flesh of the first Adam, the one who had strayed through the disobedience and disbelief of the other Eve.[21] Now it was the Spirit's turn to become accustomed to living not only *with* the children of men, but *in* them.[22] So it is that the creator's work, interrupted by man's betrayal, is taken up as from a new beginning and carried through to its blessed conclusion.

Typical of the balanced approach taken by St. Irenaeus are two assertions: "the glory of God is in the life of man" and "for man, to live is to see God."[23] We recognize here the essentially Johannine reciprocity of light and life. In reaction against the false Gnostic spiritualism, however, he made clear—and this is no less significant—that in speaking of life he always had in mind the life of the whole man, body and soul, and man in the world which God made that they might live together in it. Conversely, for St. Irenaeus, the result of sin is death, a physical death, but one caused by spiritual and moral death.

Millenarianism and Ultraspiritualism

It is therefore hardly surprising that St. Irenaeus was won over by Millenarianism, which interprets the millennium of the Johannine apocalypse as a period of regenerate life, gloriously incarnate on a luxuriant earth, the reward of the elect before the last onslaught of the satanic powers and their final eviction from the cosmos.

The most determined opponent of this type of speculation was to be Origen. Though deeply influenced by Paulinism and its insistence on the mystery of the Cross, he approached Christianity in the same intellectual environment which produced neo-Platonism which was, in many respects, despite Plotinus' protestations against the Gnostics, a highly purified form of Gnosticism.[24] For neo-Platonism also posits a strong opposition between the transcendent divinity, the One which overrides all distinctions, and matter, in which everything becomes increasingly differentiated and dispersed. Plotinus, however, tends to make matter evaporate into pure unreality, as the limit of the emanation of the pure spirit (the *nous*), then of the soul (the *psyche*), from the One, for the One can be communicated to all things only by vanishing into them.

Origen

For Origen,[25] as for the neo-Platonists and all ancient Greeks, God and the world are inseparable, like the two sides of one cloth. The Logos and the Pneuma are eternally produced by God the Father, but so is the world; in fact, the Logos and the Pneuma are produced so that the world may come into being and be vitalized. As willed by God, the whole world is but a single spiritual reality: a cluster of pure spirits, all equal, who should all have persevered in the contemplation of the Logos. But they turned from it, all except one, which was to become the soul of Christ. The rest fell into the material world, to a greater or lesser degree, according to whether they became men or angels; or more accurately, their fall made matter emerge as the place and the medium of their possible restoration. This would come about through the voluntary and compassionate descent of the one faithful soul which would lead them back to the Word, guiding them in and from this material world, to be reabsorbed into the pleroma of pure spirits.[26]

This theory Origen put forward merely as a hypothesis, but Evagrius of Pontus was to develop it into a system.[27] One is struck by its deep and obvious similarity to the constructs of heretical Gnostics—despite differences in details with relatively important implications, e.g., concerning the reality of the incarnation and the unreality of matter. Also noteworthy is the view, shared by all neo-Platonists, that neither the Spirit (although according to Origen it does not animate the cosmos, but only the holy souls), nor even the Word (who enlightens every man in this world) is truly God in the biblical sense of the term. This belongs only to the Father, or rather the Henad. The Logos and the Pneuma are but intermediaries or mediators between the Father and the cosmos, and are in fact seen not only as "immanentized," but also as increasingly immersed in the cosmos.[28]

Actually, and in spite of Origen's intentions, it may be questioned whether even his God-Father, the transcendent Henad (to use his designation), is really the biblical God, since he does not have life within himself but finds it only in the production of the cosmos. At least Arius and his more extreme successors (Eunomius of Cyzicus[29] and his followers) have the merit of bringing a semblance of logic to this contradictory attempt to adapt the God of Abraham, of the prophets, and of Jesus Christ to a cosmos that is conceptually entirely Greek; for this cosmos is but a series of reductions of a wholly impersonal divine principle (in spite of Origen's efforts to Christianize it by introducing freedom) which is alone capable of leading to a differentiation between beings. For the Arians neither the Logos nor the Pneuma can be considered as divine, even in a secondary sense. The Logos is but the first of creatures and has not always existed; God created it only to bring the world into being. In Arianism eternity (as well as perfect unity), and therefore transcendence, belong only to the Father.

Athanasius

Faithful to the entire patristic tradition of evangelic interpretation, St. Athanasius saw it jeopardized by such a system. While allowing God, the one God, to remain transcendent in relation to everything other than himself, it does not allow him to impart life to his creature, anymore than he himself is in possession of life. It should therefore be maintained on the one hand—and this was asserted by St. Athanasius more clearly than anyone so far—that God the Father possesses life and indeed *is* life (and has no need to create in order to have it), but only in that he produces eternally the Son and the Spirit,[30] and on the other hand that, although this life is God's alone, he wants to communicate it freely. This is why, alongside his eternal infinity, he creates or raises up a temporal and finite world. But he draws this world from nothingness to communicate his own life, through the gift of the illuminating Logos and the vivifying Spirit, to the created spirits, who are in a sense the soul of the world. This communication takes place despite the fall into corruption of the free creatures, who withdraw into themselves instead of opening up to the divine liberality. For the Logos was to become incarnate in the flesh of fallen humanity: the Logos would take onto himself everything which is man's, even death, to give us in return, through the Spirit of life, his own filial life, which eternally issues from the Father and flows back to him.[31]

This assumes that the filiation of Jesus, the Word made flesh, is so real that it makes him to be of one substance with the Father.[32] Athanasius' epistles to Serapion supplement his three books *Contra Arianos*, by showing that the Spirit must also be divine, in the strictest sense and for the same reasons.[33] But the risk will then be obvious—as the example of Marcellus of Ancyra would show—of simply confusing the Son and the Spirit with the Father, in the image (derived from the Stoics) of a plastic deity, by turns extended, relaxed, or reconcentrated within itself.[34] In full agreement with St. Athanasius, the Cappadocians (St. Basil and the two St. Gregorys) averted this new or renewed danger by asserting the infrangible distinction between the three hypostases or persons in undivided possession of the one divine nature, deriving its only principle from the Father.[35]

Created Wisdom According to St. Athanasius and St. Augustine

St. Athanasius, as early as the first conflicts, and St. Augustine, at the end of the confrontation, both recognized a biblical basis for the Arian description of the Logos—as a form of Wisdom, divine inasmuch as it is associated with the Trinitarian life of God, and associating the entire universe to the divine life, yet in itself created, finite, and distinct from God.[36] But this description does not fit the divine Word, by which the Father makes himself known to us in his Son; instead, it finds its fulfillment in mankind, in the whole humanized cosmos, through the divinization (*theōsis*) bestowed on it as a free gift by the Son (the eternal Logos) when he became man, and therefore one of us, a creature, so that the Spirit of his own sonship might be ours.[37]

The careful reflection inspired both in the East and the West by resistance to Arianism therefore came to an unexpected conclusion: even though the world is neither a fallen god, nor is in the process of becoming once again the transcendent One which disappeared into matter and multiplicity, nevertheless, in God's eternal thought, in the filial Logos in which by uttering his Son he thinks and knows himself, God also plans the world as a reflection of his own Godhead. Indeed, when he thinks the world into being as a creation subject to the limitations of time, God intends the cosmos—in the immanent Wisdom which causes it to conform freely, by the working of the Spirit, to the divine and eternal plan—to become the Bride, at the end of time, of the uncreated Word, the eternal Son.

Maximus the Confessor: The Logoi in the Logos

Maximus the Confessor[38] thought all created personalities and their destinies were both distinct and conjoined in God's plan for the world, a plan which, in his view, is linked to the eternal generation of the Son and the eternal procession of the filial Spirit. They are as many *logoi*, divine ideas, gathered into the unity of his unlimited Logos. Because of the Lamb sacrificed even before the creation of the world, the gift of the Spirit is bestowed on each of them individually (in spite of the possibility of rebelliousness); it is the bounty which stimulates and regenerates their freedom in the eternal Son's own freedom, and which makes them all converge in the *agape* received from the Father and returned to him in the Spirit.

Creation and Free Will: St. Gregory of Nyssa

In the period between Athanasius and Maximus, Gregory of Nyssa would conclude that creation was necessarily a creation of free wills (here Origen was certainly not mistaken), and the world, as seen in biblical revelation, is therefore essentially personal. It is the community of those persons destined, despite lapses, to be grafted all together onto the uncreated Trinity. This will happen through the incarnation of the eternal Son and the extension over all flesh of the Spirit of his sonship.[39]

This raises from a new perspective the question of the relationship between what is called the physical world, the world of bodies, and this intelligible world, posited by the ancient Greeks and early Christians—a world which is also personal, St. Gregory added. In his view, matter did not emerge after the Fall with the corporeity of created spirits, as Origen claimed. St. Gregory maintained that matter is from the start a feature of creation, but that it exists only because of the possibility of sin, in order to provide a means of atonement. This atonement became effective when the filial Logos took part in it, taking upon himself our death and defeating the corruption of sin and death. Gathering us to his own resurrected being, Jesus thus prepared the spiritualization of the entire universe. This universal liberation will be the extension to all creation of the glory bestowed on the children of God.

From this viewpoint, it seemed clear to St. Gregory that matter does not exist apart from the created spirit, but is simply the limit of its autonomous existence, revealed when man seeks to be self-sufficient, instead of heeding the inspired *eros* which answers within himself the call of the divine *agape*.[40]

Corruption and Carnal Eros

The first theologians of monastic asceticism, and particularly Maximus, extending this view, saw in the sexual *eros* a correlate of the *phthora*, the corruption which brings death to man when he refuses God. The sexual *eros* makes the division of creatures (i.e., sexuality) a temporary remedy against their total death, until the death of the incarnate creator returns them to the integrity of a virginity wholly dedicated to the divine love poured into our hearts by the Spirit bestowed on us.[41]

In the West, St. Augustine did not raise to such a high level of subtlety the dialectics of carnal lust and supernatural love. However, it became difficult in the Latin tradition to avoid seeing an outright opposition between procreation and the incarnate love of a human couple, which was thought to be a relapse into at least venial sin.[42]

Noetic Cosmos and Physical Cosmos

Though without the precise formulations of St. Gregory of Nyssa and his successors in the East, the Western tradition inspired by St. Augustine always considered the physical world as dependent on the intelligible world of guiding and guarding spirits (i.e., the angels) and the incarnate spirits (i.e., men). In other words, there is at the edge of the so-called material world a fringe or reflection of an essentially spiritual and personal universe.[43]

This is the conception first sketched by Clement and Origen and the Christian school of Alexandria.[44] We have become accustomed to calling this a Platonizing viewpoint, since it uses extensively the exemplarist terminology of the dialogues concerning the noetic world and the physical world. But their conception, as they themselves emphasize, derives much more directly from the biblical theme found in the book of Exodus in connection with the construction of the tabernacle. This is the theme of a celestial model, eternally present in the divine Wisdom, for all things terrestrial. In this vision, as interpreted by the Fathers of the Church, divine ideas are not abstractions; not only are they bubbling with life (as Plotinus said of their existence in the divine *nous*), but they faithfully represent the multitude of created personalities in the interplay of their supernatural destinies, which will lead them to share one single life with the divine Persons themselves.

The Fathers went even further in explicating what distinguishes and relates angels and men in the world of spirits. At least from the time of St. Basil's commentary on the *Hexaemeron* (the six days of creation) to St. Augustine and his followers in the high Middle Ages, a kind of consensus developed that creation is primarily of the angelic world, of the pure spirits as such. This does not mean that the first universe was immaterial, but indicates that its materiality is but the tissue of angelic thoughts, just as they themselves are a projection of the divine thoughts forever unified in the eternal Wisdom. Man appeared, in this view, to rescue the cosmos from the defection of those incorporeal spirits who, rather than responding to the call to divine association in the *agape*, were led astray by Lucifer, the first among them. He is an incarnate spirit, a free agent restored to the physical cosmos and offering it the possibility of escaping the corruption and darkness caused by the fall of the powers. But man, also yielding to satanic temptation, precipitated and consummated the fall of the sensible universe.[45]

This is where, in spite of everything, the divine plan to recapitulate all things in the eternal Son, who is himself the firstborn of every creature, finds its fulfillment. The Son, model and principle of all things, by becoming flesh in fallen mankind and making his own the death of man and of the whole universe, returns the world and man to the praise of divine glory. He thereby gives back life to all flesh and the light of glory to every being. Upon completion of the *opus redemptionis*, the angels who had been unfaithful from the start and those men who remain unrepentant to the end will be exiled from the cosmos and lost in the eternal abyss of a second death. God will then make all things new. He will cause the celestial Jerusalem, the divine Wisdom, the ideal of creation which he has carried in himself from all eternity, to descend from heaven and become the Bride of the Lamb sacrificed before the foundation of the world—the Lamb whose resurrection announces the end of all things. The kingdom will be returned by him to his Father, and God will be all in all.[46]

A shorter and simplified version of this interpretation by the Church Fathers was to be the medieval Latin view which saw the human race as a stand-in for the angels. This inspired bizarre speculations on the number of the elect, which would be complete when it equaled the number of the fallen angels.[47] Be that as it may, this view of an overall economy of creation, which extends the Pauline and Irenaean theme of recapitulation to all levels of created beings, obviously excludes the conceptions (also Latin and medieval) of an incarnation of the Word that is unconnected with man's sinfulness and ultimate atonement. Since humanity, whose spirit is natively incarnate, appears to be natively redemptive, it is obvious that one cannot imagine an incarnation of the Word in humanity which would not also be redemptive in nature. It is therefore not by chance that Rupert de Deutz, the first Western theologian to accept the idea of an incarnation independent of the Fall, was also the first to reject the idea that mankind appeared in order to mitigate the defection of angels.[48]

Chapter XII: From the Ambiguities of Scientific Theology to Modern Science

The Birth of Scholasticism

During the thirteenth century, in the West, the brilliant Patristic revival of the twelfth century was succeeded and all but replaced, in barely a generation, by the system of theology which was to be called Scholastic. Despite many studies of the subject since the last quarter of the nineteenth century—among which are some truly scholarly efforts, and some showing keen critical insight—we still have a long way to go before we can give a balanced overall evaluation of that school of theology. This is because all these studies are linked to the so-called neo-Thomistic movement—even when their authors deny belonging to it—and so suffer from the misconceptions that were basic to that earlier neo-Thomism which flourished during the Baroque period and were passed on to its modern-day successor.

The most serious error was the one Etienne Gilson had started to sense when he wrote *L'esprit de la philosophie médiévale*, and fully identified in his last works, especially his major contribution to the history of the scholastic revival, *A New History of Philosophy*, which he edited.[1] The error was to consider separately and before all else the philosophy associated with Scholasticism, without realizing that, particularly in authentic Thomism, this philosophy never appeared before and apart from theology, but occurred within the process of theological development and was guided, if not constrained, by the fundamental requirements of that development.

The great scholastic movement of the thirteenth century, as it perceived itself, was by no means a philosophy to which theology was later joined. Rather, it was from the start and in principle a theology, a traditional Christian theology, deeply biblical in inspiration, one which provided itself with a philosophy modeled for Scholasticism's own ends, i.e., for the development of an integrated system. It should never be forgotten that this system rested entirely on the traditional Christian conviction of those who developed it, while its structure was in keeping with the period's specific philosophical interests.

An earlier but hardly less persistent misconception, and one with an even greater potential for consequent errors, was the perception of this Scholasticism as a theological system conforming to Aristotelianism, whereas the theology of the Fathers (both Greek and Latin) and of the medieval Byzantines was thought to be Platonic. In fact, the alleged Platonism of the Church Fathers,[2] which has attracted far too much attention, was never anything more than a specifically adapted form of neo-Platonism, i.e., a Platonism in which the Aristotelian influence was hardly less important than the Platonic, while both ingredients were so permeated with late Stoicism that one may well wonder whether anything was left in it that was not more or less transposed into this Stoicism.[3]

Moreover, starting at least with the first generation of the fourth century, in Alexandria as well as in Antioch, it was no longer Platonism (or even middle- or neo-Platonism) which dominated the philosophical outlook of heretical or orthodox Christians, but rather a first revival of Aristotle's logic, and to a large extent of his metaphysics. In Byzantium, perhaps even more than among contemporary Latin followers of Scholasticism, it was a renewed Aristotelianism evolved by the Cappadocian Fathers rather than any form of Platonism which increasingly emerged as the only instrument suitable to an authentically Christian theology. Platonism, on the contrary, revived in Byzantium by a succession of lay and increasingly secularized thinkers, from Psellos to Gemistes Plethon, was constantly denounced by theologians as the source of the latest heresies, and indeed on occasion of a downright neo-paganism.[4]

St. Albert, St. Thomas, and St. Bonaventure

Whatever the merits of these various points, which are too often overlooked, the alleged Aristotelianism of the three major proponents of the golden age of Scholasticism—St. Albert the Great, St. Thomas Aquinas, and St. Bonaventure—was in fact nothing of the sort. In St. Albert it was an Aristotelianism so finely sifted as to be reduced to a few principles grafted onto Platonism as interpreted by St. Augustine. In St. Thomas, it was linked to a fundamental reinterpretation of Platonism, aiming at a deeper and total Christianization of both doctrines. And in St. Bonaventure, Aristotelian logic was almost completely absorbed by an Augustinianism which was itself so overlaid by a biblicized exemplarism and intuitionism that little remains of Platonism except its distinctive terminology.[5]

Yet there is another, even more serious aspect to these developments: these three great Doctors of the Church, endowed with a charisma that raises them above their scholastic contemporaries or successors, actually developed forms of scholastic theology so peculiar to themselves that it is questionable if they truly represent the movement as a whole. They had not hesitated to join it, but then they had attempted to amend the system comprehensively. They did this with varying degrees of success; they did not manage to alter the body of Scholasticism decisively or durably.

Even before the death of St. Thomas, Duns Scotus,[6] while claiming to integrate Thomas' accuracy and keenness with Bonaventure's spirituality, marked out an occasionally ambiguous path which was to allow Occam and others, almost overnight, to achieve a triumphant advance in thinking. It would not always be a Christian mode of thought, but it would link what remained of an increasingly troubled Christianity to the rationalism which had first emerged so ostentatiously a century earlier with Abelard and which had then come to an inevitable and spectacular downfall.

In contrast to Abelard's intemperate rationalism, the neo-rationalism of post-Occamian Scholasticism was more subtle, even managing to pass itself off as its opposite and to be mistaken for a pious form of neo-Augustinianism. This neo-rationalism would deeply undermine Scholasticism's entire Christian future, quite possibly including "Thomistic" revivals (in the intent of their initiators), first in the sixteenth and seventeenth centuries, then in the nineteenth and twentieth.[7]

Birth of Rationalism: St. Anselm and Abelard

These various developments should not cause too much surprise, if one notes that what we call the scholastic movement had gone blatantly off-course with St. Anselm's *Monologion*, subsequently counterbalanced, not without virtuosity, by the reverent and spirited *Proslogion*. But this first use—within the framework of Christian contemplation—not only of discursive reasoning, but of reason seeking to be fiercely independent, occurred without an open confrontation with dogma only because of a determined and partly successful effort to probe the creed from within. It became clear that a mind as lucidly critical as Abelard's—unrestricted by Anselm's timely safeguards—could reduce the entire Christian faith to smoke, under the pretext of explaining it thoroughly.[8]

In the wake of these inauspicious developments, it proved to be ultimately in vain that medieval Scholasticism was consolidated and set back on course by the three great masters, Albert, Thomas, and Bonaventure. When a fourth appeared, Duns Scotus, as deeply religious as they but also as subtle as Anselm, Scholasticism was again seized by the spirit of Occam, with its rationalizing frenzy, and there was henceforth no way to arrest its disastrous course.

The Cosmological Vision of the Great Scholastic Masters

Credit should therefore go not to the whole scholastic movement as such, but rather to those three great thinkers—Albert, Bonaventure, and especially Aquinas—for the resounding and unprecedented success of thirteenth-century efforts to offer an overall view of the world that is both deeply Christian and fully reasoned.[9]

Even the most comprehensive and sound version of Scholasticism, that of St. Thomas Aquinas, is not always free of a certain narrow-mindedness. Whatever the merit of his thinking—far richer and more complex than its form (at least in *Summa Theologica*) might suggest—it is weakened by being exclusively deductive (on a superficial level in any case). This tendency came from Aquinas' acceptance of the Aristotelianism strongly colored with Averrhoism that was being propagated by the translators at Emperor Frederick's neo-pagan court. [10]

Yet the best of St. Thomas's thinking—evident in *De ente et essentia* and mainly in *De veritate*—throws off this straitjacket forced on him by the period in which he lived. Freer still is the *Scriptum super Libros Sententiarum* written in his youth when he was still innocent of the caution and diffidence which usually come with maturity.

Birth of Modern Science

In spite of these limitations, and of the still greater ones under which St. Albert and St. Bonaventure labored, these three great masters of Scholasticism—unrepresentative though they may be of the movement they towered over—were to have, through their converging if not identical views, an unforeseeable influence both over their contemporaries and over later generations. As Alfred North Whitehead perceived with rare insight a generation ago, this influence was due to their theology, conceived and developed as a science fitting the Aristotelian definition, and which finally allowed the rise of a science of nature freed once and for all from the shackles of Aristotelian science. For their science of divine things, by becoming in fact a coherent and logical interpretation of the contents of biblical revelation, far from forcing on the natural universe the abstract principles of aprioristic Aristotelian metaphysics, suggested the need for attention to the essential contingency of the creative work, together with the total rationality of the Maker. The three major scholastic thinkers were thus the first to show convincingly that the cosmic reality depends for its necessary principle on a personal God who remains absolutely transcendent and who therefore, in his activity *ad extra*, his creative activity, can combine contingency and rationality. This gave science its first opportunity to develop into logical analysis based on experimentation that considered only its object. Pierre Duhem [11] established this point, writing before World War I in the first truly critical study of the beginning of modern science. The cosmos as it is—and not as deduced from aprioristic Aristotelian principles—was finally able to become the object of what we call science.

Although it was the best approach Greek antiquity offered, Aristotelian science was indeed incapable of casting off myths (though it attempted to do so) in its rationalization of experience in general. But the theology of the great masters of the thirteenth century, having replaced mythic assumptions as a basis for its systematization with the data of biblical and Christian revelation, made possible the emergence of a rational science of a world accepted as essentially contingent. More recently, Stanley Jaki[12] has shown that it was by continuing along the same path, after the first preliminary attempts by Galileo and his followers, that Newtonian and even Einsteinian science were able decisively to push back the limits of knowledge.

The soundness of Whitehead's insight and its historical justification have been confirmed by the phenomenological analysis found in the thinking of those contemporary scientists most capable of reflecting philosophically on their own endeavors. For instance, Collingwood in his *Idea of Nature*[13] has brought out with the utmost clarity all the implications of the methodology of modern science. As in Newtonian science, this methodology assumes the adequacy to physical reality of a mind capable of conceiving a structure both dynamic and precise, and then, as with Planck and Einstein, the possibility of linking this structure to a formula experimentally discovered, the formula for something fundamentally contingent.[14] If this science is not to be meaningless, if it is really to teach us something about the universe, and not simply about the working of the human mind, it must assume (as Collingwood points out) that the world is in effect the thought, fulfilled without impediment, of a mind that is both supremely free and totally rational.[15] Which means that the entire potential intelligibility of science is dependent on belief (at least implicit) in an omnipotent creative God, who can be described as none other than the biblical and Christian God. The great masters of Scholasticism were the first to draw from this vision of God the logical foundations for any world view that man can hope to attain.

This is being progressively recognized by contemporary scientists who reflect on their activities with truly philosophical discernment. We do not have in mind only the proponents of the so-called "Princeton gnosis,"[16] but also before them James Jeans[17] and Whittaker,[18] and in France quite separately Olivier Costa de Beauregard,[19] as well as most of those who cannot accept the utter agnosticism of the Copenhagen school, which holds that science can provide us with information only on the manner in which our mind operates.[20] One after the other, these scientists have reached the same conclusion: if our minds, after meticulously analyzed and critically examined experiments, are to understand anything about the universe, the latter must itself necessarily proceed in its entirety from what Aristotle called *noēsis noēseōs*, i.e., a thought whose first object is itself and thinks everything within itself. According to Lonergan in our time—and in this he agrees with Eckhart, and probably with St. Thomas in *De veritate*[21]—this may well be the best possible description of the Christian God considered in his creative activity.

One may add, with Einstein, that the only objection still conceivable (that of Nils Bohr and his followers), is disproved by the mere fact that science can now predict, and thus control in accordance with our expectations, the operation of the universe.

Technological Trend of Science and Late Scholasticism

However true and crucial may be these historical demonstrations justifying Whitehead's intuitions—which were guided by the comparison and confrontation between the intellectual trends of the great *Summae* we have in mind and of those that made possible not only a promising start, but also a constructive pursuit of modern science—it must be recognized that they provide us with only one facet of the reality of science, just as the three major *Summae* of the thirteenth century show us but one manifestation, superior but ephemeral, of the scholastic theological movement.

This is implicitly acknowledged by Einstein's comment referred to above. Modern science unquestionably provides us with a knowledge of the world that has never been rivaled by the scientific endeavors of any earlier period. But our science remains focused on the one aspect of the universe where our desires may operate: our longing for material gratification, our desire to use the material world to satisfy our real or imagined needs, to serve what we call our comfort. A good example, certainly, of the decisive nature, for any kind of knowledge developed by man, of the importance he gives for entirely subjective reasons to his starting point, as pointed out by Whitehead.[22]

It is therefore pertinent to ask how this utilitarian stance has influenced the way in which science looks at the cosmos and how science relates to the self-serving undertaking of modern technology. The answer is not in doubt: the fact is that science (in the sense this term has now acquired) approaches reality from an essentially quantitative viewpoint. This approach is fully consonant with the determination to draw from the world the greatest possible benefit—i.e., "comfort"—with a minimum of effort.

We are in full agreement on this point with another of Whitehead's insights, quite possibly the most meaningful of them all. This is his identification of the fateful if implicit choice made by modern science and technology of a paramount criterion of significance, i.e., of what really matters most.[23] Whitehead uncovered this choice in Locke's *a posteriori* analysis of the human mind's manner of operating. He showed that Locke simply presented an analysis of our mental operations that would foster this science and this technology. According to Locke, indeed, one should establish a distinction between primary and secondary data in our perception of the world. In his view, primary data are alone objective and therefore provide the only suitable objects for study by science. These are the quantifiable and measurable data pertaining to length, surface, volume, mass, velocity, etc. All other data are dependent on the subjectivity of our senses.[24]

In actual fact, as Berkeley was the first to establish, it is impossible, even contradictory, to demonstrate that these so-called primary qualities are more objective, or less subjective, than those Locke described as secondary, thereby seeking to justify their exclusion from the field of science. Whitehead picked up the demonstration from that point, and carried it through to an unshakable conclusion.[25]

We must then ask what it was in Scholasticism that both made possible the development of science as we understand it and gave it this very specific bent. It seems unquestionable that the decisive factor was the sudden change in direction of Scholasticism itself, when Occam and his followers (who were Franciscans like him) turned toward the most extreme nominalism. Indeed, the first venture along the path which modern science would follow was in the optical research conducted by Oxford's so-called "perspectivist" Franciscan school, with Nicholas of Oresme's *impetus* mechanics.[26] Although still tentative, this research was moving clearly toward a systematic application of mathematics to the results of experimentation, based on an assumption of a numerical relationship rather than on *a priori* metaphysical preconceptions.

Is it possible to determine why this development took place, and why the trend appeared where one specific form of the scholastic mentality was dominant, and not another? It is in fact not difficult to make this determination. Occamian nominalism held that there could be no objectivity in respect to the world of ideas. The biblical freedom belonging to God the creator which Occam claimed to have once again recognized, is actually a complete indifference to any objective good whatsoever, to any beneficence, to any beauty. The ultimate logic of this position, as will become evident, would lead to the conclusion that reality is absolutely devoid of meaning, and therefore unknowable, simply because there is nothing to be known in it. This would be to deny that any science is possible or to affirm that the only possible science—as indeed the Copenhagen school held—is one which merely tabulates empirical data and provides a classification of these data in accordance with the mind's spontaneous organization.

As long as nominalism maintained the precarious coexistence of a dual truth—opposing biblical revelation to a philosophical truth which denies that existence and the world can have any valid meaning—it was possible to retain the Christian idea of a world created by God and therefore endowed with a coherence freely willed by him. But this coherence could henceforth be defined only through laws couched in mathematical terms, since these were held to be the only laws not dependent on the pure subjectivity of concepts, that is, forms agreeable to our intelligence but lacking any connection with reality.

How can such an exception or privilege be defensible, however? To repeat, a more sophisticated criticism of concepts, and more generally of our sensible perception interpreted by intelligence, would find it easy—first with Berkeley and today with Whitehead—to show that all this is equally objective or subjective, depending on one's viewpoint. But it was characteristic of the early fourteenth century (as Pierre Chaunu emphasized), in the wake of the recent technical progress in agriculture and the resultant years of relative plenty, and following the consecutive appearance of a new social class, that of wealthy merchants and bankers—the beginnings of the modern middle class—to recognize whatever can be accumulated and counted as the *only* unquestionably tangible reality in this world.[27]

It was then, and under these circumstances, that mathematics, which during Antiquity was limited to elementary geometry and arithmetic, started to develop decisively. The very novelty and the immediately obvious efficiency of its methods allowed this discipline to give the illusion that it was above the criticism leveled at concepts, inasmuch as concepts, criticized by philosophers, belonged entirely to an outdated intellectual world.

Modern science was thus made possible, as the objective and rational science of a universe intelligible in its very contingency, by the theology of Scholasticism's golden age. This theology had just become a science of biblical revelation, thanks to which man's world view would become that of a contingency wholly imbued with rationality. But the fact that it very soon became necessary to interpret this rationality of the universe exclusively in terms of quantification, a "mathematization" pure and simple, seems due to the rapid drift of Scholasticism into a nominalism from which it could not break free, a development coinciding with the emergence of what has been called "the bourgeois mentality."[28]

Theology as Science

In conclusion, we are led to reflect on the ambiguity of Scholasticism's view of theology as a science. It must first be admitted that, as Abelard clearly perceived, if the designation is taken in a strictly Aristotelian sense, whether one interprets Aristotle along realist or nominalist lines, consideration of God as the Blessed Trinity of biblical and Christian tradition necessarily yields an interpretation which is either tritheistic or Sabellian.

The only way to escape this dilemma, as the Cappadocians had already understood, was through what Denys (who systematized their position) called apophasis, which ceaselessly corrects kataphasis. It is the negation of a trait not strictly applicable to God, yet which must be attributed to him in a certain sense and under a specific aspect, if one is to speak of him as did the divine Word itself. This is the solution St. Thomas Aquinas was to seek, with greater subtlety, by combining a moderate realism—which he ascribed to Aristotle himself, but which is more likely to be a paradoxical balance between historical Platonism and historical Aristotelianism—with an application to the divinity of concepts properly pertaining to our own experience, which would be used only by analogy. Aquinas emphasizes, however, that this can be only an analogy of the second-degree, an analogy of proportionality, i.e., one which does not liken God to man, but only compares on the one hand the relation between God and his works, and on the other the relation between man and his own activity.

In this kind of intellectual context, modern science certainly has its place and justification. But in this framework it must be seen not as the *only* knowledge of the universe, but rather as *a* knowledge of the world defined and limited in relation to certain modes of thought and to an outlook which are all peculiar to modern mankind. Today's science must therefore leave room for a number of other types of knowledge, all just as valid in principle, each according to its own frame of reference and its own field, such as artistic knowledge, moral knowledge, and finally religious knowledge. The latter, though it cannot replace or absorb the others, is the only one, if it is authentic, capable of uniting them. Rather, it joins them together, not within itself, but in respect to the single ultimate object of all reality, which it neither comprehends nor attains, but in whose direction it must always point. [29]

Chapter XIII: Decline of the Religious Vision of the World

Wisdom and Religion

The last considerations to which we have been led raise in turn one of the most vexing problems of the history of civilizations. It concerns the decline of the religious vision of the world, which occurs if not in all, then at least in a great many of them, generally from the time when they seem to have reached the peak or acme of their development. The phenomenon is no more universal than the pattern—identified and studied by Spengler—of the supposedly unavoidable decline of any civilization which has attained the highest point of its achievement.[1] Indeed, there are cases where the growth of a wisdom enriched with experience and imbued with rational criticism, far from weakening religion, would seem instead to have reinforced it. This is what happened in Egypt, where wisdom, in assessing traditional religious ideas, successfully reinterpreted them without any loss of substance, and actually grafted onto them—durably, it turned out—at least something of the monotheistic reform which Ikhnaton's religious revolution was unable to maintain for more than one generation.[2] The same process may be observed in Taoism, China's basic religion: the painstaking scrutiny attributed to Lao-tzu not only preserved the system's original religious foundation, but made it into a real mystical system by eliminating any accretions of popular or somewhat more sophisticated superstitions.[3]

A special case, as we have already mentioned, is that of Brahman India. Nowhere else perhaps has rational activity been brought to bear with such intensity on the body of popular religion. The latter was nevertheless left standing, and apparently undisturbed. True, one may wonder whether this is not the most astonishing case of what Spengler called pseudomorphosis, for the primitive substance of the religion involved seems to have been processed by rational criticism to such an extent that the result—whether pantheistic, atheistic, materialistic, or ultra-idealistic—of this quiet absorption actually replaced the religious substance, although one would not think so at first glance.[4]

Elsewhere, however, and particularly in Greco-Roman antiquity, starting with the Hellenistic period,[5] and in the medieval Christian civilization, from the fourteenth century on and, after an apparent revival, definitely after the eighteenth, events took a decidedly different course.[6] Wisdom, evolving gradually into what we call science, eventually attacked religion, with such determination that at a certain stage the latter seemed to have been dealt a fatal blow.

At this point, however, one of the strands at least of the sustained development of wisdom itself is seen to lead back toward a restoration, if not of concrete and traditional religion, then at least of the sacred: one sees not only a reversion to a religious philosophy (and philosophy is always religious in its origins), but also an attempt to evolve a philosophical religion.[7] And one may wonder today, in our own Christian or post-Christian civilization, whether a similar development is not starting to take place.[8]

The Decline of Religion

Actually, upon closer examination, one may doubt whether it is really wisdom, or science, which attacks religion and causes it to lose ground. On the contrary, might it not be the very weakening of religion which gives rise to criticism by wisdom, or its by-products such as science, before inspiring a determination (of questionable efficacy) to take religion's place?

At any rate, this is what seems to be suggested, as we shall see, by a study of this decline during the two periods referred to above, i.e., late Antiquity and Christianity. It does indeed appear that the rationalist temptation to do away with religion materializes only after a tendency (evident in all religions at a certain stage) has prevailed or started to prevail: the tendency of religion to evolve into its own opposite, i.e., into some form of magic.

In this connection, the following point, which we have already made, needs to be repeated and emphasized: magic is not an elementary form of religion (contrary to what the latter's historians long believed).[9] In fact, magic is always a debased religion in which man, though still going through ritualistic motions, no longer sees himself as the obedient servant of the gods when he carries out certain rites, which have become his while also remaining theirs, so that man's ritual activity is the very expression of his worshipful submission. Religion veers to magic when man imagines that, through ritual, he can place the gods at his disposal, to the extent of obtaining from them anything he pleases. And when magic becomes confident, its unfailing result is not only to destroy religion, even when religious forms are most carefully preserved, but also to destroy itself through its own victory. For once man is convinced that he has gained complete mastery over ritual, then the observance of rites loses all significance and substance.

There is then a progressive shift, as Freud correctly perceived, not from magic to technical expertise, which is not incompatible with it and can exist independently, but from magic to a certain technology, built on the premise that there is nothing beyond the reach of technical skill, not even what seemed to be the exclusive prerogative of the gods.[10] When it focuses on this kind of shift, Feuerbach's analysis hews to reality.[11]

This being so, it is indeed true that man regains (or has the illusion of recovering) as his own that which he had first projected outside and above himself, as an ideal but inaccessible possibility, and ascribed to the divinity. Once this process of regaining what had been relinquished is set in motion, it promotes rational criticism of religion. The converse does not hold, although it may be true that once this criticism has gathered momentum, it can but accelerate and complete the process (both magical and technological) at which it was aimed.

Decline of Greco-Roman Religion

The development we have just sketched out took place for the first time during the Roman decadence, and was in prospect when Greek civilization was turning into what is known as Hellenistic civilization. When the very heart of the earliest mysteries (which were derived from the cult of natural fertility) evolves into a mere agricultural technique, one that is virtually desacralized and profaned, the cult itself, which had first come to be enacted in religious theater, is then reduced to a theater that ceases to be religious in the traditional sense of the word. This may be verified by viewing the evolution of Greek tragedy from Aeschylus to Sophocles and Euripides.[12] Aeschylus depicts men as wholly dependent on the gods and finds this state of affairs quite natural. Sophocles first rebels, then becomes resigned to the unaccountable fatality governing human life. Euripides finds this subjection unacceptable and would gladly, if he but dared, do without these gods who treat humans so shabbily.

If we turn to epic poems, the development is even more striking. In Homer's *Iliad*, the gods are the true agents of history, and humans are merely the instrument, either willing or reluctant, of their plans. In the *Odyssey*, things are somewhat different: man, such as Ulysses, becomes the protagonist, and the gods are simply his auxiliaries or opponents. In the Alexandrian epics, the gods provide no more than a setting, and the entirely human plot is that of an adventure story pure and simple.[13]

There were occasional revivals, variously successful and often contrived. In the *Aeneid*, the most notable attempt, Virgil willingly fell in with the wishes of Augustus, and attempted to present human initiative and effort as once again dependent on the old gods, which he rather artificially reinstated for the purpose.[14] At the same time, however, Ovid showed all the ancient myths downgraded into a mythology, i.e., barely more heroic versions of human stories, or even into mere fables written simply to cater to our imagination, or rather to what Schelling or Coleridge would have called fantasy.[15]

Xenophanes made every effort to discredit mythology, and advocated a more philosophically oriented religion, but not irreligion.[16] Philosophers found in fables only a justification for disbelief. This is obvious in many of Cicero's orations, where religious concern is certainly not absent, but where there is also an admission that religion no longer offers anything to answer this deep concern.

In the Greco-Roman world, all these developments appear as the consequence of what we have called civilization, when its progress exceeds a certain point. When mankind, in the cities which it had established, succeeded in humanizing the world to such an extent that man believed he could control the gods or do without them, they inevitably became totally inactive gods, *dii otiosi*, as in the poem written by Lucretius.[17] And since everything goes on, at least ostensibly, as though they did not exist, it was to be expected that rational wisdom would suggest, or even seemed to demonstrate, that the gods might indeed be, or probably were, inexistent.

Survival of the Religious Sense

It would be a serious mistake to conclude that the religious need or instinct was thereafter to vanish, a view which has never been held by first-rate thinkers. It is true, however, that this need henceforth had to find indirect or covert channels and outlets, which could hardly be fully satisfactory.

The sages would either recognize the failure of their thinking, and on their own initiative would advocate a return to the ancestral religion—which happened in the time of Augustus, but one is then left merely with the view that "the common man needs a religion"—or, if they were to go so far as to resume personally the observance of the old religious practices, they would generally be guided by considerations more esthetic in nature, or at best ethical, than truly religious.[18] To obtain a more substantive result, the reflection of the wise men would need to be buttressed by a renewed and directly religious inspiration. But this seldom took place. When it did—as with the tendency of many philosophies of the declining Roman Empire which, starting with Stoicism, changed one after the other into philosophical religions—the successful outcome was limited to intellectuals. Even so, the latter rarely derived a true sense of fulfillment from what they had produced for their own use—but which would not have been acceptable to the masses—because these intellectuals somehow sensed obscurely within themselves that what they had brought forth was nothing more than an inferior substitute.[19] Somewhat uneasy and ashamed, they would then follow the lead of the non-intellectuals and seek solace in debased practices, whose real or apparent exoticism or archaism gave the impression of ensuring the survival or revival of something they had come to realize one can neither dispense with nor obtain through one's own efforts. It is enough to read Catullus or Propertius to see how easily the most intellectually gifted, subtle, and civilized men, unable to find a respectable religion, fell back into the most primitive or absurd superstitions.[20]

The Religious Crisis of Christianity

Much of what we have just described, but with other and much more disturbing factors, recurred at the end of our Middle Ages, and even more so in the eighteenth century, when what has been aptly termed the crisis of Western civilization broke out. As early as the fifteenth century, and much more markedly still after the period of the Renaissance, first in the ruling classes (or rather in their art and literature), in spite of the Protestant Reformation and the Catholic Counter-Reformation, we see Christianity in its turn degenerate into a mere support or cover for a society which has lost its Christian soul and frame of reference, and even sometimes into a superficial ornament of culture.

This time, the crisis was not due simply to a success of civilization so marked and apparently so secure that the humanization of the universe acted as a screen against the radiance of the divine glory, so that God became as though absent, if not inexistent. It was quite specifically the result of the first emergence in history of what one may call a bourgeois or middle-class civilization, one based directly and perhaps exclusively on money. Wealth became the supreme means of gaining, in this world, not only a much coveted (though rarely if ever attained) security, but also what was to be called comfort, perhaps the most novel feature of this unprecedented civilization.[21]

Yet it must be emphasized that this change in attitude came about in an environment where Christianity held sway, a religion implying, nay demanding—through the central role played by the mystery of the cross, which assumes a detachment from the things of this world, in preparation for the world to come—a particularly exacting form of self-denial and ascetic discipline. The need for this self-denial was first emphasized when the prophecies of the Old Testament, starting with Jeremiah's, began to point unmistakably toward the future Gospel. Foreshadowed by Isaiah's paradoxical "woe to the rich," this call to otherworldliness, with all its demands and promises, became fully explicit in the Beatitudes. After centuries dominated by a preparation for martyrdom, monasticism was to be, in the early Church, the witness and preserver of this calling to poverty.

In the fifteenth and sixteenth centuries, however, early monasticism can be considered to have reached a standstill. The great abbeys were among the wealthiest landowners, and the Cistercian abbeys, in less than a century, had become worse than the Benedictine ones, whose opulent tendencies Cîteaux had initially inveighed against.[22] As for the new Franciscan or Dominican orders, in spite of their "mendicant" designation, they were already hardly any better, and soon reached the height of corruption, their supposed mendicity having promptly given way to a most profitable urban industry.[23] In the Western Church, this was matched by a widespread secularization of the ecclesiastical institutions, which resisted the encroachments of the nobility and the sovereigns only by gaining for themselves a princely or quasi-imperial status of power and wealth.[24]

Weakened from within by what was to emerge increasingly as the most destructive vice of the coming age—the progressively stronger craving for riches which seemed easier to acquire as time went on—the Church and Christianity were to be no more successful in protecting the world than they had been in defending themselves against the rising tide of a new civilization, in which a quantitative approach would ceaselessly undermine qualitative criteria. Infiltrating and consolidating itself everywhere under the outward appearances of Christianity (appearances which would last for a few centuries), this new civilization was progressively to inactivate all specifically Christian characteristics, simply by substituting the worship of Mammon for that of Christ, while maintaining Christian forms.

Under this influence, strengthened by the development of scientifically-based techniques which conversely held science in thrall, there would be a trend, starting in the eighteenth century with its industrial revolution, to consider the world simply as a source of sense satisfactions. The task was then merely to take stock of them, then to channel and exploit them, under the impulse of the most predatory instincts.

The end result was to rob man of his ability to see the world as a meaningful cosmos oriented toward transcendence, a sense of which had previously been imparted to our lives by contemplation of the universe. Henceforth man saw in the world no more than a collection of "things," soulless objects to be greedily seized for maximum gratification at minimum cost. We do not even realize that we thus destroy living realities under the pretext of taking them for our own use. Far from thus nourishing our own true life, we inevitably undo it and bring about our own undoing, we become as increasingly unraveled skeins of more and more irrational instincts.

The Crisis of Technological Civilization

This realization suddenly burst upon even the most forewarned observers, when the world fell in danger of becoming the victim of a technology we have set in motion but obviously can no longer control.[25]

The proliferating machine built by us from the remains of a universe fragmented by our greed not only escapes our control, but is actually developing in ways we had not foreseen, even less intended. It is not only destroying the world by reducing it to a mass of lifeless scraps, but is destroying us in the bargain.

More precisely, this machine deprives us of our innate possibilities of specific development by likening us to itself. It turns us into robots, or rather, into passive and inert parts of the colossal robot we have by now virtually constructed to replace the cosmos set in position by God. The only predictable future for this all-consuming robot and ourselves is to be reduced together, sooner or later (but the prospect draws closer, since the process exhibits an irreversible acceleration), to spent and useless matter.

The meaning of this ominous development, whose full implications are by no means clear as yet, has suddenly been brought home to us in connection with present threats to the environment. And this is precisely not a problem which, however serious, can remain external to us. Indeed, it is basically a problem of our own inner disintegration, together with the deterioration of the world, which we have brought about. Because we have been unable to resist the anarchic diffusion of our blind desires, our apparently complete rationalization of the universe brings about an unproductive exhaustion of the world. In the very destruction of the universe, it is therefore not simply through a fated consequence that the process of mankind's own extinction is inevitably initiated. It is rather because human life, having become a welter of conflicting desires, had already acquired a propensity toward death, or even had reached a state of incipient decay, that man has drawn the universe along with him into this doom.

Indeed, how could we live as persons in a world where, through our own perverse will, only things can subsist? As we have already indicated (and we shall return to this topic), the person can exist only in a reciprocity or mutuality of relations between individual conscious beings. We ourselves therefore become things, i.e., we have no more value than the same barren ash to which we reduce the universe, when we refuse to recognize in the world anything more than a consumer product, as it were.

Such have been, from the very first, the consequences of the bourgeois civilization and its increasingly immoderate craving for wealth and for the comfort money can buy. The world brought forth by this civilization, or rather reshaped by it, would no longer be a cosmos recognizable throughout as God's creation, one which reminds us of our own creaturehood the more we penetrate its substance. It would make a sacral interpretation of reality unthinkable since it rules out the possibility of the religious attitude which such an interpretation assumes in man, when he discovers himself belonging to the world as God made it.

The death of God proclaimed by man was to be the last word of the venture into the infernal circle we have described.[26] But this statement would hide an implicit acknowledgement of man's own death, just before his disappearance into nothingness.[27]

Culture Becomes a Substitute for Religion

As though he had a premonition of the threat hanging over him, modern man, middle-class man—and Marxist man would be but an attempt to extend to all mankind the spiritual condition of the bourgeoisie as a privileged class—tried to guard against the impending danger through what he called the development of culture, which was never really anything more than the widespread breakdown of all the true cultures, drawn one after the other into the vortex of a monstrous civilization, where they successively drowned without any lasting benefit.

For a bourgeois civilization, based exclusively on wealth, culture is only a possession, which empties it of meaning, since true culture is essentially an activity which enables us to live more fully. Admittedly, since the establishment of cities assumes increased specialization, art or poetry in the original sense of the word (i.e., true creation) will be for most people something that can be bought rather than the result of their own inspiration. The priest and the warrior, however, in the same way as the farmer and the craftsman, devote their time to activities akin to artistic or poetic creation, either because they inspire it, or because they draw inspiration from it. Even if a work of art or literature is bought by or for them, they can enjoy a deep sense of closeness to, and participation in the creation of the work. For the merchant or the banker, on the other hand, the work of art is only something which may be purchased. It is significant that modern art, in particular, has become nothing more, to many of its buyers, than a speculative commodity among others. But the most meaningful sign of the times is that even those philosophies that try, in a commercial world, to uphold the great transcendental ideals of truth, good, and beauty do so by calling them "values"!

This explains the rootlessness of modern culture, an image which emphasizes the implied contradiction. For how can one possibly cultivate anything without first allowing it to take root? But a culture which only acquires, instead of creating, will tend to enrich artificially a cosmopolitanism and a historicism incapable of multiplying, or rather accumulating, these riches without first dealing them a mortal blow. For when these elements are torn away from the native soil which gives them nourishment and are separated from the moment of their creation, they lose not only their vitality, but also their meaning.[28]

Which is not to say—as some of our contemporaries, reacting at times to their own follies, seem inclined to believe—that a culture, in order to develop soundly, must do so in isolation. Quite the contrary. The characteristic of both vital cultures and creative geniuses is not to avoid imitating anything, but rather to produce the inimitable.[29] Even so, a culture, to remain fully alive, must maintain the continuity of its development; to do so, it must spread its roots in space, and also reach the lives of those who will truly benefit from that culture only if they also contribute to its development. Failing which, the culture which was to preserve the quality of life turns toward the quantitative, whose influence is thus further strengthened. Nothing is more revealing of this inversion process than the current role of museums: they have become—for a civilization that accumulates capital indiscriminately and unduly extends the concept of capital—the specific place for esthetic enjoyment. This is all that remains of a communion with the deepest realities of this world, a communion that was formerly found not in the mere ownership of art produced by others, but in a participation by non-artists in the very process of artistic creation.[30]

It should be recalled that museums had already been established by the time of Antiquity's cultural decline. At least officially, however, Alexandria's *Mousaion* remained a temple, the sanctuary of the Muses, and to the extent that this exceeded a simple convention, the treasures of art and literature gathered there had not yet lost all their communicative vitality. In contradistinction, our museums, and the imaginary museum mentioned by Malraux, (i.e., in effect, our overloaded memory), are hardly more than cultural refrigerators where apparent life is actually preserved in a state of death. Except in rare individuals, gifted with exceptional powers of re-creating through imagination, a museum and the art it contains (including music and poetry) now merely arouse stale emotions incapable of regenerating in us that instinct of created life that impelled man to seek throughout the universe, to recognize in myths, to capture in wisdom and to express in art this current of cosmic life through which our life can hope to re-establish a connection with its eternal source, i.e., with divine life.[31]

Many things we learn through a bourgeois education, which seeks merely to store them in our memory, can provide no more than notional knowledge, or labels in place of the realities of true experience. The desiccated and emasculated art available to a patron who is no more than a collector provides him with shimmering but empty husks, carrying none of the cosmic life which might find an echo in our human life, a reminiscence or a preparation (and generally both together) of the life of God, without which no truly creative art would ever have been able to develop.[32]

The clearest symptom of this deep cultural degeneration is to be found in an abundant artistic activity, frantically but vainly seeking a distinctive creativity which is reaching exhaustion in a torrentially productive out-pouring, whose ever-increasing quantity and rate of production cannot hide a fundamental inner sterility. Here, too, the machine has invaded, so to speak, the spirit's corporeity, which in this senseless and purposeless flow is now losing what was left of its soul.[33]

All this explains the cultural conditioning which brought about the devitalization of myth in Antiquity and that of the biblical and evangelical Word in modern times. But these considerations are not enough to allow us to understand the process of self-destruction without which neither myth nor the Word would have succumbed, as they did, to the degradation of the cosmos, when man fell prey to the illusion that he had mastered the universe.

From Myth to Polytheism and Idolatry

To start with myth, one may well say that it became vulnerable when man's self-centeredness led to a literalist interpretation, going hand in hand with the boundless presumption of a pedantic and overly subtle form of reasoning, prevailing over the normal use of a reason in touch with reality. This literalism operates on two levels. Either it focuses on the multiplicity of images, of hierophanies (to use Mircea Eliade's term), through which myths express the divine activity that gives rites their content. In which case religion sinks into polytheism, i.e., into its own contradiction, since religion is but the result of man's deep inner sense of the transcendent unity linking his experience of the life of the world and his own life in the world.[34] Or, worse still, this literalism can reach the point of outright idolatry: the confusion of the divine with the humanity of its representations.

We are faced here with an even deeper contradiction than that of polytheism. For religion, in its very principle, and on this point Schleiermacher is certainly not mistaken, implies a relationship with, and more precisely a dependence on,[35] the Other without whom we cannot be ourselves. But now religion is faced with a mere projection of ourselves, distorted and involuted as we are as a result of the Fall. No longer can there be a revival or reawakening of the fundamental conviction that God made us in his image. Instead, we worship a god who no longer commands belief, since he is not even a reflection of our truest and innermost self, but only of the self's superficial distortion, for which we are responsible.[36]

From Realism to Idealism

It is true that this excessive shift observable from the start in the perceived significance of myths, caused by mankind's alienation from its true source, inevitably brought about a reaction, obviously encouraged by the best critical development of discursive reasoning. This reaction eventually led to the realization that, in the divinity reduced to an idol, we worship only ourselves, and perhaps the worst part of ourselves. As a consequence, the opposite temptation then arose, that of moving from naive realism, from the objectivism which is instinctive in human thinking, to an assumed idealism arising from the fact that, when we indulge, as we actually do, in wrong thinking about the world and the supra-cosmic divinity, we are still thinking only of ourselves, so that in the final analysis we are the only object of our own thinking.[37]

This idea that the whole of reality, the entire world, is but a product of our thinking—which, far from opening our being to a reality that transcends us, is simply a projection of ourselves—did not await the German philosophies of the nineteenth century to take shape. It was already one of the theses most familiar to a whole trend of Indian, Buddhist, and Brahman thinking.[38]

Any such idealism, however, is but an unstable transition from realism to mere solipsism. And solipsism itself, for a personal being such as ours, i.e., one that intrinsically assumes a reciprocity of relations between conscious beings, is a theory impossible to live with, and therefore soon shows itself to be unthinkable.[39] Hence the final plunge into agnosticism pure and simple, the fate of a culture which reaches a supreme degree of decadence when its myths completely fade away.

All these developments occurred at the twilight of the culture and religion of Antiquity.[40] And a parallel evolution, if anything in heightened form, may be noted in what has been correctly called the post-Christian civilization, prepared and indeed made inevitable not only by the breakdown, at the emergence of the bourgeois civilization, of the ascetic conditions implied by the Christian faith, but also by the concomitant waning of this very faith among believers.[41]

Biblical Literalism Against Theological Analogy

A first point is the literalism with which those who in fact no longer seek comfort and strength in the God they confess, but rather in the material things of this world, pay more attention to the formal expression of their faith than to its actual object.[42]

Philosophy refined by Thomistic theological thinking, by its treatment of the *analogia entis* and its interpretation of the concept, should have made such a confusion impossible. According to these principles, what we know are not the concepts, nor do we reach knowledge in the concepts, but only through them; and where the possible knowledge of things divine is concerned, a transposition is also needed, and (it should be recalled) of the kind characteristic of analogy of proportionality, so that through concepts faith may reach its transcendent object. This was consonant with the Church's entire traditional exegesis, in the wake of Judaism and its reinterpreted heritage, which found significance in the formulations of revelation only through a deepening of the literal sense. Thus the underlying mystical sense was brought out, pointing to Christ in his incarnation, and requiring in turn to be extended into a tropological sense involving our experience of life with him in his grace. Finally, one would reach the anagogical sense, orienting us from this experience initiated in the Spirit toward its eschatological plenitude, accessible only in eternity.[43]

But all these insights were ignored by the obtuse materialism of a literal interpretation of the Bible and of dogmatic formulations, an attitude which passed for orthodoxy and would become increasingly dominant in the Church, even starting as far back as the second half of the thirteenth century.[44]

The first result was an essentially fragmented or compartmentalized conception of the faith, no longer leading toward the organic oneness of a mystery in which our total experience of the world and of ourselves is taken up again in Christ, the incarnate Word of God, but on the contrary splintering into a multitude of disjointed or heterogeneous propositions that could lead only to the perception of a shattered world.[45] In other words, a downright irreligious vision of the whole of reality, a vision affecting the very heart of the faith.

From that point, there was to be a further deterioration—in the area of apologetics and more fully in an implicit and fundamentally concordistic philosophy of religion—a deterioration from an atomization of the faith that was a counterpart of ancient polytheism, to an imitation which attempted to establish the truth of its assertions by identifying them with those that human intelligence makes, when left to its own devices—in science, or what passes as such—concerning its experience of the world. This would be the post-Christian equivalent of ancient idolatry.[46] The way in which a great many Christians currently identify their faith with some contemporary ideology reflects the last degree of this degeneration.[47]

After which, as we see today, an idealistic reaction was inevitable, convincing us either that the assertions of the faith are necessarily meaningless to modern man,[48] or that we should see in them merely a particular formulation, of indifferent value in itself, of the spontaneous convictions which in any case he harbors, and which are his as long as he remains sincere and faithful to his own truth; for each modern man, indeed, there can be, in this view, no truth that is not precisely his.[49]

On this basis, Christianity is clearly no longer possible, because there is no longer an acceptable God and because the world itself has vanished, for an intelligence or a human consciousness that has become, in relation to reality, similar to a stomach incapable of digesting anything but itself.[50]

At this low ebb, it may be assumed that we have reached the last stage of the decline modern man has brought upon himself, since mankind has become essentially grasping and acquisitive.

Post-Christian Mankind

One may, however, wonder why this pitiful humanity, potentially present in every human being since Adam's sin, did not become manifest in all its poverty and misery until the post-Christian era.

The adage *corruptio optimi pessima* provides, we believe, an answer to this question. It is not the ignorance of Christianity among those who were never evangelized, nor its negation by those who were never able to accept it, but rather the betrayal of Christianity by those who received the Gospel and were brought up as Christians which was to show with the utmost clarity the fate of a godless world and a godless mankind. More specifically, the refusal by Christians of the ascetic conditions necessary to the life of faith, or worse still their travesty, inevitably produced a world blind to the revelation of the divine glory. The lust for power too often apparent in churchmen (preferably under the pretext of promoting their mission) for an absolute power over the things of this world, along with the contempt or at least the practical misunderstanding shown by the "religious" for evangelic poverty, which they should have been the very first to uphold, could but promote the emergence of a mankind devoted to the exclusive pursuit of wealth, and therefore to the worship of material riches, a humanity bent on an unprecedented desacralization of the world. An orientation of the life of Christians (and prominently that of their consecrated guides, of their supposed spiritual directors) so completely at odds with the spirit of their faith could not fail to promote the development of a humankind more deeply perverted than ever before. Man would then turn creation not simply into a broken world, which it has been since the Fall, but into one which is damned, where everything proclaims the absence of God. Since the worship of Mammon has fully preempted the life of twice-fallen man, where might he still find in this world any recognizable trace of the God of truth?

Chapter XIV: From Positive Theology to Philosophies of Nature

Failure of Seventeenth-Century Reforms

As early as the fourteenth century, circumstances were favorable not only to a rejection of the traditional Christian conception of the world, but also to a systematic nihilism, or at least to some form of dogmatic agnosticism quite unknown to pagan Antiquity, even during its decline. All this was already present in the immanent logic of Occam's nominalism, and it is difficult to read the latter's writings without suspecting this presence under the excesses of his verbal theism. The *potentia absoluta* he ascribes to his falsely biblical God is all too obviously nothing but a worship of chaos under the name of God. This would, however, not be formulated as the accepted framework of a school of thought, rather than the hesitant endeavor of a few individuals, until the beginning of the seventeenth century, with the so-called free-thinkers.[1]

Wherever the Protestant Reformation, through the excesses of a pseudo-transcendentalism imbued with nominalism, did not evoke a second wave (even stronger than the first) of formal impiety, the Catholic Counter-Reformation, or rather the true Catholic Reformation, seemed for a time to raise an effective bulwark against the flood of unbelief.[2] Among the Anglicans[3] and the Lutherans,[4] a reform of the Reformation, more successful as an effort to return to its own roots than was Calvin's attempt to do so, made a significant contribution to this reconstruction. During the eighteenth century, however, the industrial revolution in England, then spreading to the continent, following the ravages, both cultural and material, of the Thirty Years' War, gave impetus to a second wave of free thought, the philosophy of Enlightenment. Against this assault Christianity did little more than survive.[5]

In the nineteenth century, with German Romanticism, came a Christian renewal, whose harbinger was the Pietism of the late eighteenth century. Although at first it seemed more widespread than the seventeenth-century resurgence, it is doubtful whether this renewal was as deeply rooted.[6] Not until the twentieth century, amid the clamor of an unbridled if not frenetic nihilism, did "a return of the Angels"[7] occur.

Catholic Reform and Reform of the Reformation

Prepared and supported by what was best in Erasmian humanism, and inspired by the mystical and missionary renewal of the preceding period, the most decisive factor in Catholic reform, was the development by the Jesuit Denys Petau and the Oratorian Louis Thomassin[8] of positive theology. Equivalents may be found in various Catholic countries, especially in Spain, but mainly it is found in the Anglican school of the Caroline Divines who continued the work of Richard Hooker, and in the neo-Lutheran school of which Johann Gerhard is the foremost representative.[9]

This positive theology was quite different from the mere history of theology which was to be similarly named (for reasons which remain unclear) in the nineteenth century. Petau's and Thomassin's theology was traditional, not in the sense of being simply repetitive, but in the very different sense of replacing Scholasticism's largely illusive endeavor to produce a definitive and logical overview of the entire Christian doctrine— with an undertaking more attuned to the nature of Catholic theology. Its purpose was to follow and explain the emergence of detailed foundations of Christian doctrine by tracing their development in the Church's own awareness of these formulations, manifest in its evangelization of the world.

The only weakness in Petau's admirable efforts is that in wishing to avoid scholastic theology's entrapment in a philosophy which became increasingly abstract and less Christian, he did not sufficiently recognize the need to provide any theology with a philosophical instrument adapted to its own requirements and suitable for communicating with one's contemporaries. In contradistinction, the most inspired theologians of the Patristic age (such as the Cappadocians) and of Scholasticism (such as St. Thomas himself) had been deeply aware of this need.

Thomassin, on the contrary, merged with the theology of the Church the facile syncretizing of neo-Platonism (all too easily adapted by Marsillo Ficino) an amalgam which could satisfy neither the critical sense of believers, nor that of unbelievers or agnostics.[10]

The Philosophical Decline of Christians

There was no lack of Christian philosophers during the late sixteenth and early seventeenth centuries. The first neo-Thomists, such as Cajetan, the Salamanca Carmelites, or John of St. Thomas were interested in philosophy at least as much as in theology itself.[11] Unfortunately, none of them did much more than extract their master's philosophy from its theological context, apparently without wondering whether the two elements were separable, or whether the philosophy they sought to define was not distorted in the process.

The only Christian thinker of that period who had more ambitious aims was undoubtedly Suarez.[12] Though exceptionally intelligent in the strictest meaning of the term, Suarez sought to reconcile the views of contemporary as well as earlier thinkers through quasi-diplomatic compromise, instead of attempting a true synthesis. The result was an extraordinarily flexible philosophy, but Janus-like, affirming with one mouth what he is simultaneously denying with the other.

The same applies, even more strongly, to Pierre Ramus,[13] the Protestant philosopher who was among the victims of the St. Bartholomew's Day massacre. Ramus provided the emerging Protestant orthodoxy with a logic which at first sight seemed capable of lifting it out of the nominalist rut, something the Reformers themselves, including Luther, had been unable to achieve. But since its logic was linguistic rather than ontological, Ramism proved no more helpful to Protestants than the work of Suarez had been to Catholics in consolidating theologies which, in spite of excellent intentions, were built on sand.

Hereupon Locke's empiricism makes its appearance, prompted by the many successes of science, which expanded rapidly during this period following lines suggested by Descartes, even more than Bacon, though it remained basically realistic, as may be clearly seen in the thinking of the real founder of science, Sir Isaac Newton. Science therefore agreed to be wedded to technological endeavor, whose quasi-magical aim was defined by Bacon, then by Descartes.[14] Locke subsequently claimed to reveal its logical and metaphysical requirements.

Two philosophers, however, both sincerely Christian, were to denounce and attempt to correct the alleged philosophy of science, which was in fact only a philosophy of blindly accepting modern technology. These philosophers were Berkeley and Leibnitz, and it is hardly surprising that they have remained until now largely misunderstood, for they worked against the prevailing current of their time. But it may be that future generations will recognize them—and especially Berkeley, the less understood of the two—as anticipators of the discoveries or rediscoveries which must come soon if modern mankind is to survive.

Berkeley

Berkeley is remembered only through the travesty of his thinking popularized, though not originated, by Hume, who chose to concentrate exclusively on the critical aspect of the doctrine he was supposedly analyzing. Berkeley's immaterialism therefore remains foolishly confused with an obviously absurd negation of the existence of the physical or material world. It was not until the recent publication of the critical edition of his works, and of the commentary by its initiators, T. Jessop and particularly

A. A. Luce, that the incredible misunderstanding of Berkeley's ideas has finally come to light.[15]

What Berkeley established, so rigorously that no one has even attempted to disprove it—simply because, as Whitehead has pointed out, the insight is indisputable—is not that the world does not exist independently from its observers, but first and foremost that this objective existence cannot be reduced (as Locke insisted it could) to its so-called primary qualities, such as extension, mass, and velocity, i.e., those that can be expressed in mathematical terms. As the *Three Dialogues Between Hylas and Philonous* clearly show, in a demonstration exhaustively completed by the later dialogue *Alciphron*, it is impossible to maintain, except arbitrarily, that these qualities are any more objective than the so-called secondary qualities, be they sensory (e.g., color, sound, smell) or affective (e.g., beauty). This completely invalidates the idea of matter existing objectively, simply through its so-called primary qualities, and independently from our mind. In Berkeley's view, however, it emphatically does not follow that the world of material objects does not exist; on the contrary it exists just as we are able to perceive it, not merely by our senses, an artificial abstraction which has been confused with the concrete reality of experience, but by our entire mind focusing on the input of the senses. This does not mean in any way that the physical world is a product of our mind, for conscious thought is not separable in our mind, except through another abstraction, from what we will. And it is obvious that the world we perceive is in no way dependent on will. The conclusion is, quite clearly, that the material world is itself spiritual—in the sense that its existence is inseparable from that of spiritual beings—and must be recognized as a language through which the spirit which has created the whole universe communicates with the society of created spirits, and allows them to communicate with one another.

This is Berkeley's only authentic conception. As the last developments of *Siris* were to show, it is not an idealistic view, in the modern sense of the term, but a highly original realistic conception, distinguishing ideas proper from mere concepts, which according to Berkeley are simply constructs through which we seek to reach ideas and make them our own.

Berkeley's conception was therefore a remarkable restatement of the interpretation of cosmic reality toward which the thinking of all the Church Fathers was striving, in the light of biblical revelation; it was a view that St. Gregory of Nyssa had already sythesized in terms very similar to those Berkeley was to use.

Leibnitz

In his *Monadology*, Leibnitz was to set forth independently a vision of the universe at first sight different from that of Berkeley, but which in the final analysis converges with it.[16] His presentation is of particular interest to us since it offers the first explicit formulation of a factor modern psychology was to bring to light: the presence, underlying our clear consciousness, of a complex subconscious or unconscious, which might aptly be called a penumbral or nocturnal consciousness.

For Leibnitz considered it essential to distinguish what we perceive, what affects our consciousness in one way or another, from whatever impinges on it and directly captures our attention. Every spirit implies, or is involved in, a total perception of the universe. But this perception merely tends toward consciousness without being able to achieve it altogether, in this life at least. For our consciousness never reaches a static level of completion; it is in a constant process of growth, both as consciousness of ourselves *and* of the rest of the universe, and as consciousness of ourselves *in* the universe.

This being so, the material world must be considered as the shared externality through which all the spiritual monads composing the universe form a single world. Considered from this material viewpoint, the world is essentially determined, for materiality is the key to its coherence. But considered from the spiritual viewpoint, and more specifically from that of each of its constituent spirits, the world is pure freedom. On the level of the all-encompassing divine spirit, for whom there is no externality, necessity and freedom are reconciled in what Leibnitz sees as grace. This leads him to the concept of what he calls, perhaps unfortunately (since the designation invites misunderstanding) "pre-established harmony." Through this the monads, while remaining independent from one another, are yet associated in one world, by virtue of its very creation.

Having failed to understand Berkeley's immaterialism, contemporaries proved even less receptive to Leibnitz's concept of a pre-established harmony, which admittedly bears an uncomfortable resemblance to the excessively ingenious reconciliation of all contradictions in the philosophy of Suarez, whom Leibnitz greatly admired.

Although neither Berkeley nor Leibnitz were able to resolve all the problems raised by the collapse of traditional worldviews, their insights were pregnant with possibilities which neither their contemporaries nor their successors have sufficiently explored.

The "Naturphilosophien" of German Romanticism

During the first half of the nineteenth century, German Romantic thinking attempted unsuccessfully to supplement or even replace the scientific reconstruction of the world according to Newtonian physics with a philosophy of nature that made room for matter's "secondary qualities" and everything they might imply. And this at a time when Locke and his followers believed they had once and for all eliminated these qualities from the realm of science.

The results of these attempts were most disappointing. The efforts nevertheless deserve attention, if only because they show continuing resistance to a doctrine that reduces reality exclusively to what can be counted and measured. These efforts therefore bear witness to the unacceptability of such a doctrine, which is repugnant to the human spirit, as well as to Christian faith.

Goethe

The philosophies of nature drew special inspiration from Goethe, who, though far from traditional Christianity, was nevertheless anxious to avoid any view of reality which would be less than comprehensive.[17] He therefore attempted to oppose a science of qualities to the Newtonian science of pure quantities which in his view emptied cosmic reality of its richness and variety; he specifically attacked Newton's theory of color, which reduced it to vibrations of various frequencies.

More successful perhaps, though not entirely convincing, was Goethe's theory of the *Urpflanze*, the primitive or, more precisely, ideal plan, a theory he developed in order to synthesize into a single vision, without reducing their variety, all the forms of plant life.

These attempts, though questionable, benefited from their initiator's personal prestige, and were perhaps the most worthy of truly scientific consideration among all the endeavors of the German *Naturphilosophien*. (The most worthy, that is, until their revival in a new form with the dynamic psychologies of the twentieth century.) We will not review the contributions of the most famous philosophers of nature, such as Schelling, since their views are already well known. But it may be worthwhile to survey some of the features of less publicized systems which sought explicitly to bridge the gap between traditional Christian thinking and the worldview persistently promoted by nineteenth-century science. This is the aspect we shall stress in summarizing the conclusions of several largely forgotten thinkers whose influence, however, was much greater and more lasting than is generally recognized: Franz von Baader and Louis Bautain at the beginning of the century, and Lotze in its closing years.

From Renaissance to Romanticism

Before turning to these thinkers, one should point out their shared background. Explicitly or not, they all owe much to Renaissance, and particularly Florentine, neo-Platonism, to the Jewish Cabala (in which Pico della Mirandola was one of the first to see parallels to neo-Platonism), and to the various schools of empirical medicine—some more "magical" than others, but all akin to alchemy—which were inspired by Paracelsus (even more than by the rather impractical "magi" such as Agrippa von Nettesheim[18]). Henry More,[19] the last of the Cambridge Platonists, and Jakob Boehme, the mystical shoemaker of Görlitz, kept alive these two currents of thought and were the first to attempt to reconcile them.[20]

Baader

Franz von Baader[21] was the earliest and most influential of those who tried, in Germany at the beginning of the nineteenth century, to revive and rehabilitate this more or less occult tradition. It was he who succeeded in gaining a certain mainstream acceptance for it, so that its influence on respectable schools of thought was more enduring than is generally realized. This tradition reached Baader through Arnold's Pietism and various late eighteenth-century thinkers who had already been affected by it, the most prominent among these being J. G. Hammann, the magus of the North.[22] The latter's thinking was shaped largely by the analogy between the biblical Word and creation itself, that fundamental word of God. The following is typical of his outlook:

> Socrates' wish (Speak, so that I may see you) was answered by creation, which is an utterance to the creatures through the creatures: one day speaks to another, and one night to the next. The word of creation reaches all climes, to the very end of the universe, and in every language its voice is heard.[23]

Another quotation from the same source is even more significant:

> The world is therefore composed of scattered fragments animated by the divine breath and spirit. We cannot grasp the whole. There is in this regard a lack, a gap, whether the fault lies within or outside us, and this is reminiscent of original sin, which is both internal and external to ourselves. Be that as it may, we find in nature only verses to be completed or set straight, *disjecta membra poetae*. And this is consequently how the shares of the sciences, of philosophy and of poetry are apportioned: the role of the scientist is to assemble these fragments; that of the philosopher is to interpret them; and that of the poet is to imitate them, along the lines of ancient poetics, or still more boldly to put them in order (*sie in Geschick bringen*) and reestablish their new poetic unity.[24]

In this spirit, Baader's system has been described as one of relative supernaturalism. According to him, indeed, any reality is defined by the region or circle where it is situated. But each reality draws its life from above and is nourished from below. In this sense, we are supernatural in relation to animals, just as God is in relation to us. Ideally, every creature is in an organic or dynamic relationship of free and obedient subordination to God. The germ of a higher life then quickens in the creature and makes it reach toward that life, as a seed seeks the sun. This is a second birth, a supernatural one. But a universal law of polarity makes it possible to refuse the call. If supernatural growth is rejected, below us everything organic becomes mechanical, and above us the way is totally closed.

The only salvation will then be in an infusion of love from above. This implies the death of our hardened or armored mode of existence, so that life may recover its ductility. Instead of being consumed, we will then be fulfilled in our higher individuality, while divine transcendence will yet be maintained.

Any authentic knowledge is dependent on this organic life and assumes a perfect union between subject and object (which Baader frequently likens to sexual union).

Three major and inseparable criteria of truth derive from this theory: 1) God's immediate testimony to the mystic soul; 2) the verdict of society's common sense; and 3) the conclusions of individual reason. Only God is infallible in himself. When organized in relation to God, society is endowed with a communicated infallibility. And the individual, to the extent that he participates in this society, enjoys a conditional infallibility.

Louis Bautain

Organic concepts of the universe, more or less in accordance with the model just described, are common features of all these philosophies. One of the most intriguing but least known of the concepts was developed by the Strasbourg philosopher Louis Bautain, who was led to the Catholic faith and the priesthood by philosophical thinking based on medical studies. Bautain is generally remembered only in connection with his theory of faith, falsely accused of irrational fideism, but which makes him a fore-runner of Blondel in this respect. This other facet of his doctrine is today largely overlooked. It is not even mentioned in the recent study by Msgr. Poupard, but an American Protestant theologian, W. M. Horton, analyzed Bautain's often highly original ideas and recognized their value.[25] The fact is that, apart from Goethe's efforts, which we have briefly outlined, Bautain's natural philosophy is virtually the only one of its time to have a truly scientific basis.

The developments of Bautain's views were inspired by both organicism and, even more, vitalism. His central idea, as Horton has quite rightly shown, was that all life is a reciprocating movement between subject and object. The subject's reaction depends on the object's action, but the subject, once stimulated by the object, develops through a continual intussusception and polarization. Bautain first applied this principle to biology. But there is no doubt that a spiritual experience led him to the insight which set him against Fichte (whom he had first followed) by convincing him that life does indeed develop from the being of a subject, but always (on the level of the human and the created) because the subject in question started by being passive before a given object.

Bautain generalizes this insight by saying that all life is male, objective, and universal, but that it gains existence only by joining with a being which is feminine, subjective, passive, yet in its own way no less universal. The passive agent provides the basis, the malleable element, the place for the generative act, while the active agent is the organ of life and contributes all its qualities. When the center of the maternal being is reached by the active agent, its concentration is vanquished, and conception occurs through intussusception.

According to Bautain, this biological process has its counterpart in the realm of thought, which he defines as life that is also light. And the same process is again present on the level of moral and spiritual life. On the basis of this analogy he successively studied the generation, then the growth of the embryo, distinguished by a secondary polarization process. Every living being, he asserted, has its center of indifference, on an axis with one pole pointing toward stimulative life and the other toward the matrix. In man the result is head, heart, and abdomen, just as in plants we have the shoot, the seed, and the rootlet.

Childhood continues this development outside the maternal womb, but within the family structure. Adolescence follows, and leads to adulthood under the twofold influence of language, which awakens the intelligence, and of God's Word, which quickens the soul. After life has blossomed in this way, decline and death cut it off from its natural foundation.

Four main points derive from this analysis of growth, after the birth of man in the world. The first is the conjunction of nature and spirit. The nature of anything is the divine idea, latent within, of all its possibilities. The spirit is what the fecundating action of life draws from subjective nature. Two types of spirit match the two types of nature, the heavenly and the earthly. Hence the animal, plant, and mineral spirits, and that of Mother Earth, made fruitful by the rays of the sun. And hence also the celestial spirits, the angels, nourished by divine life itself. The spirit of the world (or macrocosm) and the spirit of man (or microcosm) partake of both types.

We then come to the idea of being, which is God. The laws of the universe are but copies of the law by which the three divine Persons are eternally produced by the indivisible One. In their interrelationship these Persons are indeed, in a manner of speaking, essence, existence, and life: the center, its poles, the axis joining them; the one, duality, duality returning to unity; the subject, the object, and their relationship.

God is totally self-sufficient, Bautain emphasized, and did not need the universe, which was nevertheless created out of pure love, and which is therefore entirely dependent on divine love. However, Bautain held, God cannot have created this world bearing the blemishes of time, space, death, and suffering. The heavenly world is perfect and changeless, eternally conceived and begotten in the bosom of divine Wisdom, and forever fertilized by the influx of divine life, by the Spirit. Each point of the sphere of Wisdom is a potential center of life. Fertilized by divine life, it reaches eternal existence and becomes an immortal spirit. In other words, the ideas harbored in the divine mind are actualized as angels. The spatial and temporal universe derives from the contemplation of an angel falling back upon itself: the spirit of the world, in which our organisms are all involved. For evil is but the isolation of the particular in the universal. The first effect of evil is time, produced by the introversion of the creature, and the product of isolated reflection is space.

A third essential element in Bautain's system is his anthropology. In his view, man is a threefold spirit. As intelligence, he reaches intelligible truths; as animal spirit, he is in touch with the phenomenal world through his senses; and as a mixed spirit, his reason combines and sorts the data of the senses.

As may be seen from the foregoing, the concept of relationship is the final key idea of the system. It is essential to Bautain's biological views, according to which life is simply a relationship between an organism and its environment. The concept is no less fundamental to his entire view of the world and of the divinity from which the world proceeds, and of which it offers an image. All this shows how close Bautain's thinking is to Baader's. The same ideas recur, more or less explicitly, in the various *Naturphilosophien* of the period.

Reappearance of the Theme of Wisdom

Also noteworthy is the cardinal role Bautain ascribes to a certain notion of Wisdom, as both presence and vision, in God, of the entire creation. We have seen how the concept originated with the Church Fathers who drew the final conclusions of the struggle against Arianism. After them, this theme seems to have virtually disappeared from theology. In fact, it was to be a major influence in a large area of Marian liturgy, in both Eastern and

Western Christendom. In the wake of some of the most unusual visions of St. Hildegarde of Bingen, related in her *Scivias*, the theme reemerged in the theological cosmology of Bernard Sylvestris. Subsequently (no doubt borrowed from Heinrich Kuhnrat's disconcerting *Amphitheatrum Sapientiae*), it was exuberantly illustrated in Jakob Boehme's theosophy, whose main popularizer was to be Gottfried Arnold.[26] It is probably through Arnold that this concept of Wisdom reached Baader, then Schelling, and through him probably Bautain, and later Soloviev.[27] Among Soloviev's followers, this view of Wisdom was to be most recently orchestrated, during the first half of the twentieth century, in two major contributions made by Russian Orthodoxy, those of Paul Florensky[28] and Sergei Boulgakoff.[29] We have already discussed this theme on several occasions and in earlier works, and will attempt to dispose of the question, insofar as possible, in the conclusion to the present book.

Hermann Lotze

At the very end of the nineteenth century, and in closer contact than Bautain with the developments of contemporary science, we find in the works of Hermann Lotze what may be seen as the last attempt to evolve a philosophy of nature. While its aspirations were still those of Romanticism, its inspiration proper was resolutely drawn from post-Newtonian science. Lotze's key work is *Microcosmus: An Essay Concerning Man and His Relation to the World*.[30]

Writing at a time when scientism was in full swing, it is remarkable that Lotze sought, with brilliant arguments, to establish that the living unity of human consciousness cannot be reduced to some combination of physical elements.[31]

More generally, Lotze held that a truly scientific knowledge of the world is incompatible with anthropomorphism which likens the universe to what we ourselves produce and sees it in purely mechanistic terms.[32] But he also rejected the idea of a world soul unconsciously tending toward ideal ends through determinism.[33] The unity of the cosmos, combining the determinism of material phenomena with the freedom of the spirit, postulates a God who is not only transcendent, but whose transcendence belongs to the only conceivable perfect personality.

Particularly noteworthy, in this context, is Lotze's demonstration of the widespread error that there is limitation inherent in personal existence.[34] He showed that it is God's infinity alone which allows him to be perfectly and uniquely personal, by excluding from his being any trace of dependence, in contradistinction to cosmic being in general, including created persons.

Anton Günther

In all this Romantic cosmological thinking, which was explicitly religious in inspiration and aimed at a rediscovery of traditional Christianity, it seems to us that the deepest insights were those of a theologian of the Vienna school who, after an extraordinary vogue, fell into a most unjustified discredit. This was Anton Günther. After his condemnation by Rome, he was considered a proponent of semi-rationalism, along the lines of Hermes and Froschammer,[35] but in truth his views were entirely opposed to theirs. He did not believe in an *intellectus quaerens fidem*, expecting through intellectual effort to reach the goal of faith, but in a *fides quaerens intellectum*, an endeavor that exactly parallels that of St. Anselm. For in Günther's view the demonstrations this undertaking suggests are possible only for reason illumined by faith and within the practice of faith.

It is nevertheless true that Günther may have inadvertently distorted the revealed truths whose supernatural nature he sought to emphasize. On this question, however, of interpretation of a cosmos created by a transcendent God, whose transcendence is above all that of a boundlessly generous love, it must be recognized that Günther has many important insights. His entire thinking must be seen as an effort to assimilate the element of truth in nineteenth-century German idealism, and mainly in Hegelianism, while decisively correcting its extreme immanentism. Much more so than Barth's, his doctrine may be described as a dialectic theology.

Günther first tackled Kant's objection that no knowledge of phenomena, i.e., what is apparent to subjective consciousness, can allow us to reach the noumenon, i.e., objective reality as such. To which Günther replied that the self is precisely a noumenon (and possibly the only one) the knowledge of which coincides with the object. He concluded that if we are to reach a true knowledge of the world, we must be able to examine it where it enters our consciousness and thus to see it from within, as it were. This holds true for our bodies, with their organs and sense appetites, which are both alien to us and yet ours. If therefore I see myself as the microcosm through which the nature of the cosmos can be revealed to me—as an idea coinciding with reality, and not merely as a concept replacing reality—I must necessarily view the world as composed (as I am myself) of spirit, of nature, and of their synthesis in consciousness.

It follows that matter is not conceivable without life, but that nature, seen from within, would everywhere show the same vital impulse, the same tendency to self-development that I find in my physical organism and my animal instincts. From this I must conclude that the world, although threefold in substance, is one in form, for my body and spirit are formally linked in my consciousness. Yet the world cannot be the ultimate being, for it is dependent and imperfect in its finitude, as I am myself. The world assumes as its *Urgrund*, or original foundation, an infinite, independent, and perfect being, which is God. This being so, divine nature may be inferred from the nature of the cosmos, just as the nature of the cosmos may be inferred from mine, though this time not through a direct analogy, but through a reversed analogy. As Günther puts it, the world is *der contraponierte Gott*, the counter-position of God. And so, since the world is one in its form and threefold in its substance, one can understand that God is one in substance and threefold in form: the Subject, the transcendent Object, and their Unity—in the Father, the Son, and the Holy Spirit.[36]

After Hegel

The similarity between Günther's approach and Hegel's, in trying to fit the philosophy of nature into a comprehensive phenomenology of the spirit, is obvious, but the difference between them should be no less so. What Günther attempted, renewing St. Anselm's endeavor in a new intellectual context, was to revive and, at the same time, reinterpret within a theological cosmology and anthropology Descartes' *Cogito ergo sum*, Kant's critique of pure reason, and the phenomenology of the spirit. The undertaking was unprecedented in its boldness, and intoxicated a whole generation of Romantic Catholics in the Germanic countries. It is also understandable that in the eyes of the Roman censors—who saw salvation, amid the apparent disarray of modern philosophical systems, only in renascent neo-Thomism, Günther was confused with those he sought to oppose by utilizing their own weapons. It must be recognized that as yet he had provided but an outline of his contemplated work, and that his terms were not always free from ambiguity. But even more than St. Anselm had foreshadowed and initiated the best of scholastic syntheses, Günther anticipated a theological vision of the cosmos in the context of modern philosophy in general and modern science in particular. His efforts may well have done more than even the apparently promising attempts of the contemporary and openly Christian *Naturphilosophien*.

Chapter XV: From Positivist Science to the Rediscovery of the Spirit

The various philosophies of nature developed during the age of Romanticism failed to replace an increasingly mechanistic and materialistic science, which at the end of the nineteenth century seemed to have an unlimited future. Remarkable enough, however, the development of positivist science reached a point where it not only burst the constraints of mechanism, but also sublimated the notion of matter so much so that the idea of materialism has today become meaningless.

Scientific Cosmology at the Beginning of the Twentieth Century

At the start of this century, many scientists felt that in physics and chemistry man had reached the knowledge of virtually everything there was to know.[1] The matter of the universe was made up of molecules, which were themselves the result of a combination of elemental atoms whose properties, and in particular the ability to combine with one anther, could be predicted from the element's position in Mendeleyev's periodic table. This table made it possible to know the precise number of elements still to be discovered and to determine what their properties would be.

Basic to this view of the universe was the concept of the atom developed by Niels Bohr, continuing the work of J. J. Thomson (Lord Kelvin).[2] Each atom was seen as a miniature solar system, with a heavy nucleus made up of positively-charged protons, around which negatively-charged electrons gravitate, matching in number the protons of the nucleus and traveling in concentric orbits. The number of electrons in each outer orbit indicates the element's valence, i.e., the proportions in which each metal can combine with a metalloid, and vice versa.

By yielding to or receiving from a neighboring atom some loosely bonded electrons, which are the key to chemical combinations, each metal atom, changed into a positive ion by the loss of electrons through electrolysis in a liquid medium, was attracted to the negative pole. In a conducting solid or liquid, the electrons, transferred from one static atom to another, created an electric current. Thus, this system explained all chemical reactions and made it possible to predict the widest range of possibilities, it also accounted for the phenomenon of electrolysis and for electricity in general.

Moreover, radiations such as light or X-rays were simply waves in a field of electromagnetic vibrations emitted by the shift of electrons from their normal orbit. In this coherent overall view of the constitution of matter, it seemed that science had established the principle of all the chemical and physical operations through which we perceive the universe. It appeared that the laws precisely governing these operations would soon be completely unified through the development of formulas accounting for the behavior of the proton and the electron, just as Newton had been able to reduce all astronomical phenomena to a system of celestial mechanics based on his gravitational formula.

It did not seem unrealistic to hope that Newtonian physics of the macrocosm and the new physical chemistry of the microcosm could be unified in an all-embracing formula of universal determinism.[3] After which it could be confidently expected that biology, the science of life in the widest sense of the term, would also be subsumed by this fully-developed physical chemistry, and that psychology, and finally sociology, could then be drawn into the unified conceptual framework. At that stage, positivist science would have produced a full explanation of nature, and of man in nature. Technology would then offer unlimited possibilities of deriving benefit from knowledge of the universe.

Today, all thinkers—except those belonging to the Marxist-Leninist persuasion—have abandoned this dream. But it must be recognized that the mirage, far from being the ultimate in a scientific vision of the world, was nothing but a quasi-mythological degradation of science, which was immobilized on the threshold of developments that were to make earlier expectations totally unrealistic.

Waves or Particles?

The first difficulty to emerge could be considered as already latent when the impressive synthesis referred to above seemed closest to perfection. The problem was the persistent ambiguity in the very concept of vibrations or electromagnetic waves. The theory of waves assumes the existence of an elastic medium in a state of vibration. As far as sounds are concerned, there is no difficulty; it has been long known that air is the medium. But for what we now call electromagnetic waves (light, heat, X-rays or gamma rays, radio-frequency waves, etc.), it had been necessary to postulate a medium (not material according to the above definition) enveloping all things. This medium, which was named ether, required such contradictory characteristics, however, that the concept had to be abandoned toward the end of the nineteenth century. Henceforth, only electromagnetic waves would be referred to—no longer as an explanation, but simply as a description of the manner in which an electromagnetic field is propagated, i.e., a series of phenomena or of possible phenomena.

A closer study of light transmission did even greater damage to the theory of vibrating fields. The wave concept—though it was no longer possible to specify what was oscillating—still provided an adequate explanation of the transmission of light and of related phenomena, but to account for their interaction and for the way in which such interaction occurs, one had to revert to a theory developed during Antiquity, with light considered as an emission of particles. But how could the same phenomenon be explicable in some cases in terms of waves, and in others in terms of particles?[4]

From Quantum Physics to Relativity

This problem would lead to the introduction of the so-called *quanta* in expressing the laws of physics. For the benefit of nonspecialists, the clearest thing to be said about them is that they made it impossible to establish at the same time the position and the velocity of a given particle. Two consequences followed, both equally disconcerting. The first is that (on the level of the microcosm, at any rate) any determination is necessarily the obverse of a more extreme indetermination. And the second is that we cannot obtain any information about the world without modifying the relevant data. This precludes any sharp distinction between the subjective and the objective in scientific knowledge; the latter is and can be only the knowledge available to a given observer under a certain well-defined set of circumstances. These discoveries, attributable to Max Planck[5] and Heisenberg[6] among others, disrupted the concept of physicochemical science developed by nineteenth-century Positivism even more profoundly than did Einstein's subsequent discovery of special, then general relativity.[7]

Einstein's theories of relativity, which introduce time into calculations as though it were simply a fourth dimension of space, inevitably lead one to consider space itself as curved, like the surface of a sphere, or (which comes to the same thing) relegate any speeds greater than that of light, although perfectly conceivable, outside the realm of the possible. Actually, however, these conclusions are simply projections into the imagination of calculation techniques which have become necessary if one is to continue progressing in the mathematical formulation of phenomena.

The precise implications of these theories are fundamentally less spectacular, but even more disconcerting: we can no longer calculate certain aspects of reality investigated by science without at the same time making this reality totally unrepresentable. Which is to say that the modern scientist should no longer, and indeed can no longer, interpret waves and particles as concrete realities, but rather as strictly symbolic figurations.[8] This does not necessarily mean, as maintained by the Copenhagen school, that they do not relate to any objective reality but only to the wholly subjective modes of thought through which we come to grips with the real.[9] It certainly does mean, however, that these models, through which we picture reality in accordance with the most recent advances of physical science, are endowed with a purely symbolic objectivity, similar to that of a graphic curve representing the variations of a mathematical function. In other words, what we persist in calling matter has completely vanished as far as its materiality is concerned, if materiality is defined in relation to sense-perception. Matter no longer subsists, except in "forms" (in the Platonic sense), which have meaning or reality only to spirits. Berkeley could not have hoped for a better confirmation of his views, coming through the mere development of experimental physics aiming at strict scientific formulations.

Nor is this all. The changed outlook means that matter, far from being able of itself to produce thought, resolves into thought, when thoroughly analyzed in the light of the latest scientific findings. Furthermore, the concept of scientific information implied by quantum physics requires us to recognize that, quite simply, we alter the world to the extent that we succeed in making it the object of our own thoughts, under any of its aspects.

At this point, it must be admitted either that these considerations no longer make any objective sense (as alleged by Niels Bohr's followers), or else that in the last analysis the world is but a language between limited minds, which can offer a coherent meaning only if all those minds are included (in the sense Jaspers gives the expression) within an unlimited mind. This brings us back to Aristotle's *noēsis noēseōs*, the God of pure thought who "thinks" the universe into existence by being the object of his own thinking.

It is most remarkable to see these conclusions reached quite independently by both American and Soviet scientists, since they still believe it possible to give meaning to their assertions in the realm of pure science.[10]

New Complexities

These conclusions appear to be assumed by the present state of science, which certainly can and must progress further. On the other hand, there is not the slightest chance that science will ever regress to a stage where materialism might regain some of its credibility. Nevertheless, it is clear that the scheme of the world that science had evolved by the end of the nineteenth century has since then grown singularly more complex. The day is past when it seemed that everything in the universe could be explained in terms of positive and heavy protons concentrated in the atomic nucleus and negative and light electrons revolving around that nucleus. First it became necessary to take into account the isotopes, i.e., elements with the same number of peripheral electrons and therefore the same chemical properties, yet with different masses. Attempts were made to explain this through additional combinations of proton-electron pairs embedded in the nucleus. But it was soon realized that this explanation failed to resolve all difficulties. Scientists had to bring themselves to add to the two elementary particles—by which it had once seemed that everything could be accounted for—an increasing number of other particles, defined in terms of more and more sophisticated properties.[11] The result is that the scientific conception of the universe, a rigorously simple one which seemed to provide final answers, maintains its determinism—only in appearance—as the obverse of a radical indetermination.

It is difficult to escape the feeling that what has happened to the atomic theory is like what happened to the Ptolemaic astronomical system at the end of the sixteenth century, when it was maintained only at the price of increasingly arbitrary epicycles, then collapsed altogether as the simpler theory of heliocentrism gained acceptance. It is clearly impossible—and in this regard the present situation parallels the one which prevailed before Kepler and Galileo—to forecast what may in the future invalidate and supersede our present cosmology. We may be sure, however, that any new system will carry us even further away from the nineteenth century's materialistic absurdities, whose contradictions have become obvious.

The Expanding Universe

Another consequence of recent discoveries in the fields of astronomy and physical chemistry is that the world as we know it cannot have existed from all time, even if such a thing were conceivable. The progressive dispersion of the nebulae composing the cosmos seems to imply that it originated, at a time which can be determined with some degree of accuracy, from a state of maximum concentration through an irreversible process. This conclusion, first reached by Father Lemaître of the University of Louvain,[12] was so disconcerting to some thinkers, still influenced by a belated scientism, that all kinds of fanciful theories were put forward in order to justify the *a priori* assumption of a stationary universe. Most symptomatic of the rather desperate nature of these attempts is the theory advanced by Fred Hoyle, the Cambridge astronomer,[13] which posits an unceasing creation, or rather the spontaneous appearance of new matter to compensate for entropy, the progressive exhaustion of the energy available for maintaining movement and life in the world. Not only are these theories quite impossible to verify, but in addition it is increasingly clear that they ignore the most reliable data on the present state of the universe, as well as the significance and the chronological pattern of its evolution.

Determinism and Counterdeterminism in Biology

We now move from physicochemical studies to biology. Clearly, the remarkable development of organic chemistry in recent years, with the discovery of amino acids and their exceptionally complex and specific molecular structure, has made it possible to understand, to an extent that would have been unthinkable just a short time ago, the mechanics through which life diversifies and progresses and in particular the workings of heredity. This has led such an eminent scientist (and poor philosopher) as Jacques Monod to assert that it is only a question of time before vital phenomena are reduced to a chemical process, and therefore to complete determinism.[14]

There is one thing Monod failed to take into account: life, though we know better and better how it "operates," nevertheless seems stubbornly to challenge the principle, set forth by Carnot and Clausius, that the process of energy degradation is irreversible; moreover, and this actually comes to the same thing, life appears consistently and forcefully to suggest the objective reality of every organism's overall finality. The latter can be disguised under the name of *teleonomy*, but will nevertheless continue, not to counter the operation of physicochemical determinism, but rather (and this is much more significant) to include it in a mode of existence where the whole, which as such cannot be materialized, governs its parts, instead of depending on them, which could lead only to its death.

This leads straight to the equally insoluble contradiction facing neo-Darwinism,[15] when it seeks to salvage a transformistic evolution that would be the result merely of blind chance or pure randomness. In the first place, Darwin's principle of the survival of the fittest is not even a begging of the question, but only a disguised definition: the fitness in question can become manifest only through actual survival, so that the principle eludes verification, which means that it lacks any scientific value.

Moreover, there is a latent contradiction in suggesting that the development of life was already "contained" in its initial data, while acknowledging tacitly that at the conclusion of the process there is something which did not exist at the beginning, since it is precisely this novelty that neo-Darwinists claim to explain. It therefore becomes necessary either to acknowledge that in the interval there occurred a creative intervention which cannot be made fully immanent, or simply to accept the utter irrationality of additional life with no antecedent to account for it.

It should be added that a mere phenomenological analysis of Darwinian and neo-Darwinian concepts shows that they are based on a worldview that must be pronounced not only mythical, but mythological, or else these concepts have little significance. For "the survival of the fittest" implies, as a basis for its assumed rationality, an underlying divinity who is not only in the image of man, but in the image of a typically Victorian man. The principle takes it for granted that life is a kind of competition carried out according to the "laissez-faire" policies of nineteenth-century economic liberalism. The fact that the theory uses such a naive anthropomorphic model should be enough to discredit it.[16]

If then, as seems to be the case, there is indeed an evolution of living beings toward forms better and better integrated in their increasing complexity, it can be only what has been called an emergent evolution, i.e., one in which the advance toward resultant order is not explained by initial disorder, but rather by final order, determined by an intelligence which is both immanent and transcendent for the development of the species, an intelligence which must have governed and programed the structure and mix of determinants so as to produce the history of the species. Consistently, and more and more clearly as one ascends the scale of integrated complexity, it is therefore the spirit, rather than either chance (which is nothing really) or matter considered to be alien to any spirituality (a meaningless assumption), which can make the development of the world intelligible.

The Human Sciences at a Dead End

This picture reemerges on a higher level when we move from living beings in general to the being endowed with a rational consciousness, i.e., to man. Behaviorism, which long inspired those psychologists claiming to be scientific, was in its very concept altogether arbitrary and contradictory, since it seeks to provide a rational explanation for something that, though rational *per se*, excludes rationality as the principle of its explanation. For it should be obvious that to explain human consciousness (with its basic attributes of thought and will), while excluding any reference to the immaterial, is to necessitate an explanation focusing exclusively on what man shares with non-human beings.[17]

The development and the partial therapeutic success of the depth psychologies evolved by Freud, Jung, and Adler were to establish as an experimental fact that, in order to function effectively, psychological phenomena, far from being mere epiphenomena, must constitute in man, and in the world through man, a primary datum. Man's psyche now appears irreducible to any other reality and capable of influencing and even governing his physiology, and through it his biology, and therefore of having a decisive impact on the outward appearance of the living body, and even of inanimate bodies. These conclusions increasingly compel recognition as we work our way backward from immediate individual consciouness to its wellspring in the subconscious of the individual past, then to experiences completely submerged in the unconscious memory of early childhood, and finally to some form of collective unconscious which is actually the inherited or atavistic consciousness of the entire race, finally emerging from the pre-conscious state of a physical universe which must now be recognized as having no meaning or existence unless they derive from a mind and will without which the phenomenality of matter would be inconceivable.

In this connection, it is illuminating to consider the progressive development of *Schicksalanalysis*, Szondi's analysis of hereditary destiny.[18] Having realized, in his earliest investigation, the inherited conditioning of all our behavior patterns, and even of our apparently most personal leanings and decisions, he had prematurely concluded that individual consciousness was subject to determinism. But subsequent experience of creativity, restored by accession to the conscious level, and of deliberate acceptance of all the hereditary background of our individual consciousness was to convince him that the freedom of the individual grows through the progressive discovery and the conscious assimilation of all the determinants from which it emerges. This can have no other conceivable meaning than to reflect the primordial inclusion of these psychophysiological determinants in a creative liberty that is prior and superior to all these organisms and to the cosmic system from which the body and soul of each individual human being finally derive, within what we call the social body and the collective animation of all mankind. Prompted by an "oversoul" remaining enigmatic as long as it does not become manifest as the divine Spirit, calling from the beginning of time and throughout the history of the cosmos for the appearance of the soul of Christ, through which all human souls are to be reconciled with each other and with the invisible Father, this collective and universal animation will finally show itself in the Wisdom of the creature becoming one, when its evolution is completed, with the eternal Word in which God reveals and offers himself forever.

Mutation of the Model of Science

One should however draw attention to a highly ironical peculiarity of the evolution of sciences. At the end of the nineteenth century, just when it seemed that the natural sciences had been permanently established on a materialistic basis, and that the same basis would soon be recognized as the only suitable one for all other sciences as well, the latter sciences appeared to resist this development. Yet the prestige of modern physics was such that any different conception of science was soon overshadowed. The so-called human sciences, still in their early stages at that time, gradually sought to adapt to the ready-made and apparently definitive mold of the natural sciences, particularly mathematical physics. It is amusing to note that by resorting to various devices they managed to convey the impression that their efforts were succeeding, at the very moment when physicists had to recognize that their own supposedly ideal model was in the process of disintegration.

The result was paradoxical. The scientism of positivists and materialists seemed about to force its approach even on psychology, through behaviorism, just when virtually every reputable physicist had ceased to believe in such outmoded patterns of thought. Similarly, at the precise time when the hope of reducing physical phenomena to pure determinism had to be abandoned, biologists believed that their parallel efforts were about to succeed in the area of the phenomena of life.

In spite of this inertia and time-lag of the human sciences in relation to the physical sciences, psychology demonstrated, through the development of dynamic or depth psychologies, the validity of the romantic hopes that the nineteenth-century *Naturphilosophien* were unable to satisfy with their clumsy attempts to invent a non-Newtonian version of physics. It is all the more significant that the development of physics promoted recognition, at the very foundation of the study of the cosmos, of the reality of the spirit obvious at the highest level of that study, and this despite the most stubborn preconceptions. For the cosmos cannot accommodate the manifestations of the created soul unless it is itself a creation of the uncreated Spirit who has left his stamp on it. The world transmits the impulse of that Spirit, and reveals the Spirit's presence and intention, namely, that the world in itself should call forth the response elicited from us by the Spirit who created both ourselves and the cosmos.

Chapter XVI: From Technological Magic to Cosmic Mysticisms

The last comments in the previous chapter remind us of a point we have already mentioned but must now examine more closely: it is not as a secondary effect of science that modern technology came into existence. In fact, almost from the beginning, technological research, proceeding by trial and error, was to guide scientific research. If the various *Naturphilosophien* of Germanic Romanticism never reached the status of a true science—except, perhaps, for the later depth psychologies—it was precisely because the technological bias of civilization was too strong to allow the human mind to pursue a different path of knowledge.

Science and Technology

Contrary to what is often alleged, neither Francis Bacon nor Descartes laid the foundation of modern science, as Jaki has shown. Instead, the credit should go to men of a completely different turn of mind such as Galileo and Newton.[1] They are legitimate heirs of the fundamentally biblical and Christian cosmology propounded by the great scholastic masters of the thirteenth century. These scholastics had been mindful of reality in all its contingency and, at the same time, convinced of its deep rationality, since their worldview was shaped by the fully developed idea of an omnipotent and omniscient God who created all things out of the pure liberality of his love. However, Bacon and Descartes are the first spokesmen for (if not the prime movers of) the decisive course taken by modern technological development, which was to subject to its own goals the early progress of physico-chemical science. And it should be made quite clear that these goals, attitudes, or approaches were definitely not religious, particularly in the biblical and Christian sense. Rather, they were magical, if magic is understood as an effort to subordinate all things, even realities in which the hand of God may be recognized, to the self-centeredness of an arrogant and sensual mankind.

Bacon and Descartes made much of religion, but this should not deceive us. The religion of Descartes, a complex and curious individual, is probably more sincere. But Descartes typically calls on God only to get the world started initially, then if it breaks down, to get it moving again. It has been humorously said that his God was no more than a divine plumber, useful simply for the installation of the system and the repair of any leaks which might occur. On the metaphysical level, he is only the guarantor of the objective reality of the operations of the human mind, which becomes so involved in its self-awareness as to be incapable, without this divine guarantee, of perceiving any other reality but its own. Thus assured, however, the Cartesian technocrat, who is interested in science essentially for the advantages to be drawn from it, attempts without scruple or compunction to take the place of the creator as master of the universe.

As for Bacon, his essentially acquisitive mind assumes a religion which is not much more than an appurtenance or bulwark of government, or rather of those who have infiltrated it for their own benefit, and who see no reason why they should not selfishly use the world in the same manner. Despite his unctious protestations, it is therefore a lust for power and wealth which is the driving force behind Bacon's technology. Technological development was to be the goal of his *Advance of Learning*, the increase in knowledge which he advocates, but it would never have been achieved on the basis suggested by him. For this basis continued to combine an insufficiently or improperly critical empiricism with various *a priori* considerations, somewhat different from but no better than Aristotle's.

These comments are equally applicable to Descartes' physics based on a theory of vortices, to his mechanistic view of animals, and to many other concepts of his which, far from contributing to the contemporary progress of science, produced a virtually insuperable intellectual inertia in his followers, much to the detriment of their scientific acumen. Even today, these concepts color the views of many reputable thinkers and result in a scientism which proves to be the worst enemy of true science.

Bacon and Descartes share one trait, hypocritically veiled in the former and ineffectively repressed in the latter, which is the worship of money and its power and the possibilities of unlimited material gratification it seems to offer. As we have noted, this attitude is characteristic of the bourgeois civilization starting to emerge at the end of the Middle Ages. It was to reach its fullest expression in England during the industrial revolution of the mid-eighteenth century, and in France when the Revolution, followed by the Empire, sought to fulfill the ideals of the *Encyclopedia*. Bourgeois civilization found its justification in nominalist philosophy. And Marxism, which claimed to revive the idealism spawned by nominalism, was in fact to preserve and even consolidate this civilization of mammon, by asserting that there exists nothing real outside economic reality. Thus for technological civilization, the ends—i.e., the aims of a self-centered and alienated mankind—were to justify any and every means; what is more, one of these means was to become virtually an idol and to replace all the conceivable ends of human activity.[2]

From Technique to Technological Civilization

And so not only was bourgeois civilization ruled by money, but also (and even more, if possible) Marxist civilization became likewise materialized with matter itself devitalized in a soulless mechanism. It is important to see how all this came about; in other words how, with attention concentrated more and more exclusively on technical progress, purportedly for the "good" of mankind, the result was to be a civilization in which absorption with technique becomes the entire life of man and of the cosmos itself.

At this point we observe a psychological and sociological phenomenon similar to one frequently described in connection with money. But since both occur together, their joint effect is more than cumulative, and the result is raised to the second power, as it were. During Antiquity, it had been noticed that men seek money for its power, as a means of obtaining gratification of the senses or satisfying their wish to dominate. But eventually they seek money for itself, and in its pursuit seem willing to give up any other pleasure. Finally they become the slaves of what they had first pursued simply as an instrument of power.

Technological development in modern society offers a greatly heightened or intensified version of this alienation. It reveals, more clearly perhaps than anything else, how man's determination to achieve complete autonomy and to make himself the center of all reality leads him into a slavery that is ultimately demonic, robbing him of his humanity, and making him into a thing or object. This does not mean that technique in itself is in any way evil. We are taught in Genesis that man is born in this world, by the will of the creator, in order to cultivate it. This means that he is a born technician, technique being simply the art of understanding nature so as to make it serve a consciously pursued purpose. But this purpose, in the context of creation, was to glorify the creator by developing what he has wrought in a spirit of mutual service between men, thereby leading them all together to fulfill in their lives God's plan. This is what St. Irenaeus expressed in a formulation which unfortunately is seldom quoted in full: "The glory of God is for man to live. . . . But for man, to live is to know God." This should be understood in the biblical sense: to live is to know God as he has known us from the beginning of time, i.e., to acknowledge his love by loving him and by loving everything he loves.

Christian Justification of Technological Civilization: Teilhard de Chardin

Some modern Catholic theologians, wishing to justify progress, particularly technological progress, and writing before it had begun to arouse widespread concern or criticism, submitted that the development and expansion of technology within a Christian civilization (at least, initially so) is an effort to recapture the preternatural gifts which man had before the Fall. Having lost his supernatural vocation as adoptive son of God, and reduced to the level of his own nature (or worse, since human nature was itself diminished by the Fall), man redeemed by Christ and returning to the Father is destined, in this view, to regain everything he had lost through his transgression.[3]

The most optimistic systematization of this theology of earthly realities is the one put forward by Teilhard de Chardin.[4] Since the development of technology proceeds *pari passu* with an increasing socialization, the end result of which should be what Teilhard calls the "planetization" of human life, this development, while not leading directly to the coming of God's kingdom, should nevertheless promote it.

Even more optimistic is the concept of a Russian Orthodox thinker, which leaves one wondering how much it owes to genius and how much to unbridled imagination. According to Fedorov, the famous St. Petersburg librarian who lived at the end of the nineteenth century, technological development should bring about the resurrection of the dead, which is achievable by human effort based on scientific progress.[5] More formally and consistently than Teilhard, however, Fedorov assumes that mankind must make a deliberate choice concerning the direction of research, and must then accept an individual and collective ascetic discipline which is essential to the success of these efforts.

Vladimir Soloviev was to pursue this approach in the so-called theurgic phase of his Christian philosophy. He advocated that civilizations impose a strict ascetic discipline on their activities, to conform them to the Christian outlook of free fulfillment of the divine kingdom.[6] But it is significant that the deepening of his experience was to lead him gradually to abandon these hopes in favor of an apocalyptic eschatology, as in his *Three Conversations on the Antichrist.*[7]

Although he does not approach the vigor of their thinking, Robert Hugh Benson's apocalyptic novel, *The Master of the Earth*, written at about the same time, may be compared to the works of these two Russian thinkers. It is true that when his critics accused him of being too pessimistic, Benson did put forth in *The New Dawn* an alternative vision of a world progressing in the fullness of rediscovered joy toward the Parousia, Christ's glorious return at the end of time. It is perhaps not surprising that Benson's imagination, in spite of his talent, leaves one with a sense of superficiality, even childishness.[8]

The truth of the matter is that, behind all the efforts to make human progress, and particularly technical progress, coincide with the fulfillment of the supernatural destiny awaiting man and the universe, there is a dual error, bearing both on this destiny and on the actual condition of fallen and redeemed man. Indeed, the filial adoption by God in his only-begotten Son, offered to all mankind, and including man's entire relationship with the cosmos, does not imply a mutilation of anything in human nature; instead, it holds out the promise of transfiguration. Nevertheless, as St. Maximus the Confessor well explained,[9] no creature can be associated with divine life and uplifted in the Father's *agape* to a new level of being without going through a metamorphosis. This transformation, even if it does not mean death as we know it, will always require a heroic alteration, an agonizing reappraisal. Our God is a "consuming fire," according to Deuteronomy, and Job warns us that the angels themselves cannot endure God's gaze without being scoured in the deepest recesses of their being.[10]

All the more does the idea of a painless eschatology, allowing fallen man to be led back to God by Christ without having to follow his example and bear his cross, appear totally fanciful and unrealistic. We must always remember that Christ did not die and suffer to exempt us from suffering and death, but to enable us to suffer in a redemptive way and to die as he did, experiencing the kind of death which vanquishes death and restores life to those lying in their graves, as the Byzantine Easter tropary expresses it. Moreover, if technology *per se* and its development properly belong to the development of human nature, one cannot say the same of the particular bent given technological development in modern society. For this progress has been distorted from the first to cater to the uncontrolled gratification of man's sensuality; furthermore, it has been covertly governed by man's Promethean desire to wrest from God mastery over the universe.[11]

Nor is this all. The desire, in essence, to resume construction of the tower of Babel—reappearing in a society which still claims to be Christian, and just when it seemed to have reached the highest point of self-awareness—this technical project of modern man is clearly from the start not really a Christian but rather a pre- or post-Christian one. Just as, during the first centuries of our era, heretical Gnosticism had simply made use of biblical and Christian terms and ideas to revive and strengthen the old cosmic and anthropological vision of myths, in which the original Fall was reflected, one can say that modern technology, from the beginning and with increasing emphasis as time went by, sought to convert the most typically Christian hopes and expectations into a neo-magical undertaking.

Significance of Feuerbach's Ideas

Feuerbach's works are unusually significant in this respect.[12] The naive enthusiasm they inspired, first in Karl Barth then in his followers[13] (the originators of the theologies of desacralization and of the death of God), shows the danger of noncosmic transcendental systems. Their only lasting effect is to force man, who cannot survive if deprived of every form of divine immanence, into an unrestrained immanentism in which he seeks to reabsorb and merge the divine into himself.

In Feuerbach's view, indeed, the idea of God, and specifically the biblical and Christian idea of God, is nothing more than a projection which mankind, while still in its infancy, makes of its unfulfilled and as yet unrealizable possibilities. Progress, and particularly social and technological progress, must lie in the recovery and fulfillment, through man's conscious effort to transform himself and the cosmos, of the divine image. This image, projected into an entirely imaginary transcendence, can turn into reality only if it is made immanent through our conscious and deliberate assertion of control over our own destiny. This obviously does not apply to the Christian God in his biblical and evangelical authenticity. But it is all too clear that Feuerbach's views apply perfectly to the God imagined by Bacon and his followers, and that these views are the temptation to which faith in Descartes' God would inevitably fall prey.[14]

Technology Turns Against Man

Evidence of this explosive and demonic progress of a technology that is good in itself toward an exclusively technological ideal is shown in the increasing tendency to substitute a wasteful economy of conspicuous consumption, destructive of natural resources, for the various economies, now considered obsolete, which allowed or positively promoted renewal of these resources, by respecting the natural rhythms of plant and animal life.

At the same time, there is a gradual degradation in the quality of manufactured or processed goods, and particularly of foodstuffs, which is the price paid for a steep and constant rise in productivity; the result is a quantitative abundance of frequently unusable goods and a simultaneous scarcity of essential products. From this deterioration in consumer goods— supplied to meet a demand artificially stimulated—we are now moving to the manipulation of man himself. Under the pretext of offering mankind unprecedented opportunities for gratification, particularly of a sexual kind, the very means of ensuring propagation of the human species are being subverted. In a catastrophic paradox, a so-called population explosion in the underdeveloped countries coexists with a deliberately induced and seemingly irreversible sterility in the nations that claim to be the prime movers of civilization.

The most spectacular and alarming consequence of this loss of control over technological development in the post-Christian civilization (which is really a post-humanistic civilization) is the manufacture and senseless stockpiling of weapons capable of polluting the world forever, and even of destroying mankind altogether. Threatening as this aspect of technical progress may be, what it implies is even more disturbing for the integrity of mankind and the cosmos. The lust for power, which is even stronger than the search for gratification (and is thus a directly demonic trait) is reflected in the feverish proliferation of new weapons, both nuclear and conventional, and shows the influence it now exerts not only over technology but even over basic scientific research.[15] Idealists among the proponents of a technological society claim man's concern for so-called defense has led to discoveries which can be turned to fruitful and peaceful purposes. But the ends which have mobilized these means are so economically compelling that they can never allow these means to support other and opposite ends, except as a temporary cover for the true purpose policymakers have in mind.

Worse still is the fact that the unrelenting and uncritical development of technology, for instance in the area of nuclear energy, leads to an autocratic growth in the power and responsibilities of government. This replaces a responsive and effective democracy with a "massification" of the entire population, which is subjected to a deliberately misleading propaganda that outdoes the most inquisitorial police systems in its dehumanizing effects.[16] Here we reach the ultimate in the deterioration of all creation toward which a civilization such as ours, absorbed in technology, is inevitably moving. Not only does it replace the original vitality of the cosmos with an accumulation of machines—in fact turning the entire cosmos and all human society into a monstrous machine operating to no useful purpose—but also, although in principle this machine was developed to serve mankind, when man allows himself to be caught up in the momentum of its development, this veritable Moloch absorbs man, reducing him to the status of a mere part or cog of its all-invading machinery. So that in the end not only does the world become a pile of useless scrap, but man is simply one more lifeless object among many others.

A particularly revealing symptom of this trend is the disproportionate and truly idolatrous importance ascribed by contemporary mankind to means of transportation, to ceaseless motion, to a fascination with speed. The purpose of travel is no longer simply to go from one place to another for some specific purpose; it is to avoid remaining where we are, or simply to move at ever greater speed. This unwillingness to stay in the same spot is not the sign of a true creative freedom, but of an inability to put down roots. It is a pointless exhaustion of human resources, tantamount to a flight from the qualitative in favor of quantitative proliferation.

The continuance of those living communities that are the physical and moral matrices of personal development becomes impossible. Hence the uniform miscarriage of all individuals, piling up in a perpetual reproduction or cloning of the same low-quality man, to use the expression coined by Musil.[17] This pitiful man may then establish increasing numbers of mock societies, more and more artificially specialized, but they will be as so many Procrustean beds to which he will try to adapt, and where what is left of his humanity will be amputated.

When this development reaches completion, one can foresee the emergence of a totally fossilized universe resembling an immense concentration camp, a caricature of the mystical body of Christ in a colossal *corpus diaboli* entirely immobilized, like Dante's Satan, in a prison of ice.

The Ecological Reaction

A panic-like reaction was inevitable, once a dim awareness of what awaited mankind became widespread. This seems to have occurred over the last few generations. And it was predictable that it would first come about in North America, where the destructive process was most advanced, and where a rootless society was in headlong and indiscriminate pursuit of technological progress,[18] first in scientific circles, then among technologists startled out of their optimistic dreams into a waking nightmare.

This explains the emergence—not only among hippies and other marginal groups, but also among a growing number of craftsmen who had been convinced of the desirability of unlimited technological advance—of a true naturist mystique, and a passionate rejection of all technologies as well as of technological society. This reaction has gone beyond a rational ecological concern for the preservation of misused and dwindling natural resources or the safeguarding of the natural environment. In an extreme form of neo-Rousseauism, these new zealots seek to withdraw from civilization as such, without realizing that the search for a pristine nature untainted by man is an obviously unattainable and unrealistic endeavor, one that could be pursued, moreover, only at the cost of ceasing to be human. To avoid the dire consequences of a spurious humanization of the cosmos—which is simply its materialization by men and women who have lost the sense of their own spirituality—many still cling to the perverse choices that have led to the predicament they are now desperately trying to escape. Symptomatic of such contradictions is the fact that these illogical ecologists, who idealize an unpolluted nature, nevertheless persist in fighting for a sexuality in which both contraception and abortion are freely available.

In fact, the switch in idols is more apparent than real. Whether man, in a simplistically euphoric spirit, worships himself, or adores instead a nature acclaimed and sought for its inhumanity, it is still the same demon under various masks. The world some now seek to return to is not really the cosmos of divine creation, but a projection onto all things of rootless man, stripped of mystery and denied his true being as a creature called to divine filiation.

In the last analysis, there is nothing more pathetic and ominous than the mystiques of sexuality (such as that advocated by D. H. Lawrence), of blood (such as that of neo-pagan nationalists), or of the earth-mother worshiped by the more extreme naturists. In order to halt an evolution which has gone off track, their only solution is to reverse all evolution.[19] We are running around in circles with all these new gospels, which are returns to the ultimate confusion of the ancient myths, i.e., the confusion of salvation with decreation, and of the search for the source of living waters with a regression into primal chaos, or into nothingness pure and simple. For it is senseless to claim that one must choose between a secularized civilization where technology is seen as an end in itself, and a desacralized cosmos alienated from anything outside or above itself. These two destructive alternatives go together. In fact, they promote each other.

Man can recover true life and preserve the cosmos only by rediscovering that a certain voluntary poverty is the condition for possessing the world in a way that will not reduce it to ashes. Man can again find the true measure of his own humanity only in a new respect for and awe of what lies beyond the world. Acknowledging in the world the signs and forgotten presence of transcendent love, and recognizing in oneself a person created and called by the Person from whom all proceeds and by whom everything exists, are two endeavors which go hand in hand. Without self-detachment and disso-ciation from all things there can be no revival in us of the mythopoetic or the poetic, which alone can put us back in touch with true reality by making us part of it.

Outside Christianity, an outstanding example of the revival of the human spirit in a rediscovered cosmos is evidenced by the flowering of Chinese painting during the Sung period. It is significant that this devel-opment derived from a merging of two fundamental Chinese strains: Taoism, with its sense that man is rooted in a cosmos that, although transcendent, reveals itself only to him and through him, and Buddhism, the greatest pre-Christian doctrine of liberation from the all-invading ego. This merger was to lead to a distinctive concept of man's absorption into the cosmos. Far from dissolving or destroying personality, this absorption regenerates and purifies it, enabling it to overcome its limitations in a world where there seems to emerge from some mysterious depth another pres-ence, sovereign yet personal, tacit yet unmistakable.

This was also to be the message of a school of cosmic poetry, ultrapersonal and yet intensely traditional in its essence, which flourished throughout the nineteenth century and remains vital to this day. It implies that the poet seeks detachment from our technological society, a dissociation without which he cannot hope to escape from its coils, or reverse its spread.

Chapter XVII: Renewal of Poetic Experience and Liberation from Technological Bondage

From the outset, the poetic view of reality has led man to see in the world the result and the permanent manifestation of God's loving wisdom, which is his glory. Far from being some sentimental musing, poetic intuition and imagination (as Schelling or Coleridge understood it)[1] should be considered not as irrational but as a higher form of reason. It is an intuitive grasp of the deeper meaning of things and of existence. Opening the way to a truly human existence, it must maintain that focus failing which our life no longer reaches its full potential. This is because myth, the primary creative result of poetry, provides a symbolic vision of the world in God. In myth, poetry fulfills its fundamental purpose, though it is true, as we have seen, that no myth is free from the ambiguities attributable to the Fall.

Poetry and the Sacred

Traces of this origin, or rather of this intrinsic nature, of all poetry remain even in what may be called its humanistic manifestations, in the sense that mankind's self-awareness, attained during the classical ages of civilization, is the dominant element in poetic inspiration.[2] Poetic creation's specific logic, the logic of all living symbols, universally preserves man's experience in this world as a unifying experience. And this unity, which only poetry can make us sense, is the organic—indeed, a spiritual—unity which man in the world feels and makes his own, through his primal, constant, or renewed experience. Be it explicitly religious or not, poetry is always an intimation that we come from God, that everything reminds us of him or leads us back to him. This is indeed why all poetry, even when not an expression of praise, imparts a sense of wonder.

In classical poetry, however, and particularly in Greek poetry, the cosmos is always present as such, in its harmony with the human soul. The soul is thus awakened and impelled to sing the mystery of existence, even when the sense of the divine is not made explicit. However, in this immediate unity of human experience, not as yet fragmented by a rational or even a merely reasoning criticism, the world itself is but fleetingly the direct focus of the poet's concern. Nevertheless, the intensity of the poetic perception of the world, although at most half conscious, is reflected in revealing images such as "the sea's innumerable smile" of Aeschylus, or the *flammantia moenia mundi* (flaming ramparts of the world) of Lucretius, the most Greek of the Roman poets.[3]

In Latin poetry, and particularly during the age of Augustus, when a first attempt was made to revive the weakening religious view of the world, something more was expressed, for instance by Virgil: "...majoresque cadunt altis de montibus umbrae" (longer shadows fall from the mountain heights).[4]

Dante would continue in the same vein. His unceasing comparisons are a reminder of how the cosmos accompanies the wanderings of the human soul as it seeks its God and the lost paradise.[5] Paradoxically, in the mechanized world that denies God, rediscovery of the sense of a cosmos disintegrating in man's greedy hands was to become a major theme of a new poetry. This trend initially surprised and shocked those whose contrived versification merely expressed their own satisfaction with a world where man becomes the focus of everything without feeling the curse of his solipsism. The rediscovery came about through the poet's deliberate withdrawal from the world as it is, cultivating a separation which alone can allow one to rediscover the world as God made it.

A Forerunner: Henry Vaughan

Among the very first to strike this distinctive chord of cosmic poetry was "the Silurian," as he liked to call himself, the Anglo-Welsh poet Henry Vaughan, who lived in the middle years of the seventeenth century.[6] Vaughan had intended simply to follow in the footsteps of his master, George Herbert,[7] the quintessential saint of Anglicanism. But Herbert, in spite of his cultured mind and of the worldliness he had all but overcome, remains one of those Christians beset with interior difficulties. Whatever the torment of his soul, in the presence of his God, into whose hands he finally committed himself with all the trustfulness of a child, Herbert's world remained God's world. It was the world of the village church, of the walled garden in Bemerton, of the spire of Salisbury cathedral rising in the distance between the trees.

As for Vaughan, he lived in a damaged world, not yet that of technology, but certainly one of strife and revolt, where man, even when claiming to remain devout, accepts only *his* personal religion and avoids reminders of the faith in which God was universally acknowledged as Lord of heaven and earth. Puritanism wounded Vaughan deeply, and in his scientific studies he foresaw a rampant materialism. He reacted in two ways: by holding to a hermetic science[8] which, despite its dream-like remoteness, does retain a vision of that spiritual unity elsewhere being totally lost; and by holding to the Celtic lore of sprites,[9] by which, strangely enough, his fidelity to the most traditional part of Anglicanism was strengthened.

In his better moments, however, Vaughan was much more than a reactionary. He lacks Herbert's miraculous ability to conjure up a world where

God is ever present under the humblest manifestations of everyday reality. But he has occasional flashes of insight into the invisible which appears through the visible. Herbert is the mystic of a faith always approaching contemplation, but probably never quite reaching it, and certainly never becoming lost in it. Vaughan is the ecstatic contemplative to whom the world suddenly reveals the glory ready to burst forth from it.

Nothing could be more striking in this regard than Vaughan's poem precisely entitled "The World." It opens with one of his rare but supremely felicitous surprises, a truly apocalyptic stanza:

I saw Eternity the other night,
Like a great Ring of pure and endless light,
All calm, as it was bright...

Immediately the vision fades, however. We are faced simply with the temporal world of politicians, speculators, social climbers, and dandies, the world of the vanity condemned in Ecclesiastes. Then the last verses briefly revive Vaughan's vision, and the poem ends in a kind of twilight glow:

And round beneath it, Time, in hours, days, years,
    Driven by the spheres,
Like a vast shadow moved, in which the world
    And all her train were hurled...
Yet some, who all this while did weep and sing,
And sing and weep, soared up into the Ring;
    But most would use no wing.
'O fool,' said I, 'thus to prefer dark night
    Before true light!...'
But, as I did their madness so discuss,
    One whispered thus,
This ring the Bridegroom did for none provide
    But for his Bride.[10]

Even more revealing is Vaughan's extraordinary vision of the transparent waterfall. The abundant waters flowing through the world in a vital current are, for the multitude, scattered and lost. But the elect are like white pebbles in the basin where the water of life gathers, cleansed, cooled and polished by the current, so that they resemble drops of light.[11]

The most startling of Vaughan's poems is probably "Ascension Day." The loss of all his departed friends he sees as a premonition, a call, and even an anticipation of entry with them and with Christ into glory, which already bathes in a golden radiance the far reaches of the world where they have disappeared with Him:

They are all gone into the world of light!
    And I alone sit ling'ring here;
Their very memory is fair and bright,

And my sad thoughts doth clear...
O Father of eternal life, and all
    Created glories under thee!
Resume thy spirit from this world of thrall
    Into true liberty.[12]

"The Retreat" presents a rediscovery of the world in God, rather than of God in the world. This occurs through a renewal of that spirit of childhood which the Gospel seeks to bring about in us. Platonic reminiscence and the recapitulation of lost innocence are combined with Christian faith to bring us back to the universal beginning, the coming into being of man and all things within God himself—what has become once more the birth of God:

Happy those early days, when I
Shined in my angel-infancy!...
When yet I had not walked above
A mile or two from my first love,
And looking back, at that short space,
Could see a glimpse of his bright face...
Some men a forward motion love,
But I by backward steps would move;
And when this dust falls to the urn,
In that state I came, return.[13]

In this vision the apparent regression to the deepest past is but an anticipation of the eschatological expectation. In Newman's words: "It is not that they regret the past or wish to revert to childhood, but that they long for the future: they can hardly wait to be angels crowned with amaranth and carrying palms, before God's throne, and they long to see him...."

Wordsworth

Early in the nineteenth century, Wordsworth, disappointed by the French Revolution (which had ushered in the worst kind of oppression), was deeply concerned over his own country's industrial revolution and the moral and physical deterioration it led to. Just as Vaughan had returned to the river Usk and the Cimmerian valley of his childhood, Wordsworth turned back to his native Cumberland with its mountains and lakes, the river Duddon and the faraway sea. Wordsworth would perpetually sing a poetry in which the Savior, who is first and foremost God the creator, shows himself in a world that bears everywhere the stamp of his active presence.

Coleridge, that other genius so comically and pitifully associated with Wordsworth, was more a philosopher than a poet, and had the good sense to recognize in his friend the kind of writer he had longed to be. He constantly pestered Wordsworth to compose the philosophical poem he himself wished to produce but lacked the ambition to tackle. Amazingly enough, Wordsworth meekly and solemnly devoted the better part of his life to this major undertaking, without realizing that the outcome would fortunately turn out to be something entirely different from what he had in mind.

The result of this fanciful project was to be "The Prelude," an autobiographical poem of his early life, to be followed many years later by "The Excursion," the account of a "recluse" who leaves home just to have the pleasure of returning to it. This paradoxical epic of self-discovery taught Wordsworth that he was actually more interested in the external world than in his interior self and that the manifestations of God in the world fascinated him more than anything else. Among floods of aphorisms, one is struck by the poetic outbursts of truly disconcerting power and magnificence. Direct communication of the experience which inspired them is the key to his works, and particularly to those brief, impersonal (or perhaps suprapersonal) lines whose richness of inspiration seems inexhaustible. These rare verses are interspersed among a mass of disquisitions, frequently valid and pertinent but generally tedious, and of images meant to be dramatic but often in fact quite comical.

Keats writes in his letters of the undeniable literary stature of this strange and good-hearted man, as well as his awkwardness, most appealing when it is on the verge of becoming unbearable.[14] The following generation, however, accused Wordsworth of having betrayed the convictions of his early life, thereby losing his poetic genius. But as Mary Moorman, the latest and most perceptive of his biographers, has pointed out, there had always been something of the moralizing pedant about him, particularly during his radical youth, but true poetic vision came to him truly when he had lost his illusions. And if he lived on for many years after having said all he had to say, that does not mean the source of his inspiration ever ran dry. But he had expressed himself fully and well on most of his preferred topics, and it was perhaps a sense of modesty which led him into rambling and somewhat repetitive dissertations which, even if far from his generous adolescent dreams, at least never contradicted them.

The Ode on Immortality

Admittedly, the famous ode on "Intimations of Immortality from Recollections of Early Childhood" does not contain the sum total of Wordsworth's message. But it does provide a starting point to explore his vision, i.e., renewal of the world within one's experience. This ode is in the tradition of the May songs found in English poetry from its earliest days. Their first fruit is in a page by Chaucer,[15] and their most delectable in a number of short poems by Herrick. Here, however, from the very first stanza, a new chord is struck: spring itself is still the same, but the eye of the beholder has changed:

> There was a time when meadow, grove, and stream,
>   The earth, and every common sight,
>   To me did seem
>   Appareled in celestial light,
> The glory and the freshness of a dream.
> It is not now as it hath been of yore—
>   Turn wheresoe'er I may,
>   By night or day,
> The things which I have seen I now can see no more.[16]

Yet these things, which he describes in a few deft strokes, remain intrinsically what they have always been:

> The rainbow comes and goes,
> And lovely is the rose,
> The moon doth with delight
> Look round her when the heavens are bare,
> Waters on a starry night
> Are beautiful and fair;
> The sunshine is a glorious birth;
> But yet I know, where'er I go,
> That there hath passed away a glory from the earth.[17]

The poet then immediately regrets his melancholy mood:

> The cataracts blow their trumpets from the steep;
> No more shall grief of mine the season wrong.[18]

As an imaginary young shepherd might do, he then calls upon all creatures, so that they may impart their happiness to him. But they themselves force him to recognize that, though it is still present, he can no longer find in this world what he used to perceive:

> Ye blessed creatures, I have heard the call
>   Ye to each other make; I see
> The heavens laugh with you in your jubilee;
>   My heart is at your festival,
>   My head hath its coronal,
> The fullness of your bliss, I feel—I feel it all...
>   I hear, I hear, with joy I hear!
>   —But there's a tree, of many, one,
> A single field which I have looked upon,

Both of them speak of something that is gone:
    The pansy at my feet
    Doth the same tale repeat:
    Whither is fled the visionary gleam?
    Where is it now, the glory and the dream?[19]

He answers this question, as Vaughan might, with what seems to be a reminiscence, the Platonic reminiscence. Still more explicitly, however, his reply takes on the wholly Christian meaning of a longing for the creator from whom we and all things proceed, but from whom life seems to be increasingly drawing us away:

Our birth is but a sleep and a forgetting:
The Soul that rises with us, our life's Star,
    Hath had elsewhere its setting,
        And cometh from afar:
    Not in entire forgetfulness,
    And not in utter nakedness,
But trailing clouds of glory do we come
    From God, who is our home:
Heaven lies about us in our infancy!
Shades of the prison-house begin to close
    Upon the growing boy,
But he beholds the light, and whence it flows,
    He sees it in his joy;
The Youth, who daily farther from the east
    Must travel, still is Nature's priest,
        And by the vision splendid
        Is on his way attended;
At length the Man perceives it die away,
And fade into the light of common day.[20]

This fading of the vision is caused by man's countless occupations, which children imitate in their games: words of commerce, or of love or hate, which they repeat without grasping their full significance, just as they copy what their friends do, reproducing in their lives a pattern which will persist until the decline and paralysis of old age. So it is that in children the opaque layers successively superimposed by adult habits gradually smother and betray the innate light of their souls.

    Mighty prophet! Seer blessed!
    On whom those truths do rest,
Which we are toiling all our lives to find,
In darkness lost, the darkness of the grave.[21]

Yet there remains in us a spark under the ashes, a spark revived in a springtime meeting with nature:

O joy! that in our embers
Is something that doth live,
That nature yet remembers
What was so fugitive!
The thought of our past years in me doth breed
Perpetual benediction: not indeed
For that which is most worthy to be blessed—
Delight and liberty, the simple creed
Of childhood, whether busy or at rest,
With new-fledged hope still fluttering in his breast—
    Not for these I raise
    The song of thanks and praise;
    But for those obstinate questionings
    Of sense and outward things,
    Fallings from us, vanishings;
    Blank misgivings of a creature
Moving about in worlds not realized,
High instincts before which our mortal Nature
Did tremble like a guilty thing surprised;
    But for those first affections,
    Those shadowy recollections,
    Which, be they what they may,
Are yet the fountain-light of all our day,
Are yet a master-light of all our seeing.[22]

A favorable time and place can trigger the memory of these childhood impressions, and they come flooding back, with an unprecedented awareness of their significance, but without the initial intimacy and freshness, which cannot be recaptured:

Hence in a season of calm weather
    Though inland far we be,
Our souls have sight of that immortal sea
    Which brought us hither,
    Can in a moment travel thither,
And see the children sport upon the shore,
And hear the mighty waters rolling evermore.[23]

The conclusion is unexpectedly optimistic, and carries us again—more surely than ever—from regret for the past to the hope of an immortal future:

And O, ye Fountains, Meadows, Hills, and Groves,
Forebode not any severing of our loves!
Yet in my heart of hearts I feel your might;
I only have relinquished one delight
To live beneath your more habitual sway.

I love the brooks which down their channels fret,
Even more than when I tripped lightly as they;
The innocent brightness of a new-born Day
    Is lovely yet;
The clouds that gather round the setting sun
Do take a sober coloring from an eye
That hath kept watch o'er man's mortality;
Another race hath been, and other palms are won.
Thanks to the human heart by which we live,
Thanks to its tenderness, its joys, and fears,
To me the meanest flower than blows can give
Thoughts that do often lie too deep for tears.[24]

Tintern Abbey

The essential role of memory, which the Ode did no more than touch upon, was the theme of the equally famous lines penned a little earlier by Wordsworth, when for the second time he visited the valley of the Wye and the ruins of Tintern Abbey. During his years of stultifying life in the city, the vitality of earlier memories had been simmering. His return to the abbey brought them flooding back:

            These beauteous forms,
Through a long absence, have not been for me
As is a landscape to a blind man's eye:
But oft, in lonely rooms, and 'mid the din
Of towns and cities, I have owed to them
In hours of weariness, sensations sweet,
Felt in the blood, and felt along the heart;
And passing even into my purer mind,
With tranquil restoration: —feelings too
Of unremembered pleasure; such, perhaps,
As have no slight or trivial influence
On that best portion of a good man's life,
His little, nameless, unremembered acts
Of kindness and of love. Nor less, I trust,
To them I may have owed another gift,
Of aspect more sublime; that blessèd mood,
In which the burthen of the mystery,
In which the heavy and the weary weight
Of all this unintelligible world,
Is lightened—that serene and blessèd mood,
In which the affections gently lead us on—
Until, the breath of this corporeal frame
And even the motion of our human blood
Almost suspended, we are laid asleep

In body, and become a living soul:
While with an eye made quiet by the power
Of harmony, and the deep power of joy,
We see into the life of things.[25]

At this point it seems that we have reached the very heart of what has been called a cosmic mystique.

Pantheism . . . or Panentheism?

The following poem expresses perfectly, though in deliberately enigmatic terms, the paradox of this world, which we are so used to that we no longer really see it but which on special occasions still provides wholly unexpected revelations:

The world is too much with us; late and soon,
Getting and spending, we lay waste our powers...
For this, for everything, we are out of tune;
It moves us not. —Great God! I'd rather be
A pagan suckled in a creed outworn;
So might I, standing on this pleasant lea,
Have glimpses that would make me less forlorn;
Have sight of Proteus rising from the sea;
Or hear old Triton blow his wreathèd horn.[26]

These lines would of course be eagerly pounced upon by misguided critics who, on behalf of an obsolete Puritanism, took Wordsworth to task for his alleged pantheism or, in support of a spurious neo-paganism, upbraided him for later adopting Anglo-Catholic orthodoxy.[27] To both factions he replied sharply in a letter written in 1815 answering criticism leveled at "The Excursion":

I am being censured for supposedly failing to make a distinction between God's creation and God himself. But there is no such assertion or implication in my writings. How can one possibly conclude that the author of "The Excursion" considers that nature and God are one and the same? The only truth of the matter is that indeed he does not view the relationship between the Supreme Being and the universe in the same light as the connection between a clockmaker and his clock.[28]

A key section of "The Prelude" makes his thinking more explicit:

Wisdom and Spirit of the universe!
Thou Soul that art the Eternity of Thought!
That givest to forms and images a breath
And everlasting motion! not in vain,
By day or star-light thus from my first dawn

Of childhood didst thou intertwine for me
The passions that build up our human soul,
Not with the mean and vulgar works of man,
But with high objects, with enduring things,
With life and nature, purifying thus
The elements of feeling and of thought,
And sanctifying, by such discipline,
Both pain and fear, until we recognize
A grandeur in the beatings of the heart.
        Nor was this fellowship vouchsafed to me
With stinted kindness. In November days,
When vapors, rolling down the valleys, made
A lonely scene more lonesome; among woods
At noon, and 'mid the calm of summer nights,
When, by the margin of the trembling lake,
Beneath the gloomy hills I homeward went
In solitude, such intercourse was mine;
'Twas mine among the fields both day and night,
And by the waters all the summer long.[29]

In lines remarkable for their psychological insight, Wordsworth reflects on the communion between a child and the mother holding it in her arms to express the relationship between man and the universe,[30] as well as the imprint of beauty on an awakening mind:

I held unconscious intercourse with beauty
Old as creation, drinking in a pure
Organic pleasure from the silver wreaths
Of curling mist, or from the level plain
Of waters colored by impending clouds.[31]

It has been noted that these impressions of Wordsworth's focus more on awesome beauty—such as the threatening mountain which seems to follow him when in "an act of stealth and troubled pleasure" he rowed his little boat across the waters of the lake,[32] or the coming of a storm[33]—than on a superhuman serenity such as he felt at the sight of tranquil Windermere.[34]
        Both types of impressions are found in another of his descriptions:

                    . . . I was only then
Contented, when with bliss ineffable
I felt the sentiment of Being spread
O'er all that moves and all that seemeth still;
O'er all that, lost beyond the reach of thought
And human knowledge, to the human eye
Invisible, yet liveth to the heart;
O'er all that leaps and runs, and shouts and sings,
Or beats the gladsome air; o'er all that glides

Beneath the wave, yea, in the wave itself,
And mighty depth of waters. Wonder not
If high the transport, great the joy I felt,
Communing in this sort through earth and heaven
With every form of creature, as it looked
Towards the Uncreated with a countenance
Of adoration, with an eye of love.
One song they sang, and it was audible,
Most audible, then, when the fleshy ear,
O'ercome by humblest prelude of that strain,
Forgot her functions, and slept undisturbed.[35]

Wordsworth clearly gave considerable importance to sounds, as well as to visual impressions, which he admitted he received more spontaneously to the extent that at one time they "often held [his] mind in absolute dominion."[36] In one of those extraordinary effusions of his waning years—though relatively rare by then, they showed he had lost none of his poetic sensitivity—he developed this theme, for the only time, but in a way which surpasses anything ever written about the harmony of the spheres. At the same time, this unusual poem explicitly establishes the link, so seldom acknowledged, between Wordsworth's panentheistic (rather than pantheistic) mystique and the increasing dogmatic precision of the traditional Christian faith. It was this that impelled this Northern Protestant, imbued with Miltonian memories, to accept so readily the tributes paid him by Keble and Faber:[37]

By one pervading spirit
Of tones and numbers all things are controlled,
As sages taught, where faith was found to merit
Initiation in that mystery old.
The heavens, whose aspect makes our minds as still
As they themselves appear to be,
Innumerable voices fill
With everlasting harmony...
Break forth into thanksgiving,
Ye banded instruments of wind and chords
Unite, to magnify the Ever-living,
Your inarticulate notes with the voice of words!
Nor hushed be service from the lowing mead,
Nor mute the forest hum of noon...
As Deep to Deep
Shouting through one valley calls,
All worlds, all natures, mood and measure keep
For praise and ceaseless gratulation, poured
Into the ear of God, their Lord...

A Voice to Light gave Being;
To Time, and Man, his earth-born chronicler;
A Voice shall finish doubt and dim foreseeing,
And sweep away life's visionary stir . . .
Though earth be dust
And vanish, though the heavens dissolve,
[Harmony's] stay
Is in the WORD, that shall not pass away.[38]

From Cosmic to Christian Mysticism

Wordsworth's steady progress from his cosmic mystique toward an increasingly full and explicit discovery of Christian contemplation was manifest even in his early youth, and in spite of Protestant preconceptions; he recognized in the venerable Charterhouse near Grenoble the symbol of an openness (prepared by natural contemplation) to the Gospel, and saw in the cross planted on the mountaintop by the sons of St. Bruno the epitome of the divine word which all things whisper to a receptive soul.[39]

In this light, the somewhat timid but significantly consistent lines he wrote on the value of myths and their fulfillment in the revealed Word of the Bible and the Gospel should not be minimized nor misunderstood as a sign of lingering pantheism. He clearly knew exactly what he wanted to say, even if he did not quite know how to say it, in what is quite possibly the most unexpected page of "The Excursion." He praised the element of truth contained in ancient myths in words which might have been penned by Clement of Alexandria: they perpetuate and revive what remains of God's initial communication through the angels with man, and pave the way for the Word vouchsafed to the patriarchs and prophets, to become incarnate forever in the Son of God made man.[40] Testimony to how much this conviction meant to him is found in the most Catholic of Wordsworth's poems, "The Processions," written on a theme which suggested itself to him one Sunday morning in Chamonix.[41] (Wordsworth's awareness of how openly he is expressing his religious views here obviously causes him some trepidation.)

Though he did not realize it, Wordsworth's feelings closely paralleled those of another poet with an even more inspired cosmic vision, one who seemed utterly alien to the straightforward Northern Englishman. Wordsworth spent only one winter in Germany, trailing after the tireless and scatter-brained Coleridge, but what a winter it was! Seated next to his stove, unable to understand a word of what was being said in his presence, he was to remain forever unaware of and unknown by his surprisingly like-minded contemporary. Had he been able to read something of what this true soul-mate had started to write at that very time—and moreover in close geographical proximity—it is not certain that he would have recognized its consonance with the element in his own writings which was to immortalize him.

During that terrible winter of 1798-1799, while desperately trying to keep warm and putting up with the dubious comfort of his Württemberg lodgings, Wordsworth had composed the most enigmatic part of his writings, the beautiful and limpid elegiac poems to the mysterious Lucy, whose real or imaginary identity no one has been able to unravel.[42] This is probably the only instance, among countless vain attempts, when he succeeded fully in describing the unblemished innocence which he felt should come to artless souls from a life lived deliberately close to nature.

Hölderlin

At precisely the same time, in Homburg, Hölderlin, after his tragic separation from Diotima, was starting to write *Empedocles* and his major Odes, not far from the insular Wordsworth in Würtemberg. A few years earlier, in Tübingen, he had held endless discussions with Hegel and Schelling, those two other budding geniuses, about the new religion which could be made to replace a Christianity that seemed exhausted beyond any hope of revival.[43]

Hegel was to die with the comforting conviction, which few others shared, that he had succeeded in the undertaking. Schelling would bluntly acknowledge that he had failed. He would then try, with more good will than success, to revive the lost tradition through speculation in which boldness and humility blend somewhat explosively and fruitful intuitions alternate with bewildering verbosity.

It may well be that Hölderlin, fleeing from their increasingly intemperate celebrations into an ineffable form of poetry, drew closer to a solution, at the price of madness and a shattered life. More applicable to him than to Keats is the line written by Shelley, Hölderlin's unknown intellectual brother:

He has outsoared the shadow of our night![44]

As J. C. Shairp perceptively noted, in one of the most discerning commentaries on Wordsworth's poetry, his power to convince and move us stems from the fact that he depicts nature not (as is the case with Lamartine, for instance) in a general or atopical way, but precisely in terms of his most personal experience.[45] The same may be said of Hölderlin. His insistence on the essential complementarity between the Greece of his dreams and his native and nurturing Swabia, attests to his deep sense of the openness of the limited to the unlimited, and particularly of the descent and communication of the infinite in the finite, which is central to his poetic experience. Wordsworth, though he loved rivers and oceans, generally preferred to turn back to the serene beauty of "his" lakes of Windermere and Derwent-water, while Hölderlin was enthralled by the mightier rivers and their valleys. He attributed the first poetic experience of his childhood to his discovery of the Rhine and the narrow path it cuts through the mountains. Yet, the more familiar Neckar would always symbolize his homecoming after an escape to the dreamland of a timeless Greece, a return that revived the wellspring of his own existence through celebration of the feast that made the gods feel at home among men. But it was the Danube, or the Ister—to give it, as he did, its Greek name—which conjured up for him, as for Keats, the inner search for the land of celestial light that transfigures the earth: the Greece of his *Empedocles* and *Hyperion's Song of Fate*.

Hölderlin met, then lost Diotima, who through an earthly love led him to the radiance of the Father's love, descending from the Ether where he dwells onto those who dedicate their lives to him. The poet was inspired to sing of a luminous "Archipelago":

> ...Every one of them lives, those mothers of heroes, the islands,
> Flowering year after year, and if at times the subterranean
> Thunder, the flame of Night, let loose from the primal abysses,
> Seized on one of the dear isles and, dying, she sank in your waters,
> You, divine one, endured, for much already has risen,
> Much gone down for you here above your deeper foundations.
> And the heavens, too, the powers up above us, the silent,
> Who from afar bring the cloudless day, delicious sleep and forebodings
> Down to the heads of sentient mortals, bestowing
> Gifts in their fullness and might, they too, your playmates as ever,
> Dwell with you as before...
> When the all-transfiguring, then, she, the child of the Orient,
> Miracle-worker, the sun of our day-time, is present,
> All that's alive in a golden dream recommences,
> Golden dream the poetic one grants us anew every morning,
> Then to you, the sorrowing god, she will send a still gladder enchantment,
> And her own beneficent light is not equal in beauty
> To the token of love, the wreath, which even now and as ever
> Mindful of you, she winds round your locks that are greying.
> Does not Aether enfold you, too, and your heralds, the clouds, do
> They not return to you with his gift, the divine, with the rays that
> Come from above?...[46]

It would be naive to interpret these lines simply as romantic nostalgia, like Winckelmann's, for an imaginary paganism. What riveted Hölderlin's interest in his idealized vision of Greece was his radiant Apollinian fore-knowledge and ecstatic Dionysiac premonition of the hidden God finally to be revealed. Greece was nature flooded with the light from on high and thrilling to a call from depths beyond any abyss, a golden landscape where the human and superhuman splendor of the original paradise seemed permanent.

The elegy "Bread and Wine" tells of the expectation of life reappearing from death and defeating it. It is an expectation vibrant in the eternal symbolism of wheat and the vine—and which would at last find its fulfillment in Christ, freed from the pseudo-orthodoxy that had belittled him and from the Pietism that had diminished his humanity:

> Nothing succeeds, because we are heartless, mere shadows until our
> Father Aether, made known, recognized, fathers us all.
> Meanwhile, though, to us shadows comes the Son of the Highest,
> Comes the Syrian and down into our gloom bears his torch.
> Blissful, the wise men see it; in souls that were captive there gleams a
> Smile, and their eyes shall yet thaw in response to the light.[47]

The last and possibly the most moving of the unfinished poems, abandoned when the poet's mind entirely gave way under his excruciating trials, stops just short of the avowal that it was Patmos, the island of the Christian apocalypse, which received the true revelation, one that must forever be recognized anew:

> But around Asia's gates
> There murmur, stretching here and there
> In the uncertain plain of the sea,
> Sufficient shadowless streets,
> Yet the boatman knows the islands.
> And, when I heard
> One of the nearest
> Was Patmos,
> I desired greatly
> There to be lodged and there
> To approach the dark grotto.
> For not like Cyprus,
> Rich in sources, or
> One of the others,
> Lives glorious Patmos.
> Hospitable, nevertheless,
> In the poorer house,
> Yet is Patmos...
> ...So once she tended
> The beloved of God,

The seer, who in blissful youth had
Walked with
The Son of the Highest, inseparable, for
The bearer of thunder loved the disciple's
Ingenuousness, and the attentive man
Saw the face of the God distinctly,
When by the mystery of the vine
They sat together at the banqueting hour,
And calmly foreknowing in his great soul, the Lord
Pronounced death, and the last love, for never he had
Enough words to say of goodness,
At that time, and to soothe,
When he saw it, the wrath of the world.
For all things are good. Thereupon he died. Much might
Be said of it. And to the very last the friends
Beheld him as he gazed triumphant, gladdest of them all.[48]

After this glimpse of ultimate reality, Hölderlin slipped away into the silent night. For the poet who had suffered so deeply and rediscovered so much through his suffering, the existence he had "outsoared" was to continue here below for many long years, and his contemporaries looked upon these as years of madness. Yet his gentle and ironical wisdom, mocking theirs, so vain and pretentious, would henceforth sing only of a recovered or anticipated childhood:

Like the bright day that brings down from the heights
Clear, shining light and in its radiance wraps mankind,
So that it binds together all earth's glimmering sights,
Is knowledge wholly granted to the striving mind.[49]

Once again and more than ever, these two poets suggest a close relationship between mysticism and poetry. Wordsworth's sudden explorations of an experience so different from his usual, occasionally insightful but uniformly prosaic and often tedious meditations, reflect his premonitions of what mystics call illuminative meditation. Through the realities of this world, an intuition of the mystery of the creator starts to emerge. The impetus driving Hölderlin along the same paths was so intense, fed and purified by his agonizing trials, that he reached the goal. But he was too exhausted by the course he had taken, as well as by his secularized Christianity, the uncertain cerebrations of the age's best minds, and his own insufficient preparation for encounter with the numinous. It could but overwhelm his reason, even though his broken heart found a certain peace, and even a modicum of joy.

Shelley and Keats

The poetry of Wordsworth and Hölderlin probably represent the most remarkable achievements in modern man's efforts to reactivate a sense of the lost or hidden world. We have already drawn attention to the similarities between Shelley and Hölderlin which, though real enough, should not be overemphasized. Shelley's poems, even at their best, are the attempts of an inspired but spoiled child. In these works, daydreams and play mimic life experience in an astonishing manner, but an obvious rhetorical facility casts doubt on almost every one of his poems. This youth who constantly spoke of love seems to have been an incorrigible egotist. The atheism in his "Epipsychidion" is entirely verbal, and he is the first to be taken in by the essentially literary nature of the ecstatic mood the poem evokes.[50]

After ignoring Keats during his lifetime, Shelley lavished eloquent posthumous praise on the unpretentious poet who had been in real need of his friendship—if indeed this Ariel (as Maurois dubbed him) was capable of bestowing friendship on anyone. Keats appears to have been captive to an exceptionally intense sensuality. Yet he was obviously lacking in neither intelligence nor heart. If life had been kinder to him, and particularly if it had granted him more time, it is possible that the springtime of his major Odes would have matured into a wider and fuller version of Wordsworth's cosmic vision, whose immediate significance he may well have been the only one to grasp.[51]

Novalis, Baudelaire, and Nerval

It is tempting to see Novalis as another Keats. His spiritual, religious, and openly Christian intuition seems in him more distinct from sensuality, but it is doubtful whether this intuition ever really jolted, as it did in Keats, his self-complacency. It is not surprising that for him there was a certain confusion or overlap between religion and magic. Without doubt Baudelaire and Nerval often reached the areas where Wordsworth and Hölderlin were at home. This is particularly true of Nerval, though he may have entered the realm of the sacred only in a dream tinged with madness.[52]

Claudel

Among all French poets, and not only the modern ones, Claudel is unquestionably the most cosmic, yet his vision never quite equals that of Wordsworth and Hölderlin. In La ville and especially in Tête d'Or, it seemed that he would reinstate the world's original meaning, turning it once again into a way to God, an encounter with Christ seen with new eyes. But in any event this did not prove to be the nature of his post-conversion poetry, even of the *Cinq grandes Odes*. These are no more than a magnificently orchestrated revival—one might almost say an imitation—of traditional biblical and liturgical poetry. Indeed, Claudelian versification is based on a somewhat contrived imitation of the Vulgate and its psalter, including deliberately preserved mistranslations and instances of syntactic awkwardness. In *L'Epée dans le miroir* and other works written in the same vein, an imitation of the exegesis of the Church Fathers, leaning on oversimplifications and approximations in order to promote edification, engages the poet's meditation. The Bible was his Sunamite, Claudel would humorously say. Quite so, a critic replied: he sleeps with her, but does not know her!

There can be no doubt that the imitation was sincere. It remains troublesome nevertheless, and makes Claudel's cosmic Christianity a baroque and contrived survival, or relic, rather than a renewal. This seems to be confirmed by the fact that the only other poet suggestive of Claudel and owing his own inspiration to him is, so far at least, Saint-John Perse, composer of faceless, antiquarian verse.[53]

T. S. Eliot

Quite the opposite is the poetry of T. S. Eliot, notwithstanding its archaic and deliberately reactionary features. Eliot's poetic form—and in poetry form can never be separated from substance—is quite unlike anything ever seen before. Eliot's starting point is always present-day man and his world, and nobody else has expressed so well the irreparable wear and tear of both, the impression they give of a corroded and burnt-out reality. This is the theme in "Ash Wednesday." But true faith—not some gnostic, deceptively disincarnate, inward-looking substitute—faith in a savior of the world who remains its creator, faith found in the journey of the Magi and reflected as crucified love in Becket's sacrifice, finally wins out in "Little Gidding." Here, despite his own disavowals, Eliot invokes and touches the world of resurrection.[54]

Rilke

Though he never embraced the Christian faith, Rilke may be compared with Eliot. The parallel is more valid for some of his works than for others. In the *Sonnets for Orpheus*, for instance, the poet appears to seek escape from the alternative between salvation and damnation by turning to a purely aesthetic contemplation. Duino's *Elegies*, on the other hand, even if they do not rediscover the way to God through the cosmos, do recognize in it the divine element, the Ether as Hölderlin called it, the spirit without which matter would be naught. This spirit is the angel, the counterpart of Hölderlin's Greek "gods," whom he also sometimes calls by the same name: cosmic powers. It is a name whose ambiguity attests that the world in itself—however we may use or misuse it—remains sacred, and is in fact *the* sacred, the sign of God, both absent and present.[55]

These sudden songs from a voice fading into the void, a void of our own making, suggest what Heidegger, commenting on Hölderlin, was to call the fourfold nature of the world, constituted of the twin relationships between heaven and earth on the one hand, and gods and men on the other.[56]

Retrospections

Here ends our survey of the history of salvation, which is also that of revelation. We undertook it in the hope of discovering, through the accomplishment of the divine plan, a shadow or image of the divine figure which projects itself through the thrust of that love which God *possesses* as his own, so much so that he *is* that love. Our meditation on the Paraclete has given us a glimpse, through his superabundant grace, of God's unfathomable depths: the *Grund* of mystics, the *Urgrund* or better still the *Ungrund*, from which everything not only in ourselves but even in God derives. Our reflection on the Cosmos will end in a rediscovery of the world in God, whose Love produced, redeemed and adopted it. Such is the purpose of the following Retrospections.

Chapter XVIII: Wisdom in the Trinity

Immanence and Transcendence

Greek philosophy seems to have substituted *logos* for *mythos*, but actually it only simplified and clarified myth by eliminating superfluous accretions. This is proved by the fact that Greek philosophers were never able to stop confusing God with the world, and never really grasped the omnipresence of God in the world. Spinoza, the first to define the divine transcendence and immanence,[1] was true to his Jewish heritage in asserting that they are inseparable attributes. But he showed himself to be still bound by Greek rationalism when he failed to maintain fully the distinction between them.

Platonic ideas—and even the idea of the Good, which sums them all up by transcending them—were cut off from the world, in relation to which they remained pure abstractions. Yet they are nothing but the substance of the sensible world, the other side of it, as it were.

Aristotle's prime "unmoved-mover" exists only in and for itself, and nothing else exists for it. Nevertheless, this "unmoved-mover" is the entelechy, the final outcome toward which all in this world tends, its inaccessible perfection.

The stoic god, both as *pneuma* vivifying all things and as *logos* endowing them with sense and reason, is indeed in all things, but in an increasingly diluted state, except in the fiery sky, where it exists fully and purely. Yet this sky, which moves and encompasses everything, is only the outer envelope of the world, inseparable from it.

The dialectics of transcendence and immanence is more subtle in neo-Platonism, especially in Plotinus.[2] But their relationship seems to lie only in two complementary views of one and the same reality. The One is God, and God is the One. In fact, the One has and is no other reality than that of the world. The One is the world considered exclusively in terms of unity. Conversely, the world is simply the One in a dispersed state. If a being of this world, or the world itself, condenses and concentrates, not only will the being or the world become God as a result of the operation, but the process itself will simply reveal that it was God all along, since everything that is exists as one, and by virtue of its existence partakes of that unity.

On the other hand, the world, whose multiplicity distinguishes it from the One, no longer partakes in any way of the One, as a result of this distinction. The world and the One are therefore distinct or not, depending on the point of view. But they each have their identity precisely because they are not coextensive, and in fact precisely because each has nothing of the other.

The mediator, the *nous*, intelligence, is much nearer to the Jewish and Christian idea of God, while implying a concept of the world approximating even more closely the biblical and evangelical vision. For the Plotinian *nous* is but the One open to multiplicity, encompassing it, yet without dissolving or losing itself in multiplicity. All the distinct beings subsist in the One, and do so in unity. And they subsist not as mere abstractions, but instead remain bubbling with life, as Plotinus emphasizes.

It is highly probable that this *nous* owes much, if not everything, to the biblical teaching, and most precisely to the fundamental concept of the Word in which God expresses himself and brings forth all things. It seems that in this instance the biblical current in the thinking of Ammonius Saccas, Plotinus' Alexandrian master, was able for the first time truly to penetrate Greek thought.

Even so, God and the world, according to Plotinus, are both distinct and indistinct from each other. To the extent that they appear distinct, they become alien to one another. Either God makes himself known to us and his identity changes, or we return to him and are no longer ourselves. The alternative is inescapable.

Person, Love, and Trinity

What is lacking here, though intuitively sought after, is personality, both ours and God's. The recently coined word "personalism" has unfortunately been already debased. The opposed meanings of person (one living in interpersonal relationships) and individual (one essentially partitioned off and alienated from others) have been turned—by the same Christian thinkers who drew attention to the contrast in the first place—into a fawning and unseemly apologia for Marxism. The only one in this group to hold his own was Maurice Nédoncelle; supremely discerning, courteous and discreet, he was not easily taken in.[3] Far from holding that the person has the exclusive ability and duty to merge into the crowd, he developed with subtlety and depth the theme of the reciprocity of consciousnesses as the leitmotif of his personalism.

What St. Gregory the Great said of charity holds true of the human person. Love and person are thus connected: one person alone is inconceivable, and at least two are needed to love one another. This is not to say that a person can exist only in such close reciprocity. And here may well be where we reach the unique feature of Christianity's affirmation concerning God, as he is in himself and as he shows himself in relation to the world. For the struggle against the earliest of the great heresies was to lead Christian thinkers to the reasoned conviction that God is triune, as was immediately grasped and asserted by the Cappadocian Fathers who were engaged in the defeat of Arianism and its sequels; this means that God transcends both unity and multiplicity.[4] The fact that he is above multiplicity had been at least glimpsed by Plato, then fully brought out by Plotinus and his school. (Though sympathetic to neo-Platonism, the Cappadocians were also critical of it.) But biblical and especially evangelic revelation was required in order to complete this fundamental certitude, accessible to unaided natural reason, but only with difficulty.

To start with, St. Athanasius seems to have been the first to realize this formally, or in any case to state it expressly: though God is one, he yet encompasses, both in his relationship to the world and within himself absolutely, something which, while not multiplicity, cannot be reduced to mere unity as we experience it.

Plato held that God, identified with the Good, necessarily produced the world, because the Good is diffusive of itself and therefore cannot remain sterile. All the more so, the God who revealed himself as *agape*, the love which gives itself without reservation, cannot be alone.[5] However, paternity is so essential to him that he can only be the Father of a Son who is really an *alter ego*. The production of all possible and imaginable worlds would not satisfy this infinitude of God's love. Only by being entirely communicated and projected in his only-begotten Son is the paternity of the only God Who is Father, and only in this way perfected.

Nor is this all. From the Father in the Son proceeds the Spirit of sonship. This means, first of all, that to this Son who receives everything from him God even gives that which is the soul of his own life: the ability to give himself as he does, to answer the paternal love with a love that is not only its reflection, but its living image. Moreover, in the Spirit the divine love does not appear simply as a perfect reciprocity in a community of love; it becomes apparent that this reciprocity implies a communication of the very community established by love, for this community cannot be inward-looking, any more than those by whom and in whom it is founded.

It is in this sense that the Spirit is love, which is not to say that the Father and the Son are not already love, nor that the Spirit is not also, like them and with them, both the subject and the object of divine love. But it is in the Spirit that the fullness of love shows itself to be the plenitude not only of a mutual love, but also of a shared openness of this reciprocity of love to yet another person. So it is that the Spirit fulfills the personal unity of the union of the Father and the Son.

Since the Father is thus fully projected in the Son, the Son expresses him perfectly. This is why the Son is eternally his Word, and this Word is first of all the divine Name. The Spirit, which rests eternally on the Son, attests the reality of this expression of the Father by irradiating the paternal glory in the Son. The Spirit itself is therefore the luminous effulgence of the divine life in the Son, as Beauty shining in the Truth of the Goodness which is its source and the source of all things. For everything which can be from the being of the Father is translated into the Son, and in him is life and light through the Spirit, as in the Father.[6]

Taken in this sense, the Augustinian formulations, enshrined in later Latin tradition, on the Son begotten through intelligence and the Spirit proceeding through loving will are certainly faithful to the biblical and patristic tradition, as some of the most punctilious spokesmen of the Eastern Church, such as Gregory Palamas, have clearly recognized.[7] And still in the same sense, it is understandable that St. Thomas asserted that the Father and the Son are still fully love just as much as the Spirit, though differently, in the same way as the Father and the Spirit are no less wise than the Son, although eternal Wisdom is fulfilled in him and eternal Love in the Spirit, in a manner specific to them.[8]

It will also be clear that in this perspective one meets the affirmation voiced by Boulgakoff, among others, to the effect that the relations which allow us to distinguish the divine persons, the paternity-filiation and the procession (*ekporeusis*), active and passive, even if they are at first relations of origin, are really something quite different: exchanges so rich and deep as to defy totally our attempts at analysis.[9] What we can say of the subject, far from exhausting its mystery, simply indicates and conjures up the inexpressible and inconceivable plenitude of these exchanges. Thus, the concept of personality, far from raising questions regarding how it applies to God, applies only to him in its most rigorous sense. It applies to us only because we carry within ourselves, as conscious and spiritual beings, an analogical participation in the divine mystery.[10] But like all analogies between the creator and his creature, this analogy cannot be a direct one. Man, the human individual, is not properly speaking an image of the Trinity; rather, it is the relationships between men which makes humanity a natural image of the Trinity. And within the Church (humanity's supernatural society), this relationship is elevated in each member to a participation in the divine life (i.e., the trinitarian life), which turns this static image into a living resemblance.

Immutability, Impassibility, and Agape

The result of all this is undoubtedly the divine immutability and impassibility, for such a God has in him no lack and no imperfection. But it also follows that in the Christian God these two attributes take on a meaning utterly different from the unconcern of the Aristotelian God about whatever gravitates toward him, or even of Plato's Good or Plotinus' One about what proceeds from him, but without involving an act of will on his part. This is where we shall discover how this transcendence of God, which is that of his *agape*, is on a par with his immanence in the world, which it would be better to call (in accordance with a comment in St. Thomas' *De veritate*) a presence of this world in himself.[11]

It is most significant that such a subtle analyst and skillful defender of quietism as Father Varillon, S.J.,[12] seemed determined in his last writings to project onto God the anxiety which he had so brilliantly praised the mystics for having overcome.[13] Modern man, even when he no longer believes in God, is more starved for divinization than any generation before him.[14] At the same time, he feels strictly entitled to it. This being so, he inevitably has the greatest difficulty in accepting the fact that God himself is indeed God.

But how could he be God unless he were absolutely perfect? Or if anything outside himself could have any effect on him? The biblical assertion that he is King, the King of heaven and earth, the King of ages, the only King, would then lose all meaning. Either God, the God of biblical and evangelic revelation, is unchanging forever and the one exclusive source of every being—since he is the source of all being and indeed is being itself—or he is no longer himself.[15] But this perfection, this sovereignty—and the omnipotence deriving from it—must be correctly understood. And these attributes can be so understood only if they are related to love, to the *agape* in which God made himself known above all else, as St. Paul emphasized, in the cross of Christ, by which St. John did not hesitate to define him, asserting that "greater love has no man than this, that a man lay down his life for his friends."[16]

This is tantamount to saying that divine impassibility has nothing in common with indifference, any more than God's immutability is the immobility of a statue or of a dead body. From this viewpoint, one can understand the indignation of Laberthonnière, among others, at certain neo-Scholastic translations of Thomism which, while claiming the opposite, reduce the theology of St. Thomas Aquinas to an uncritical Aristotelianism.[17] In actual fact, these translations wrongly interpret the deference Aquinas felt for certain Aristotelian expressions in which he perceived an undeveloped sense of God's absolute transcendence—a sense which until then had always been lacking in the Greek concept of the divine. In so doing, these translators sought to explain St. Thomas' views in a manner totally contrary to his intended meaning.

For St. Thomas and for the entire authentically Christian tradition, the divine plenitude is indubitably that of the infinite, and not some kind of ultimate limitation, just as God's inaccessibility to any causality other than his own derives from the fact that the latter, being the first cause of all the others, remains the basis of them all.

One should therefore understand precisely what is meant by some absolutely orthodox Christian authors when they say that God finds all his happiness in himself, knows nothing outside himself, cannot love anything alien to him, can have no other purpose but his own glory, etc. This means that in his triune life God is—and therefore has within himself—everything that can exist, so that not only can nothing be added to him from without, but also it would be totally meaningless to assume that he might himself undergo some kind of progression.

But because this plenitude is that of love, and because the love unfolding in the life of the Trinity is pure gift and pure gratuitousness, there is nothing to prevent God from being the creator of other beings. This implies, indeed, that having created them out of pure love—in the same way as everything he does *ad intra* or *ad extra*—he knows them in the biblical sense of the word, i.e., he takes an interest in them, delights in them, takes pleasure in their welfare and happiness, as no other conceivable lover would or could do for the beloved.

At this point, we can and must denounce the sophistry of the *potentia absoluta* which nominalist Scholasticism deemed it necessary to ascribe to God so that he might actually be the sovereign described in the Bible, as though he could fulfill this representation only by holding for naught everything other than himself. Behind this idea—or rather this pseudo-idea, for it truly lacks substance—is our own inability to conceive of the infinite. As a consequence, in order that what we conceive of as extremely large (larger than anything imaginable) may in fact seem indescribably vast, there is in us a tendency, a temptation, to reduce or even essentially to annihilate everything else. But only a limited magnitude could be "offended" or "feel belittled" (to speak anthropomorphically) by the existence next to it of another equally real magnitude. For however small the latter may be in comparison, it can but emphasize that the former does not encompass everything and is not absolute.

The real infinite, on the other hand, is in no way diminished by such a comparison, simply because it is completely unaffected by the existence next to it (so to speak) of the finite. Moreover, and this is the basic significance of what we call creation, the greater the number of finite entities produced by the infinite—which alone can bring them into being, with no assignable limit to what it can thus call forth—the more these finite entities, by their very existence, which can derive only from the infinite, will attest that the latter is in fact infinite.[18]

In the same sense, however, it can be said that any relationship between the creator and the creature is real only in and for the latter.[19] This does not in any way mean that God is unconcerned in the relationship, but that he enters into it in no way as effect but entirely as cause. In other words, it is

indeed God—and even in the last analysis only he—who produces something in his creature, since he has gone so far as to produce the creature
itself. The creature, on the other hand, cannot produce anything in God,
since everything that can be is already there, from all eternity.

This does not mean that God does not know or love his creatures, that he
does not feel for them in their afflictions nor share in their joys. Precisely
the opposite is true. God the Father knows and loves us, delights in us, only
by knowing and loving his Son, in whom he is eternally well pleased. But
the converse is that by knowing and loving his only-begotten Son, the
source of all his joy, he has eternally known and loved us, and has included
us in this joy.

It is vain to object that one cannot love beings who are the victims of
suffering unless one can suffer with them and as they do. For God, including our freedom and all its effects in his will to impart existence to us,
initially consented to the sufferings this would bring down on us only with
a view to the "eternal weight of glory" which these very sufferings would
bear as fruit, as St. Paul expressed it.[20] Above all, however, God accepted
the prospect of our sufferings only in the context of his plan to join us in
historical time, through the incarnation of the Son inseparable from himself, and to make our sufferings his own, to bear them with and in us. He
would even bear them in our place, in the sense that he would make them
contribute—as only he could do, by making them, as it were, fully and
exclusively his—to the final and total good of those he loves.[21] And it is
because he loves them to this extent that he thus infuses into them, as into
the Son, a love answering his, a love rejoicing at and in his own joy.

Preexistence in God of His Creation

This amounts to saying that in eternally begetting his Son, the Father
was already conceiving us all in him. Better still, in begetting him, in
projecting himself fully in his Son as the Name in which he gives and reveals
himself, he made him by the same token the Word which expresses us all
with him, in him, and which expresses us as destined to be adopted in him,
united to him and in him, in order to be in return adopted and united in his
Father and our Father, as the Son is in the Father.

Once again, by begetting his Son and Word, the Father produced him
with the intention that he would become incarnate in our flesh, in our
sinful humanity, so as to bring it back to its origin and its original purpose,
and thus to complete our interrupted adoption, which is literal and not
figurative.

But since the Father begets the Son only by producing in him the Spirit of
filiation—the substantial Gift through which the Son perfects his resem-

blance to the Father by loving him, as well as everything the Father may ever love, with the same devotion lavished on him—the Father also produces this Spirit with the intention that it be imparted to us. We thereby receive the gift of being not only known and loved by the Father in the Son, as the Son is by the Father, but also of knowing the Father and loving him in return, through the Son in the Spirit, as the Son alone knows and loves him. This is why the Spirit, the Love both beloved and loving, loving because beloved, linking all things to the love which is itself, will associate us all in the Son with the trinitarian life, a life which eternally descends from the Father in the Son and returns to the Father with him, in him, through the Spirit.

Neither is this all. These various future occurrences have meaning only in relation to us, to our temporal existence. Since it is in eternity that God creates us, sends us the Son and the Spirit, decides our adoption in the Son, as well as his redeeming incarnation and the universal fulfillment in the gift of the Spirit, it is also in eternity that he knows and loves us and, thus knowing and loving us, that he changes us into everything we are called upon to become in time.[22]

If therefore God is immutable, and strictly speaking can receive nothing from any of his creatures, it is quite simply because he is what he is and lives his own life only by knowing (with the closest and most understanding knowledge) and loving with his all-participating love, everything he will ever create for evermore.

For God himself, what difference is there then between the life he begets in his Son and animates in his Spirit, and the life he creates in us to adopt us in him? The difference is simply that the former directly expresses the necessity inherent in his essence (which is to love), while the latter reflects foremost its sovereign freedom. And it is only from our viewpoint that this distinction involves an apparent opposition. Just as the necessity of the eternal unfolding of his love is in no way a constraint, the freedom of its communication to us is absolutely not fortuitous or accidental. All that we can say, without being able to conceptualize our insight in the slightest, is that in God freedom is but the obverse of the deepest necessity in his being, just as necessity is but the infinity of his sovereign freedom.

It is obvious that we are here at the heart of the mystery of God, that eternal and unfathomable mystery which only the cross of Christ can express in a way that is not totally inadequate, in our world defined by space and time. In the light of the cross, we may catch a glimpse of what St. Maximus the Confessor meant when he asserted that the Lamb sacrificed even before the creation of the world was the principle of that entire creation.[23]

This leads to a consequence which is itself profoundly mysterious though absolutely concrete, for it has a fundamental bearing on the Christian vision we should have of the world: as we have already noted, the eternal generation of the Son, considered as the Word in whom God expresses to himself everything he is, involves two distinct though inseparable facets.

From a first viewpoint, this Word of God, or its "content," is the Name of God, since it is the Father himself who, as Father, expresses himself in the Son. But from a second viewpoint, the same Word of God, from all eternity, contains everything he will ever call into being through the Son, in the Spirit, and above all this being who is quintessentially made in the image of God, i.e., the human being, including an innate vocation to a living likeness of his model, in the incarnate Son, by the Holy Spirit. The designation of Wisdom fits this second aspect of the divine Word expressed from all eternity in the Son before echoing in history, which the Word was to bring to its highest point.

Wisdom in the Word

For Wisdom, when its revelation in Scripture was complete, appeared as God's eschatological plan for his work: the perfect model of creation (as it already existed before the beginning of time in the eternal divine mind) and the architect of its accomplishment, since this plan is to be fulfilled in history through a free effort of construction in which we, the creatures, are called upon to play an essential role, in a joint endeavor with God himself. Daughter of the Father in the Son, divine Wisdom in its predestination will therefore be at the same time, under the incubation of the Holy Spirit, the Mother of his redeeming incarnation, and thus of redemption fulfilled and bearing fruit in the universal adoption of a new mankind, as the new Eve in the second Adam. And finally, Wisdom was to be that very Eve in the recovered purity of her virginal nuptials with the eternal Son, at the end of history.

The one divine and eternal Wisdom is thus oriented toward a succession of historical developments, from the Virgin Mary as Mother of the incarnate Son of God down to the eschatological Church, his predestined Bride, descending at the end of time from the side of God to be joined to the Son in the nuptials of the Lamb, which are both at the end of all things and their end, the long-awaited fruit of the eternal immolation of the Lamb, the principle of creation.

Wisdom in the meantime appears in the body of Christ stirring in the depths of mankind and of all creation, pending his conception in the Virgin by the Spirit. Then, through the ascent to the cross and crucifixion, this body, glorified in the Savior's resurrection—or more precisely in the saturation of his humanity (received from us) through the superanimating presence of the Holy Spirit after he descended upon the apostles—gathers all flesh into itself.

In the total humanity of the Second and Last Adam who will reach his own fullness (so as to be all in all) in his countless members on the last day, this body will assume the entire physical creation, "Christified" in the Christ of the Parousia, glorified in the Spirit through whom God will finally be all in all, just as through the Son we are eternally all in him and nothing exists except in him.

Gradually forming the body of the total Christ from the entire substance of the Universe, Wisdom thereby builds herself up, throughout history, into the Temple of the Spirit.

Turning back to the principle of this sublime process, to that which alone could bring it about and account for it, Wisdom is, in God and from all eternity, first and foremost everything which will ever exist outside him, and is destined to revert fully to God, not to be reabsorbed and lost in him, but to live in him with only one life, the divine life itself.

Divine Essence, Wisdom, and Glory

There can however be in God nothing which is not his essence and eternal existence, an essence and existence that can be considered the very nature of the Father, who transmits it consubstantially to the Son and to the Spirit. And the Spirit *is* this transmission.

In God himself, Wisdom may therefore be identified with this essence. But it represents this essence from a doubly mysterious viewpoint, whereby God's eternal existence is extended, or rather transposed, in the temporal existence of the world, which is itself obviously incapable of adding anything whatsoever to God's own essence, but is destined to return to God in the ultimate Man, in the perfect Humanity of God's Son made man; and the world will revert to God not to melt away, but to blossom forth by participating in the eternal plenitude of divine being as such.

The divine essence therefore appears in the Son and Word as divine Wisdom, inasmuch as this essence, eternally begotten with the Son, will bring him forth in time and will build up his individual, eucharistic and mystical body, so as to be revealed at the end of history as his eternal Bride.

But since the Spirit, proceeding eternally from the Father in the Son, rests on Wisdom, and through this overshadowing projects onto it the divine maternity, multiplied into a maternity of grace, and moreover is finally to bring about the nuptials of the Lamb as the perfect conjunction and identification of the Word with Wisdom, the latter will be revealed at the end of time, through the Spirit, as the eternal Glory of the Father in the Son.

Wisdom is therefore the glory which was the Son's at the side of the Father before the creation of the world, a glory the Father bestows on him through his crucifixion in historical time, a glory which the glorified Son will then impart to the faithful when he gives them the Spirit, the Spirit of filiation, the Spirit of the Father and of the Son. Or rather, Wisdom tends through its whole being, in God as in ourselves, toward that divine glory which God gives to no other, but which is nevertheless destined to clothe all things, since all things, as we have said before, derive from the Father through the Son only to return to him in the Spirit.

Thus, may we say, as Wisdom is eternally begotten in the Son, in the eternal Word, as in the latter God utters the divine Name and calls forth all things, inasmuch as they proceed with the Son from the Father, source of all paternity in heaven and on earth, therefore this Wisdom returns to him through the history of creation, of the Fall, and of salvation, as a universal Eucharist where all things come together in glory, fully responding to the Word from which they proceed, through the Spirit that recapitulates the Son himself in the Father, and with the Son, in the Son, everything which is and ever will be.[24]

Of course, in this divine essence encompassing every possible essence, in this divine existence calling forth in the Son and gathering back into itself through the Spirit the specific existence of all things, these remain in an infrangible unity. But just as this unity of the divine essence does not negate the Trinity of the Father, Son, and Holy Spirit—the distinction between unity and Trinity being purely notional, though the three divine Persons are really differentiated—it does not negate the distinction between creatures, neither in God nor in themselves. On the contrary, since all things exist in God's pure thought and more really and in a more perfect manner than they do in themselves,[25] it is in God and in him only that the distinction which makes for the irreplaceable perfection of each thing is itself perfect. This distinction will be perfect in us only when we cleave perfectly to God in blessed eternity, i.e., when we coincide, each and every one of us, in our temporal existence once it has succeeded in rejoining its eternal model, with that prototype. Indeed—as St. Thomas demonstrates in a page of *De veritate* which is one of the high points of his work—if what we think of any being is true only to the extent that this thought of ours coincides with the being as it is in itself, conversely, no being is itself, its true and authentic self, except to the extent that it coincides with God's eternal thought concerning it.[26]

Wisdom and the Divine Energies

Divine Wisdom, such as it exists eternally in God, is therefore in the final analysis nothing but the uncreated whole, the fundamental and primal unity of those divine energies which unfold successively, through the gift of the Spirit, in the course of creation and its history, and which by the same token become distinct from God's immutable essence, but distinct only in a notional sense.[27] Their activation and proliferation have but a single purpose, however, which is to gather all things together in the same Son, in whom everything was created, so as to bring about a universal recapitulation in him, with him, in the Father, through the Holy Spirit. The divine energies will therefore return to a blessed state of rest, as to the great Sabbath in which God the creator intends to introduce all his creatures, along with the Son, into the unity of his essence, in the ultimate glory of that freedom of the children of God, which is no other than the glory the Father himself gives his Son in begetting him and in having his Spirit rest on him.

Since the world and what it includes are intrinsically limited, their essence is necessarily material in the world's temporal existence. This essence and existence are both forever distinct from God's existence, which is eternally one with his unlimited essence. But since both proceed from the latter, they can but strive toward it, for they can subsist only in a state of dependence on the divine existence. So it is that God created everything in his Wisdom, for his glory, and that the world can add nothing, through either its essence or its existence, to God's conjoined existence and essence; the world can only express freely, in a temporal framework but for eternity, the necessary existence of God's eternal essence.

Chapter XIX: Intelligible World and Physical World: The Angels

Personality and Personal Relations

Since God is the quintessential personal being, the only world he could conceivably create is a world of persons. And through the gift of his grace he makes it possible for them not only to imitate the Trinity in their interpersonal relationships, but also to participate in the intercommunication between the three divine Persons. So it is that in God we find the Father's fundamental relation with the Son, mysteriously fulfilled in the procession of the Spirit, as proceeding from the Father in the Son and returning toward the Father with the Son.[1] But these divine and uncreated relationships include and involve—in the essential Wisdom begotten by the Father in the Son, in whom this Wisdom is suffused with the glory of the Spirit—the fundamental created relationships of the Mother with the Son and of the Son with his Bride.[2]

In this sense, one may say that femininity, in its dual aspect (both maternal and spousal), expresses the activity and existence characteristic of the creature, in the relationship of grace between creator and creature.[3] In the same way masculinity expresses the activity deriving from the very being of the uncreated, considered in the same relationship with the created. This in turn shows how filiation, though having its eternal model in God, is open to direct participation by the creature. However, the ineffable procession of the Spirit projects, in maternity and sponsality, what might be termed an inverted image.[4] In this context, it is appropriate to apply Anton Günther's principle of the contraposition of the world in relation to God, the concept of the created reflecting the uncreated, i.e., the infinite, in the mirror of its finitude.[5]

Wisdom, in God, is not itself personal. It subsists, in the persons of the Father, the Son and the Spirit—as Essence, Wisdom and Glory—only in relation to the creature, onto which it is projected as a dual (maternal and spousal) personality. From the first viewpoint, it encompasses and produces countless individual personalities, which will all be summed up and gathered together in the eternal person of the Word and Son, once he has been brought forth by Wisdom.[6]

From the second viewpoint, Wisdom is to join all these individual personalities to the Son at the end of time.[7] We are thus all called upon in divine Wisdom, and all creation with and in us, to receive the divine filiation through the universal communication of the Spirit of the Father. Overshadowed by the Holy Spirit, Mary becomes in history the perfect expression of eternal Wisdom as Mother of the incarnate Son and Mother of the divine filiation extending through him to every creature. On the cross mankind, dismembered by sin, but made one again by Christ as his members in his body sacrificed so that the world may be reconciled with the Father, is reborn from his pierced heart as the Church of the predestined whose names are written in heaven.[8] At the time of the Parousia, when mankind has reached the maturity of Christ in all its members, it will be presented to the Son as an immaculate virgin, to be brought to perfection in a freely accepted union with him.[9] The entire creation will then express the perfect fulfillment in history of eternal Wisdom as the Bride of the eternal Son, and she shall be clothed in glory.[10]

This will be the ultimate revelation, in God's totally manifest Wisdom, of the Spirit as glorifier: glorifying the Father in the Son by imparting to all of us all the Son's glory, which he possessed before the world was, with the Father.[11] This glory will thus belong to all the children of God, assembled and perfected.[12] God will henceforth be all in all, through the historical fulfillment of Wisdom, just as everything was in him eternally through the Wisdom hidden in him from all eternity, the "Wisdom in mystery," as St. Paul called it.

In this will consist the completion of the created world in the creation of mankind, and the completion of mankind in the total epiphany, at the time of the Parousia, of the Son of God made man.

From the Human World to the Angelic World

The human world itself, however, must be recognized as proceeding from an earlier world and, in a sense, as intended to replace it. This primal world is obviously the physical world in and from which man appeared. But according to all Scripture and tradition, the physical world, i.e., nature, is much more than a mere material universe. In fact, its material aspect is but the envelope, the external clothing of a wholly spiritual world, without which the existence of matter becomes incomprehensible, for the essence of the cosmos then falls back into nothingness.

This primeval world, recognized in all its dimensions, is what the Greek Fathers and St. Augustine still called the intelligible world, following the Platonic terminology.[13] From their description and interpretation of it, however, it is clear that what they have in mind is the angelic world, whose invisible presence the Bible assumes as the background of all visible reality.

Whatever use these Fathers may have made of all the terms coined by Plato to deal with the mysterious reality of the invisible world, which holds sway over the visible one and is known to us through it, the intelligible world (as they continued to designate it) was for them actually quite different from what it meant to the ancient Greeks.

This distinction probably emerges most clearly from the writings on the created universe by St. Gregory of Nyssa, though among all the Fathers he was unquestionably the one who understood Plato best.[14] The difference is a simple one: for Plato, the invisible world was one of ideas, whereas the invisible world Christians believe in is one of persons. With the eyes of faith, Christians see these created persons forming a great luminous cloud,[15] a kind of halo, around the figure of the creator himself, before whom the Seraphim, standing in his immediate presence, must cover their faces. They are truly personal, truly in the image of the creator, because they are free, just as he himself is free.[16]

As pointed out by Maximus the Confessor, among others, the difference between Plato's immutable ideas and these created persons is that the latter are God's eternal thoughts, forming the essentially one yet infinitely varied complex of his eternal Wisdom. Moreover they are all included in the Son, the living Word through whom God expresses himself. They are therefore living thoughts, for everything in the Word is life.[17] The Spirit of filiation which rests on the Son forever descends on each of these thoughts. And so that they might all recognize, as the Son does, the enveloping love of the Father, he endowed each of them with its own specific freedom.

The exact number of these individual thoughts, these countless *logoi*, is known and determined only by God; for he knows each and every one of them as though it were the only one, within the single, eternal and only-begotten *Logos*. They made themselves unconditionally available to the divine call from the moment of their joint awakening to a distinct existence under the influence of the Spirit. All together, but each on its own behalf, they awaken to this distinct though unanimous existence, in adoration and praise of their creator.[18]

From the first moment of its existence, the created universe is forever a single chorus praising God, freely answering the eternal Word, who is the expression of the Father himself. It is given in a joyous assent of love returning to its source, love extending to all things and drawing them along with it, love which belongs to the Spirit of the Father, who is the Spirit of filiation resting on the Son from the eternal instant when he was brought forth from the bosom of the Father.[19]

These created but blissful spirits are in the only-begotten Son like countless sons of God, the *benê Elōhim* of the Bible, the sons of dawn who sang together, according to Job,[20] on the first morning of the universe. And this universe itself, as we know it from the outside, in its corporeal visibility, resonates with their singing, their *melos amoris*, set afire by the divine Spirit's *ignis amoris*.[21]

From the very start, however, as we shall soon see,[22] a fault or split occurred in this visible creation where we live. It was caused by the original failure of some of the created luminaries meant to shine upon our universe, and foremost among them the prince of this world, Lucifer, the bearer of light.

This does not, however, modify the fundamental state of everything created. It is to be the chorus of the first-born sons of God united in the only-begotten, radiating the glory of the creator recognized as Father, perfectly responding to his love, totally given in the Holy Spirit.

Intelligible World, Order, and Materiality

We have already pointed out that Origen, in reacting against Greek fatalism, had somewhat overstated his description of the universe of individual freedoms deriving from the eminently loving freedom of the Father, the creator of all things. In Origen's view, all the created spirits were necessarily similar and equal, at the time of their creation. It was their fall, or rather the various degrees of their unfaithfulness, which freely diversified the world as we know it, producing a gradation of creatures, from the highest angels of light down to the last spirits of darkness, with men an intermediate category.

St. Gregory of Nyssa, though influenced by Origen in several respects, perceived and asserted that this view was not in harmony with biblical tradition. From the first page of Genesis, it is clear that the creator intends the diversity and inequality of creatures. Diversity is actually fundamental to the harmony through which the created world is meant to reflect the glory of the uncreated.

Though not asserting with Origen that matter is the result of the fall in creatures which are, in the image of their creator, essentially spiritual, St. Gregory yet maintained that matter was associated with the spirituality of human souls only in anticipation of their fall. It, as it were, prevents man's fall from being as total and final as the angels', by slowing it down and thus allowing the possibility of penance and rehabilitation.[23]

On the whole, tradition did not follow St. Gregory on this point. Always seeking faithfulness to revelation, tradition developed the position held by the great Scholastic masters of the thirteenth century: matter is an essential and original part of creation, in addition to spirit. St. Thomas was to assert[24] that when the final resurrection occurs, the human body will not be absorbed and disappear in the spirit, but will be spiritualized, as will the entire tangible universe, being transfigured even in its materiality by the radiance of God's glory.

Other Scholastic masters, such as St. Bonaventure, went further and said that even in incorporeal beings such as angels, the created spirit cannot be completely immaterial, either now or in the blissful eternity which it is called upon to enter.[25] It seems that the difference on this point is due simply to two conceptions of matter.[26] Even though St. Thomas does not acknowledge the materiality of angels, nor even their mere corporeity, he does see them in a close relationship with the material element in the universe.[27]

Though the temptation of an immaterialistic angelism was even greater than in the West, the development of the Eastern tradition was to lead independently to the same certainty, and this at the time of the successive controversies surrounding Evagrian Origenism, then iconoclasm,[28] or perhaps even because of these. In the tradition of the iconophiles, and later in Hesychasm, the view that human bodies, and more generally the physical universe, were to be entirely redeemed and imbued with the divine glory became even more explicit, and therefore more biblical, than in Western spirituality and theology.[29]

Taboric Light and the Creatures' Canticle

This theme of the ultimate glorification of all creation, in the inseparable union of the created spirit and the physical cosmos, would be developed in both the East and the West, in a real theology of light and an outline at least of what might be called a theology of music.

The theology of light became explicit in the East, paradoxically enough, mainly in the writings of Dionysius and pseudo-Areopagite—who was to ascribe such importance to the mystical theme of the divine darkness—although it was first and most eloquently expressed in the homilies of St. Macarius.[30] In the West, it owes much to St. Augustine,[31] but was fully developed by St. Bonaventure.[32]

The two currents had already merged in the thinking of John Scotus Eriugena.[33] One of the earliest results of this is found during the twelfth century in the theology of physical beauty as an expression of God's glory. It is a theology characteristic of Suger,[34] the famous abbot of St. Denis, but it merely formalizes the inspiration of all Romanesque art, and particularly that of Cluny. Initially Cistercian art, with its concern for asceticism, barrenness and poverty, seems to contrast with this approach. But in fact it simply evolved an unadorned, clearer, and even more distinctive version of the earlier architectural style.

It may be maintained that Cîteaux, with the musicality so typical of St. Bernard's prose, introduced pure music as another channel exceeding the capacities of the sung word, for the material translation of the glory of God in this world.[35] This too had been prepared by St. Augustine in his comments on the Jubilus of alleluias.³⁶ It was echoed in both early Gregorian and Byzantine chant,³⁷ even before pseudo-Boethius and his successors attempted to evolve a theory of it.³⁸

It is noteworthy that the iconoclastic tendencies of Protestantism did not prevent—and indeed seem to have encouraged (just as with the Cistercians) —this religious exaltation of music.³⁹ It is indeed in the polyphony of Goudimel⁴⁰ in France, and of Byrd and Purcell⁴¹ and later of Handel⁴² in England, that the so-called Reformed Christians, whether Calvinist or not, were to pursue this trend. During the nineteenth century, Joseph-Henry Shorthouse, a Quaker convert to Anglicanism, said in one of the most inspired pages of his spiritual novel entitled *John Inglesant* that melodies were like the bodies of angels.⁴³

In Lutheranism—whose piety, particularly at the beginning of the seventeenth century, remained so Catholic in inspiration, in spite of its strengthened personalism—the musical glorification of the creator produced its most extraordinary flowering in the works of Johann Sebastian Bach, and perhaps even more so in his organ music than in his choral compositions.⁴⁴

The theology of invisible light coming from the transfiguration of the Savior and glorifying even the face of the visible world was to reach its ultimate development in the East, at the end of the Byzantine Middle Ages, with the apologia of the Hesychast saints by St. Gregory Palamas. His theology of Taboric light systematized the elements that had already been suggested by St. Symeon the New Theologian.⁴⁵ And the same Symeon, in his *Hymns of Love*, had linked this to the glorification of God in his creatures (closely resembling in this the Englishman Richard Rolle).⁴⁶

Created Hierarchies and Uncreated Thearchy

In order to define more accurately the positive significance ascribed to diversity, and particularly to that of the various levels of being, St. Thomas had shown that in a world limited by its very nature, this diversity is essential for that world to express in its way the glory of the God who, in himself, transcends both unity as we know it, and multiplicity.⁴⁷ But once again it is pseudo-Dionysius who deserves the credit for being, if not the first to reach that insight, then the first to justify its importance. This is the basic thrust of his generally misunderstood concept of a cosmic hierarchy, which he developed in two closely related treatises, *The Celestial Hierarchy* and *The Ecclesiastical Hierarchy*.⁴⁸

Pseudo-Dionysius undeniably borrowed many details of the neo-Platonic view of the chain of beings connected by degrees, from the transcendent One to sheer nothingness, which is indistinguishable from what could be called pure matter. There is however a total opposition between his "hierarchies" and the neo-Platonic "series." The latter are the layers of a strictly compartmentalized universe, and cannot be transgressed without bringing about the abolition of all differences and of any distinct existence, by a return to the One which amounts to a reabsorption and disappearance of everything individual in this world.

It is fundamental that the various degrees of the hierarchy, or rather of the Dionysian hierarchies, are simply so many relays for communicating what the higher beings can keep for themselves only by sharing freely with others (as pseudo-Dionysius explicitly asserts). And though these others can receive the gift from above only in proportion to their capacity, it is still the gift of God, i.e., not only something he gives, but in the final analysis his very self. This is what Endre von Ivanka, among others, has clearly established, in contrast to many superficial commentators.[49] And the insight follows logically from the central Dionysian assertion that, through creation, the created hierarchies are but the communication and extension of the uncreated thearchy, i.e., of the eternal exchanges between the divine persons.[50]

This is not to say that one should take literally the elaborate description which pseudo-Dionysius developed of the various incorporeal spirits, divided into nine angelic choirs. We can be sure that in his own mind it was but an attempt to express the discontinuous continuity linking even the lowest of the first created spirits to the uncreated itself, a continuity which subsequently was to extend through the ecclesiastical hierarchy to the world of bodies. Though deeply influenced by many traits of contemporary Christian and non-Christian thinking, the Dionysian vision ultimately draws its cogency from the cosmology of the Fathers[51] and from the biblical outlook which inspired it.

Cosmic Liturgy

The first and most important characteristic shared by their thinking, and which they owe directly to the tradition of the Hebrew prophets and apocalyptic seers, is that the whole world is essentially liturgical.[52] The entire cosmos, in this Jewish and Christian perspective, appears first of all—in the very plan of eternal Wisdom working toward its fulfillment through all cosmic history—as a celebration of uncreated glory through the whole time of creation. The cosmos, seen as basically angelic, exists only for the glory of the creator, who is first the invisible Father of his only-begotten Son in whom everything was created in order to be immediately vivified in the Spirit who is the Spirit of light and life, precisely because he is the Spirit of the Father and of sonship. From this viewpoint, the very beauty of the world—not only the static beauty of its unchanging forms, but also the living beauty of its development and fruitfulness—appears as an ultimate radiance extending to the edge of nothingness, a reflection on its surface—through the angelic world, the intelligible cosmos—of the very glory of the Trinity's *agape*.[53]

It is important to emphasize that this vision systematized by pseudo-Dionysius—far from being the result of a wholly Hellenic intellectual contemplation, or even the end-product of an Iranian gnosis through the apocalyptic tradition—originates in the earliest prophetic and Mosaic (or even pre-Mosaic) tradition. It derives directly from the vision of the Seraphim surrounding God's throne, in chapter 6 of Isaiah, and from that of the Cherubim and *Ophanim* in Ezechiel who became the coursers and fiery wheels of the throne, tracing a flaming furrow throughout the world. But both these books reflected in their visions a much earlier tradition, according to which Moses himself built the tabernacle and organized the rites of worship in conformity with his vision of the celestial sanctuary on Sinai.[54] And this in turn seems to have been anticipated in the vision of Jacob's ladder, with the angels descending and ascending by it, from the earthly sanctuary which was to be Bethel, to the heavenly house of God.[55]

After the extraordinary proliferation, in the Jewish apocalyptic writings, of cosmologies revealed through dreams,[56] the picture cleared and was unified in the vision vouchsafed St. John while he was in Patmos.[57] Proceeding from the throne, upon which sat the Indescribable One, there was a rainbow, "in sight like an emerald," illuminating all things, and round about the throne were four living creatures (who seem to match the elementary spirits of the cosmos referred to in St. Paul's epistles to the Galatians and Ephesians)[58] and four and twenty ancients upon as many seats—probably the guardian angels of nations—singing their canticle day and night, each striking his cithara with a plectrum—and these musical instruments must represent everything that lives and moves in the world. The ancients also "fell down on their faces" and "cast their crowns before the throne" of the Father of light, himself invisible, then presented him with "golden vials full of odors, which are the prayers of saints."

"And in the sight of the throne was, as it were, a sea of glass like to crystal," resembling the translucent vault of heaven that both separates and joins the visible world and that which lies above.[59] "And there were seven lamps burning before the throne, which are the seven spirits of God," the angels of the Presence, as lamps of the Spirit in whom the adoration and love of all creation rise toward him from whom all derives.

Then, before the throne, among the ancients, in the midst of the candlesticks, holding in his hand the seven stars which are the angels of the seven mother churches, there appeared the One who was dead and who now lives forever, the Lamb sacrificed even before the creation of the world, who is both the beginning and the end of all things created, the alpha and the omega.[60] The ancients fell down on their faces before him and before the One sitting on the throne, and glorified them together.

With him, in the glory radiating from the invisible Father, and as the perpetual flames from the seven lamps on their seven candlesticks glorified him, all the witnesses, the martyrs of the Lamb who follow him wherever he goes, rose up in turn.[61] This cosmic contemplation, interpreting the deeper significance of the ultimate revelation, is reflected on the facade of many Romanesque churches of the West, from Moissac to Chartres, including Vézelay, Autun, and many others.[62] From the basilicas of Ravenna, it has spread to the churches of the Byzantine East,[63] in which the iconography regulated by St. Theodore the Studite[64] attempted to make visible this ecclesiastical history (i.e., this description of the invisible Church made present to the visible Church through the eucharistic celebration) such as it had been set in a treatise by St. Germanos of Constantinople, with gradual enrichment, along the developments of Byzantine liturgy.[65]

Indeed, cosmic contemplation condenses the entire traditional theology of the Church celebrating the eucharist as mankind's sharing in cosmic and supra-cosmic liturgy. Through sacramental participation in the Savior's glorifying cross, mankind thus joins the faithful angels, themselves forever celebrating, from the first moment of creation, the Ancient of days.[66] Whether at Cluny or Cîteaux, St. John of Stoudios or the Trinity-Saint Sergius in Zagorsk, this apocalyptic vision was to become the inspiration of cenobitic monasticism, leaving the city of Babylon, where the entire cosmos was increasingly viewed as anthropocentric and magically allied to a civilization that was not only Promethean but diabolical.[67] And wherever this monasticism took root, it was to become in effect the nucleus of a new city, the city of God among men, a culture ploughed by asceticism and sowed with mysticism, the only means capable of restoring the cosmos to its primitive nature as a sacred sign, by returning it to its eschatological destiny as an instrument of divine praise and saving charity.[68]

The occasionally over-subtle speculations which Dionysian developments of the vision were to inspire in the Latin Middle Ages may seem just as "Byzantine" as the discussions on the sex of angels, to which the Eastern Roman Empire reputedly devoted much attention, at the very time when conquering Islam was already at the gates of the New Rome. The Thomist and Franciscan schools endlessly compared the relative merits of the Seraphim, absorbed in the love of God, and the Cherubim, rapt in his contemplation.[69]

Later schools of religious thought would appear, and end a debate deemed pointless and interminable, by shifting the priority from contemplation to action, before eventually sinking into vain activism. Yet one should recognize, with Soloviev, that the only possible salvation for the world is by a renewal of the spirit in which the Church is called upon to give witness and which requires that the Church be rededicated to the cosmic vision of early Christianity, deriving from the very wellspring of revelation.[70]

Newman and Angelological Cosmology

In two of his most unforgettable *Parochial and Plain Sermons*, Newman has brought out, in terms perfectly accessible to modern minds, the basic principles and permanent implications of this cosmic vision. The two sermons in question are "The Powers of Nature," in the second volume, and the more comprehensive "The Invisible World," in the fourth volume. Henri Brémond himself, though very much a modernist, particularly at the time when he wrote his essay on Newman, considered the second of these not only one of Newman's most impressive works, but also one of the most inspired Christian sermons of all time.[71]

In "The Powers of Nature," Newman notes that the scientific and technical view of the universe, which has become our usual frame of reference, has made us virtually forget the existence of angels and their active presence in this world. Yet consideration of the angelic world as a fundamental reality in the cosmos—whose mere surface is touched by scientific studies, fascinating and obviously valid on their own level, and which technology looks at only from a narrow utilitarian viewpoint—remains essential to any religious approach to the universe and the life we are called upon to live in it.[72]

If nothing else, the beauty of this world—if we were still capable of gazing upon it with new eyes—should be enough to make us recognize the dynamic presence of the angels, just as we acknowledge in the world, through various elementary signs, the presence of the embryonic consciousness of animals, as well as the consciousness of other human beings.

Scripture itself teaches us to discern this angelic activity as the background of the visible cosmos, whose deeper meaning it gives us: all things created are in the service of God.[73] Realization of this significance allows us to see in the visible world a first and fundamental revelation of God.[74] This revelation carries the certainty that we are not the only spirits in this world, and that we are not and cannot become the masters of this world, as our wayward and frenzied technology would have us believe.[75]

How startled we would be if these angelic presences, hidden but hinted at by all the realities most familiar to us, suddenly became visible![76] There is nothing utopian about the possibility: according to biblical tradition, this is how divine revelation started. Before the prophets, the patriarchs of Israel were forced to recognize that all things acquire meaning only if they contribute to the glorification of God, as indeed they do in the hands of the angelic powers,[77] whose helpmates we are called upon to be.[78]

The second of Newman's sermons, "The Invisible World,"[79] begins by picturing this visible world, one we are so accustomed to that we readily assume there is no other reality beside it.[80] Yet our experience, if only we were to ponder it as we should, would be enough to convince us that many things, and possibly the most important, in what we call the visible world are in fact invisible, e.g., the feelings in our heart and the working of our mind.[81]

All the more so, the world known to us only through faith is more important than the world accessible to our senses.[82] For it is in this invisible world, or rather in the invisible part of the one world, where God dwells and Christ entered, where the souls of the faithful will join him, and where the angels reside from all time.[83]

At this point Newman introduces, with consummate art, an episode drawn from the earliest sources of biblical tradition, one we have already referred to: Jacob's vision, in Bethel, of the angelic ladder rising from the earth to heaven. He stresses[84] Jacob's exclamation: "How terrible is this place! This is no other but the house of God, and the gate of heaven... *and I knew it not!*" In other words, the invisible did not suddenly invade (as it were) the visible; it was always there from the beginning, and still is, "behind" the visible, long before we become aware of it, and even if we were to persist in ignoring it.

Once again, is this not something that simply continues and extends our everyday experience? In the midst of our human world, do we not see the unquestionable and highly mysterious presence of the animal world, whose depths are at least as impenetrable to us as the angelic world? And this world we call our own is made up of many different worlds. We can live in each of them as though the others did not exist: the political world, the scientific world, the world of scholars, of poets, of religious men.[85] So it is with the world of the spirits, which cannot but appear as the most important of all when we consider it seriously.[86] And one day soon that world, in which the angels habitually abide, in the very presence of God, along with the saints, will be revealed to us as it once appeared to Jacob, as the truest of all, the only one which is to last forever.[87]

Let us but think of our repeated experience of springtime. During winter, how could we possibly believe, or even imagine, unless we had previously experienced it, that the world could once again become what it does every springtime?[88] Christians can but live in the expectation of the eternal springtime which is to come.[89] Only then shall we discover the world as it is in its deepest reality, as it will last forever. It is the world as the angels have always known it, and as God's elect who have reached perfection are beginning to discover it...and as we are all called upon to do in our turn.[90]

This is the fundamental vision of the cosmos in Christian faith. But the same Newman who knew how to express its beauty and luminosity so incomparably is also the one who saw its dark face more fearsomely than perhaps any Christian thinker at any time. His essay on "Anthony in the Conflict" makes this obvious.[91] This is the topic we must now approach.

Chapter XX: The Fall and Rehabilitation

The Fall of the Angels and of the Cosmos

In this world which was meant to be, and fundamentally remains, a harmonious and unanimous chorus, a dissonance has crept in. The world shows that the angels, whose song of adoration and praise it expresses, have had to add to their liturgy and their function of glorification a completely different service: they are required to be soldiers of God, the *militia Dei*, whose leader, the *dux bellorum*, is, according to the Bible, the Archangel Michael.[1] For the world is visibly divided, not just in its present structure, but in its entire temporal development. There is a break in its continuity, a cleft or fault splitting it asunder, which hostile forces are trying to widen and protective forces are attempting to mend.

The definition that biologists have given of organic life—the sum total of the forces resisting death—is typical. Actually, the truth requires a more extreme statement: the contradiction is so deep-seated in the universe today that life subsists only at the cost of a mortal struggle. Life feeds on death.

The explanations we are offered simply do not hold water. Some say it is all a matter of one's viewpoint in observing reality.[2] The suffering of animals, an innocent suffering surely, would be an unacceptable scandal in a world made by the God of wisdom and love, if we persist in asserting that the world today is just as God willed it and brought it into being. On this point, Buddhism shows a lucidity which could be envied by many Christians whose convictions have lost their edge. The very concept of an initial and faintly remembered paradise, far from being uniquely biblical, emerges, in one form or another, in all mankind's religious traditions. It testifies to the deep and universal awareness that the world is no longer what it should be, or indeed what it was when the Almighty made it.[3] In words reminiscent of the first pages of the NT, the Gospel asserts that "an enemy has done this," and ascribes the saying to the Creator.[4]

As yet we have made no mention of man's part or responsibility in the deterioration of the world. There are misfortunes—and these are precisely the most problematic—that we simply cannot imagine as due to a failure of ourselves alone. Yet the irremediable perversion of mankind and its universality inevitably suggest that, in this world, evil is the consequence of a captivity or bondage to which man, along with all other creatures, is subjected.

As we have emphasized, none of this can be explained—and biblical teaching is quite clear in this respect—by some form of metaphysical dualism, an omnipresent assumption underlying all myths. Everything which exists, both matter and created spirit, proceeds exclusively from the benevolence of the creator of all things. Even the most debased of creatures—at least those of which we have immediate experience—bear witness to this infinite benevolence by showing evidence of an irreducible core of goodness remaining within them.

The Fall of Man and the Fall of the World

Biblical teaching, from Genesis to the book of Revelation, clearly assumes and unequivocally asserts that man—each individual man, as well as human society as such—bears a share of responsibility for the Fall. But the Bible states no less clearly—though this necessarily carries a mystery much deeper even than that of our fall—that the fall of man is but a part and consequence of another, earlier, and more comprehensive Fall.[5]

How can we possibly understand what happened, at least enough so as to properly appreciate the predicament we are in, and from which we must extricate ourselves? Here more than ever, it is essential to remember that the revelation we believe in was not granted to satisfy our curiosity—even on a scientific level. Rather it was needed to lead us to salvation, i.e., to a fully accepted awareness of God's plan for us.[6]

Yet it is surprising to see how many priests and professed theologians today assert that it is necessary, if the Gospel is to be made acceptable to our contemporaries, to get rid of the notion of diabolic intervention, if not the very notion of original sin.[7] This attitude simply shows the extent of clerical ignorance, an ignorance which often makes men of the cloth incapable of fulfilling their ministry. In contrast, it is enough to speak to our contemporaries (particularly the younger ones) whose spontaneous reactions have not yet been deadened by experience, to realize that as they face the weightier questions of life, this is one of the foremost. They often find it difficult to believe in God, because they are convinced that it is in fact the devil, even if they do not call him by this name, who now rules the world.

Among these same men, nevertheless, there is a deep sense—without which they would not be shocked by the present state of affairs—that things could and should be better; that a benevolent God, in spite of everything, must retain control over all that exists. The traditional teaching of the Church appeals precisely to this indistinct though intense and fundamentally sound feeling. In order to be understood, however, this doctrine requires careful consideration, of which many modern theologians no longer seem capable due to their short-sighted humanistic views. Only "men of God" indifferent to their own mission can possibly imagine that, in the eyes of most people, all is well with the world.

Biblical Testimony on the Fall of the Angels

According to the Bible and Tradition, the fall of the angels, beginning with Lucifer, who became Satan[8]—"the accuser of our brethren,"[9] the devil,[10] the gainsayer and corrupter—is closely connected with the Fall of the world and of man. But what is the exact nature of the connection? This is not an easy question to answer.

To start with, it does not seem that a Fall of the world simply followed the angelic fall. The fall of the angels appears intimately linked to the world and implies a bond between the angels and the world through creation, a bond they sought to break. This much at least is evident from Genesis 6, the most enigmatic text in the Bible.[11] The shift is reflected in the contrast between two of Satan's designations in the NT. One of them, "the ruler of this world,"[12] is found in the Gospel according to St. John. The other appears in an extraordinary passage of the Second Epistle to the Corinthians, in which St. Paul calls him "the god of this world," or more literally "of this age"—for we have here the word *aiōn,* instead of *cosmos* as in St. John.[13]

Does this not assume that the quintessential fallen angel, who was the first of creatures with authority over all others, had sought to acquire divine status in their eyes? He has in fact become the god who is worshiped, followed, and served by the world, at least in the present economy of *aiōn houtos.*

The Fall and Spiritual Creation

How did this come about? The first point to elucidate is the original connection between the angels and the cosmos. According to the entire tradition of the Church and its reading of Scripture, the world is a kind of projection of angelic thoughts into objective existence, just as the angels were the manifestation of the thoughts of God the Creator in a free and distinct existence.[14] This requires us to review in greater detail what we have already said of God's Wisdom, as distinct in one respect from his Word and Son, i.e., from the living Word in which the Father expresses himself,[15] though identical with him in another respect.

To recapitulate, since everything in God is necessarily his eternal essence, Wisdom is simply this essence (indwelling as source in the Father) as it is projected into the Son through his eternal generation. The Name of the Father is thus revealed in the Son. At the same time, since the Father's thought and will imply the creation from all eternity, in the Son uncreated

Wisdom comprehends the form of every creature and of all creation as a unified whole, in the complete fulfillment in history of God's creative plan. We are faced here with what may well be for us the most mysterious aspect of the Godhead. We can understand that the finite posits the infinite, for the conditioned is conceivable only in relation to the unconditioned. But since the unconditioned itself is beyond our intelligence, we cannot possibly understand how it contains and produces our limited being. We can but acknowledge the fact, and from the unfathomable admiration this recognition evokes in us we can draw, not an image of the infinite, for that could be only an illusion and an idol, but a sort of presentiment. Even less are we able to grasp how, in projecting his thought and will in his Son, God thinks into being this finite creation. Neither can we comprehend why he brought forth this particular world rather than a different one.

These comments are valid for the whole of the cosmos and for each of the personal beings in it, starting with the incorporeal spirits at the core of its existence. All attempts made to connect the existence of a definite cosmos with the existence of the infinite God are but intellectual exercises—including the most sophisticated, such as Leibnitz's efforts, inspired by integral calculus to posit the infinite in the very structure of the finite.[16] They help us to maintain God's superior rationality which is certainly the obverse of his sovereign freedom. If we take these exercises literally, however, our concept of him can but suffer, while we are forced to recognize that we are not even capable of harmonizing our interpretations with the extraordinary richness of the finite created by God.

These considerations also apply to the Pythagorean speculations centering on the so-called golden numbers, on geometric figures generating one another, on the harmonies of sounds, and to all the intriguing ideas developed along similar lines.[17] The most that can be said for all these cerebral constructs is that at times they seem to approach the reality that commands our admiration, but finally always eludes our speculations. These constructs never actually coincide with reality, any more than a polygon inscribed in a circle, even if the number of its sides is increased indefinitely, can ever quite become identical with that circle. The overwhelming mystery of God and what links the universe to him (without linking him to the universe) is echoed by a mystery inherent in the universe itself. This mystery is principally the enigma of the angelic personalities, each one in particular and all together in their community, as it were, which sustain the sensible existence of this world. From the viewpoint of its structure, the most valid comparison is of the world to a shimmering white light which breaks down into countless colors that remain distinctive only by merging imperceptibly into each other. And from the viewpoint of its development in time, we can liken it to an immense polyphonic choir, which sings in tune and on beat only as long as all its members keep their eyes constantly on the silent choirmaster.[18]

The most suggestive symbolic expression of the infinite in the finite is that of Dionysius. It is that of a hierarchy of choirs, each one bringing together in harmony a hierarchy of inseparable individuals grouped together to form an immense concert. Not only does this concert replicate, to the extent that the finite can reproduce the infinite, the divine thearchy of the blessed Trinity itself, it also captures, reflects, and transmits something of the Trinity's own current of life, ceaselessly descending and re-ascending, like a fountain of clear water, multiple yet one.

But these images must always conform to the biblical assertion that God alone knows the precise number of beings that compose the universe in the image he chose to give of himself, and also how each one of these beings is a particular image, reflecting, from a specific viewpoint, all the others both individually and together. God willed all these images together, yet also willed each one singly. It seems that this duality reflects two aspects of reality, both essential to the plan of his eternal Wisdom.[19]

These symbolic representations afford us a glimpse of the way in which the physical universe itself can reflect the intelligible world to which it owes all its content, one thus being the expression of the other. The world of incorporeal spirits is but the total and harmonious combination of the individual thoughts which God, in his Wisdom, chose to include in the one thought wherein he recognizes himself in the person of his Word and Son. Conversely, the physical universe is but a symphony of the thoughts through which the first of the created spirits commune with each other. Their hierarchies are reflected in the harmonious beauty of the forms and the laws which adapt them, and the flow of life which fills and animates these spirits finds an echo in the interplay of melodic changes in which the whole cosmos is involved in a single concert.

This being so, what we call the universe's materiality is but the paradoxically translucent opacity by which the relative exteriority of our human world (in relation to the intelligible world of angels) allows contact with the cosmos. For the angels themselves, however, it is simply the harmony of reciprocal distinctions in which they live, by the grace of their joint creation in the Son and their joint assumption in the Spirit: a mutual transparency, illuminated by the glory of God, which shines forth from both.

Lucifer's Fall

All this is an imperfect representation of the universe created by God and as yet untouched by evil. The prevailing order, an essentially fluid order, involves a reciprocation of all things among all beings within God's communication of himself to all. It assumes a First, a Beginning of this creation, a foundation or cornerstone, which could be only the divine Word, gathering and coordinating around himself, through the Holy Spirit, all those living thoughts issuing from him and called upon to live through the divine life of the Trinity.

Such being the case, one may say that evil entered the world from the time of the first sin, the original lie through which the prince of this world sought to become its God.[20] In accordance with the plan of creation, the world was a concert of unanimous praise rising toward the Creator. Lucifer himself should have been the choirmaster of this concert, but he tried to turn it into a mere reflection of his own beauty. Instead of holding up his own faithfulness as an example for the converging contemplation of the invisible uncreated by all those created beings, he attempted to draw their attention to his own splendor.[21] All the evil in the world derives from the ambition of the prince of this world desiring to become its God, and from his pernicious influence over a number of his followers in the celestial hierarchy. But he succeeded only in becoming the false god, the first phase in a history whose ending was as much outside his control as its start.

Clearly evil may be equated principally with sin, with the creature's rejection of the Creator's call to reciprocate the love bestowed on him. The first sin is pride: the determination of the highest among created beings to add further to his own stature. It is equally clear that pride, both in the tempter himself and in those who are led into temptation, turns into greed and unscrupulous ambition, which enslave and debase whoever lusts for power and position.

The Fall of the Benê Elōhim

This provides a key to the deeper meaning of those strange lines in Genesis 6 concerning the *benê Elōhim*, who allowed themselves to be led astray by the beauty of "the daughters of men." In the first place, the text shows that whoever represents the creator to and in the created takes on a masculine role in respect to the rest of creation; creation as a whole, on the contrary, appears as feminine. Moreover, we see that the mere desire to possess, caused by pride, leads the covetous person into subjection and makes him even more of a slave than those he dominates.

Lucifer, the first liar and the father of lies, failed to realize that every creature is fundamentally incapable of really possessing any other one. God, the creator of them all, possesses them fully only to grant them their freedom and to enable them to give themselves. What the prince of this world forgot to take into account, in his inordinate pride, is that it is generous love, rather than greed, that makes one divine. Furthermore, he overlooked the fact that this world, just like himself, is exclusively the creature of God, so that, even when superficially corrupted by the seductive schemes of the powers, it remains wholly in the hands of God.

Two consequences, apparently unforeseen by Lucifer, followed this *prōton pseudos*, or first lie. In the first place, even after the defection of the first of the powers to whom it had been entrusted, and the subsequent and consequent defections of a whole series of lower powers, the created world still did not represent Lucifer's pride and domination. Instead, the created world henceforth merely expressed the existence of a conflict: the unrelenting struggle between the unfaithfulness of Lucifer and his supporters, and the constant loyalty of the rest of the "choirs," now become angelic armies. Secondly, through God's own fidelity to the purpose of his love, encompassing in his grace the loyalty of the angels who had remained steadfast, Satan's very unfaithfulness was to provide the opportunity for a manifestation of divine love even more extraordinary than the initial creation.

The Battle Between Michael and the Demons

To start with, there is what the Bible describes as the battle fought by Michael. He was the first to cry out, after Lucifer's lie: "Who is like unto God?" The battle is found in Daniel's apocalypse,[22] then in that of St. John,[23] and, as the immediate result of the struggle, Satan "was thrown down to the earth."[24] This would seem to mean that the prince of this world kept authority over all that was originally his, but that his dominion—unlike that belonging to the other and inferior spirits—was henceforth reduced, so that it amounted to a kind of immanence devoid of any transcendence whatsoever. So it is that the enemy was cast to earth, and that death thereby entered into this world.[25] But the unceasing opposition of the faithful spirits, who had become the guardians of this world and everything in it, succeeds in integrating death itself, as it were, into the development of life, which we see constantly surviving worldly death, and even feeding on it. This seems to be where the mysterious link occurs, which man has always dimly sensed, between death, ceaselessly extinguishing life, and sexual activity, ceaselessly regenerating it. And this in spite of lust, the antithesis of true love, which at first seems to rule sexuality but is actually the source of death.[26]

Resurgence of Life in the Fallen Universe

The remaining forces of life—represented by the faithful angels entrusted with guarding the universe and protecting it against the demonic treason—succeeded in achieving much more than a mere static equilibrium in creation. Supported and nourished by the creative grace to which the angels' fidelity contributed, their struggle was to bring about the consistent triumph in this world of the forces of life over those of death. It was also to achieve the ascent of life, a steady development that seems to be the essence of the entire history of the physical world—in spite of entropy, the deterioration which appears inevitably to accompany creative energies.

Hence, the first stage in the reassertion of the forces of life in the world (even though it is under the control of the one who holds the power of death) was the emergence of man. For, as so many Fathers understood it, he was a surrogate angel.[27]

Originally, the spirituality which defines personal being created in God's image was projected onto materiality (the boundary between finite being and nothingness). Conversely, an incarnate spirit, having a synergetic relationship with the faithful powers, was to arise in the world, notwithstanding the fall of the rebellious powers. This incarnate spirit was to be in the image of the faithful created spirits, as well as in the image of their own model. This incarnate spirit was man, in whom it can be said that a new freedom emerged in the world, which would oppose from within it that which sought to pervert and enslave it. For God is and remains the creator of the entire cosmos, including the angel whom he had made its prince, but who could not become its sovereign.

Creation of Man and Redemption of the Cosmos

In this view, which seems solidly based on Scripture, man is, by virtue of his creation and its conditions, a first potential redeemer of the world. If he had been faithful to the call of God, who intended him to fill the place left by the prevaricator, his faithfulness would have erased the initial transgression.

This is the meaning of paradise, the restoration of the world around man.[28] As the high point of the divine re-creation, man, regaining control from within over what had been taken away from him—for God alone is more intimately linked to his own work of creation than any other created spirit can be—would have reinstated this world in its original condition, and would therefore have thrown Satan and his legions back into the outer darkness. The very emergence of man's created freedom initiated the restoration of the cosmos in its original truth, which the satanic prevarication had obscured but not entirely destroyed.

Yet God could not, without abolishing the fundamental order of the cosmos, spare man the temptation of following the fallen prince, who is still active in this world. To defeat this temptation, however, man needed only to have faith in the divine Word reinstating in this world the truth of its original purpose.[29]

Man reflected from this world the created spirit which had descended to meet him and draw forth his ascending word of praise to answer the creative word. For man therefore, it was carnal seduction which enveloped the inspiration of pride, instead of deriving from it as with the demon. The attraction of a worldly forbidden fruit, a sensual domination over the earth he should have cultivated as the garden of God, was immediately to concretize for man the deceptive promise: 'You will be like God!'"[30]

This attitude found its first manifestation in the human couple's seeking of mutual gratification instead of extending God's creative work in all its generosity.[31] The result was to be a kind of disjunctive conjunction of the entire human society, organizing only for the endeavor of dominating the world.[32] This reverse humanization, effected by a supremely successful technology, resulted in a deadly mechanization of man himself. He would sink into matter, along with the whole universe which he exploited instead of leading it to liberation, in joint praise and mutual charity.[33]

So it is that all human history has shown a persistent tendency to reverse the progressive evolution which had set the stage for man, by being victorious over the forces of destruction. History, through the weight of accumulated sins, would turn this evolution backwards by materialization of the human spirit, which placed it increasingly in thraldom to death, even when man claims to control life.

Redemption of the Fallen Redeemer

Though the physical world was in the power of the demon, its evolution remained ultimately in the hands of God, who from this evolution produced man. In the same way, God would bring forth from the history of sin a Savior who would turn it into the history of salvation. Supporting by his creating grace the powers who had remained faithful to him, God projected into this world an incarnate spirit native to it and able to become its first savior by giving it, as though from within, a new spirituality. Similarly, God would now carry forward on a still higher level the evolution of man. Through a new incubation of his Holy Spirit, God was to prepare in mankind, beguiled by the devil, in his sinful flesh, the incarnation of his Son. From the depths of fallen mankind, from a world which had regressed even further than it had with the fall of its prince, God was to call forth a lineage of believers and prophets. A long line of sinners—each successive generation being begotten in sin—was to prepare the coming, at the culmination of history, of the One who was the very principle of the whole process, the Lamb sacrificed from the foundation of the world.

From twice-fallen creation God was to produce, through a supreme kenosis, a third and definitive creation. It is the creation of the incarnate

Son of God who is the Son of man, "born of woman, born under the law,"[34]—that is, God's law which the angels had awakened in human consciousness,[35] though by it they had been able only to revive the hope of salvation. This new Man would become the Savior of the world by first becoming the Savior of man. This is the recapitulation referred to by St. Irenaeus,[36] one which was first outlined when the world, fallen along with its prince, was summed up in a created but natively incarnate spirit. It is a recapitulation which would now raise up and save, along with its would-be savior, the world which he had plunged into an apparently irreversible decadence.

It has been maintained, not without justification, that the creation of the world was a first divine kenosis, since God in producing created liberties placed a limitation on himself, so to speak, by making his search for a response to his love dependent on those liberties.[37] A second and more complete kenosis involved the recovery of the world to the freedom imparted to it after its fall, in the person of mankind, its first leader. But the supreme kenosis was for God in his Son to identify with fallen mankind, to the extent of becoming its second Adam, in and by whom mankind and the cosmos were to be brought back to their principle. For this could be resumed and fulfilled only in the immolation consented to by God, at the origin of all things, as the only principle of history capable of leading it to the outcome he intended, not by abolishing freedom but by consecrating it in himself.[38]

This series of kenoses culminates in the supreme manifestation of uncreated love as the gift of self which is its divine essence. In the last phase of the history of salvation, all mankind and the entire cosmos follow and join their leader, the incarnate Word, from the cross to the glory of his resurrection. The kenosis of the Son would bring about, however, the possibly even more mysterious kenosis of the Spirit of love. The ultimate kenosis will end in the death and transfiguration of the physical universe, with redeemed mankind following the steps of its redeemer. In the ultimate Parousia of the Son of God, the Spirit of God will appear as the Glorifier of the Father in his Son and in all things, when the eternal Wisdom will appear with the Saving Word in the divine glory which, though not given to anyone else, will gather back into God everything which has ever proceeded from him. Wisdom will then become the Bride of the eternal Son, at the end of time, for the consummation of all creatures in him through the Holy Spirit.[39]

Symbolism and Reality

Our treatment of this problem of the fall of the cosmos and its rehabilitation, though directly inspired by the converging testimony of the Scriptures in the meditation of the Fathers, may seem to many too closely related to the figures of ancient myths. But these things can be spoken of only in images, and—we repeat it for the last time—for the Word of God to be understandable to man, it was necessary to introduce through familiar terms the truth he himself was not able to provide.

It will be noted that we have abstained from raising and discussing in detail assertions concerning the angels as guardians of individuals and communities,[40] as regulators of the heavenly bodies, and as generally responsible for the most diverse natural phenomena.[41] This is because any direct correlation between the visible and invisible worlds must be viewed with the utmost caution, even though such correlations have been taken seriously by the greatest theologians.

On the other hand, the Fathers were convinced, following the prophets and St. Paul, that the convictions underlying various forms of paganism were far from being only illusions. Though nature is not strictly speaking filled with gods, it is indeed inhabited by spiritual powers, by "rulers of the world of this darkness," as the apostle put it, by "elements" belonging not to mere materiality, but to a spirituality more mysterious than ours, though it is not directly God's.[42] In the view of the Fathers, these gods were simply demons, taking from God the exclusive adoration and submission which are rightfully his.[43] When some real good resulted from the cults of what St. Paul called "ignorance," their influence was mitigated and overcome by a more discreet but never absent angelic influence.[44] From this viewpoint, there is some truth, though hidden or even perverted, in the fables of paganism.

Man and the Angels

A final question is whether man is ultimately superior to the angels. Father Sergei Boulgakoff recently asserted this human superiority, because man provided his flesh for the incarnation of the eternal Son, and also because mankind is naturally incarnate, which gives him a fullness of being the angels cannot experience.[45]

One of the most remarkable religious thinkers of the last century, the Danish Lutheran bishop Martensen—unfortunately remembered mostly for Kierkegaard's sarcastic comments about him—went somewhat further. In his *Christian Dogmatics,*[46] deeply orthodox in spirit yet often extremely original in thinking, he suggested that angels should be considered as spiritual powers in the process of development, rather than as completed personalities. This completion was, he felt, the exclusive privilege of human beings, who are called upon to reach their full stature in union with the divine person of Christ.

It does not seem that either opinion can be accepted as it stands. The element of truth in Martensen's view is that the angels are predominant in a merely provisional economy of the world, which in any case was restored and fulfilled only through man and the role God assigned to him. But in turn this economy is carried forth and completed, in accordance with an eternal predestination, only through the incarnation of the Son of God within it.[47]

On the one hand, even if they are considered as pure spirits, angels are not alien to the physical world, which exists only in conjunction with the angelic world and in dependence on it. Conversely, the angels— independently of sin and therefore of the final redemptive incarnation, as well as of our own incarnation which was meant to be redemptive—are called upon to enter through grace into a participation in divine life, by being assimilated to the Son and receiving the Spirit, just as man does.[48] The two inferiorities assumed by Boulgakoff therefore lack substance.

In relation to the divinity, the grace of the angels is the same as that of men, but in relationship to the physical world, our situation and theirs are mirror images of each other. However, the angels are, as individuals, higher in grace through their greater capacity to receive it and correspond to it—with the exceptions of the Virgin Mary personally and of the mystical body of Christ, the Church militant in union with Christ.[49] They nevertheless remain relatively superior to mankind, in spite of the completion which men contribute to the angels, and in spite of the consummation which the Savior's incarnation brings to the entire work of creation.

It is certainly true, for instance, in accordance with the perceptive views outlined by Dionysius and deepened by St. Thomas, that on the level of creation the divinity can be "imitated" only by a world in which multiplicity harmonizes with unity.[50] Moreover, only the humblest personal creatures could provide the divine *agape*—made available through a superabundant grace—with the opportunity to demonstrate, through kenosis, the inconceivable extent of its generosity. In a sense, the grace received by men and spread in mankind brings the creator a maximum of extrinsic glory.

Yet it is only when divine grace is considered in the whole breadth of creation, in the pure spirits and the physical cosmos (in which they are projected, just as God is projected in them), and finally in the creation of man, all recapitulated together in Christ, that divine grace glorifies God with all possible glory. So it is that God's creature responds to the Word made flesh, in whom are communicated all the treasures, hidden in him, of eternal Wisdom in its inherent variety (*polypoikilē*), through the gift of the Spirit, who is the Spirit of unity because he is the Spirit of love.

Chapter XXI: Created Spirit, Matter, and Corporeity

Having spoken at such length of spirit and matter, it becomes inevitable to wonder precisely what is meant by those terms. Admittedly this is an area shared by theology and philosophy, a field in which theologians have few landmarks in revelation and tradition. They can do no more than make conjectures. Yet they must do so or even their most confident assertions will lose credibility.

What is the Meaning of "Matter"?

Though the notion of "spirit" developed slowly in philosophical and even theological thinking, that of "matter" was even slower to develop—contrary to what modern minds fondly imagine. In fact, the truth should be unambiguously stated: we still do not know exactly what is meant by "matter." One may even wonder whether we might not be further than ever from reaching an acceptable definition.

To realize this, it is enough to outline the semantics of the term. Curiously enough, this is something nobody has yet seriously attempted, apart from A. A. Luce, the outstanding modern editor and commentator of Berkeley's works,[1] and even he has provided only a first draft. In availing ourselves of his valuable groundwork, without always agreeing, we do not lay claim to any substantially improved results.

To start with, we shall return to the disagreement between St. Thomas and St. Bonaventure on whether the angels themselves are purely immaterial. We noted that these two thinkers, who were contemporaries working with similar methods and on the basis of shared principles and identical sources, probably showed in their divergent views that the same word held a different significance for each of them.[2]

More disconcerting still may be the remark made by Collingwood, one of the most distinguished historians of cosmology, to the effect that what present-day scientists mean by "matter" is not only quite different from Plato's or Aristotle's understanding of the word, but virtually the opposite. Today's "matter" is something they would both unhesitatingly have categorized under the heading of "forms" or "ideas"—entirely immaterial for Plato, and for Aristotle existing only in the mind—God's mind or ours.[3]

These two comments should cause us a certain degree of disquiet over the manner in which we constantly use this term. Collingwood's comment, in particular, implies that it makes little sense for some philosophies to claim to be materialistic, while at the same time being based on science. In fact these philosophies habitually use the identical word in mutually exclusive meanings, sometimes even in the same sentence. Both Piper[4] and Collingwood[5] have made it clear that these various forms of materialism, either mechanistic (e.g., Haeckel's system) or dialectic (e.g., Marx's) manage to stay out of difficulty only by surreptitiously giving the term "matter" connotations which traditionally belong to the concept of spirit, or even of God.

The best historians of the pre-Socratic philosophies, starting with Burnet,[6] have shown that these philosophies remained totally unaware of an opposition between spirit and matter. And specialists in the history of Stoicism (which must however be credited with originating the concept of *pneuma*, one of the main words translated as "spirit") must recognize that this holds true of this relatively late philosophy, except when influenced by the later developments of neo-Platonism.[7]

Nevertheless general agreement attributes to Plato the first reference to a distinction and opposition between spirit and matter. In fact, this betrays a disconcerting survival, in Plato's most recent exegetes, of a neo-Platonic reinterpretation by Renaissance "Platonists," starting with Marsilio Ficino.[8] The influence of this reinterpretation is felt in all commentaries and even in a good many translations of the dialogues, including some of the most recent. This is undeniably a flagrant case of reading into a text something that is not really there.

Starting with the *Phaedo*, Plato indeed discusses the *nous*, a concept he borrowed from Anaxagoras, although giving it a more active role.[9] However, Plato's *nous* does not contrast with anything we could legitimately call matter, but rather with the activity of our senses, which give us nothing but an opinion (*doxa*), which contrasts with idea (*eidos*), which alone is pure and true and accessible only to the *nous*.[10] Even so, the system implies a strict discipline, which is the rationale of Platonic dialectics.

The later *Timaeus* is the first to introduce the word *hylē*, which was subsequently to be translated as "matter." But in that dialogue the term keeps its original meaning of "wood" or "foliage." At the most, it tends toward a vivid transposition applying to the imprecise objects of sense knowledge. In this sense, Plato writes of the *hylē naupēgēsimē*, the material (rather than matter) of which ships were made.[11] But it is never with the *hylē* as such that he contrasts the transcendent "forms" or "ideas," but rather with an undefined receptacle (*hypodokhē*),[12] which seems to be simply what we call space.

In Aristotle's works, we find for the first time a truly philosophical use of the word *hylē*, which allows us to translate it as "matter." We are far from the end of our troubles, however. For it seems that Aristotle himself is hardly consistent in his use of the word. In his works, one may distinguish three different meanings of *hylē*, related to a certain extent, yet not reducible to each other.

First, it is the element underlying decline or change. Matter therefore appears as a relative term, varying with the different degrees of being, so that what is form from one viewpoint will be matter from another. For instance, the steel of a knife will be its matter, and the cutting edge its form. But in relation to the constituent particles, steel is the form and they are the matter. And in a murder, the edge of the knife becomes merely the matter.

The next step is matter as being *in posse*, which was to lead—when these speculations were translated into Latin—to a play on words with *mater* and *materia*: paternity, the origin of beings, represented being in action, and maternity being *in posse*.

Finally, matter is interpreted as the substratum or suppositum of everything visible or tangible, but with no qualities itself—to the extent, according to Aristotle, that it cannot exist independently.[13] The most explicit statement concerning this is found in *Metaphysics*:[14]

> By "matter" I mean that which in itself is not stated as being the whatness of something, nor a quantity, nor any of the other senses of "being." For there is something of which each of these is a predicate, whose being is other than that of each of the predicates; for all the others are predicates of a substance, while a substance is a predicate of matter. Thus, this last is in itself neither a whatness nor a quantity nor any of the others...

These lines seem to draw inspiration from the *Timaeus*,[15] from which the word "matter" (*hylē*) is absent, however:

> ...the mother and receptacle [*hypodokhē*] of all created and visible and in any way sensible things, is not to be termed earth, or air, or fire, or water,[16] or any of their compounds or any of the elements from which these are derived, but is an invisible and formless being [*eidos*] which receives all things and in some mysterious way partakes of the intelligible, and is most incomprehensible...[17]

The evanescence of Aristotelian matter is such that it is difficult to say whether matter is really a substance, in Aristotle's opinion, or the fundamental substance of all things.[18]

Plotinus was to resume the discussion in the context of what Plato has to say of the receptacle of forms. But since matter was for him, in the last analysis, that which reduces and therefore degrades the fundamental unity of being, it seems to be simply an abstract limit of being, in itself indistinguishable from nothingness,[19] and difficult to differentiate from evil. None of which, we must admit, is particularly enlightening.

It should be noted, moreover, that the biblical writings—except for the last deuterocanonical texts, and particularly the Wisdom of Solomon—do not use *hylē* in the philosophical sense of matter.[20] They simply refer to heaven as the abode of God and his angels, and to the earth as that of men, but where God manifests himself through his angels. In the case of man, these writings contrast "flesh and blood," his terrestrial and mortal nature, vivified however by the created soul (*nephesh*) and the transcendent divine Spirit (*rûah*).

And What is the Meaning of "Spirit"?

Let us now turn our attention from matter to spirit. It should first be noted that the English word "spirit," in the same way as words derived from the Latin *spiritus* in other languages, combines the meanings of the two Greek terms *pneuma* and *nous*. In Stoic philosophy, *pneuma* is essentially the vital breath, always considered by that school as a material and sensible reality, a particularly subtle kind of fiery air. And *nous* applies specifically to intelligence. However, the biblical custom of using *pneuma* (the equivalent of the Hebrew *rûah*) to designate only the divine Spirit in its transcendence— as opposed to the human soul (*nephesh*)—together with the New Testament idea of the communication of this Spirit to all the faithful Christians, has considerably nuanced the modern use of the word. Conversely, this use has sometimes been affected by the meaning of the word "soul" (the translation of *anima*, the Latin equivalent of the Greek *psychē*), which similarly desig-nates the breath of life, both human and animal.[21]

St. Augustine was most instrumental in giving "spirit" the meaning it has acquired in Western thinking: an angelic spirit or a human soul, essentially in the image of God, retaining its ability to animate the body, yet combining inseparably the intellectual qualities of the Platonic *nous* and the volun-tarism implied in the biblical "heart." This created spirit will therefore quite naturally appear susceptible, through grace, to the action of the divine Spirit.

What should one conclude from all these considerations? The first obvious point is that the word "matter," for those who have attempted to define it—and in the entire history of philosophy it would seem that no one has achieved anything more than Aristotle in this area—has never desig-nated anything but an abstraction, which may be made into a substance only at the cost of inextricable contradictions.

More specifically, as St. Gregory of Nyssa was the first to discern and to assert, it is impossible to conceive matter except by separating from the human spirit some of the elements of its experience, although they are endowed with consistency and sense only in the context of its living unity.

Personal Being and Cosmic Being

To use a different terminology—which seems required by the elaboration of the concept of person through Christian theology—we would say that person, as we experience it, i.e., the human person, is a living whole whose center is what we rather imprecisely call "spirit," and whose periphery is what we, even more imprecisely, call "matter."

Faced with Locke's foredoomed endeavor to reach a rational view of the universe based on pure sensism, Berkeley expressed this by saying that a being neither perceptive nor perceived is properly unthinkable. His most recent and most rigorous interpreters have restored the true significance of Berkeley's thinking, so clearly explained by him initially that its misrepresentation had to be virtually deliberate. Just as untenable would be the view that there might be perceptions unperceived by any perceptive being.

This obviously does not mean that what we call the material world—i.e., the world which our senses reveal to our intelligence—does not exist, but only that its existence is not independent of a society of spirits.[22] It cannot even be maintained that matter does not exist, as Berkeley contended in his earliest writings, which gave rise to the misunderstanding that has persisted to our day, ever since Hume, who had his own reasons to entertain it. But it is true that matter, or more accurately the entirety of the so-called material realities, exists only as a common content given to the created spirits by the one uncreated Spirit from whom they and matter both derive.[23] One may therefore assert, as Berkeley did in his last writings, thereby coming around specifically to St. Bonaventure's view,[24] that the material world, or rather the world considered in its materiality, i.e., in its sensible existence, is but a shared language among spirits.

It is principally, we will add, the language of the first-created spirits, the angels, a language in which they communicate, belonging to, or constituting a simple world.[25] Moreover, it is the language through which the divine Word calls us forth, as spirits immersed in matter, or rather emerging from it. And the entire physical cosmos thereby appears as a fundamental language through which the uncreated Spirit calls upon all humanity to be an exclusive reception of his Word and a response to it.

Body and Cosmos

We have now reached the point where we can attempt to understand the significance of this corporeity essential to our human spirituality, and which distinguishes our spirituality from that of the angels. Then we will try to grasp the meaning of the hoped-for resurrection of our bodies which, without abolishing their reality, will perfectly harmonize the human world with the angelic world, or with that part of it that remains faithful to the creative plan. We have already indicated our view that organic life, and its unceasing and progressive victory in the evolution of the various species, is the outcome of the struggle between angelic and demonic spirits, a struggle in which the world is at stake. For each body, taking and changing shape in spite of the forces of death weighing on it, reaches, through this evolution, ever higher stages of corporeal being, increasingly integrated in their very complexity, in a universe apparently doomed to degradation, and is in fact the germination of a new universe.[26] However, this renovated universe can succeed in bursting forth from the original world—whose prince, in spite of everything, is still the devil—only through the achievement of a corporeity coadapted to a new freedom.

But this assumes a second creative intervention, acting in combination with the angelic struggle, but which alone is capable of allowing this contest to lead to a new creation, breaking clear from the first as a butterfly emerges from its chrysalis.[27] This is what took place in the appearance of man. Had he proved faithful to the Word which called him forth from the cosmos, man would, in cultivating the paradise-like garden which the universe would have become around him, have banished death from this earth and regained his own immortality. One may say that the victorious freedom of men, having become children of God, would have retrieved the entire universe from the fallen *benê Elōhim*, and would have made it or remade it into the Temple of God.

Events took the opposite course. Due to man's sinfulness, death gained the ascendency over mankind and is now dominant, through fallen man, over the whole universe, which is involved in his ruin. A second saving evolution then started, however, one intimately connected with the regressive evolution which reflects within humanity the fall of angels. This blessed development was to lead to the incarnation in fallen mankind of the very Son of God, in whose likeness man was fashioned.[28]

From Physical Bodies to the Mystical Body

By making his own the body animated by an immortal soul in the womb of the Virgin, the Word made it the shared body of mankind renewed in him. This body was to develop, by associating with it, into the mystical body of the Second Adam, the eschatological Man. This saving process will be comprehensively discussed in a final chapter. For the moment, we must draw the conclusions—for the situation of mankind in the universe, and for the overall future of the universe—of the introduction of this process, as we see it, in the conflict between the faithful and unfaithful powers.

Once again, the ascent of matter toward life and the ascent of life toward an animality readying itself for hominization seem to continue on earth the combat of St. Michael and his angels against the demon they cast forth into its midst. Plant life's mysterious reproductive ability is a preliminary form of sexuality and represents the first sign of the animation elicited by the angels' descent along Jacob's ladder, which initiates the rehabilitation of a world held until then in night and death by the fall of Lucifer, its prince. Mobility in the animal world is linked to an embryonic consciousness which is like a muted reflection of the angels' superconsciousness and provides an outline of what the human world was to become. As such it may seem the high point of this angelic conquest or reconquest over the forces of death.[29]

But from the very moment of the fall of the powers, the condescension of the divine Word (what the Fathers of the Church called his *synkatabasis*), surrounded this descent and brought about, within the offering of their cosmic praise, the incubation of the Spirit over chaos. Whence the yearning of the creature for deliverance "from the servitude of corruption," in the words of St. Paul.[30] At the confluence of the descent of the Word and the outpouring of the Spirit, man was to appear. Incarnate image of the eternal Son in this worldly flesh, vivified by a breath of life capable of being caught up and carried away in the very breath of divine life, man was thus to reinstate the cosmic eucharist into the eucharist of angels, and even in the eternal reascent of the Son through the Spirit to the bosom of the Father.

Man failed to respond to this calling. But God's gifts permit no regret, and the incarnation of the Word in person was to fulfill the divine plan, in a manner more marvelous than anything the angels themselves could have hoped for.

In this perspective, the insignificance of human duration (whether individual or collective) in relation to geologic or astral ages, as well as the spatial insignificance of the human body in relation to the inconceivable dimensions of the universe, seem no more than a twofold illusion. Until the awakening of human consciousness, historical time, our time, simply could not exist.[31] The years and centuries we can account for in this prehuman genesis are but the extrapolation of a reality inevitably coextensive with mankind's consciousness. As Einsteinian science has established, without such consciousness time is but an imaginary variable: it simply appears in equations as a fourth dimension of the space where the human body was in gestation, so to speak, but into which historical time, the field of our freedom, had not entered.[32]

Similarly, the infinitesimal dimensions ascribed to man in relation to the universe to which he now belongs are the result of a confusion. As Kant observes in the first pages of his *Metaphysics of Ethics*, we have to start with a particularly crude confusion between a metaphor and the reality it conjurs up, as if it were possible to compare spiritual greatness, which appears in the world with man, with merely material magnitudes.[33] Pascal had already stressed the lack of any common measure between the realm of thought and mere dimension, pending the new and final mutation involved when we reach the order of charity.[34]

But ever remaining in the spatial order, man's alleged spatial insignificance is but an optical illusion. For one thing, as Pascal noted, man, between the microscopic and astral infinities, is neither large nor small; instead and quite simply, his position is much more "central" than imagined by Ptolemaic cosmography, which assumed that the earth was at the center of a world which we consider to have been extraordinarily limited.[35]

The ultimate truth in this respect is simpler still, although at first sight it may appear incredible. Since personal consciousness, as we have seen, encompasses all exclusively material realities, man as person includes within himself the entire universe. For the universe is not only devoid of any conceivable existence outside the society of spirits, but (as Leibnitz expressed it) the universe exists as a whole only in the consciousness of each spirit, and in a manner specific to each one of them.[36]

And for those who are unsatisfied with this explanation, we will return to what we have already said of corporeity, which recreates, within a universe that had reverted to chaos, what may be called its cosmicity. We may add that the human body itself, the body of each individual in mankind —through the roots sensible consciousness gives it in the entire cosmic reality, which both penetrates us through these senses and is entirely accessible to them—actually extends to the limits of the universe. In fact, the latest findings of science indicate not only that there is theoretically no limit to our ability to act upon the world, but also that any information has the effect of modifying whatever it conveys to us.[37]

What will be the situation when the Word is incarnate in the flesh of man and when he instills into our spirit the very Spirit of his Father, the Spirit of filiation? The universe will henceforth be entirely seized by mankind and returned to the praise of its creator: Father, Son, and Holy Spirit. This will come to pass when human history, which started, as did the cosmos, as a history of sin, is recapitulated into a story of promised salvation, carrying the pledge that everything which exists will find its eschatological reconciliation in the universal feast of the Lamb's Nuptials.

Chapter XXII: The Nuptials of the Word and of Wisdom

Consciousness of the Universe and of the Word

Human consciousness is spiritual in the sense that it is inseparably free and rational. Moreover, it is personal; it can live and develop only in interpersonal relationships with similar conscious beings. And human consciousness is called upon to enter into the interpersonal relationships which constitute the divine personality in whose image every created personality has been fashioned.

Yet our consciousness originates and remains (here below at least) as though immersed in a merely animal consciousness, the consciousness of a body, of one of those specific organisms in the cosmos which, from a certain viewpoint, espouse it in its totality. Each of these viewpoints reflects one of the principal divine ideas which are the angelic personalities. The microcosmic organization of each body, or perhaps of each kind of body, is like an inverted image of one of those angelic forms in the material mirror that is the web of the cosmos. Moreover, the entire cosmic reality is simply their harmonic manifestation, one that is at present out of harmony.[1]

This implies, in the sensitivity and reactivity which together are characteristic of bodies, the imprint of a spirituality, and more precisely of a definite personality. But it is God's creative intervention which has projected, in this image of an image, a direct reflection of the Word and Son himself, their divine model, while the divine Spirit awakens in them a new freedom.[2]

This freedom arises in the finite, the limited, in the sense that is bestowed in a particular perspective, in a place determined among all others by this material network where it is assigned a specific location. However, since the entire network in question is made up of the projections of various angelic personalities, and since each of its parts is capable, in its own way, of including all the others, this freedom is nevertheless real, because it is open to everything and can embrace all of reality.

Furthermore, beyond the limited whole of the created cosmos, the freedom in question remains open, through the reflection of the Word impinging upon it, to every possible form and level of being and, therefore, if the grace of the Spirit awakening and stimulating this freedom actualizes its openness, it shall itself have a capacity for infinity.[3]

Moreover, mankind does not originate in an individual, but in a couple, so that the free spirituality of the immortal soul is expressed in the sexual polarity of two naturally incarnate individuals. Therefore, primitive man carried in his flesh, and in the duality of the two souls defined by the fundamental community and complementarity of their bodies, the original vocation of a reconciler. Femininity was, in the unblemished fullness of its virginity, a potential assumption, both maternal and spousal of everything created, returned in principle to its immanent unity.[4] And masculinity was a sign of conjunction with the uncreated, in which this immanent unity was to become actual again. To bring about this result, it would have been enough if the coming together of Adam (*man*, "formed. . .of the slime of the earth" by an imprint of the divine Word) and Eve (cosmic *life*, called by the grace of the Spirit to commune in divine life) had taken place with faith in the creator. The latter urged them to cooperate, on the basis of their union (seen in this light), in the completion of his creation by restoring its integrity, i.e., by consenting, in the obedience of faith, to carry out finally the divine plan of universal adoption which had been frustrated by the default of Lucifer and his angels.

Had the first man and woman consented, had they submitted freely to the divine plan, their union would have been blessedly fruitful, instead of being but the artificial joining of two egotisms locked into an unshared gratification. Their joining activity, in progressive knowledge of the creator through his creation, would have been conducive to the reconstitution of the society of created spirits in their participation, through the cultivation of the cosmos, in the development of a human civilization which would have built all things into a single Temple of the one divine glory.

The spirit of division and lies would have been banished from the cosmos through faith in the Word which, by bringing them into existence, called them to a communion with and in divine existence. And man in his union with woman (a union which would have become the sacrament of universal reconciliation) would have been the redeemer of the world. In human history the cosmos would have recovered its harmony and congruence with the plan of divine Wisdom.

Needless to say, we can have no inkling how this might have taken place. What we can assert is that man and woman, in their union and by cooperating in the completion of creation, would have reconciled the cosmos with itself and with its maker, thus becoming the agents of a spiritualization of their own bodies and of the entire material universe, and therefore the instruments of universal divinization.

Misfortune of Man's Fallen Consciousness and Fulfillment of Wisdom

But none of this came to pass because of the seduction of woman by the first fallen one of the "sons of Elohim," then of the other women by their entire cohort, and because of complicity by later men in that initial adultery in which lust for power was inseparable from sensuality. And so civilization, the organization of the world through human effort, could but result in the proud tower of Babel project, destroyed by greed, by mortal divisions in the body social, by activities immersed in a materiality which had changed from servant to tyrant.

In the background, however, in spite of all this, and even through these developments, the divine plan progressed toward its unfailing fulfillment notwithstanding the deviation on all levels of the created freedoms, because it used their very failings to promote their ultimate salvation. From the time of man's Fall, as St. Irenaeus remarked, the Word of God started to approach fallen mankind and grew accustomed to living with the children of men. And thereby, this descent to earth of the Son of God, toward and in pursuit of fleeing mankind, prepared the reawakening in man, in mankind's own unfaithful heart, of the Spirit of sonship.

In a first phase, that of the Old Testament—which continued and corrected the era of primitive paganisms—the Word, in order to be heard by us when we were still utterly incapable of recognizing him, first became an angel, as Origen disconcertingly expressed it.[5] Which is to say that he addressed us through his angel rather than directly, and finally through the first among them, Gabriel, the "strength of God." He it was who openly showed himself only to the Virgin Mary, at the high point of the history of salvation, and whom Moslems therefore take for the Word in person. At the same time Michael ("who is like unto God?"), "the Prince of the heavenly host," who guarded God's people in the making by continuously driving away the idolatrous and corrupting images raised by the Demon[6]— thereby opened the way to a first, indirect, but real inspiration of the faithful hearts by the very Spirit of God. Hence the preparatory revelation of the law "given by the angels,"[7] as the authors of the New Testament repeatedly emphasize. It is so called in the sense that it restored to human consciousness the law immanent in the first creation, entirely dependent on the incorporeal spirits, but which diabolical phantasms had obscured.

This also led to a correlative inspiration which impelled the patriarchs— at first negatively, or so it seems—to break away from the cities of allegedly divinized men, which can therefore be nothing but successive manifestations of the city of the devil.[8] Hence the still essentially symbolic promises which supported the demands for detachment, exile and failure, accepted in the constantly increasing hope, from one prophet to the next, of a decisive deliverance, a total renewal of man and the entire cosmos.[9]

Hence finally—when the meditation of wise men and inspired scribes had finally destroyed all human hopes of a merely human victory in an essentially unchanged world—the last prophecy, which held forth the paradoxical solution of a salvation through the suffering of the Innocent One, of the faithful Servant broken by suffering and abandoned to death.[10]

In the agonizing crisis of Maccabean times, the apocalypse—still a symbolic revelation, but one whose symbolism was already so luminous as to match the awesome demands of prophecy now reaching its highest point—announced the coming of a "Son of Man" on the clouds of heaven, to meet the Ancient of days and deliver unto him the Kingdom which is his, but which also belongs to the "saints," through their acceptance in faith of obscure suffering and of a death apparently without remission.[11]

Though the divine Word is dominant in all this and the divine Spirit inspires acceptance of it, it is still only an angelic revelation, i.e., a revelation of the divine plan reflected in knowledge, and refracted through the images of this carnal world, for which God's messengers, even the highest among them, can do no more than clear the way.

In the person of John the Baptist, however, a kind of incarnate angel, we have the "messenger," the *angelos* whom God himself sends immediately before his countenance. He purifies the temple of the world by emptying it of all idols, through the example of a life freed from earthly attachments, as he abides in the desert, drawing crowds and preparing the way for the One who is to come.[12] And with the Virgin, elevated higher even than the angels through her divine motherhood, there is the Angel Gabriel appearing for the first time to mankind, whose eyes are now opened by absolute faith. He is merely a "Friend of the Bridegroom," though indeed the greatest, who stands aside for Him.[13]

Until then the faithful angels could do no more than ceaselessly oppose the demons, to counter the influence of their spurious oracles, and allow flashes of the repressed truth to shine through from time to time.[14] In Israel, the angels had given many hints of this truth, but now, on Christmas night, as the very Word descends from heaven,[15] the eternal Eucharist is revealed to the shepherds, the humblest of the obscure faithful, rather than to the wise men of Israel. And through dreams the angels reveal the coming of the Word to the pious Joseph,[16] and to the Magi in search of a truth that has always eluded them, and who do not hesitate to leave everything and follow the unfamiliar star.[17] It leads them to the manger where they find an infant wrapped in swaddling clothes; they offer him the gold, frankincense and myrrh they had prepared for the King of all ages.[18]

All is thus in readiness for the revelation of the Word, the Son in whom the Father is well pleased. And in this revelation the Father adopts us, and the entire universe with us, despite its Fall, consummated in our own fall. This incarnation of the Word, who in the fullest, most literal sense of the term takes upon himself all the infirmity of the world, reveals the divine fatherhood and prepares through the Cross the glorification of all God's children.[19]

Indeed, the Incarnation prepares the final revelation to both angels and men of the mysterious Wisdom which God had conceived in begetting his own Son, to whom that Wisdom will finally be espoused, when the history of sin is transfigured into the history of salvation.[20]

The Body Assumed in Time by the Eternal Word

The Virgin asked the Angel: "How can this be?"[21] And the answer came: "The Holy Spirit will come upon you, and the power of the Most High will overshadow you; therefore the child to be born will be called holy, the Son of God."[22] In the first human couple, the image of the Word drawing Adam's body to freedom could have fashioned it to God's actual likeness only by a reunion with the whole cosmos through and with Eve, the mother of all the living. This would have been accomplished in the epiphany of the Spirit of divine love filling the entire reality of the terrestrial *eros*.

In the body of the immaculate Virgin, entirely available to the re-creative *fiat* through the *fiat* of her faith, now takes shape the body of the Word and Son, by which he would bring together those shattered fragments of mankind.[23] For the body of the child then born, being from the first moment of its existence the body of the eternal Son, becomes again the body in which all mankind, adopted in the only Son by the invisible Father, must be and can be reconciled with its creator.

On the Cross, Jesus made this reconciliation effective, by consecrating his offering exclusively to the will of the Father in the Holy Spirit, who had watched over Jesus from the instant of his conception and dwelt in him since his baptism in the Jordan.[24]

Once resurrected, manifested and effectively established in his glorified flesh as the eternal Son, he draws all men to himself as he ascends again toward the Father.[25] Through baptism and faith, he makes them part of himself,[26] conforming them to the mystery of his death and resurrection. In the Eucharist—extended through the "logical" sacrifice in which, by their individual lives and deaths, they complete what remains to be endured of the sufferings of Christ for the Church, his mystical body[27]—he assimilates them so completely to the temple of his own body, that their bodies also become even now "the Temple of the Spirit."[28]

When this mystical body—in which is found the extension of Christ's physical body in the Eucharistic body—reaches its cosmic fullness, when the last of the elect have been absorbed and conformed to it, then Christ will have reached maturity in all his members, and his own Parousia, the event toward which this entire growth had been straining, will finally take place.[29]

Appearing with Christ, and descending with him from the side of the

Father, will be his eternal Bride, the eschatological Church, the redeemed, saved and glorified cosmos. And eternal Wisdom will be revealed as the goal of all history both for the cosmos and for mankind.[30]

Ultimate Revelation of the Polypoikilē Wisdom

This Wisdom, in the eternal origin of all things, was mysteriously enclosed in the Word, as Eve was in man, although paradoxically it was she who would be called upon to bring him forth in time, and although this same Word could not reach his full potential without being united to her at the end of time. All creation is actually the development of Wisdom from the initial stage when the distinction between it and the Word is purely rational, to the final stage when it becomes real. But Wisdom reaches this separation only to strive—through the entire history of the created world, taken up finally into the flow of divine life, of which it is only a reflection— to be reunited to the Word again, this time forever. The Nuptials of the Lamb are the goal of history, just as the principle of history is in the Lamb's immolation, decided before the creation of the world and carried out at the highest point of historical development.

From this viewpoint, it is understandable that sexuality is indeed, in the cosmos, the sign of its supernatural destiny, of which mankind's natural fate is an outline. All creation tends toward man, all mankind tends toward Christ, and in turn Christ, as he has revealed himself to us, tends to unite with all mankind, and through it with the universe. In and for this union the cosmos becomes what the Father had in mind when he conceived Wisdom in his own Son, a Wisdom from and for all eternity both distinct and inseparable from Christ.

It is in this sense that the eternal Son of God, on two crucial occasions, appears as the Son of man. He appears at the height of history, under the features of the humiliated Servant, which shows in the very sin which blatantly scorns God's love the infinity of that love in its source. And he appears at the end of history as the celestial Man, who draws to himself all redeemed mankind and in it every creature.

The world is not God, but the world is permeated with God—although his presence generally remains at best indistinctly sensed—because it is immersed in him. God besets the world on all sides, so to speak, to be finally all in all—just as everything, from all time, exists for him and existed only in him. Time is but the mysterious transit in which the created freedoms signify their consent to the uncreated liberty, in a process of Love calling Love.

At first sight time seems to be filled with sin, initially that of the angels, then the transgressions of men, and it seems that Wisdom, left to its own devices and abandoned to the creatures, has become folly. But this degrading folly of angels and of men, through the sublime folly of God's love made manifest and incarnate in the Crucified One, is uplifted and transformed in the eternal Wisdom where everything is brought to completion just as in it all things originated.

In eternity, God's love descends from the Father into the Son and rises again in the Spirit, with the Son, toward the Father. In time, the same love, descending with the Son, returns to him in the eschatological appearance of his Bride. Thus taken up again with the Son through the Spirit, the whole of creation, the entire cosmos, is included in this eternal eucharist of the Spirit, which responds to the eternal Gospel of the Word. In the Spirit, Wisdom, the Bride of the Son, who has herself become perfectly filial, shines throughout the cosmos with the same glory that belongs to God, and to him alone, from all eternity.

The Second Death

What may be said of the ultimate fate awaiting the fallen angels and the stubborn men who join them in their persistent refusal of the *Agape*? When the Bridegroom appears in all his glory, received from his Father before the creation of the world, and shares it with his Bride, attired in the shimmering cloak made up of all the creatures returned to their creator, then the doors of the banquet hall will be closed. Outside, there will be only darkness. As Revelation expresses it, the devil and his angels, together with all those who have followed him, will be cast into the pool of the second death.

What does this mean? One cannot imagine that a temporal end awaits any personal being created by God, for it is his eternal will to make any such being a free echo of his love. But if this free creature refuses, it remains forever trapped in time. And precisely in time leading nowhere, since time no longer exists for all those who have accepted God's love and have entered eternity. All we can say of the others is: *Habent mercedem suam, vani vanam.* In other words, they have what they wanted, but all that is left for them is to realize its nothingness, without even having the option of ceasing to be. They do not die, in the sense that their existence does not end. But they exist only to tend toward a nothingness they can never quite reach, though they may draw closer and closer to it. This is what Revelation calls the second death.

Eternal Life

In what Scholastics called the *aevum*, divine eternity as shared by creatures, the cosmos has recovered its unity. The elect have left the world where time slips away, and all together have reached the other shore, where everything endures. The transfigured universe, all around the resurrected bodies, is swathed in a kind of rainbow in which the indivisible glory of God shines forth, and in which the sparkles are as numerous as the elect. There is now but a single harp and its strings hum in the breath of the Spirit. In an endless procession, the angels descend and rise again with the Son of Man, who comes down alone from the Father and returns to him with his Bride, who is in perfect union with the Son through the very unity of the Spirit which eternally connects the Son to the Father. Everything old and worn has ceased to exist. The One who sits on the throne has made all things new, and on the banks of blessed immortality, the elect sing forever the hymn of Moses, the psalm of victory, of enthronement of the King who finally takes possession of his Kingdom only by also allowing all his children to take part in it through his only-begotten Son.

*   *   *

We have now reached the end of this series of essays in which we have attempted to study the many facets of the Mystery of God and his creation. At best, we have been able to do no more than suggest a way into the silence where all of us—including the one who has held forth at possibly excessive length—shall await the moment when God himself will grant us the repose and peace of his eternal Sabbath.

As we await this outcome in the evening light of faith, may we recognize—in experiencing the love poured into our hearts by the Spirit sent to us—the shadowless light of the eternal day, in order to prepare for the impending night to which we are drawn in joyful hope of the resurrection.

Joyous light of the eternal Father's hallowed glory:
heavenly, holy, and blessèd Jesus Christ,
reaching the sunset hour,
as we gaze at the evening light,
we praise you, O God, Father, Son, and Holy Spirit.
You are indeed worthy of the holy voices' everlasting song,
O Son of God, giver of life,
Wherefore does the whole world ceaselessly extol and magnify
your name.

NOTES

Chapter I

[1]Concerning this formulation, so frequently and completely misinterpreted (by commentators who do not even seem to realize that many masters of Christian spirituality, from the desert Fathers to St. John of the Cross, expressed similar views), one should refer to the perceptive comments made by Charles Stephen Dessain in *Newman's Spiritual Themes*, Dublin, 1977, pp. 14 and 46ff. The quotation is from *Apologia*, p. 4 of the Longman edition. Newman had earlier developed the same thought, even more strikingly, in the second of his *Parochial and Plain Sermons*, p. 210: ". . . [Progressively] we see that, while [the world] changes, we are one and the same; and thus, under God's blessing, we come to have some glimpse of the meaning of our independence of things temporal, and our immortality. And should it so happen that misfortunes come upon us (as they often do), then still more are we led to understand the nothingness of this world; then still more are we led to distrust it, and are weaned from the love of it, till at length it floats before our eyes merely as some idle veil, which, notwithstanding its many tints, cannot hide the view of what is beyond it;—and we begin, by degrees, to perceive that there are but two beings in the whole universe, our own soul, and the God who made it." The most valuable commentary on these lines is given implicitly, in the second volume of the same series of Newman's Anglican sermons, by the one on *The Natural Powers*, and in the fourth volume (see below, pp. 203ff.), by the sermon on *The Invisible World*, where clearly the reality of the tangible world is not denied, but on the contrary where its true significance—or what we might call its essentially significant reality—is affirmed. The same theme recurs, in the identical sense, in Julian Green's insight that God actually makes the world for each of us, as though each existed in it uniquely with him.

[2]1 John 2:15 and 5:19.

[3]John 3:16.

[4]S. Alexander's unusual philosophy is expressed in his paradoxical yet penetrating book, *Space, Time, and Deity* (new edition in two volumes, with a preface by D. Emmet), in his 1916-1918 Gifford Lectures, London, 1966.

[5]*Confessions*, book III, chapter VI, paragraph 11. Compare book II, chapter II; book IX, chapter X; book X, chapter XVII and chapters XXV-XXVII; *De Genesi ad litteram*, book V, chapter XVI.

[6]See Antoine Guillaumont, *Les 'Kephalaia gnostica' d'Evagre le Pontique et l'histoire de l'origénisme chez les Grecs et les Syriens*, Paris, 1962.

[7]This term, which Eckhart made familiar, seems to have been borrowed by him from Hadewijch of Antwerp. Cf. *Spiritual letters*, in *The Complete Works of Hadewijch*, translation and introduction by Columba Hart, preface by Paul Mommaers, New York, 1980.

[8]The concept was given considerable importance by a theologian of the generation preceding ours, Paul Tillich, who may be considered the last and the most brilliant of their disciples. In developing it further, he relied on the modern depth psychologies, and particularly that of C. G. Jung (see the latter's *Modern Man in Search of a Soul*, translated by W. S. Dell and Cary F. Baynes, New York, 1933). Cf. Paul Tillich, *Systematic Theology*, London, 1953, vol. I, pp. 122ff.

⁹See Alexandre Koyré, *La Philosophie de Jacob Boehme*, Paris, 1929, pp. 320ff.
¹⁰It seems that this was not only the interpretation of St. Thomas Aquinas, but also Aristotle's own view, according to A. Chroust, the latter's most recent commentator.
¹¹This was the opinion maintained by Karl Barth in his earliest works, and particularly in his commentary on the Epistle to the Romans. As his thinking subsequently evolved, he explained his initial viewpoint in a way that increasingly limited its scope.
¹²As far as the Koran is concerned, cf. A. Schimmel's contribution on Islam in Vol. II of *Historia Religionum*, edited by C. Blekker and G. Widengren, Leiden, 1976 (see in particular paragraph 2 of chapter VI). Concerning the contradictions faced by fundamentalists, see James Barr, *Fundamentalism*, London, 1977.
¹³Such was obviously the view held by the nineteenth century popularizers of Darwin's transformism, e.g., Thomas Huxley in England, and Haeckel or even more so Engels (K. Marx's authority on this point) in Germany. Regarding the difficulties currently facing both neo-Darwinism and Darwinism in its original form, it is illuminating to read Arthur Koestler's essay entitled *The Case of the Midwife Toad*, (London, 1971). Concerning the internal contradictions, and in the final analysis the utter verbalism, of the philosophies deriving from this viewpoint, see among others R. G. Collingwood, *The Idea of Nature*, and Piper, both of whom we shall subsequently return to.
¹⁴This is the typically Platonic view, inspired by the supposedly Orphic myth, dear to Pythagoreans, a view the entire *Phaedo* seeks to illustrate (see also the *Gorgias*, 493a).
¹⁵Drawing on Aristotle, but inspired mainly by St. Paul and the entire biblical tradition, Aquinas was to define and maintain this position: *Summa Theologica*, Prima pars, question 76, and particularly articles 1 and 5ff. Cf. E. Gilson, *Le Thomisme*, 1944 edition, pp. 266ff.
¹⁶Starting in the thirteenth century, this controversy was to divide the entire Latin Middle Ages, pitting Thomists on the one side against Augustinians of various hues (such as St. Bonaventure) on the other.
¹⁷These various views, which separate orthodox Christianity and Judaism from the positions considered gnostic by the moderns, but which actually originate in the whole body of ancient myths, will be discussed subsequently, starting with Chapter IV.
¹⁸This problem will be dealt with in Chapter VI, in connection with the emergence of the so-called apocalyptic literature.
¹⁹In the history of Christian thinking, Origen raised these problems for the first time (see Chapter X).
²⁰This will be the specific topic of Chapters XIXff.
²¹These questions will be addressed in Chapter XIV.
²²This is what Etienne Gilson had already more than outlined in *The Spirit of Mediaeval Philosophy*, New York, 1936; he pursued the undertaking with increased vigor and accuracy in some of his last works, e.g., *The Philosopher and Theology*, New York, 1962.
²³In this connection, see our previous volumes: *The Eternal Son, Le Père Invisible*, and *Le Consolateur*, the last two to be published in English by St. Bede's Publications.
²⁴See particularly Chapters V and VI.
²⁵This topic is developed in Chapter II.
²⁶In this connection, see Arnold Toynbee's frequently illuminating and insightful comments in *Tradition and Change*, New York, 1954.

[27]We have already discussed this problem in *The Church of God*, pp. 331ff., and *Le Consolateur*, pp. 381ff. and 416ff. In Chapters II and III, we shall pursue the topic further, both in its widest implications and in its concrete historical reality.

[28]These and the following questions will be the main topic of Chapters II through VI, as well as VIII and IX, and finally XII through XV.

[29]Alfred North Whitehead, *Science and the Modern World*, Cambridge University Press, 1946.

[30]Stanley L. Jaki, *The Road of Science and the Ways to God* (1975 and 1976 Gifford Lectures). All quotations will be to the American edition of this capital book (Chicago, 1978). See also, by the same author, *The Origin of Science and the Science of the Origin*, South Bend (Indiana), 1979, and *Cosmos and Creator*, Chicago, 1980.

Chapter II

[1]On this topic see below, Chapters XIIff.

[2]William James, *Psychology*, New York, 1892 (an abridgment of his larger work, *Principles of Psychology*). See pp. 301 and 408ff. of the French edition, (10th ed., Paris, 1946).

[3]On this point and the rest of the chapter, we are particularly indebted to A. N. Whitehead, *Process and Reality*, New York, 1929, and *Modes of Thought*, New York, 1938 (with a new edition in 1968).

[4]Concerning myths, see first of all Mircea Eliade's chapter devoted to the subject in *The Quest*, Chicago and London, 1969, pp. 72ff.

[5]See in particular Chapter I in C. G. Jung's *The Integration of the Personality*, English translation, London, 1940.

[6]R. Amadou, *La Parapsychologie*, Paris, 1954.

[7]This is the direction in which authentic Aristotelian-Thomistic epistemology was already moving. According to this school of thought, we have no knowledge of concepts as such, but only of objects in and more precisely through concepts. See Jacques Maritain, *Les Degrés du Savoir*, Paris, 1932, pp. 231ff. See below the entire Chapters XIX and XXI of the present book.

[8]Cf. supra, note 3.

[9]Ludwig Wittgenstein, after meticulously analyzing the implications of the modern conception of the world in his *Tractatus logico-philosophicus*, London, 1947, and seeming to support—in agreement with Mach, and even more strongly than the Vienna school's somewhat restrictive views would allow—Alfred Ayer's logical positivism, completely turned away from this doctrine in *The Blue* and *The Brown Books*, Oxford, 1958. With an integrity all too rare in founders of metaphysical or other systems, Ayer himself eventually recognized that the equation of truth to scientific truth—in the strictest sense of the term, the sense logical positivism gives it—is not only impossible, but also inherently contradictory. For the assertion that such a system is true obviously eludes any effort to reduce truth merely to statements verifiable through the experience of our senses...an experience which is, however, the system's only criterion!

[10]A. N. Whitehead, *Symbolism*, Cambridge, 1928.

[11]See our own book, *Le Rite et l'Homme*, Paris, 1962, pp. 135ff.; also S. Hocart's *The Life-Giving Myth*, published in *The Labyrinth* (under the editorship of S. H. Hooke), London, 1935, pp. 261ff.

12E. O. James, *Myth and Ritual in the Ancient Near East*, London, 1958 (the entire first chapter is especially pertinent).

13On this point, see Mircea Eliade, *loc. cit.*

14This is not to be confused with any form of pragmatism narrowing down the truth to whatever is successful. If the truth of any being is fundamentally inseparable from existence *per se*, however, it follows that this submission of the human mind to reality—which is the prime requirement for us to reach any truth whatsoever— directly implies, even if we are not always or immediately aware of it, a religious attitude of our limited intelligence. But this is precisely what remains inconceivable except as the attribute of a free and therefore responsible being. The basic condition for an effective quest for truth, in any field, is therefore an attitude of the soul which in the final analysis can recognize itself only as a striving toward divine praise and service. This is what Plato (and even Socrates before him) sensed when he said that one cannot philosophize save with one's whole soul (*The Republic*, VII, 518C). And this is exactly what Maurice Blondel had in mind when he wrote his first *Action*, in spite of the work's obscurities or ambiguities. See in this connection Henri Bouillard's excellent demonstration, *Blondel et le christianisme*, Paris, 1961.

15See *Le Rite et l'Homme*, pp. 137ff.

16This has been noted more particularly in the case of children abandoned at a very early age, who were saved and fed by a female wild animal.

17Maurice Nédoncelle, *La réciprocité des consciences*, Paris, 1942.

18*Le Rite et l'Homme*, pp. 105ff. and 140ff.

19*Ibid.*, p. 107.

20*The Eternal Son*, p. 70, and *Le Père Invisible*, pp. 27ff.

21José Ortega y Gasset, *¿Qué es Filosofía?*, Madrid, 8th ed., 1978.

22See in this respect Liu Kia-Hway, *L'Esprit synthétique de la Chine*, Paris, 1961.

23On the role of myths in Plato's thinking, see P. Frutiger, *Les Mythes de Platon*, Paris, 1930, and P. M. Schuhl, *La Fabulation platonicienne*, Paris, 1966.

24On the connection between myths and philosophical speculation in India, see Anne-Marie Esnoul, *L' Hindouisme*, in *Histoire des Religions*, Vol. I (La Pléiade series), Paris, 1970, pp. 1002ff.

25The reconciliation, or even symbiosis, between myths and wisdom in Egypt is discussed by Ph. Derchain, *La Religion égyptienne*, pp. 107ff. of the volume referred to in the previous footnote.

26On the opposition between Confucianism and Taoism, see Max Kaltenmark, *Le Taoïsme religieux*, in the same volume referred to above, pp. 1218ff., and Jean Grenier, *L'Esprit du Tao*, Paris, 1957, pp. 85ff.

27Cf. *Le Père Invisible*, pp. 140ff. and footnotes.

28A. C. Graham, *Reason in Chinese Philosophical Tradition*, p. 51 in *The Legacy of China* (edited by R. Dawson), Oxford, 1964.

29On Amidism, see H. de Lubac, *Aspects du Bouddhisme*, Paris, 1951, and particularly his *Amidisme et Christianisme*, Paris, 1954.

Chapter III

1See Mircea Eliade, *The Quest*, pp. 8ff. and 68ff.

2See C. G. Jung, *Modern Man in Search of a Soul*, translated by W. S. Dell and Cary F. Baynes, New York, 1933 (Chapter 1 in particular).

[3]On the role of archetypes and their development in Jungian psychology, see for instance Yolanda Jacobi's books.

[4]This fact is emphasized in the volumes Gaston Bachelard has devoted to the various forms of poetic imagination: *L'Eau et les Rêves, L'Air et les Songes*, etc.

[5]Wilhelm Schmidt, *Der Ursprung des Gottesidee*, 6 vol., Münster-in-Westfal, 1925-1936.

[6]R. Pettazoni, *Dio*, vol. I, Rome, 1922, pp. 367ff.

[7]On the importance of these divinities, particularly in the ancient Near East, see W. F. Albright, *Yahweh and the Gods of Canaan*, London, 1968.

[8]E. O. James, *The Cult of the Mother Goddess*, New York, 1959. On hierophanies in general, see Mircea Eliade, *Patterns in Comparative Religion*, translated by Rosemary Sheed, New York, 1958.

[9]On the mythical role of the blacksmith in the earliest civilizations, see Mircea Eliade, *The Forge and the Crucible*, New York, 1971.

[10]See *Le Consolateur*, pp. 16ff., in which we have summarized M. Eliade's *Shamanism: Archaic Techniques of Ecstasy*, New York, 1964.

[11]The study of the primitive king's sacred nature was first undertaken by Sir James Frazer in *The Golden Bough*, 2nd ed., London, 1902. The two schools of S. H. Hooke in England, then of H. Frankfort, first in Germany and later in America, comprehensively developed its general and local charateristics. No exegete has used these insights to better advantage to illuminate the meaning of the Old Testament than Sigmund Mowinckel, particularly in *He That Cometh*, Oxford, 1956.

[12]S. Mowinckel, *op. cit.*, pp. 28ff.

[13]*Ibid.*, pp. 32ff.

[14]The ideas developed by René Girard on the nature of sacrifice (*Des choses inconnues depuis la fondation du monde*, Paris, 1978) have recently created a considerable stir in learned circles. But his brilliant speculations overlook virtually all the contributions made in the last hundred years on this undeniably fundamental aspect of religion. Which may be why he considers supremely indicative of the meaning of sacrifice the apotropaic rites now recognized by all specialists as never having been looked upon as sacrifices by those who practiced these rituals. Quite simply, scapegoats and all variations on the same theme, far from ever being considered as sacrifices to God, were always sent to the devil! On the materiality of sacrifices—the necessary starting point before any attempt to unravel their meaning—one may refer to works such as R. K. Yerkes' *Sacrifice in Greek and Roman Religions and in Primitive Judaism*. This kind of factual study inevitably leads to a firm conclusion: it is not the killing which determines the sacrifice, even when the victim is put to death, which is far from always being the case (see in this respect E. O. James, *Origins of Sacrifice*, London, 1953, pp. 256ff.). Neither is its nature established by the oblation to the divinity. Instead, a sacrifice is a meal, but a meal considered sacred because the divinity partakes of it, whether the sacrifice is exclusively intended for the deity (as in the holocaust), whether priests alone also take part (as in the Hebrew sacrifices for the expiation of sins), or finally whether the entire people participate with them, as in the sacrifices of communion. Or indeed in the Passover, and this seems to have been a characteristic of the very earliest sacrifices, in which all is consumed by the participants, with no role clearly reserved for the divinity.

This explains why, in the most ancient mythic expression of their significance, sacrifices are far from appearing as tremulous attempts of terrified humans to placate a bloodthirsty divinity through some kind of ritual murder. Instead, the gods themselves, acting either directly or through kings deemed to embody or represent them, are the initiators of sacrifices, and thereby show themselves as the quintessential benefactors of mankind, and more particularly the sources of human life, in that which maintains it (nourishment) and produces it (sexuality). The idea of sacrifice as a ritual murder is nothing but the fabrication of self-styled scholars, who thus prove that they belong with the pathetic dupes who persist in taking seriously the alleged *Protocols of the Wise Men of Zion.*

¹⁵Typically claiming to offer up a sacrifice in the place of the priest-prophet Samuel, Saul bears witness to the temptation felt by the kings of Israel to revert to the original role of monarchs among other peoples. Cf. 1 Samuel 13:8ff.

¹⁶Cf. the description of David as the "inspired singer" in 2 Samuel 23:1, expanded upon in Sirach 47:8ff.

¹⁷Girard's excuse, which also explains the confusion of theologians (or allegedly such) when faced with his diatribe, is that late medieval theology, and particularly the theology of the Baroque period—the Protestant even more than its Catholic counterpart—distorting virtually the entire biblical and ecclesiastical tradition (of which it was largely ignorant) in an exacerbated doloristic sentimentality, was the first to develop the nightmarish vision which St. Anselm's extravagant theology of satisfaction had greatly helped to accredit, of a god who sees red at our slightest peccadilloes, and who can be appeased only by blood, preferably innocent blood.

In the first quarter of the twentieth century, however, M. Lepin showed that early biblical and Christian tradition presented no such picture. But since he superimposed a Sulpician and essentially psychological spirituality upon the texts being studied, he was bent on reading into them, as the essence of sacrifice, the pure intention of the offering on the part of the participants in the sacrificial act, an offering of themselves and of their entire being to the one from whom they receive everything. This is admittedly an inspired thought, without doubt one of the purest though belated results of Christian meditative reflection on the topic of sacrifice. Subsequently, starting with Gustaf Aulén's masterful *Christus Victor*, commentators began (but how timidly, even today!) to rediscover what should have been quite obvious to them throughout the Bible, from Genesis 22 (the account of what is improperly known as the sacrifice of Isaac, since the whole purpose was to show Abraham that only God can make an "offering") to Romans 5, namely, that the sacrifice (etymologically the quintessential sacred action) can be performed only *by God*. It is therefore an eminently creative and saving action, the supereminent sign and fulfillment of his love for us, and not in any way some monstrously blessed crime demanded of man for the appeasement of a divinity apparently even more vicious than ourselves!

Which is indeed why—as Joachim Jeremias gradually succeeded in showing, through the various editions, increasingly enriched with facts and quotations, of his impressive book on the Eucharistic sayings of Jesus—the sacrificial rite, offered or rather celebrated by man, could be only, in our hands, a memorial of the properly divine, initial and founding act. Even so, as Jeremias superbly established, this memorial possesses value and reality, as given by God himself in his creative and re-creative intervention in the life of man, only because it mysteriously envelops the continuation of the divine act through the deed of man. And (this aspect is decisive) it is thus placed in the hands of man only so as to be presented again to God in grateful faith, so that God himself may complete its fulfillment in the definitive salvation of man and of the entire cosmos.

Needless to say, this was to become fully luminous in the Christian interpretation of the cross of Jesus and in the light of his resurrection. But the germ was in Chapter 22 of Genesis (which had already inspired the whole Hebraic and Jewish vision of sacrifice, and of ritual in general).

It may be said, however, that the biblical inspiration simply gave an unhoped-for confirmation and a new irradiation (which was henceforth to grow constantly) to an interpretation of sacrifices always held by those we can call "the good pagans." Indeed, this interpretation is the explicit presupposition underlying the entire Vedic literature, primitive Mazdaism and later Mithraism, as well as pre-Colombian religions such as those of the Incas in the Andes, or of Ce Acatl in the Toltec civilization. In turn, it states clearly what virtually all myths adumbrate: the gods are not only the initial institutors of sacrifices, but remain their sole and true agents, though through priests who are only human. And these sacrifices, far from expressing some murderous intent toward mankind, simply reflect the overwhelming generosity with which these gods themselves impart life to man, a life which remains fundamentally theirs.

The repeated lapse of sacrificial religion into mere magic, i.e., into a claim, on the part of man, to obtain from the gods whatever is expected of them by presenting them with vast quantities of the most valuable gifts of food, makes sense only on the basis of the earlier religious conviction, which still underlies even the distorted forms of the ritual: the sacrifice is a sacred deed (*sacrum facere*) because it is a divine action, if ever there was one, as a vitalizing act, a communication of life in its source. All the rest is but a caricature of spiritualities veering on hysteria, or but a speculation by followers who have lost all understanding of what they believe they are trying to develop.

[18]See two of our previous books, Le Rite et l'Homme, particularly pp. 127ff., and Eucharist, Notre Dame (Indiana), 1968, pp. 104 and 463ff.

We are aware of having been accused of admitting, in these two books, that we believe neither in the sacrifice of the Cross nor in that of the Eucharist! It goes without saying that we do not for a moment hold with the idea of sacrifice advocated by some theologians, who therefore claim to be super-orthodox (the fury already evoked by a contribution of such obvious integrity as that of Louis Hardy, La Doctrine de la Rédemption chez St. Thomas, Paris, 1938, was most revealing in this regard). But it is enough to read—starting with St. Thomas himself and going back to the early Fathers—everything that the greatest witnesses of both Latin and Eastern tradition have written on the subject, and to recognize to what extent their views are in harmony with biblical tradition (such as the most ancient and best elements of the synagogical tradition on Abraham's *abodah* always understood it) to see where the truth of faith is to be found. We shall repeat it once again: if there is a point where biblical revelation corrects, illuminates, supernaturally elevates, and also confirms the intuitions of the most universal human religiousness (as the comparative history of religions has allowed us to trace them), it is certainly this question of the meaning of sacrifices.

[19]Cf. our attempted summary and analysis of the work of Father Schmidt, showing how, at each stage of cultural development, man's conception of the divinity is directed or even shaped by the specific means of sustaining life in the context being considered: Le Père invisible, pp. 117ff.

[20]This well-known comparison originated with Wilfred Monod. The mere reading of Leviticus is sufficient to verify the considerations reviewed in this paragraph. The fact that some theologians or philosophers of religion claim to determine the significance of sacrifice without any knowledge of this fundamental biblical book should be enough to discredit their theories.

[21]Pedersen was one of the first to bring out the original nature of the Passover and the development it was to undergo (Israel, Its Life and Culture, new edition, 1959). See also J. B. Segal, The Hebrew Passover, Oxford, 1963.

²²E. O. James, *Origins of Sacrifice*, referred to above. It is revealing to note that this book is generally ignored by theologians discussing the nature of sacrifice, and even more so that the profession treats with marked disdain the more recent study by Yerkes (also referred to above in note 14), because he simply shows which rituals have in fact always been considered as sacrifices. The mere acknowledgment of this reality obviously shatters or destroys the abstract theories which obstinately ignore it. It is the sempiternal story of the theories of the golden tooth! Bayle should definitely be required reading for whoever is working toward a university degree in theology, either Protestant or Catholic.

²³On this fundamental point of the Vedas, see Louis Renou, *Hymnes spéculatifs du Véda*, XXXI, Paris, 1956, pp. 127ff.

²⁴*Le Père invisible*, p. 45. G. Gargam's *L'Amour et la Mort: Eros et Thanatos*, Paris, 1959, unfortunately provides only a preliminary treatment, both superficial and most incomplete, of a field of study which offers a considerable and scarcely suspected potential for much productive and substantive research. Freud's few suggestions on this topic, in a book which most disconcerted his own followers (*Jenseits des Lustprinzips*, Vienna, 1920), are characteristic of the astonishing intuition this unusual mind could occasionally bring to bear even in areas alien to him; in these instances, his approach was clearly much more imaginative than strictly scientific.

²⁵All these peoples were ruled by kings, and their forms of monarchy were fairly characteristic of the group, as noted by the English school of S. Hooke. The rival German and American school led by H. Frankfort underscored the local differences between these kings and their specific functions. On this entire subject and on what follows, the best introduction remains S. H. Hooke's admirable little book, *Middle Eastern Mythology*, London, 1963.

²⁶On the Egyptian king, see Mowinckel, *He That Cometh*, pp. 28ff.

²⁷On the kings of both Mesopotamia and Canaan, *ibid.*, pp. 32ff. and 52ff.

²⁸It will prove profitable to consult the new abridged edition of *The Golden Bough*, completed and corrected in the light of later research, a remarkable contribution by Theodor H. Gaster, Garden City (New York), 1961.

²⁹Cf. Mowinckel, *op. cit.*, pp. 76ff.

³⁰Mowinckel, *op. cit.*, pp. 80ff. and 139ff. For a critique of these views, see particularly Norman H. Snaith, *The Jewish New Year Festival, Its Origins and Development*, London, 1947.

³¹On this subject, see the various volumes of Mowinckel's *Psalmenstudien*, and especially his last work on the topic, *The Psalms in Israel's Worship*, 3 vols., Oxford, 1962.

³²Mowinckel, *He That Cometh*, pp. 143ff. See our more detailed comments in *The Eternal Son*, pp. 92ff., and *Le Père invisible*, pp. 171ff.

³³Cf. Mowinckel, *op. cit.*, pp. 85ff. and 152ff.

³⁴*Le Rite et l'Homme*, pp. 125ff.

³⁵Genesis 9:4ff., and Leviticus 1:5ff.

³⁶Cf. The Wisdom of Solomon 15:14ff.

³⁷Exodus 3.

³⁸Jeremiah 2:13 and 17:13; cf. Isaiah 8:6.

³⁹See our study, *Woman in the Church*, San Francisco, 1979, pp. 40ff.

⁴⁰Typical is the account of the apparition of the Angel of the Lord to Manoah, Samson's father, Judges 13, particularly verses 22ff.

⁴¹See Isaiah 25:8 and 26:19. Cf. Ezekiel 37 and the entire end of the book, from chap. 40.

⁴²On this theme of the divine glory, the book by Arthur Michael Ramsey (former

archbishop of Canterbury) entitled *The Glory of God and the Transfiguration of Christ*, London, 1949, is unusually informative and insightful.

⁴³S. H. Hooke *op. cit.*, pp. 146ff. See also N. J. Phythian Adams, *The People and the Presence*, Oxford, 1942. The main biblical references are Exodus 13:21-22 (cf. 14:19-20); 19:9ff.; 40:34ff.; Numbers 9:15ff., and 10:34-36. Cf. 1 Kings 8:10ff., and the visions of Isaiah 6 and Ezekiel 1 (particularly verse 26). See also Exodus 24:10ff.

⁴⁴Exodus 34:29ff.

⁴⁵2 Corinthians 3, from verse 13 to the end of the chapter. The transfiguration of Jesus is described in the Synoptics (Matthew 17:1-8; Mark 9:2-8; Luke 9:28-36) and commented upon in 2 Peter 1:16ff. We have discussed this theme in *Le Consolateur*, pp. 110ff.

⁴⁶1 John 3:2.

⁴⁷Cf. Plato, the *Phaedo*, 66-67.

⁴⁸Psalm 36 (35):9. We have developed (particularly in *Le Consolateur*, p. 112) this contrast between knowledge leading to resemblance—in the Bible—and knowledge as a result of resemblance—in Platonism.

⁴⁹This is precisely the effect expected from wisdom by the ancient Semites: wisdom is to establish in the lives of men the same divine order which prevails in the cosmos.

⁵⁰Psalm 147:15-18.

⁵¹Psalm 19 (18):1-4.

Chapter IV

¹Such images are common, simply because woman, the snake, and the tree are everywhere the symbols of life.

²This was to be the totally unrealistic notion of traditionalism, which would receive the most surprising appearances of justification during the nineteenth century in Germany from Creuzer, and which Lamennais in France would develop to the point of absurdity, claiming to justify Christian revelation, by asserting that it never revealed anything that the whole of mankind had not already always known!

³See mainly C. G. Jung, Chapter III of *The Integration of Personality*, London, 1940.

⁴See in *The Quest*, pp. 32-34, Mircea Eliade's assessment of G. Dumézil's work.

⁵This is what Msgr. Cerfaux and his school achieved, with outstanding results. The most remarkable example of a comparison justified by this method is quite possibly the demonstration by D. Deden of the origin of the Pauline mystery, which is to be sought not in the mystery religions of late Hellenism, but indeed in the apocalyptic literature, as is shown by the similarity between Chapter 2 of the First Epistle to the Corinthians and Chapter 2 of the book of Daniel. In these two texts, the mystery is placed and defined in relation to divine wisdom as object of apocalyptic revelation, focusing on the decisive moments of history (*kairoi*), and more particularly on its ultimate end (*ta eschata*). Cf. note 28 of Chapter VI.

⁶G. Dumézil, *Mythe et Epopée*, Paris, 3 vols., 1968-1971-1973.

⁷On this and everything that follows, see mainly S. H. Hooke's most illuminating synthesis, *op. cit.*

⁸H. Frankfort's school has shown precisely how the basic themes of the royal myth—first in Sumer, then in the entire basin of the Euphrates and the surrounding area—developed, due to the special circumstances under which the first cities were established there, this special coloration.

⁹Cf. pp. 39 and 43.

[10]One may note, however, particularly in all the ancient cultures of the Near East, the same ambiguity in the theme of water which still appears to color its image in the unconscious musings of our contemporaries: on the one hand spring water, bringing life to the arid desert, and on the other the marine abysses or overflowing rivers in which life is destroyed. S. H. Hooke, *Middle Eastern Mythology*, pp. 19ff.

[11]*Ibid.*, pp. 38ff.

[12]James B. Pritchard, *Ancient Near Eastern Texts Relating to the Old Testament*, Princeton, 1955, pp. 60ff.

[13]Mowinckel, *He That Cometh*, pp. 139ff.

[14]Cf. N. H. Snaith, *op. cit.*

[15]See particularly H. Gunkel, *Schöpfung and Chaos*, Gottingen, 1922. It should be noted that a new text, closer to the Bible in its expressions than any other, has been discovered more recently: W. Lambert and A. R. Millard, *Atra-Hasis: The Babylonian Story of the Flood*, Oxford, 1963.

[16]Cf. Genesis 1:2.

[17]As soon as light was made, in verse 4, and throughout the developing work of creation, there is a recurrent assertion of the fundamental goodness of its successive products.

[18]In this respect, Genesis 2:15 simply echoes 1:26.

[19]Cf. Genesis 1:2.

[20]This is the meaning of the ability received by Adam to call all beings by their names in Genesis 2:19.

[21]We have developed this viewpoint in *Le Trône de la Sagesse*, Paris, 1957, pp. 21ff. (cf. p. 30) and in *Woman in the Church*, pp. 39ff.

[22]Starting with Hosea. See below, pp. 67ff.

[23]This is linked (and the converse is true) with the fundamental conviction evoked by the biblical word: God is the only King, and therefore has only to speak for his will to be done.

[24]This idea that all things are the work of the Word, and in the final analysis are but an expression of the Word, is basic to Psalm 19 (18). In the Bible, it underlies all praise of God as Creator.

[25]It should be noted that anthropomorphisms—e.g., God shaping clay to create man, or breathing life into him—are frequent in this other version, which would seem to indicate that it predates the first.

[26]The final compiler, assumed to be sacerdotal, clearly did not hesitate to include this document, whose style was markedly different from the usual one of his own school. This fact shows that one should not exaggerate the tension between the various schools, a tension modern critics have felt they could detect in the biblical tradition.

[27]One should therefore consider as a whole Chapters 2ff., rather than separate Chapters 1 and 2 from everything that follows.

[28]On these various points, see Hooke, *op. cit.*, pp. 105ff.

[29]It should again be emphasized, however, that the word *rûah* is here also used only for the breath of divine life: after being transmitted to man and incorporated into him, the breath of life becomes simply *nephesh*, "a living soul," as St. Paul was to say, contrasting it with the divine and transcendent "Spirit," the one source of life, in I Corinthians 15:45. However, in Genesis 6:3, *rûah* applies to the very "spirit" which God imparted to man. But this remains exceptional in the Bible.

[30]On the importance of the name, for primitive man in general, and especially for the ancient Semites, as a means of operational knowledge, see Gerardus van der Leeuw, *La Religion dans son essence et ses manifestations*, Paris, 1948, pp. 142ff.

Chapter V

[1]Cf. above, p. 38. See Hooke, *op. cit.*, p. 29.

[2]Hooke, *op. cit.*, p. 22.

[3]*Ibid.*, cf. p. 39.

[4]*Ibid.*, pp. 31ff.

[5]*Ibid.*, pp. 46ff.

[6]Cf. on these various symbolisms, Mircea Eliade, *Traité d'Histoire des Religions*, Paris, 1949, pp. 15ff.

[7]S. H. Hooke, op. cit., pp. 55 and 110ff.

[8]Many modern versions lose sight of this opposition when they translate '*ārûm*, as applied to the serpent, simply by "wily" or "artful."

[9]Genesis 3:23-24.

[10]On these various points, see Hooke, *op. cit.*, pp. 121ff.

[11]Genesis 4.

[12]See *Woman in the Church*, pp. 40ff.

[13]The prophets' usual word to designate idolatry is the Hebrew term *zānāh*, "to commit adultery," translated into the Greek of the Septuagint as *porneia*; both apply properly to any kind of sexual debauchery, adultery as well as prostitution.

[14]Hosea 1:2ff; Jeremiah 3 (cf. 6:2); Ezechiel 16. Cf. Isaiah 50:1 and all of 51-52, as well as 54 (especially verses 5ff.) and 62:4.

[15]Hooke, *op. cit.*, pp. 133ff.

[16]Genesis 6:8ff.

[17]Genesis 6:13ff.

[18]Cf. Genesis 7:2-3 and 7-9.

[19]Genesis 7:12.

[20]Genesis 7:11.

[21]Compare Genesis 7:12 and 8:10ff. with 7:24 and 8:3ff.

[22]Genesis 8:4.

[23]Genesis 8:10 and 20-22.

[24]Genesis 9:9-17.

[25]Genesis 11:1-9. See Hooke, *op. cit.*, pp. 136ff.

[26]This identification recurs in the Pythagoreans, then in the entire Platonic and Platonizing tradition, and finally in the writings of the heretical gnostics.

Chapter VI

[1]S. H. Hooke, *Middle Eastern Mythology*, pp. 28ff.

[2]Dom Hilaire Duesberg, *Les Scribes inspirés*, 2 vols., Paris, 1938, has shown better than anyone else this duality of aspects in wisdom.

[3]Cf. above, p. 20.

[4]Duesberg, *op. cit.*, p. 59 of vol. I.

[5]*Ibid.*, p. 69.

[6]*Ibid.*, p. 27.

[7] See 1 Samuel 8:6ff.

[8]Isaiah 29:14 and Jeremiah 9:22-23. Cf. Isaiah 44:25 and 47:10.

[9]Mowinckel, *He That Cometh*, p. 89.

[10]Ecclesiastes 12:13.
[11]Duesberg, *op. cit.*, pp. 501ff. of vol. I.
[12]Cf. *Le Père Invisible*, p. 125.
[13]Mowinckel, *op. cit.*, pp. 48ff.
[14]Cf. 2 Samuel 12:13ff.
[15]1 Kings 3:5ff.
[16]Cf. *The Eternal Son*, p. 76.
[17]Cf. particularly Ecclesiastes 1.
[18]Ecclesiastes 12:13.
[19]*The Eternal Son*, loc. cit.
[20]*Ibid.*, p. 77.
[21]Duesberg, *op. cit.*, vol. 2, pp. 53ff.
[22]Job 42:7ff.
[23]Mowinckel, *op. cit.*, pp. 201ff.
[24]See D. S. Russell, *The Method and Message of Jewish Apocalyptic*, Philadelphia, 1976.
[25]Mowinckel, *op. cit.*, pp. 155ff.
[26]*Ibid.*, pp. 345ff.
[27]Cf. Isaiah 49:6.
[28]See first in this respect D. Deden's entire *Le "Mystère" paulinien*, in volume 13 of the *Ephemerides Theologicae Lovanienses*, 1936.
[29]Daniel 2:28; cf. 2:20-23.
[30]Daniel 2:29.
[31]Daniel 2:36-44.
[32]See *The Eternal Son*, p. 81.
[33]Cf. Russell's work referred to in note 24; also Mowinckel, *op. cit.*, pp. 270ff.
[34]Mowinckel, *op. cit.*, pp. 348ff.
[35]Cf. Daniel 7:27.
[36]See *Le Consolateur*, pp. 391ff.
[37]See *The Eternal Son*, pp. 125ff. and 141ff. Cf. Joachim Jeremias, *New Testament Theology*, book 1, *The Proclamation of Jesus*, New York, 1971, paragraphs 23 and 24.
[38]Mowinckel, *op. cit.*, pp. 134ff.
[39]Cf. *Le Père Invisible*, pp. 171ff. and *The Eternal Son*, pp. 92ff.
[40]*Testament de Lévi*, 17, in *Testaments of the Twelve Patriarchs*, London, 1908.
[41]Matthew 12:29; Mark 3:23-27; Luke 11:17-22.
[42]See *Le Père Invisible*, pp. 180ff.
[43]Mowinckel, *op. cit.*, p. 435.
[44]This was to be expressed in concise form by St. Paul when he said that the celestial or spiritual Man—the counterpart of the Son of man of the apocalypses, who was to overthrow the demonic rule—was not the original Man, but the "ultimate Adam," the Man of the end of time (I Corinthians 15:46).
[45]Mowinckel, *op. cit.*, pp. 422ff.
[46]On this entire subject, see *The Eternal Son*, pp. 91ff.
[47]Cf. Revelation 21 and 22, the vision of the new heaven and the new earth.
[48]*Le Consolateur*, pp. 42ff., and *The Eternal Son*, pp. 101ff.
[49]Cf. Maurice Goguel, *Eschatologie et Apocalyptique*, in *Trois études sur le christianisme primitif*, Paris, 1930.
[50]Isaiah 26:19.
[51]*The Eternal Son*, pp. 144 and 276ff.
[52]*Ibid.*, pp. 83 and 233.
[53]See below, Chapter IX.
[54]Nathan Söderblom was one of the first to see that original Zoroastrianism was

radically different from the metaphysical dualism of the later magi. Cf. N. Söder-blom, *Dieu vivant dans l'histoire*, French ed., Paris, 1937, pp. 191ff.

[55]*Ibid.*

[56]1Samuel 18:10ff.

[57]See N. P. Williams, *The Ideas of the Fall and of Original Sin*, London, 1929, pp. 59ff., and especially 67ff.

[58]See the second part of paragraph 24 in J. Jeremias, *New Testament Theology*.

[59]Cf. what we have said above, pp. 33ff.

[60]See the following chapter.

Chapter VII

[1]Cf. above p. 46.

[2]Cf. D. S. Russell, *op. cit.*, pp. 283ff.

[3]See our *Spirituality of the New Testament and the Fathers*, pp. 13ff. (Vol. III of *History of Christian Spirituality*, New York, 1982).

[4]The wording is by Jules Lebreton, *Lumen Christi*, Paris, 1947, p. 173.

[5]Genesis 49.

[6]Psalms 127 (126) and 128 (127).

[7]See our *Eucharist*, pp. 58ff.

[8]Hosea 2:8-10.

[9]Hosea 2:14-15.

[10]Isaiah 2:7-8 and 17.

[11]Isaiah 5:8, 18 and 20.

[12]Jeremiah 16:2.

[13]Jeremiah 20:7-9.

[14]Cf. especially Isaiah 49:1-6, 52:13, and 53.

[15]Cf. note 58 of the previous chapter.

[16]Luke 2:25.

[17]Jeremiah, *loc. cit.*

[18]Psalm 86 (85). On this theme, see A. Causse, *Les Pauvres d'Israël*, Strasbourg-Paris, 1922, and A. Gelin, *Les Pauvres de Yahvé*, Paris, 1954.

[19]Cf. particularly the specific form of the Beatitudes in Luke 6:20ff.

[20]Cf. Hosea 2:14ff.

[21]Genesis 12.

[22]See our *Spirituality of the New Testament and the Fathers*, pp. 343ff.

[23]See our *Le Sens de la Vie monastique*, Paris, 1950, pp. 74ff. and *Introduction à la vie spirituelle*, Paris, 1960, pp. 131ff. and 137ff.

[24]On this topic, see Dom Jean Leclercq, *Mönchtum und Peregrination im Frühmittelalter*, in *Römische Quartalschrift*, LV, Rome-Freiburg, 1960, pp. 212ff.

[25]This theme has been admirably brought out by Sergei Nikolaevich Boulgakoff in his book on St. John the Baptist, *The Friend of the Bridegroom* (in Russian).

[26]See Annie Jaubert, *La Notion d'Alliance dans le Judaïsme*, Paris, 1963.

[27]See *Woman in the Church*, p. 47.

[28]Hosea 2:16.

[29]Ezechiel 16:3-6.

[30]Ezechiel 16:60ff.

[31]Isaiah 54:11-12.

32Isaiah 60:1-19.
33Isaiah 62:3-4.
34Cf. Revelation 21:2 and *Baruch's Syriac Apocalypse*, 4.
35Proverbs 8:22-31.
36Cf. Proverbs 7:17ff.
37See *Le Consolateur*, pp. 42ff.
38Sirach 24:3-10.
39Cf. the end of Daniel 7.
40Isaiah 62:5.
41Wisdom of Solomon 8:2-4.
42See Adolphe Lods, *Histoire de la littérature hébraïque et juive*, Paris, 1950, on the fact itself, and on its value, A. Feuillet, *Le Cantique des cantiques*, Paris, 1953, pp. 248ff.
43See our *Eucharist*.

Chapter VIII

1R. G. Collingwood, *The Idea of Nature*, Oxford, 1945 (new edition, 1970). Our page references relate to the 1976 American reprinting.
2*Ibid.*, pp. 30ff.
3P. 33.
4Pp. 33ff.
5Pp. 48ff. Cf. p. 39.
6Pp. 65-66.
7P. 66. Cf. John Burnet, *L'Aurore de la philosophie grecque*, French ed., Paris, 1919, p. 165.
8*Ibid.*, pp. 161-162.
9Collingwood, *op. cit.*, pp. 63-64 and 68-69.
10Cf. Burnet, *op. cit.*, pp. 373-374.
11Collingwood, *op. cit.*, pp. 20-21.
12*Ibid.*, p. 18.
13Cf. Burnet, *op. cit.*, pp. 379ff.
14Collingwood, *op. cit.*, p. 18.
15*Ibid.*, pp. 63-68.
16See the depiction of Socrates in *The Clouds*, in which he is described as having the characteristics of the Sophists, and also—curiously enough—as sharing the traits of the ancient natural philosophers.
17The *Theaetetus*, 152a. See W. K. C. Guthrie, *History of Greek Philosophy*, vol. 3, Cambridge, 1969, p. 171.
18Guthrie, *op. cit.*, pp. 272ff. of the same volume.
19See A. J. Festugière, *Socrate*, Paris, 1932.
20Aristotle, *Metaphysics*, 987a, 32ff.
21See L. Robin, *Le Pensée grecque*, Paris, 1948, pp. 210ff.
22Cf. Guthrie, *op. cit.*, vol. 1, 1971, pp. 311ff., and vol. 4, 1975, p. 35.
23Burnet, *op. cit.*, pp. 126ff.
24Cf. fragments 11 to 16 of Xenophanes (in Burnet, *op. cit.*, p. 133) and fragments 124 to 130 of Heraclitus (*ibid.*, p. 192).
25Cf. Festugière, *op. cit.*

[26]W. Lutoslawski, *The Origin and Growth of Plato's Logic*, London, 1897. Cf. Collingwood's note, *op. cit.*, p. 58.

[27]Collingwood, *op. cit.*, pp. 63ff.

[28]In this respect, see A. Diès, *Autour de Platon*, vol. 2, Paris, 1927, pp. 523ff.

Chapter IX

[1]See Werner Jaeger, *Aristotle*, second edition, Oxford, 1948, and the recently published last volume in Guthrie's *op. cit.*

[2]Jaeger, *op. cit.*, pp. 219ff.

[3]Guthrie had already published two articles on the subject in the *Classical Review* (1933 and 1934).

[4]William David Ross, *Aristote*, French ed., Paris, 1930, p. 221.

[5]A. Chroust, *Aristotle, New Light on His Life and on Some of His Lost Works*, London, 1973.

[6]*Lambda Metaphysics*, 1072b.

[7]On this entire topic, see Collingwood, *op. cit.*, pp. 80ff. and 87ff. Cf. *Nicomachean Ethics*, X, 7.

[8]Collingwood, *op. cit.*, pp. 91ff.

[9]Guthrie, *op. cit.*, vol. 2, Cambridge, 1965, pp. 386ff. (particularly p. 415).

[10]Cf. J. de Vogel, *Greek Philosophy*, vol. 3, third edition, Leiden, 1975, pp. 17 and 33ff.

[11]G. Verbecke, *L'évolution de la doctrine du Pneuma de stoïcisme à Saint Augustin*, Paris-Louvain, 1945, pp. 223ff.

[12]*Ibid.*, pp. 115ff.

[13]*Ibid.*, pp. 12ff.

[14]*Ibid.*, pp. 62ff.

[15]*Ibid.*, pp. 90ff.

[16]M. Spanneut, *Le Stoïcisme des Pères de l'Eglise*, Paris, 1957.

[17]G. Verbecke, *op. cit.*, pp. 41ff. and 90ff.

[18]In particular, this is the view of Emile Bréhier, *Les idées philosophiques et religieuses de Philon d'Alexandrie*, Paris, second edition, 1925.

[19]H. A. Wolfson, *Philo*, second edition, Cambridge, MA, 1948; E. R. Goodenough, *By Light, Light*, New Haven, CT, 1935; Jean Laporte, *La doctrine eucharistique chez Philon d'Alexandrie*, Paris, 1972.

[20]A number of recent authors, such as John Dillon (*The Middle Platonists*, London, 1977, pp. 139ff.), followed in particular by David Winston (*Philo of Alexandria*, New York, 1981), strongly disagreed with the scholars we have referred to, and emphasized again Philo's debt to Middle Platonism. Although this influence is undeniable, the very texts collected, translated and explained by Winston show clearly that Philo nevertheless remained fundamentally inspired by the biblical vision of God the Creator.

Chapter X

[1]See *Le Consolateur*, pp. 45ff.

[2]J. Jeremias, *Abba. The Prayers of Jesus*, Philadelphia, 1978.

[3]See the study by Dom Jacques Dupont, *Les Béatitudes*, second edition, Paris, 1973.

[4]Luke 12:27.

[5]J. Jeremias, *The Parables of Jesus*, translated by S. H. Hooke, revised edition, New York, 1963.

[6]Cf. John 3:16 and 17:3.

[7]Romans 8:21.

[8]I Corinthians 3:22-23.

[9]All the works of St. Theresa of the Child Jesus and her very life are probably the best commentary one could find on this evangelical theme. See Hans Urs von Balthasar, *Thérèse of Lisieux, the Story of a Mission*, translated by Donald Nicholl, New York, 1954.

[10]Luke 10:21-22.

[11]Matthew 11:25-27.

[12]Matthew 4:1-11; Mark 1:12-13; Luke 4:1-13.

[13]Mark 1:12. Cf. H. Riesenfeld, *Studies in the Gospel Tradition*, Philadephia, 1968.

[14]See our study titled *Harpagmos*, in *Mélanges Lebreton*.

[15]Mark 6:7-13.

[16]Matthew 12:29ff.

[17]A. Feuillet, *Le Christ Sagesse de Dieu d'après les épîtres pauliniennes*, Paris, 1966.

[18]Cf. D. Deden, *Le "Mystère" paulinien*, in *Ephemerides theologicae Lovanienses*, 1936, and Dom J. Dupont, *Gnosis*, Louvain, 1949.

[19]On St. Paul's notion of the body, see J. T. A. Robinson, *The Body*, London, 1963.

[20]On the Pauline view of the cosmos as created entirely in the Son, see Feuillet, *op. cit.*, pp. 202ff., as well as J. B. Lightfoot's commentary on the Epistle to the Colossians, in connection with Colossians 1:15, regarding the Son as firstborn of the entire creation.

[21]Romans 8:22-23.

[22]See the whole context of Romans 8:18-27.

[23]Romans 8:19.

[24]On this theme, see our study, *Les Deux Economies du Gouvernement divin*, in *Initiation théologique*, vol. II, Paris, 1952, pp. 504ff.

[25]Romans 5:12ff.

[26]See the entries on *Sarx, Kosmos,* and *Aiōn*, in Kittel's *Theological Dictionary*.

[27]Galatians 4:9 and Colossians 2:9 and 20.

[28]I Corinthians 2:6 and 8. Cf. Ephesians 2:2 and 3:10.

[29]Ephesians 6:12. Cf. Colossians 1:13.

[30]II Corinthians 4:4.

[31]Gustaf E. H. Aulén, *Christus Victor: An Historical Study of the Three Main Types of the Idea of the Atonement*, translated by A. G. Hebert, London, 1970.

[32]Cf. Colossians 3:6 and Ephesians 2:3.

[33]Cf. Ephesians 2:5 and the entire context.

[34]Colossians 2:14.

[35]Cf. Colossians 2:15.

[36]II Thessalonians 2:7.

[37]Galatians 3:19.

[38]Acts 7:53.

[39]Hebrews 2:2.

[40]Colossians 2:16ff.

[41]Cf. Galatians 4:2ff., and particularly 8ff.

[42]Hebrews 2:5.

[43]I Corinthians 15:45.

[44]This is certainly the meaning of I Corinthians 2:8, concerning the princes of this

world, who "crucified the Lord of glory," but who would doubtless have refrained from doing so, had they understood that the Cross would lead to their dispossession.

45Cf. Colossians 2:15.
46I Corinthians 15:24ff.
47Theme of Romans 5:12ff.
48Theme of I Corinthians 15:45ff.
49Philippians 2:5ff.
50See Markus Barth's introduction to his commentary on the Epistle to the Ephesians, in the *Anchor Bible* series, Vol. 1, New York, 1974.
51Colossians 1:13-17.
52Colossians 1:15.
53I Corinthians 15:45.
54Cf. Romans 5:8 and Philippians 2:5ff.
55Cf. Colossians 1:15 and 18, and I Peter 3:22.
56Revelation 14:4.
57Revelation 7:9ff.
58Cf. Revelation 5:6ff. and I Peter 1:19ff.
59Revelation 12:9.
60Cf. Revelation 20 and 21.
61John 1:5.
62John 12:35; cf. John 9 and its context.
63I John 1:5.
64I John 2:15 and 5:19.
65John 3:16.
66John 1:14.
67John 12:31.
68John 8:44.
69*Ibid.*
70Cf. John 17:2 and 22.
71John 14:19.
72I John 3:1-3 and 4:7 and 10.
73Cf. John 12:32.
74Cf. John 17:22.
75Cf. I Thessalonians 4:13 to 5:3, and I Corinthians 15:23ff., as well as Colossians 3:4.
76I John 3:2.
77II Corinthians 3:18.
78Cf. II Corinthians 1:22, Ephesians 1:14, and Romans 2:23.
79John 14:8-10.
80R. M. Grant, *A Historical Introduction to the New Testament*, London, 1963. Also illuminating, even if his reaction may seem somewhat excessive, is J. Carmignac's *Le Mirage de l'Eschatologie*, Paris, 1979.
81C. H. Dodd, *History and the Gospel*, London, 1938.
82O. Cullmann, *Le Salut dans l'Histoire*, Neuchâtel, 1966, pp. 210ff.
83Matthew 11:12.
84Colossians 1:27.
85II Corinthians 4:16.
86Mark 13:32.

Chapter XI

[1]R. P. Casey, *The Study of Gnosticism*, in *Journal of Theological Studies*, Vol. 36, 1935, pp. 45ff.

[2]See our *Spirituality of the New Testament and the Fathers*, pp. 238ff.

[3]Adolf von Harnack, *Lehrbuch der Dogmengeschichte*, third edition, Freiburg-Leipzig, pp. 215ff.; also Eugène de Faye, *Gnostiques et Gnosticisme*, second edition, Paris, 1925.

[4]Wilhelm Bousset, *Hauptprobleme der Gnosis*, Gottingen, 1907, and R. Reitzenstein, *Die Hellenistischen Mysterienreligionen*, third edition, Leipzig, 1927.

[5]Cf. the third edition, referred to in the previous note, of his major work.

[6]G. Quispel, *Gnosis als Weltreligion*, Leiden, 1954.

[7]R. M. Grant, *Gnosticism and Early Christianity*, New York, 1966.

[8]M. Friedländer, *Die religiösen Bewegungen innerhalb des Judentums im Zeitalter Jesu*, Berlin, 1905.

[9]O. Cullmann, *Le problème littéraire et historique du roman pseudo-clémentin*, Paris, 1930.

[10]See Nock and Festugière's edition of *Hermès Trismégiste*, Paris, 1945, Vol. 1, pp. 1ff., and Vol. 2, pp. 257ff.

[11]Carsten Colpe, *Die Religionsgeschichtliche Schule: Darstellung und Kritik ihres Bildes vom gnostischen Erlösermythos*, Gottingen, 1961.

[12]See E. de Faye, *op. cit.*, for a complete description of these systems.

[13]Cf. this word's entry in Kittel's *Dictionary*.

[14]See M. Sagnard, *La Gnose valentinienne et le témoignage de saint Irénée*, 1947. Even more illuminating is Adelin Rousseau's introduction to the edition—in *Sources Chrétiennes* (263)—of a new French translation of St. Irenaeus' work, under the title *Contre les hérésies*.

[15]In his Epistle to the Ephesians (1:10), St. Paul uses only the verb, *anakephalaiō sasthai*. The noun is frequently used by St. Irenaeus, however (see the following note).

[16]*Adversus Haereses*, 3, 18, 1; cf. 4, 34, 1; 5, 14, 2.

[17]*Ibid.*, 5, 16, 1-2.

[18]See the whole of Chapters 6 to 12 in the fifth book.

[19]See *Le Consolateur*, pp. 138 and 142.

[20]*Demonstratio*, 45.

[21]*Adversus Haereses*, 3, 22, 3-4.

[22]*Ibid.*, 3, 17.

[23]*Ibid.* 4, 20, 7.

[24]On this point, see H. Langerbeck, *Aufsätze zur Gnosis*, Gottingen, 1967.

[25]*De Principiis*, 1, 2, 10; 1, 4, 3; 2, 9, 1. Cf. J. Daniélou, *Origène*, Paris, 1948, pp. 208ff. and 250ff.

[26]*De Principiis*, 2, 6, 3; 2, 9, 6 (cf. 1, 6, 2, and 1, 8, 4).

[27]Antoine Guillaumont, *Les "Kephalaia gnostica" d'Evagre le Pontique et l'histoire de l'origénisme chez les Grecs et les Syriens*, Paris, 1962, pp. 81ff.

[28]See *The Eternal Son*, pp. 311ff., and *Le Consolateur*, pp. 149ff.

[29]On Eunomius, see J. Quasten, *Patrology*, Vol. 3, Utrecht-Antwerp, 1960, pp. 306ff.

[30]See our book, *L'incarnation et l'Eglise corps du Christ selon Saint Athanase*, Paris, 1943, pp. 136ff.

[31]1 *Contra Arianos*, 43; 2 *Contra Arianos*, 69 and 70; 3 *Contra Arianos*, 33 and 36.

[32]*De Incarnatione*, 54, and 1 *Contra Arianos*, 39.

[33]See *Le Consolateur*, pp. 173ff. Cf. first epistle to Serapion, 10 and 11.

[34]*Ibid.*, p. 165.

[35]Ibid., p. 178.

[36]This has been clearly shown by J. H. Newman in his *Letter to Dr. Pusey, Vol. 2 of Certain Difficulties Felt by Anglicans in Catholic Teaching Considered*, London 1876, p. 85. Cf. *Essay on Development of Christian Doctrine*, London and New York, 1891, pp. 143ff. Cf. also Athanasius, 2 *Contra Arianos*, 77-78 and particularly 81-82, and Augustine, *Confessions*, book XII, c. 15 (cf. 11). On the latter text, see the commentary by Hans Urs von Balthasar, *De l'intégration*, French translation, Paris, 1970, pp. 22ff.; on the reference to Athanasius, see our book mentioned in note 30.

[37]Cf. Hans Urs von Balthasar, *Présence et Pensée*, Paris, 1942, pp. xviiff.; J. Daniélou, *Platonisme et théologie mystique*, Paris, 1944, pp. 152ff.; also A. H. Armstrong and R. A. Markus, *Christian Faith and Greek Philosophy*, London, 1960, pp. 24ff.

[38]On this point, see particularly Lars Thunberg, *Microcosm and Mediator*, Lund, 1965, pp. 77ff.

[39]Gregory of Nyssa, *Great Catechetical Discourse*, XXIIff.

[40]*De hominis opificio*, 24; *De anima et resurrectione*, III (cf. *In Hexaemeron*, I). See Hans Urs von Balthasar, *Présence et pensée*, pp. 19ff.

[41]Cf. Hans Urs von Balthasar, *Liturgie cosmique*, French translation, Paris, 1947, pp. 127ff.

[42]In this respect, St. Thomas, while attempting to remain as faithful as possible to the teachings of St. Augustine, nevertheless did not share the latter's pessimism. Cf. *Summa Theologica*, Prima pars, question 98 (particularly article 2) and IIa IIae, q. 153, a. 2.

[43]See Newman's sermon referred to below, p. 204.

[44]See in particular Ch. Bigg, *The Christian Platonists of Alexandria*, Oxford, 1913.

[45]In considering that lust rather than pride is at the root of human sin, St. Thomas followed the whole of tradition. Cf. *Summa Theologica*, Ia IIae, q. 82, a. 3.

[46]I Corinthians, 15:24ff.

[47]These speculations originated with Hilary of Poitiers (*In Matth.*, XVIII, 6) and Augustine (*Enchiridion*, 29, and *De Civitate Dei*, XXII, 1).

[48]See *Le Consolateur*, p. 243.

Chapter XII

[1]Etienne Gilson, *L'esprit de la philosophie médiévale*, Vol. 1 , Paris, 1932, pp. 1ff. and 54ff., and *A New History of Philosophy*, last vol.; *Recent Philosophy: From Hegel to the Present*, New York, 1966, the chapter on neo-Thomism.

[2]See Father Arnou's article, *Platonisme des Pères*, in the *Dictionnaire de théologie catholique*.

[3]Edwyn Bevan, *Stoics and Sceptics*, New York, 1959.

[4]Basile Tatakis, *La philosophie byzantine*, a supplementary volume to E. Bréhier's *Histoire de la philosophie*, Paris, 1959.

[5]See M. Grabmann, *Introduction to the Theological Summa of St. Thomas*, St. Louis, 1930; M. D. Chenu, *Introduction à l'étude de Saint Thomas*, Montreal-Paris, 1950; E. Gilson, *La philosophie de Saint Bonaventure*, second edition, Paris, 1943, and *Le Thomisme*, new edition, Paris, 1947.

[6]E. Gilson, *Jean Duns Scot*, Paris, 1952.

[7]See *A New History of Philosophy*, loc. cit.

[8]E. Gilson, *La philosophie au Moyen Age*, Paris, 1944, pp. 240ff. and 278ff. It is

nevertheless strange to note the surprising leniency with which Catholic historians (and even Karl Barth!) judge St. Anselm's certainly brilliant theological constructs, which however clearly initiated the unbridled rationalism that was subsequently to disintegrate the entire contents of revelation. Many nineteenth century Catholic thinkers were accused, or even condemned, on much flimsier grounds; among the first to be so treated was Günther, not to mention Rosmini or Newman. Admittedly, St. Anselm was canonized, but this distinction was based on his spirituality rather than his metaphysics, and it may be assumed that the Holy Office, had it existed at the time, would have unhesitatingly called a halt to the canonization proceedings.

⁹This was clearly perceived by a contemporary philosopher who was certainly sympathetic to Christianity but never professed himself a Catholic, Alfred North Whitehead, in *Science and the Modern World*, Cambridge, 1920, pp. 15ff.

¹⁰On this intellectual context of Thomism, see M. D. Chenu, *La théologie comme science au XIII siècle*, third edition, Paris, 1957.

¹¹Pierre Duhem, *Le système du monde, histoire des doctrines de Platon à Copernic*, 10 vols., 1914-1959. Of particular interest is Duhem's study of Leonardo da Vinci, from whom, in a surprisingly superficial and off-hand manner, Paul Valéry (who seems to have never actually read this fundamental text) believed he could draw the idea of a science whose very rationality would preclude any possibility of a spiritualistic metaphysics.

¹²Stanley L. Jaki, *The Road of Science and the Ways to God*, 1975 and 1976 Gifford Lectures, which we will quote from the American edition, Chicago, 1978; see also Jaki's *The Origin of Science and the Science of the Origin*, South Bend, IN, 1979, and *Cosmos and Creator*, Chicago, 1980.

¹³R. G. Collingwood, *The Idea of Nature*, Oxford, 1970.

¹⁴See also Max Planck, *The Universe in the Light of Modern Physics*, London, 1931.

¹⁵Collingwood, *op. cit.*, p. 156.

¹⁶R. Ruyer's *La Gnose de Princeton*, Paris, 1974, is most revealing. But the author does not seem to realize that the group of scientists he met in Princeton simply express— with spirit and flashes of wit which should sometimes be taken *cum grano salis*—a tendency of a large majority of the most eminent American scientists. More than twenty years ago, Nicolas Lossky (father of the theologian Vladimir Lossky), in his *History of Russian Philosophy* (New York, 1951), already noted a similar trend among Soviet men of science also, and this development has only grown stronger since that time.

¹⁷James Jeans, *The Mysterious Universe*, London, 1930.

¹⁸E. Whittaker, *The Beginning and the End of the World*, London, 1942.

¹⁹Olivier Costa de Beauregard, *Le second principe de la science du temps*, Paris, 1963, and *La physique moderne et les pouvoirs de l'esprit*, Paris, 1980.

²⁰Eric Mascall's *Christian Theology and Natural Science*, London, 1956, contains a particularly valuable analysis of these tendencies in contemporary science, by a theologian whose initial training was scientific. A revised edition, taking into account the latest developments in science, would be highly desirable.

²¹See Lonergan, *Insight*, London and New York, 1957, as well as *Verbum, Verb and Idea in Aquinas*, University of Notre Dame Press, 1967.

²²Whitehead, *Modes of Thought*, New York, 1938, first chapter.

²³*The Concept of Nature*, Cambridge, 1920, pp. 31ff.

²⁴Locke, *Essay Concerning Human Understanding*, 1690, chapter 8 of book 2.

²⁵Cf. G. Berkeley, *Treatise Concerning the Principles of Human Knowledge*, 1710, first part, paragraph 9.

[26]Jaki, *The Road of Science and the Ways to God*, p. 43.

[27]Pierre Chaunu, *L'expansion européenne du XIII au XV siècle*, Paris, 1969, and *Le temps des réformes*, Paris, 1975.

[28]Bernard Groethuysen, *Origines de l'esprit bourgeois en France*, fourth edition, Paris, 1956.

[29]It is remarkable that, as early as the middle of the nineteenth century, in his *Idea of a University*, Newman accurately outlined this conception of the relationship between theology and science. The first intimation of the idea may be found in the opening pages of the last of the *Oxford University Sermons* (whose wealth of knowledge surpasses that in the *Essay on the Development of Christian Doctrine*, which was to deepen and extend only a few of the sermon's many insights).

Chapter XIII

[1]Oswald Spengler, *The Decline of the West*, New York, 1934. In *A Study of History*, Vol. 9, Oxford, 1956, p. 168, Arnold Toynbee has clearly shown the simplistic quality of this theory.

[2]See *Le Père Invisible*, p. 127ff. Cf. Daniel Rops, *Le Roi ivre de Dieu*, Paris, 1956.

[3]Jean Grenier, *L'Esprit du Tao*, pp. 29ff.

[4]See H. Jon Glasenapp, *La Philosophie indienne*, French translation, Paris, 1951.

[5]V. Brochard, *Les Sceptiques grecs*, second edition, Paris, 1923. In the volume edited by A. H. Armstrong, *The Cambridge History of Later Greek and Early Medieval Philosophy*, Cambridge, 1967, see also the beginning of Chapter IV, by P. Merlan, on the Platonic Academy during the first century, page 5. The main texts may be found in C. J. Vogel's third volume of *Greek Philosophy*, Leiden, 1973, pp. 184ff.

[6]See mainly René Pintard, *Le Libertinage érudit dans la première moitié du XVII siècle*, Paris, 1943. Paul Hazard's *La Crise de la conscience européenne*, Paris, 1935, and *La Pensée européene au XVIII siècle, de Montesquieu à Lessing*, Paris, 1946, are more superficial.

[7]Cf. the works of Jerome Carcopino, particularly *La Basilique de la Porte Majeure*, seventh edition, Paris, 1944.

[8]See Peter Berger, *A Rumor of Angels*, Harmondsworth, 1971, and James Hitchcock, *The Recovery of the Sacred*, New York, 1974.

[9]The falsity of this view was already established by Raoul Allier in *Magie et Religion* (1935).

[10]S. Freud, *Civilization and Its Discontents*, New York, 1961.

[11]L. Feuerbach, *Das Wesen des Christentums*, published in 1841.

[12]A. J. Festugière, *De l'Essence de la Tragédie grecque*, Paris, 1969.

[13]C. M. Bowra, *Homer*, London, 1979, and *From Virgil to Milton*, London, 1945.

[14]Cf. André Bellesort, *Virgile*, Paris, 1936.

[15]This is certainly the major characteristic of his *Metamorphoses*.

[16]On Xenophanes and the true meaning of his protest, see Rex Warner, *The Greek Philosophers*, New York and Toronto, 1958, pp. 23ff.

[17]Cf. A. J. Festugière, *Epicure et ses dieux*, Paris, 1946.

[18]Walter Pater has strikingly expressed this point in his philosophical novel, *Marius the Epicurean*, London, 1900.

[19]Neoplatonism in the last phase of its evolution is most revealing in this respect; see Iamblichus, *De Mysteriis*.

[20]Examples of this decline are found in Catullus' Poem 63 on Attis and Cybele, as well as in the VIIth of Propertius' *Elegies* (book IV).

²¹See Groethuysen's book, previously referred to (note 28, Chapter XII).
²²See Georges Duby, *Saint Bernard: l'Art cistercien*, Paris, 1976. His Marxist interpretation should obviously not be taken at face value, but his facts are unquestionable.
²³Even if one ignores the criticism voiced by Erasmus, there remains the no less damning assessments by the *Consilium de emendanda Ecclesia*, prepared by a commission of cardinals at the request of Paul III.
²⁴See Gabriel Le Bras' comments in Volume 12 of *Histoire de l'Eglise*, edited by Fliche and Martin, Paris, 1964, pp. 571ff.
²⁵In connection with the rest of this section, it is essential to read Jacques Ellul's analysis in his *La Technique et l'enjeu du siècle*, Paris, 1954. Interestingly enough, his book, though it attracted scant attention in France, has been and remains a best-seller (under the title of *The Technological Society*) in the United States, where this type of civilization has developed to a far greater degree than in Europe. In America, Ellul is justifiably considered to rank among the greatest contemporary thinkers. One can however detect in this major work, and in Ellul's later books, a certain Manichean tendency, a typically Protestant temptation, which is present whenever Protestantism does not sink into an allegedly "liberal" humanism. Ellul's weakness is that he fails to distinguish—as we shall attempt to do—between technology *per se* and its unbridled development, in which sight is lost of its human finality.
²⁶On the short-lived craze for various theologies of secularization in the sixties, the most perceptive book written may well be E. Mascall's *The Secularization of Christianity*, London, 1965.
²⁷Nothing could be more enlightening in this respect than the conclusion of Claude Lévi-Strauss' *Tristes tropiques*, New York, 1961.
²⁸Malraux's *Museum Without Walls* reveals both the unprecedented wealth and the barrenness which together are characteristic of modern artistic culture.
²⁹It is noteworthy that whenever (as in the seventeenth century) there has been a feud between traditionalists and modernists, the period's truly creative geniuses are found among the former, and the crowd of superficial improvisers among the latter: Pradon against Racine, Chapelain against La Fontaine, etc. It happens every time.
³⁰It may be considered that the process started with the art collections of the Italian Renaissance *virtuosi*, and was to lead to a succession of increasingly decadent "neo" styles: from Palladian neo-classicism, in which creative inspiration was certainly prominent, to Gilbert Scott's neo-Gothic (not to mention Abadie's neo-Byzantine horrors), the decline is significant. This is not to say that there have been no occasional instances of resurgence (such as Sir Ninian Comper's truly astonishing combination of neo-Gothic and neo-Baroque) but these were strictly ephemeral.
³¹Particularly enlightening in this respect are the comments of Rodin in France (Auguste Rodin, *Cathedrals of France*, Boston, 1965) and Sir John Betjeman in England (see his introduction to the collection of essays published by Collins under the title of *Parish Churches*, new edition, London, 1980) on the highly unfortunate result, to say the least, of so many "restorations" seeking to draw inspiration from the rediscovery of former architectural styles.
³²The book devoted to Walter Pater by D'Hangest (*Walter Pater: l'homme et son oeuvre*, Paris 1961) and Enid Starkie's study of Baudelaire provide outstanding analyses of two profoundly different men who had both discovered the fallacy of aestheticism, an approach by which they had been tempted for a time, but from which they soon broke free.
³³Fr. Sergei Boulgakoff is one of those who have most accurately diagnosed the inner pathology—which one might be inclined to look upon as a shameful illness—of modern art, without however seeking to deny the talent of individual artists,

such as Picasso, who are eminently representative of their time, yet who transcend it through their genius, so that modern art appears hopelessly divided against itself.

[34]Mircea Eliade, *The Quest*, pp. 68ff.

[35]Cf. J. Rouge's introduction to his translation of Schleiermacher's *Reden*, Paris, 1944.

[36]See *Le Père invisible*, pp. 23ff.

[37]See Etienne Gilson, *Les Tribulations de Sophie*, Paris, 1967.

[38]H. von Glasenapp, *Brahma et Bouddha*, French translation, Paris, 1937, and particularly his *Philosophie indienne*, French translation, Paris, 1951, pp. 18ff. and 348ff.

[39]Cf. Bertrand Russell's humorous reference in his *Autobiography* to a letter he received expressing surprise at the very limited number of modern minds who agree that, in the final analysis, solipsism is the philosophy which suits them best.

[40]See the comments by A. H. Armstrong and R. A. Markus in *Christian Faith and Greek Philosophy*, London, 1960, pp. 142ff.

[41]In *La Justification du Bien* (French translation, Paris, 1939, pp. 457ff.), Soloviev showed himself to be particularly prophetic on this point. (English transl.: *The Justification of the Good; an essay on moral philosophy*, London, 1918).

[42]James Barr's *Fundamentalism*, London, 1977, abounds in valuable insights, but they unfortunately suffer from his typically Anglo-Saxon inability to see the distinction between orthodoxy and fundamentalism.

[43]The books by Father Henri de Lubac on Origen's exegesis and its legacy—first *Histoire et Esprit*, Paris, 1950, then the four-volume *Exégèse médiévale*, Paris, 1959-1964—are the first, and so far essentially the only ones, to have brought to light anew the permanently valid component of this exegesis of the Fathers (and the rabbis before them).

[44]Here we come upon the formidable ambiguity of this approach that sought to define theology as a science, in the Aristotelian sense of the term, which led many thinkers to empty of its substance the biblical and Christian mystery which theology proposes to elucidate, instead of providing a frame of reference for its consideration.

[45]This distortion predictably gave rise, by way of a reaction, to a rejection of any objective meaning in dogmatic formulations (thus seen as simply expressing our own personal and purely subjective experience of the object being considered). Such was to be the position of Schleiermacher and of the entire "liberal" Christianity of modern Protestants, against which Barth sought to take a stand (with many ambiguities, however), a position now claiming in turn, with Hans Küng and many others, to correct Catholic orthodoxy so as to make it acceptable to modern man, or to the idea of modern man prevalent in some academic circles.

[46]In spite of his excellent intentions, it is all too clear that Teilhard de Chardin is typical of this trend. In our view, the most perceptive critique of the assumptions underlying his thinking is the one produced by the American scientist and philosopher Gaylord Simpson, just after Teilhard de Chardin's death, in a largely unnoticed *Scientific American* article. Quite obviously, the eminent Jesuit's reconciliation of science and theology required such a radical extrapolation of scientific terms beyond the field in which they are applicable that it is difficult to say what they still mean. The same comment might well apply, Simpson concludes, to Teilhard de Chardin's use of theological terms. What remains of the encounter carried out under such conditions, except a joint "evaporation" of both theology and science in shared verbalism?

[47]In this connection, see our *Decomposition of Catholicism*, Chicago, 1969, Erik von Kühnelt-Leddin's *Hirn, Herz, und Rückgrat*, Osnabrük, 1962, and Alain Besançon's

more recent *La Confusion des Langues*, Paris, 1979.

⁴⁸This was already the direction in which H. Duméry was moving in his *Phénoménologie de la Religion*, Paris, 1958.

⁴⁹On this confusion between truth and sincerity, see H. de Lubac, *L'Eglise dans la crise actuelle*, Paris, 1966.

⁵⁰See M.-J. Le Guillou's conclusions in *Le Mystère du Père*, Paris, 1973.

Chapter XIV

¹See R. Pintard's book referred to in note 6 of the previous chapter.

²There is still no comprehensive history of the seventeenth-century Catholic reformation which, after the sixteenth-century divisions and the oppositions that followed, carried forth the best of the first Christian humanism. The studies by Father de Lubac on *Pic de la Mirandole* (Paris, 1974) and Georges Chantraine on Erasmus—and more specifically Chantraine's *Mystère et Philosophie du Christ*, and more recently *Erasme et Luther: libre et serf arbitre* (Paris, 1981)—would provide an essential introduction to such a history, in the wake of M. Bataillon's major work, *Erasme en Espagne*, as well as the studies by Tellechea Idigorras on Carranza, Morone and Pole, by G. March'adour on St. Thomas More, plus A. Prévost's annotated edition of More's *Utopia*, and reaching further back to the Italian sources, Garin's and Toffanin's valuable research. But we still have only a few chapters of the missing history: Father Ravier's studies on St. Ignatius and the first Jesuits and on St. Francis of Sales, those by Jean Orcibal and Father Louis Cognet on Port Royal, Cochois' and Dupuy's monographs on Bérulle, etc. Admittedly, Brémond provided a considerable number of outlines in his *Histoire littéraire du sentiment religieux en France*. But though brilliant, these outlines are also frequently superficial, and occasionally miss the point altogether; for instance, they fail to discriminate between a simpleton such as Yves de Paris, whom the author happened to find entertaining, and more outstanding thinkers and mystics.

³On the Anglicans considered from this viewpoint, there are a few essays, but only one written in depth and offering valuable insights, that of Olivier Loyer on Hooker, the master of them all (*L'Anglicanisme de Richard Hooker*, Lille-Paris, 1979). The few pages devoted to these Anglicans in our *La Spiritualité orthodoxe et la Spiritualité anglicane et protestante* (Paris, 1965, pp. 150ff.) provide at the most an idea of their major contribution.

⁴The literature is even less informative concerning the role of the Lutherans in this reform of the Reformation. However, a solid thesis on the topic has been written by Schaerleman: *Johann Gerhard and Thomas Aquinas*, New Haven, CT, 1965. See our *op. cit.* in the previous note, pp. 137ff.

⁵We have already referred to Paul Hazard's writings, which are unfortunately far from being up to the standard of what Pintard has published concerning the previous century.

⁶Alec Dru's studies show outstanding insight, though his scholarship is uneven. So far, these studies have been published only in part: *The Church in the XIXth Century: Germany 1800-1918*, London, 1963.

⁷Cf. Berger's book already mentioned in note 8 of the previous chapter.

⁸Nothing really worthwhile has been written about Petau. Father Galtier's article in the *Dictionnaire de Théologie catholique* offers a flimsy analysis, and its critique

amounts to little more than a caricature—which hardly comes as a surprise, considering the author's stand on various issues.

[9]Cf. notes 2 to 4.

[10]On Marsilio Ficino and his influence, see Raymond Marcel's works, particularly the French-language versions he edited of the *Commentary on the Banquet* (1956) and *Platonic Theology* (1970), as well as his *Marsile Ficin*, Paris, 1958.

[11]See the very brief and quite possibly too uncritical discussions devoted to them by Jacques Chevalier in his *Histoire de la Pensée*, vol. 2, Paris, 1956, pp. 824ff.

[12]*Ibid.*, pp. 665ff.

[13]Surprisingly enough, in France only one thesis has so far been devoted to Ramus. Perry Miller, in *The New England Mind*, vol. 1, New York, 1939, was the first to have grasped the major role played by Ramus.

[14]See, in *The Road of Science and the Ways to God*, pp. 351ff., Stanley Jaki's rather harsh comments on the true role of Bacon and Descartes in the birth of modern science. They are nevertheless unquestionably at the root (and may indeed be *the* root) of the technological ideology which from the start weighed heavily on the development of modern science.

[15]See the critical edition by A. A. Luce and T. Jessop, Edinburgh, 1945-1957. See also Luce's perceptive studies, especially *The Life of George Berkeley, Bishop of Cloyne*, Edinburgh, 1949. and *Sense Without Matter, or Direct Perception*, Edinburgh, 1954.

[16]It is most unfortunate that there exists as yet no comprehensive study of Leibnitz, or at least none worthy of that exceptional thinker. There is not even a complete collection of his works. As far as the *Monadology* is concerned, a book of particular interest to us in connection with this chapter, E. Boutroux's preface to the printing edited by him is eminently noteworthy.

[17]On Goethe's scientific research, see R. Michéa's outstanding monograph, *Les travaux scientifiques de Goethe*, Paris, 1943. Perceptive comments, strangely intermingled with insubstantial reveries, may be found in an initially fascinating but ultimately disappointing essay by Owen Barfield, *Saving the Appearances*, London, 1957.

[18]On Agrippa of Nettesheim, see Charles G. Nauert's *Agrippa and the Crisis of Renaissance Thought*, Urbana (University of Illinois Press), 1965. A. Koyré has produced a series of essays on several of the authors we have mentioned: *Mystiques, spirituels et alchimistes du XVI siècle allemand*, Paris, 1955. Cf. Ernst Benz, *Les sources mystiques de la philosophie romantique allemand*, Paris, 1968. Heinrich Kunrath's most unusual *Amphitheatrum Sapientiae*, published in 1602, of which there are only a few copies extant, remains still practically unknown.

[19]To our knowledge, there exists no extensive study of the most original among Henry More's theories.

[20]On Boehme, the only discussion which remains valuable is unquestionably Koyré's *La philosophie de Jacob Boehme*, Paris, 1929. He unfortunately seems completely unaware of Kunrath's work referred to at the end of note 18 (above), a book which seems to be a direct antecedent to Boehme's thinking, although the latter could have gained knowledge of it only through one of his more educated friends, such as Frankenberg, since it is written in Latin.

[21]See Baader's works edited, translated, and discussed by E. Susini in *Franz von Baader et le romantisme mystique*, consisting of 2 vols. on *La philosophie de Franz von Baader*, Paris, 1942, and 3 vols. of letters (vol. 1, Paris, 1942; vols. 2 and 3, Vienna, 1951).

[22]A stimulating study of Hammann may be found in Hans Urs von Balthasar's *La Gloire et la Croix* (translated from *Herrlichkeit*), vol. 2 of the second book, Paris, 1972, pp. 129ff.

²³*Aesthetica in nuce*, II, 261.

²⁴*Ibid.*, II, 265.

²⁵Monsignor Poupard's thesis focuses exclusively on the study of Bautain's alleged fideism. In contradistinction, W. M. Horton—in *The Philosophy of the Abbé Bautain*, which we are summarizing here—understood the surprising breadth of the Alsatian philosopher's thinking, even though much of it was never fully developed.

²⁶Gottfried Arnold, *Geheimnis der göttlichen Sophia oder Weisheit*, Leipzig, 1700.

²⁷See the perceptive articles by A. Kojevnikov (subsequently better known under the name of A. Kojève), published in Strasbourg in several 1934 and 1935 issues of the *Revue d'histoire et de philosophie religieuses*.

²⁸The Swiss collection "L' âge d'homme" has recently published a translation of his remarkable doctoral thesis, *La colonne et le fondement de la vérité* (Geneva and Lausanne, 1975).

²⁹In the periodical *Nova et vetera* (1978), we have published a review of the outstanding *Bulgakov Anthology*, London, 1976.

³⁰We have used the English translation (by Elizabeth Hamilton and E. E. Constance Jones) of Hermann Lotze's *Microcosmus: An Essay Concerning Man and his Relation to the World*, 2 vols., Edinburgh, 1897.

³¹*Op. cit.*, Vol. I, pp. 143ff., and especially pp. 158ff. (book II, chapter 1).

³²*Ibid.*, pp. 405ff. (book IV, chapter 1).

³³*Ibid.*, pp. 414ff.

³⁴*Op. cit.*, Vol. 2, pp. 678ff. (book IX, chapter 4).

³⁵On Hermes, see A. Thouvenin's article in the *Dictionnaire de Théologie catholique*, which however contains no entry on Froschammer; a few passing lines refer to him in the article entitled *Semirationalisme*, by G. Fritz.

³⁶On Günther, P. Godet's article in the same dictionary is even more inadequate than the ones just mentioned. A straightforward summary of his main writings may be found in E. Hocedez's *Histoire de la Théologie au XIX siècle*, Vol. 2, Brussels-Paris, 1952, pp. 39ff.

Chapter XV

¹A few particularly sensational statements by J. J. Thomson (Lord Kelvin) are generally quoted in this respect; these assertions now seem most unworthy of such an outstanding scientist.

²A comprehensive treatment of the subject is found, among others, in Boutaric's *L'atome* and Millikan's *The Electron*, two books typical of the better popularization efforts of the 1920s.

³Noteworthy are Marcel Boll's brilliant articles published between the two world wars in *La Science et la Vie*.

⁴The book referred to in the next note sets forth the problem.

⁵Max Planck, *The Universe in the Light of Modern Physics*.

⁶W. Heisenberg, *Physics and Philosophy*, New York, 1958.

⁷Countless attempts at popularization, frequently fanciful, were aimed at Einsteinian relativity. It must be admitted that the precise significance of the general theory of relativity, for instance, is not easy to grasp, even for those who are well-versed in modern physical research. Among the most famous to experience this difficulty was the philosopher Henri Bergson, though he had received an initial

scientific training most unusual for one of his calling; he had to abandon the idea of publishing a new version, even completely revised, of his *Duration and Simultaneity* (trans. by Leon Jacobson, Indianapolis, 1965), after recognizing that his discussion of the special theory of relativity was based on a complete misunderstanding.

One of the least misleading presentations, though suitable for the educated layman, may be found in E. Mascall's previously quoted *Christian Theology and Natural Science*, London, 1956, pp. 104ff.

[8]See Ian T. Ramsey, *Religious Language*, London, 1957, *Religion and Science: Conflict and Synthesis*, 1964, and *Christian Discourse*, 1965.

[9]A tightly reasoned though perhaps overly optimistic discussion on this point is to be found in Mascall, *op. cit.*, pp. 65ff.

[10]Refer to our comments in notes 15 and 16 of the previous chapter.

[11]Their number has now grown to well over a hundred.

[12]Cf. Mascall, *op. cit.*, pp. 138ff.

[13]Cf. F. Hoyle, *The Nature of the Universe*, new edition, New York, 1960, pp. 106ff. Jacques Merleau-Ponty's *Cosmologie au XX siècle*, Paris, 1963, is typical of a temporary hope, which seems to have collapsed for good.

[14]Jacques Monod's *The Necessity of Being*, London, 1973, created a sensation through the decisiveness of the philosophical assertions accompanying an unquestionably fascinating scientific account. Unfortunately, it was enough to read this work with discrimination to detect instances of faulty reasoning and plain verbal evasion which stood in sorry contrast to the author's undeniable scientific acumen. The substitution of the term "teleomony" for the word "finality" provides a particularly disconcerting example of a philosophically simplistic attitude (to say the least) which can go hand in hand, in some scientists, not only with an obvious ability in their field, but also with an inventiveness and skill in research that offer evidence of superior intellectual gifts. The case is not unusual, and this can occur in both credulous and skeptical individuals: one need merely mention names such as those of Crookes and Richet.

[15]For an overview of the problems raised by the development of life, see Ludwig von Bertalanffy, *Problems of Life: an evaluation of modern biological thoughts*, London, 1952. On the specific subject of evolution, see Rémy Collin, *L'évolution, hypothèses et problèmes*, Paris, 1958.

[16]Cf. Collingwood, *op. cit.*, pp. 10-11 and 134-135. The term "emerging evolution," which we use in this discussion, was coined by Lloyd Morgan. It remains valuable, whatever one may think of the latter's own theories.

[17]Floyd W. Matson's *The Broken Image*, New York, 1964, gives a sound analysis of the contradictions of behaviorism; this example of an honest and competent journalistic investigation is all too rare.

[18]Szondi's research has been described and discussed by H. Niel in *L'analyse du destin*, Paris, 1960.

Chapter XVI

[1]Stanley Jaki, *The Road of Science and the Ways to God*, pp. 349ff.

[2]Jacques Ellul, *La Technique et l'Enjeu du siècle*. Cf. note 24 of Chapter 13.

[3]This strange idea is developed by G. Thiels in *Théologie des Réalités terrestres*, 2 vols., Paris, 1946-1949.

[4]It is instructive to read the series of books by Father de Lubac on this controversial figure and his works; particularly recommended is *La Pensée religieuse du Père Teilhard de Chardin*, Paris, 1962.

5On this unusual personality and his rather fanciful books, see Basil Zenkovsky, *A History of Russian Philosophy*, translated from the Russian, vol. 2, New York, 1953. See also the more recent contribution by George M. Young, Jr., *Nikolai Fedorov: An Introduction*, Belmont, MA, 1979.

6*La Justification du Bien, loc. cit.* in note 41 of Chapter XIII.

7This development of Soloviev's thinking is discussed by D. Stremukhov in *Vladimir Soloviev and His Messianic Work*, Belmont, MA, 1980.

8*Lord of the World*, New York, 1908, reprinted 1924; *The Dawn of All*, St. Louis, MO, 1911.

9The writings of St. Maximus the Confessor are analyzed by Hans Urs von Balthasar in *Liturgie cosmique*, pp. 100ff.

10Deuteronomy 4:24 (cf. Ezechiel 1) and Job 4:18.

11This is obvious in Francis Bacon, even more so than in Descartes.

12Ludwig Feuerbach, *The Essence of Christianity*, New York, 1855.

13Cf. the preface borrowed from Karl Barth for a new English translation of Feuerbach's work which appeared in 1957. The German original is in Vol. 2 of *Die Theologie und die Kirche*, Zöllikon, 1928, pp. 212ff.

14Cf. the conclusive texts of the *Advancement of Learning* and the *Discourse on the Method of Rightly Conducting the Reason.*

15On these various points, see Denis de Rougemont, *Le futur dépend de nous*, Paris, 1978.

16*Ibid.*

17Through a somewhat gloomy description of the final period of the Austro-Hungarian empire, Musil's novel recalls the general depersonalization brought about by what was more recently to be known as the consumer society.

18See the previously mentioned essay by Raymond Ruyer, *La Gnose de Princeton.*

19On D. H. Lawrence, see the excellent study by Stuart in the last volume of the *Oxford History of English Literature.*

Chapter XVII

1Gabriel Marcel, *Coleridge et Schelling*, Paris, 1971.

2Contrary to what was long believed, it is indeed certain that Homeric poetry, for instance, does not express the worldview of the period it portrays, but rather the already very different vision which belonged to a civilization aware of itself. Cf. C. M. Bowra, *Homer*, Oxford, 1979.

3Aeschylus, *Prometheus*, v. 89; Lucretius, *De Rerum Natura*, book 1, verse 73.

4End of the first Eclogue.

5In this regard, see Dorothy Sayers' comments in the introduction to her English translation of the *Divine Comedy.*

6See F. E. Hutchinson, *Henry Vaughan, A Life and Interpretation*, Oxford, 1947.

7On Herbert, see Hutchinson's *XVIIth Century Studies Presented to Sir Herbert Grierson*, London, 1941, and Joseph H. Summers, *George Herbert, His Religion and Art*, London, 1954.

8His twin brother, Thomas Vaughan, is the same Eugenius Philalethes whose hermetic writings have consistently inspired variously eccentric alchemists and Rosicrucians.

9On this other side of Vaughan's interests, and more generally on the tradition of Celtic Christianity in Wales, see A. M. Allchin's beautiful book, *The World is a Wedding*, London, 1978.

10*The World*, first and last stanzas.

[11]*The Waterfall.*

[12]*They are all gone into the world of light.*

[13]*The Retreat.*

[14]The most enlightening book on Wordsworth is Mary Moorman's *William Wordsworth, A Biography*, 2 vols., Oxford, 1957-1965. Also noteworthy is Hunter Davies' biographical and psychological study similarly entitled *William Wordsworth, A Biography*, London, 1980, if only because it is the first to have made use of the revealing letters between the poet and his wife, the former Mary Hutchinson.

[15]We obviously have in mind the first lines of the *Canterbury Pilgrims.*

[16]*Intimations of Immortality from Recollections of Early Childhood*, first stanza.

[17]Second stanza.

[18]Third stanza.

[19]Fourth stanza.

[20]Fifth stanza.

[21]Eighth stanza.

[22]Ninth stanza.

[23]*Ibid.*

[24]Eleventh stanza.

[25]*Lines Composed above Tintern Abbey*, verses 22ff.

[26]*The world is too much with us.*

[27]In the first vein, we have Fairchild's rather inept commentary, and in the other, a criticism which has become traditional ever since it was first expressed by Hazlitt and Leigh Hunt, and which is passed on without any real effort being made to analyze more closely the specific writings this criticism is leveled at.

[28]This letter does not even seem to have been noticed by the critics we have referred to.

[29]*Prelude*, first book, verses 401ff.

[30]*Ibid.*, second book, verses 232ff.

[31]First book, verses 561ff.

[32]First book, verses 357ff.

[33]Verses 306ff.

[34]Fourth book, verses 10ff.

[35]Second book, verses 314ff. See also the continuation, down to verse 451.

[36]Twelfth book, verses 126ff.

[37]See the letters between Faber and Wordsworth, edited by Raleigh Addington.

[38]*On the Power of Sound*, written in 1828 and revised in 1835.

[39]Cf. particularly verses 458ff. of the sixth book and verses 262ff. of the eighth book, in the *Prelude.*

[40]*The Excursion*, fourth book, verses 631ff.

[41]Written in 1821-1822.

[42]See M. Moorman, *op. cit.*, pp. 422ff. in vol. I.

[43]See Jacottet's introduction to the French translation of Hölderlin's works in the "La Pléiade" series. Even more illuminating is Rudolf Hibel's *Hölderlin und Diotima*, Zurich, 1957.

[44]*Adonais*, verse 40.

[45]J. C. Shairp, *Studies in Poetry and Philosophy*, New York, 1872, pp. 53ff.

[46]*The Archipelago*, pp. 213-217, in *Friederich Hölderlin—Poems and Fragments*, translated by Michael Hamburger, bilingual edition, Ann Arbor, MI, 1967.

[47]*Bread and Wine*, in *Hölderlin—His Poems Translated by Michael Hamburger, with a Critical Study*, Pantheon Books, New York, 1952.

[48]*Patmos, ibid.*

⁴⁹In these various quotations, Michael Hamburger's translations have been fully preserved.

⁵⁰Richard Holmes' *Shelley, the Pursuit*, New York, 1975, seems to be the first study providing a clear distinction between the real Shelley and the image he had managed to project of himself.

⁵¹Amy Lowell's *John Keats* seriously undertook to disentangle the chronology of the poet's works and disproved the odious fabrications about Fanny Brawn and their love, which the stupid jealousy of several of Keats' friends had made credible and perpetuated.

⁵²On Baudelaire, see Enid Starkie's book referred to in note 32 of Chapter XIII, and on Gérard de Nerval the comments by Béatrice Didier for the 1972 edition published by the Librairie générale française.

⁵³On the relations between Claudel and Saint-John Perse, see the edition of the latter's works in the "La Pléiade" series.

⁵⁴Robert Sencourt's posthumous book entitled *T. S. Eliot*, published just after the latter's death, was the first to provide a full and factual account of the poet's life which goes a long way toward explaining his spiritual odyssey.

⁵⁵See J. F. Angelloz's *R. M. Rilke. L'évolution spirituelle du poète*, Paris, 1936; also the same author's introduction to the new edition and translation into French of *Duino's Elegies*, and the *Sonnets to Orpheus*, Paris, 1943.

⁵⁶See O. Pöggele, *La pensée de Martin Heidegger*, French translation, Paris, 1977.

Chapter XVIII

¹See these entries in Goblot's *Vocabulaire philosophique*.

²A. H. Armstrong, *Plotinus*, New York, 1953. See also what he has written on the same subject in the *Cambridge History of Late Greek and Early Medieval Philosophy*.

³Maurice Nédoncelle, *La Réciprocité des consciences*, Paris, 1942.

⁴Gregory the Great, *Homilia 17 in Lucam*; Gregory of Nazianzus, *Orat. 31* (fifth theological sermon), especially paragraph 26.

⁵Plato, *Timaeus*, 29e and 30a: the Demiurge who has created the material universe is without any particular need or inclination. It is the Good itself, according to *The Republic*, 508c, which reproduces its own likeness and (cf. *ibid.*, 509c) brings forth the essence and existence of everything which is knowable.

⁶This vision of Goodness as appropriated to the Father, Truth to the Son, and Beauty to the Spirit has been admirably developed by Sergei Boulgakoff, *Le Paraclet* (French translation), Paris, 1946, pp. 191ff.

⁷Cf. the text quite rightly noted by Jean Meyendorff, which we have quoted in *Le Consolateur*, p. 321.

⁸*In Sent. lib. I*, dist., XXXII, q. 1.

⁹Sergei Boulgakoff, *Le Paraclet*, pp. 64ff.

¹⁰This has been well brought out by Lotze, *op. cit.*, book IX, chapter IV, paragraphs 11 and 12 (p. 687 of Vol. 2).

¹¹*De veritate*, q. 4, a. 8.

¹²F. Varillon, *La Souffrance de Dieu*, Paris, 1975. Cf. J. Galot, *La Souffrance de Dieu*, Paris, 1976, and his article, *La Réalité de la Souffrance en Dieu*, in the *Nouvelle Revue théologique*, March-April 1979, pp. 224ff.

¹³See his works on Fénelon, particularly *Fénelon et le pur amour*, Paris, 1957.

¹⁴See James Hitchcock, *The Recovery of the Sacred*, New York, 1974.

[15]This theme of God's essential kingship is the central theme of biblical revelation, as we have shown above, pp. 23ff.

[16]Cf. Romans 5:8 (and the entire context), as well as John 15:13.

[17]This is what remains incontrovertible in the unfolding of his *Metaphysics of Charity*.

[18]See our book entitled *The Spirit and Forms of Protestantism*, Westminster (Maryland), 1957, pp. 153ff., and *Le Père Invisible*, pp. 319ff.

[19]Cf. Thomas Aquinas, *Summa theologica*, Ia pars, q. 45, a. 3, ad primum.

[20]II Corinthians 4:17.

[21]Cf. *Le Mystère pascal*, Paris, 1947, pp. 292ff. This is where one finds the core of truth in St. Anselm's theory of satisfaction, inadequate though that theory may be in many of its aspects.

[22]It is obviously in this sense that one should understand what we have written on the subject in *The Eternal Son*; our comments may have confused even a theologian as reliable and subtle as Eric Mascall.

[23]Maximus the Confessor, *Quaest. ad Thalassium*, 60 (PG 90, col. 620ff.). Cf. *Le Consolateur*, pp. 288ff.

[24]It is certainly true that, among the heretical Gnostics of the early centuries, this Wisdom of creation already gave rise to risky (if not always erroneous) speculations. This tendency has reappeared among contemporary thinkers who were inspired by nineteenth-century German idealism and who, according to Gottfried Arnold, proceeded on the basis of Boehme's ideas, from Schelling to Sergei Boulgakoff and all the other thinkers, particularly Russian, whom Soloviev was able to encourage (see his book in English, *Russia and the Universal Church*, London, 1948). Just as the countless Christological heresies do not dispense us from attempting to produce an orthodox Christology, these various developments cannot justify an *a priori* avoidance of efforts to account for a biblical datum which has inspired the entire Marian liturgy, not to mention the liturgy of the Dedication. The texts of St. Athanasius and St. Augustine which we have referred to show this to be incontrovertibly the case, as Newman clearly perceived. No theological cosmology evading this problem can satisfy the requirements of the biblical doctrine of creation and of its supernatural adoption in free and intelligent creatures. It must be admitted that the problem was all too often left unattended by medieval and modern theology. And however questionable some of Soloviev's and Boulgakoff's speculations may be (due in particular to an insufficiently critical response to Boehme's legacy), it would be a grave mistake to dismiss indiscriminately all their suggestions, or those of another eminent contemporary thinker, Father Paul Florensky, an Eastern counterpart (though more seriously philosophical in approach) to our own Pierre Teilhard de Chardin. Florensky's *La colonne et le fondement de la vérité* was recently translated into French (as we have indicated above, note 28 of Chapter 14), and it is fortunate that Boulgakoff's book directly devoted to this problem (*The Wisdom of God*, London, 1937) is available in English, for in this work his outlook is more purely biblical and traditional than in his two major theological treatises available in French: *L'Agneau de Dieu* (translated under the title of *Le Verbe incarné*) and *Le Paraclet*. This is so true that a Thomist as firm as Archbishop Goodier did not hesitate to approve of it virtually without any reservations.

[25]*De veritate*, q. 4, a. 6.

[26]However, should this distinction in the eternal divine Wisdom be considered real or merely notional, in the Scholastic sense? The question is not easy (any more than the one pertaining to the divine energies in relation to the essence), and the answer to it is hardly obvious.

[27]For a discussion of this point, see what we have attempted to formulate in *Le Consolateur*, pp. 430ff.

Chapter XIX

[1]*Le Consolateur*, p. 353.
[2]*Le Trône de la Sagesse*, pp. 39ff.
[3]See *Woman in the Church*, p. 47 and pp. 60ff.
[4]*Ibid.*, p. 38.
[5]See above, pp. 141ff.
[6]This concept was developed in particular by Maximus the Confessor. Cf. *Second Centuria on Theology and the Economy*, 25; *Theol. and Pol. Opusc.*, 16; and *First Centuria on Charity*, 71. In *The Wisdom of God*, pp. 119ff., Bulgakov has written excellent comments on this point.
[7]*Le Trône de la Sagesse*, pp. 285ff.
[8]On this theme, see *The Church of God*, pp. 493ff. In *Corpus Christi quod est Ecclesia*, Rome, 1946, pp. 35ff., Father Tromp has written a valuable monograph on the subject.
[9]II Corinthians 11:2.
[10]Cf. Romans 8:20-21.
[11]John 17:5 and 22. Cf. John 2:14.
[12]Cf. John 17:22 and Romans 8:21.
[13]Augustine, *Confessions*, book XII, chapter 20. Cf. Basil, *Hexaemeron*, Hom. I, 5, and Gregory of Nazianzus, *Poems*, II, 7, VII. See the article by Father Arnou, *Platonisme des Pères*, in *Dictionnaire de théologie catholique*.
[14]On Gregory of Nyssa in this connection, see Balthasar, *Présence et pensée*, pp. xviiiff.
[15]Cf. Hebrews 12:1.
[16]Origen, *De principiis*, book 1, 9, and all 1, 3. Cf. Maximus the Confessor, *Ambigua*, 65.
[17]John 1:3-4, which the Greek Fathers generally read without a break: "what was made in him was Life."
[18]Cf. Job 38:7.
[19]Cf. Ruysbroeck the Admirable, *The Spiritual Espousals*, book III, chapters V and VII.
[20]See note 18.
[21]On this formulation by Richard Rolle, see *Le Consolateur*, pp. 330ff. and 353.
[22]See below, pp. 206ff.
[23]Origen, *De principiis*, 1, 4, 1; 7, 1 and 4, as well as 8, 1 in the same book. Gregory of Nyssa, *De opificio hominis*, end of chapter XVII, as well as chapter XVIII (in S.C., no. 6, pp. 165ff.). Cf. chapter XII (pp. 131ff.) and *Catechetical Discourse*, end of chapter V and all chapter VI.
[24]Thomas Aquinas, *Summa theologica*, Ia pars, q. 76, a. 5. Cf. Supplementum, q. 85 and a. 3 of q. 91.
[25]Bonaventure, *In I Sent.*, 8, 2 un., 2, concl. Cf. *In II Sent.*, 3, 1, 1, 1, fund. 4 um. Cf. E. Gilson, *La philosophie de Saint Bonaventure*, pp. 237ff.
[26]See below our Chapter XXI.
[27]*Summa theologica*, Ia pars, q. 110.
[28]See Antoine Guillaumont, *op. cit.*, in Chapter XI, note 27, and Christoph Von Schönborn, *L'Icône du Christ*, Fribourg, 1976.

[29]V. Lossky has made valuable comments on this point in *The Vision of God*, London, 1964.

[30]For Dionysius, the superessential darkness of the divinity is inseparable from the inaccessible light wherein God dwells (1 Timothy 6:16). See his *Fifth Letter*, PG 3, col. 1073A. On "Macarius," see the texts quoted and discussed by us in *The Spirituality of the New Testament and the Fathers*, pp. 373ff. Cf. *Le Consolateur*, pp. 206ff.

[31]E. Gilson, *Introduction à l'étude de Saint Augustin*, Paris, 1929, pp. 103-120 and passim (see his index).

[32]E. Gilson, *La philosophie de Saint Bonaventure*, Paris, 1924, pp. 326ff.

[33]*Le Consolateur*, p. 239. Cf. Dom Maieul Cappuyns, *Jean Scot Erigène*, Louvain-Paris, 1933, pp. 283ff.

[34]Pierre Francastel, *L'humanisme roman*, Paris, 1970.

[35]Irénée Valléry-Radot, *Saint Bernard: Les noces de la nature et de la Grâce*, Paris, 1963. Whatever one may think of its outcome, the purpose expressed in St. Stephen Harding's *De correctione antiphonarii* is characteristic.

[36]Augustine, *Enarratio in psalmum*, 32, 8.

[37]See mainly Dom Albert-Jacques Bescond's *Le chant grégorien*, Paris, 1977, and Dom René-Jean Hesbert's recently published *Théologie du chant grégorien*.

[38]Henri-Irénée Marrou, *Saint Augustin et la culture antique*, Paris, 1938, p. 209.

[39]Paul Henry Lang, *Music in Western Civilization*, New York, 1941, pp. 207ff. and 468ff.

[40]*Ibid.*, pp. 258ff.

[41]*Ibid.*, pp. 280ff. and 416ff.

[42]*Ibid.*, pp. 461ff.

[43]*John Inglesant*, Macmillan edition, Chapter 25, p. 281.

[44]Also recommended is Albert Schweitzer's *J. S. Bach*, New York, 1911, and even more Lang, *op. cit.*, pp. 250ff.

[45]*Le Consolateur*, pp. 311ff.

[46]Concerning Symeon, see Archbishop Basil Krivochein's *Dans la lumière du Christ*, Chevetogne, 1980.

[47]*Summa theologica*, Ia pars, q. 47, especially article 2.

[48]Cf. our *Spirituality of the New Testament and the Fathers*, pp. 401ff., and Dom Denys Rutledge, *Cosmic Theology*, Staten Island, NY, 1965.

[49]E. von Ivanka, *La signification du Corpus Aeropagiticum*, in *Recherches de science religieuse*, vol. 36 (1949), p. 18.

[50]Pseudo-Dionysius, *Celestial Hierarchy*, 2, 1 and 3; 7, 3.

[51]Cf. the references in note 48.

[52]Cf. Dom D. Rutledge, *op. cit.*, pp. 24ff.

[53]Boulgakoff has written excellent pages on this point in *The Wisdom of God*, pp. 87ff.

[54]Cf. Exodus 26:9 and Hebrews 8:15.

[55]Genesis 28:10ff.

[56]Cf. D. S. Russell, *The Method and Message of Jewish Apocalyptics*, pp. 235ff.

[57]In chapters 4 and 5 of St. John's Apocalypse.

[58]Cf. Galatians 4:2-3 and Colossians 2:8 and 20.

[59]Cf. Genesis 1:6 and 7.

[60]Cf. Revelation 1:12ff. and 5:6ff.

[61]Cf. Revelation 7:9ff. and 14:4.

[62]One should refer to the series of outstanding books on Romanesque art produced by the abbey of La Pierre-qui-Vire.

[63]A. Grabar, *L'âge d'or de Justinien*, Paris, 1965.

⁶⁴Theodore the Studite, *Antirrhetics*, I, 45 (PG 99, col. 313Dff.).

⁶⁵PG, t. 98, col. 384ff. See in Vol. 2 of our *Histoire de la spiritualité chrétienne*, Paris, pp. 676ff. of the appendix entitled *Spiritualité byzantine*.

⁶⁶On this entire topic, see Erik Peterson, *The Angels and the Liturgy*, New York, 1964.

⁶⁷Cf. what we have shown, in the tradition of St. Gregory of Nazianzus, to be a fundamental theme (and quite possibly *the* theme) of original monasticism—the desertion of the city of fallen mankind, in the example of Abraham and the entire people of God—in *The Spirituality of the New Testament and the Fathers*, p. 343.

⁶⁸See our essay, bearing the title *Newman, le monachisme et Saint Benoît* and directly inspired by the great English prelate, in the volume of collected papers published on the occasion of the centennial of Newman's elevation to the cardinalate, Maredsous, 1980.

⁶⁹Depending on whether the essence of beatitude is considered to be in the vision or the love of God.

⁷⁰Vladimir Soloviev, *La Justification du Bien*, Paris, 1939, pp. xiiiff. and 445ff.; also pp. 182ff., and particularly 347ff.

⁷¹H. Brémond, *Newman, essai de biographie psychologique*, Paris, 1906, pp. 276ff.

⁷²*Parochial and Plain Sermons*, Vol. 2, pp. 359ff.

⁷³*Ibid.*, pp. 361ff.

⁷⁴P. 362.

⁷⁵Pp. 363ff.

⁷⁶P. 364.

⁷⁷Pp. 365ff.

⁷⁸Pp. 366-367.

⁷⁹*Parochial and Plain Sermons*, Vol. 4, pp. 200ff.

⁸⁰*Ibid.*, pp. 201ff.

⁸¹Pp. 202-203.

⁸²P. 202.

⁸³P. 203.

⁸⁴P. 204.

⁸⁵Pp. 205ff.

⁸⁶Pp. 207ff.

⁸⁷Pp. 208-209.

⁸⁸Pp. 209-210.

⁸⁹Pp. 210-211.

⁹⁰Pp. 211-213.

⁹¹*Historical Sketches*, pp. 94ff. of Vol. II.

Chapter XX

¹Cf. Daniel 10:13 and Revelation 12:7ff.

²Though undeniably brilliant, Father Sertillanges' *Le Problème du Mal*, Paris, 1948, is a sad example of these fundamentally pagan speculations disguised as Christian theology.

³See Mircea Eliade, *The Quest*, pp. 80ff.

⁴Matthew 13:28.

⁵See above, pp. 45ff.

⁶Thomas Aquinas, the very first question in the *Summa theologica*, especially articles 1, 6, and 8.

[7]Typical in this regard is H. A. Kelly's *The Devil, Demonology, and Witchcraft*, Garden City, NY, 1968. For the opposite view, see Stanislas Breton, *Faut-il parler des Anges?*, in the April 1980 issue of the *Revue des sciences philosophiques et théologiques*.

[8]Isaiah 14:4ff. This prophecy on the fall of the Babylonian king (who appeared as the "servant," or indeed the epiphany, of the celestial god Marduk) was interpreted by the Fathers as reflecting the primordial angelic fall. Which explains why Satan was called Lucifer, a name the king of Babylon, like his divine antitype, must have claimed (see verse 12).

[9]Revelation 12:10. This is a translation of the Hebrew word "satan."

[10]Revelation 12:12.

[11]We have provided our comments above, pp. 47ff. See also *Le Trône de la Sagesse*, pp. 22ff.

[12]John 12:31; 14:30; and 16:11.

[13]II Corinthians 4:4.

[14]Cf. above, pp. 188ff.

[15]Cf. above, pp. 190ff.

[16]Leibnitz, its inventor, saw in it a reflection of the necessary relationship between the finite such as it exists and the infinite which produced it.

[17]The moving point generates a line, the line generates a surface, and the surface a volume, so that the tetraktys appears as the revelation in this world of its relationship to the divinity. Similarly, in this view musical harmonies are seen as revelations of the congruence of the world with its principle. Cf. Burnet, *L'Aurore de la philosophie grecque*, pp. 112ff.

[18]*Enneads*, 9, 8.

[19]Cf. Psalm 147 (146):4.

[20]Cf. John 12:31 and II Corinthians 4:4.

[21]Cf. the text of Plotinus referred to in note 18.

[22]Daniel 10:13.

[23]Revelation 12:7ff.

[24]Revelation 12:9ff.

[25]Cf. Romans 5:12 and Wisdom of Solomon 1:13ff.

[26]We have already noted that toward the end of his life, in *Jenseits des Lustprinzips*, Freud seems to have had a strange intuition of this highly mysterious relationship, which all myths bear witness to.

[27]It may be said that the patristic literature is unanimous on this point. Rupert of Deutz seems to have been the first medieval author whose search for autonomous humanism had led him to challenge the traditional view. See Dom J. Gribomont's introduction to Rupert's *Les oeuvres du Saint-Esprit*, No. 161 in *Sources Chrétiennes*, pp. 40ff.

Father Bouëssé, who also could not accept the traditional opinion, nevertheless deserves credit for showing that the view he rejected was shared almost unanimously by the early Christian authors. See in this connection the outstanding essay by Raïssa Maritain, *The Prince of this World*, trans. by G. B. P., Toronto, 1933.

[28]On the Fathers' theology of paradise, see Anselme Stolz, *Théologie de la mystique*, Chevetogne, 1947, pp. 18ff.

[29]It is in this sense that the Fathers, following the lead of Irenaeus and no doubt inspired by a theme underlying the account of the Annunciation in Luke 1:26ff., saw a constant parallel between Eve, who led Adam into temptation—since she was the first to yield to the false evidence of the senses and rejected faith in the divine word—and Mary who, on the contrary, anticipated Christ's victory over the renewed Adamic temptation by accepting in a spirit of obedient faith the same

divine word, which the same false evidence may have seemed more than ever to contradict. Cf. St. Thomas, *Summa theologica*, IIIa pars, q. 30, a. 1. Also *Le Trône de la Sagesse*, pp. 179ff.

[30]Genesis 3 and especially verse 5.

[31]See *Le Trône de la Sagesse*, pp. 21ff.

[32]See the account of the tower of Babel: Genesis 11:1-9. Cf. above, pp. 49ff.

[33]We have here the entire Augustinian opposition (the basis on which *The City of God* was written) between the city founded on love of self—so all-consuming that it led to contempt for God—and the city which should have been built, and is actually in the process of emerging, thanks to divine Redemption, on the foundation of the love of God, which is conducive to forgetfulness of self.

[34]Galatians 4:4 and 5.

[35]Cf. Acts 7:30, 38, and 53; Galatians 3:19; Hebrews 2:2. These various texts are based on an interpretation of Exodus 20 and Joshua 5:13ff., as well as Deuteronomy 33:2, which was incorporated into the Septuagint, and whose antiquity is established by the importance the Samaritans attached to it. See in this connection the note in Munck's commentary on the Acts, in the series of the *Anchor Bible*.

[36]Cf. Irenaeus, *Adversus Haereses*, book I, chapter III, 4; cf. IX, 2, and X, 1.

[37]Though it seems to be much older, this is the Jewish interpretation which the medieval cabala developed further. See Gershom Sholem, *Les Origines de la Kabbale*, French ed., Paris, 1966, pp. 454 and 474.

[38]Maximus the Confessor superbly illustrated this certainty in his doctrine of redemption through Christ on the cross. Cf. J.-M. Garrigues, *Maxime le Confesseur*, Paris, 1976, p. 196. But the first expression is clearly found in Irenaeus, *Adversus Haereses*, book III, chapter V, 3; cf. XXIII, 2.

[39]Cf. Isaiah 54 and John 17:22, with Revelation 21.

[40]Thomas Aquinas, *Summa theologica*, Ia pars, q. 113.

[41]*Ibid.*, q. 110.

[42]Cf. I Corinthians 8:5 and Colossians 2:20, or Galatians 4:3, as well as Ephesians 6:12.

[43]Cf. I Corinthians 10:9ff., which simply echoes a continuing theme of the Old Testament (Leviticus 17:1, Deuteronomy 32:17, Baruch 4:7, etc.).

[44]Acts 17:30.

[45]See S. Boulgakoff's *Jacob's Ladder* (in Russian).

[46]H. L. Martensen's *Die christliche dogmatik*, Berlin, 1856.

[47]Cf. our essay on *God and His Creation*, pp. 466-497 in vol. 2 of *Introduction to Theology* (Chicago, 1955).

[48]*Summa theologica*, Ia pars, q. 62, especially a. 6.

[49]Mary's superiority over the angels has been systematically discussed by theologians at least since Theodore the Studite.

[50]*Summa theologica*, Ia pars, q. 47.

Chapter XXI

[1]A. A. Luce, *Sense Without Matter, or Direct Perception*, London, 1954. See also the more recently published volume of essays by various authors, edited by Ernan McMillan under the title of *The Concept of Matter in Greek and Medieval Philosophy*, Notre Dame University Press, South Bend, IN, 1963.

[2]Cf. above, pp. 197ff.

[3]Collingwood, *op. cit.*, pp. 14ff. and 145ff.

[4]H. W. Piper, *The Active Universe, Pantheism and the Concept of Imagination in the English Romantic Poets*, London, 1968.

[5]Collingwood, *op. cit.*, pp. 10ff. and 134-135.

[6]John Burnet, *L'Aurore de la philosophie grecque*, p. 328 note 3, and p. 340 note 2.

[7]See our discussion of the Stoic concept of the *pneuma* in *Le Consolateur*, pp. 28ff.

[8]Raymond Marcel, *Marsile Ficin*, Paris, 1958.

[9]The *Phaedo*, 97b.

[10]*Ibid.*, 100ff. Cf. *Timaeus*, 29ff.

[11]Luce, *op. cit.*, pp. 31ff.

[12]*Timaeus*, 51.

[13]Luce, *op. cit.*, pp. 144ff.

[14]*Metaphysics*, 1029a, 20.

[15]*Timaeus*, 51a.

[16]This is a reference to the pre-Socratic speculations discussed above, pp. 72ff.

[17]In other words, or so it would seem, matter is but an imperfect participation of that which is intelligible.

[18]Luce, *op. cit.*, pp. 140ff.

[19]First *Ennead*, 8, 7. Cf. second *Ennead*, 3, 17, and third *Ennead*, 4, 1. None of Plotinus' recent commentators would agree with Inge's assertion (*The Philosophy of Plotinus*, vol. 1, London, 1918, pp. 134ff.) that Plotinus had nothing to do with the idea that the root of evil is in matter. Cf. A. H. Armstrong, *Cambridge History of Later Greek Philosophers*, p. 256.

[20]Wisdom of Solomon 11:17 and 14:13, with the commentary by Luce, *op. cit.*, p. 131.

[21]Cf. *Le Consolateur*, pp. 28ff. and 37ff. and the comments by A. Louth, *The Origins of the Christian Mystical Tradition*, Oxford, 1981, pp. xvff., on the precise meaning of *nous*.

[22]Cf. Luce, *op. cit.*, pp. 115ff.

[23]Berkeley fully explained his position in the texts gathered together by Luce, *op. cit.*, pp. 161ff.

[24]On Bonaventure in this connection, see E. Gilson, *La Philosophie de Saint Bonaventure*, pp. 206ff.

[25]In this way, one can salvage what Leibnitz had to say about the monads and their pre-established harmony, in a universe which they constitute through their essential community.

[26]Cf. above, pp. 212ff.

[27]In other words, even if one ascribes exclusively to the influence of the angels the progressive development of life, rising from stage to stage toward mankind, this direction is guided by the illumination of the divine Word itself, of which the angels are the first beneficiaries, and it ends in the creative intervention of the selfsame Word who moves it toward ultimate readiness to receive the soul directly created by God.

[28]See what we have written on the Irenaean view of this process in *Le Consolateur*, pp. 142ff.

[29]On the relationship between the animal, subhuman consciousness and the angelic, superhuman consciousness, Newman—in his essay, "Antony in Conflict" (*Historical Sketches*, vol. II, pp. 44ff.)—has some illuminating comments. Cf. a paragraph of the sermon on "The Invisible World," in vol. 4 of *Parochial and Plain Sermons*, p. 205.

[30]Romans 8:19ff.

[31]This is the intuition, unquestionably sound in substance, which gives significance to Bergson's distinction between what he calls "clock time" and the concept of

"duration," although he did not succeed in satisfactorily explaining the relationship between them.

³²Cf. above, p. 222.

³³I. Kant, *Grundlegung zur Metaphysik der Sitten*, vol. 8, pp. 85ff. of the Rosenkranz-Schubert edition.

³⁴Pascal, *Les Pensées*, in the Chevalier edition (La Pléiade collection), p. 1341.

³⁵*Ibid*., pp. 1105ff.

³⁶This seems to us the fundamental truth of his *Monadology*.

³⁷In this respect, see Olivier Costa de Beauregard's two volumes referred to in Chapter XII, note 19.

Chapter XXII

¹Cf. above, pp. 196ff.

²See *Le Consolateur*, pp. 290ff. and 368ff.

³According to St. Thomas (provided he is understood properly), this is certainly the point at which grace can penetrate human nature; it is also what makes our nature both capable and spontaneously desirous of receiving grace.

⁴See *Woman in the Church*, p. 49.

⁵Origen, *Homilia 8 in Genes*., 8 and *Hom. I in Isaiam*, 5. Cf. the commentary by Huet, *Origeniana*, lib. II, cap. II, quaest. III (PG 17, col. 197).

⁶See above, pp. 211ff.

⁷See above, pp. 215ff.

⁸See above, pp. 62ff.

⁹*Le Consolateur*, pp. 386ff.

¹⁰See above, pp. 65ff.

¹¹See above, pp. 57ff.

¹²One can but refer to the excellent little book by Sergei Boulgakoff, *The Friend of the Bridegroom* (in Russian), in the hope that it will soon be translated.

¹³See the entire account of the Annunciation in Luke 1:26ff.

¹⁴Cf. what we have said of the "prophetism" somehow present in all civilizations (*Le Père Invisible*, pp. 164ff.) and of the widespread action of the Spirit (*Le Consolateur*, pp. 19ff. and 376ff.).

¹⁵Cf. Isaiah 63:19, and all that comes immediately before.

¹⁶Matthew 1:20 and 2:13.

¹⁷Matthew 2:12.

¹⁸Matthew 2:1-11.

¹⁹Cf. John 11:50, and our comments regarding the essentially concrete and historical nature of the Incarnation according to the Greek Fathers, in *L'Incarnation et l'Eglise-Corps du Christ d'après Saint Athanase*, pp. 87ff.

²⁰II Corinthians 11:2.

²¹Luke 1:34.

²²Luke 1:35.

²³Cf. *The Eternal Son*, pp. 47ff.

²⁴John 19:17ff.

²⁵Colossians 1:24 and John 12:32ff.

²⁶Romans 6:3ff.

²⁷Colossians 1:24.

²⁸Cf. John 2:21; Romans 6:5; and Galatians 3:27; I Corinthians 6:19.

²⁹Ephesians 4:15, and the entire context.

³⁰Revelation 21:2.

Index of Ancient Authors
(Up to the 16th Century)

Index of Modern Authors
(Since the 17th Century)